Entryways into College Reading and Learning

By Janet Elder

Boston   Burr Ridge, IL   Dubuque, IA   Madison, WI   New York   San Francisco   St. Louis
Bangkok   Bogotá   Caracas   Kuala Lumpur   Lisbon   London   Madrid   Mexico City
Milan   Montreal   New Delhi   Santiago   Seoul   Singapore   Sydney   Taipei   Toronto

Higher Education

Published by McGraw-Hill, an imprint of The McGraw-Hill Companies, Inc., 1221 Avenue of the Americas, New York, NY 10020. Copyright © 2007 by The McGraw-Hill Companies. All rights reserved. No part of this publication may be reproduced or distributed in any form or by any means, or stored in a database or retrieval system, without the prior written consent of The McGraw-Hill Companies, Inc., including, but not limited to, in any network or other electronic storage or transmission, or broadcast for distance learning.

This book is printed on acid-free paper.

1 2 3 4 5 6 7 8 9 0 QPD/QPD 0 9 8 7

ISBN 978-0-07-312358-5
MHID 0-07-312358-7

Editor in Chief: Emily Barrosse
Publisher: Lisa Moore
Sponsoring Editor: John Kindler
Developmental Editor: Joshua Feldman
Marketing Manager: Tamara Wederbrand
Text Permissions Coordinator: Marty
  Granahan
Production Editor: Leslie LaDow
Manuscript Editor: Judith Brown
Designer: Cassandra Chu

Cover Designer: Joan Greenfield
Interior Designer: Glenda King
Photo Research Manager: Brian J. Pecko
Production Supervisor: Tandra Jorgensen
Media Producer: Alex Rohrs
Media Project Manager: Marc Mattson
Composition: 10.5/13 Palatino by
  Techbooks, India
Printing: 45# Scholarly Matte by Quebecor,
  Dubuque

Cover image: Students on college campus: Comstock Images/JupiterImages; Yellow archway: Adalberto Rios Szalay/Sexto Sol/PhotoDisc/Getty Images

Photo Credits: p. 1T, BananaStock/Jupiter Images; p. 1M, BananaStock/Jupiter Images; p. 1B, Dennis Wise/Getty Images/PhotoDisc; p. 3, PhotoDisc/Getty Images; p. 8, © Getty Images; p. 34, Jeff Maloney/Getty Images; p. 70, Scott T. Baxter/Getty Images; p. 106, Doug Menuez/Getty Images; p. 109, © Bettmann/Corbis; p. 112, © Royalty-Free/Corbis; p. 180, PhotoDisc/Getty Images; p. 208, The McGraw-Hill Companies, Inc./Gary He, photographer; p. 244, PhotoLink/Getty Images; p. 278, PhotoDisc/Getty Images; p. 308, © PhotoDisc/PunchStock; p. 340, © Digital Vision/PunchStock; p. 378, © Image100 Ltd.; p. 384, John A. Rizzo/Getty Images

Library of Congress Cataloging-in-Publication Data

Elder, Janet.
  Entryways into college reading and learning / by Janet Elder — 1st ed.
    p. cm.
  Includes bibliographical references and index.
  ISBN–13: 978-0-07-312358-5 (alk. paper)
  ISBN–10: 0-07-312358-7 (alk. paper)
    1. Reading (Higher education)—Study and teaching
    I. Title

LB2395.3.E428 2008
428.407'1—dc22

                                                  200604492

www.mhhe.com

About the Author

JANET ELDER is a reading specialist whose teaching experience includes secondary and undergraduate levels, as well as clinical remediation. For three decades, she taught college reading improvement and study skills courses at Richland College (Dallas County Community College District) and served as a reading program coordinator for many of those years. She also implemented the Honors Program at the college and directed it for six years before returning to teaching full time. In addition to teaching reading courses, Dr. Elder periodically served on honors English and humanities teaching teams. She was a three-time nominee for excellence in teaching awards. Disability Services students also selected her three times as the recipient of a special award for "exceptional innovation, imagination, and consideration in working with students with disabilities." She is a recipient of the National Institute for Staff and Organizational Development's Excellence Award. In fall 2004, she left teaching in order to write full time, but she continues her affiliation with Richland as a professor emerita.

Dr. Elder was graduated summa cum laude from the University of Texas in Austin with a BA in English and Latin, and is a member of Phi Beta Kappa. She received a government fellowship for Southern Methodist University's Reading Research Program, which resulted in a master's degree. Her PhD in curriculum and instruction in reading is from Texas Woman's University, where the College of Education presented her with its Outstanding Dissertation Award.

Dr. Elder is also the coauthor of *New Worlds: An Introduction to College Reading* and *Opening Doors: Understanding College Reading*, and is the author of *Exercise Your College Reading Skills*. A frequent presenter at professional conferences, she has a deep interest and expertise in "brain-friendly" instruction.

Brief Contents

Contents

Each selection is accompanied by these five activities:
- Connecting with What You Already Know
- Vocabulary Check
- Comprehension Check
- Writing to Make Connections
- Web Resources

Welcome

The golden opportunity you are seeking is in yourself. It is not in your environment; it is not in luck or chance, or in the help of others. It is in yourself alone.

—Orison Marden, founder, *Success* magazine

Welcome! If you are using this book, you are probably enrolled in a beginning-level reading improvement course at a college. Perhaps you are college age; perhaps you are older. You may be a high school graduate, or perhaps you earned a GED. Perhaps you never finished high school. It doesn't matter.

There are many reasons people reach college age but do not have the skills they need for success in college. Do any of these describe you?

- I didn't attend school regularly when I was younger.
- I attended several different schools growing up.
- I had to drop out to go to work, to help my family, because of personal problems, for health reasons or other reasons.
- I was frustrated or bored with school.
- I skipped school a lot.
- I hung out with friends who weren't interested in school.
- I had family problems.
- I, or someone in my family, had a drug or alcohol problem.
- My family thought school was a waste of time.
- I didn't seem to learn the same way most teachers taught.
- Reading has been a struggle for me.
- English is a second language for me; my family didn't speak English at home.

You may have seen one or two items that described your situation, or perhaps several. Don't worry about it. You can't change your history, but you can change your future. You've made two major decisions: to enroll in college and to improve your vocabulary and reading skills. The important thing is that you're here now, and that from this very moment, you can get off to the right kind of start in college.

Everyone is capable of learning, regardless of his or her age or background. Think of the many things that you are good at, things that you have learned outside of school. You have a wonderful brain, filled with knowledge, and the same abilities that helped you learn things outside of school can help you be successful in school.

This book is different from other reading improvement books. It is designed to be "brain-friendly." In other words, it has several features that make learning easier, more interesting, and more enjoyable. It presents information in ways that match a variety of learning styles. Following this introduction, you will find out more about learning styles and more about your particular learning style. You will learn about each of the book's special, brain-friendly features. You will also learn a bit about how your marvelous brain works.

It takes a lot of courage to start college, especially if you are one of the first ones in your family to go to college, if school has been hard for you in the past, or if you have not been in school for a while.

At this point, you may be thinking or feeling some of these things:

- I don't have family members who can tell me how to prepare or what to expect at college.
- I'm scared about asking questions or speaking in class.
- I don't know how to study.
- I don't know how to participate effectively in a group.
- I don't read; I spend my free time watching TV.
- I've never read a book; I don't know how to check one out from a library.
- I don't read magazines or newspapers.
- I'm going to be embarrassed in class.
- I put things off until the last minute; I don't know how to manage my time.

You may be relieved to know that most of your classmates share some of the same worries. The good news, though, is that most fears never come true. Moreover, you can learn the reading and study skills you need for success in school. This book will help you gain and strengthen those skills.

Regardless of where you're starting from, you can feel proud of yourself for taking the first step. You can also take comfort in knowing that even if you feel nervous or even a little scared, that's normal. Most people feel both excited and a bit uneasy when they start something new.

People attend college for many reasons. Perhaps you want to improve your job skills, find a career, or change to a new career. You may simply want to feel better about yourself. You may want to set an example for your brothers and sisters, or for your children. Perhaps you just have a curious mind and want to learn more about the interesting things college courses have to offer. Whatever your reason, you've taken the important—and brave—first step of starting right now. Congratulations and, again, welcome!

Warmest regards,

Janet Elder

To the Instructor

Every teacher wants students to be successful, and every student wants to succeed. Even after years of schooling, however, some students reach adulthood with only limited reading and learning skills. Current research offers new insight about working effectively with these students, about working with them in ways that truly respect the fact that not all students learn the same way. Recognizing that each brain is wired in its own unique way, *Entryways* uses brain-friendly, student-friendly strategies that address a multiplicity of learning styles and intelligences.

Description

As its name suggests, *Entryways* is an entry point for underprepared students who are likely to need one or more additional developmental reading courses. Its purpose is to strengthen students' basic reading abilities, as well as begin equipping them with general learning strategies that will serve them in a variety of ways and settings.

Assumptions

Entryways assumes that students have had reading instruction in public elementary schools and that many of them have had additional help in reading in middle school or beyond. It also assumes that these students have, for whatever reasons, not profited adequately from that instruction and that providing more of the same instruction (which they have been recycled through for many years) is not a productive approach. For that reason, this book takes a fresh and different approach, not the same one that has been unsuccessful for them in the past.

Users of this book are also most likely first- or second-semester students who not only need to strengthen their reading and learning skills but also need support in their transition into college. They do not necessarily have parents or other people in their lives who can guide them through the college experience.

Instructionally, *Entryways* is based on certain pedagogical assumptions derived from research on how the brain learns:

- Learning is an inborn ability in human beings.
- Human beings *want* to learn because learning is inherently pleasurable.
- Learners must start from wherever they are because in order to learn new information, they must connect it with their existing knowledge.
- The brain is a better pattern seeker than data gatherer.

- Appropriately challenging problem solving combined with collaborative learning opportunities is the best way to help students' brains grow.
- Given appropriate instruction, all students can learn.

Approach

As indicated earlier, *Entryways* capitalizes on current research. More specifically, it is based on research on multiple intelligences, natural learning, brain-compatible learning, as well as research pertaining to learning differences, dyslexia, and gender. This research base is reflected in an emphasis on inductive learning, on connecting new information with what is already known, and on building schemata. (*Schemata* are generalized mental blueprints or scripts. They help us make sense of events and experiences and shape our expectations of what is to come. The more schemata readers have, the more quickly they can comprehend and the more accurately they can predict.) The tone of *Entryways* is supportive and encouraging, with a generous dose of humor. Humor reduces stress, which in turn enhances learning. Special attention has been paid to factors such as font style and size, layout, and the use of color because these factors can aid comprehension and make learning easier.

Most entry-level reading textbooks present strategies and skills in the same way that hasn't worked for students in their previous years of school. The material is watered down—written at a simplified level. At first glance you may have been surprised that *Entryways* appears to be more challenging than other books aimed at significantly underprepared students. Such books are typically written in very short sentences, often in a very restricted vocabulary. Reading research long ago revealed that using short, choppy, "simpler" sentences can actually make material more difficult for younger readers and older remedial readers. For example, "It's raining. We canceled the picnic." is harder to understand than, "It's raining, so we canceled the picnic." Although the second version is one longer sentence rather than two shorter ones, it is easier to grasp because the word *so* signals the relationship between the two ideas. In the first version, the reader must supply the connection between the ideas.

Entryways is designed to appropriately challenge struggling readers because "doable challenge" is an optimal learning situation. The brain likes solving problems, especially those at the outer edge of the person's competence. When an activity involves manageable challenge, it simultaneously produces feelings of frustration and pleasure—a provocative combination that keeps the brain engaged. (For more on this important topic, see "What Video Games Can Teach Teachers about Instruction" under Instructor Resource Center of the Online Reading Lab.)

The curriculum of *Entryways* is constructivist. That is, the foundation is laid before a subsequent concept or skill is introduced. A major problem in instruction is that students are often pushed ahead when they do not yet have the prerequisite knowledge or skills for comprehending (learning) the new material. For example, students who cannot tell whether they have written a sentence will not be able to formulate main idea sentences. To know when they have written a sentence, they must first understand the concepts of subjects and predicates, and they must understand that a sentence conveys a complete thought. An all too familiar scenario is that of a frustrated teacher who continues to exhort frustrated students throughout the semester to "write a sentence for the main idea"—a task students cannot do unless the teacher stops and deals first with students' missing schemata. Approaching learning in a constructivist manner is not simply a nice idea; it's a necessity.

The learning strategies in *Entryways* are more concrete, active, and hands-on so that male students in particular have a greater likelihood of success. (Male students make up the majority in many remedial reading courses, according to *Condition of Education, 1998,* published by the National Center for Education Statistics in Washington, DC, 1999.) Terminology is introduced after students have inductively arrived at a concept, principle, or strategy so that they have the cognitive framework to which to attach the terms. Rather than memorizing rules, students add self-derived strategies to their own "toolbox" at the end of each chapter. Students can use these tools to help them construct meaning and to correct the situation when they are not comprehending. There is recursive review and integration of skills.

A key feature of *Entryways* is that whenever possible, it uses an inductive approach that allows students to figure out the "rules" for themselves. This methodology appears in Part Two, Chapter 3, and in all the chapters in Part Three except Chapters 6 and 12. An inductive approach parallels real-life learning, promotes deeper understanding, and results in better recall.

Using an inductive approach may be new to you. If so, commend yourself on being open to what cognitive research has to offer teachers and their students. (You are what Steven Johnson would describe as a "key influencer," one who is willing to go ahead of the curve.) You may find, though, that initially using an inductive approach takes restraint. It can be hard to resist *telling* students the very thing they need to discover on their own. (For obvious reasons, trying to speed up the process that way simply doesn't work.) It may be a change for you to become more of a question-asker and coach, one who is continually assessing what is happening with students. You will need patience and faith that students, especially when they work together cooperatively in small groups, can arrive at correct insights about how reading works—and it's thrilling to see them make those discoveries. (The ORL Instructor Center has extensive resource material on informal assessment techniques.)

In Chapter 3, the first time students use the inductive approach, I compare it to the process they use when they are playing—learning—a complex video game. In fact, the *learning processes* are very similar. (I'm certainly not advocating playing video games over reading; nothing can or ever will replace the experience of sustained reading and its benefits.) Research indicates, however, that it's virtually impossible to find a college student who hasn't played a video game or who doesn't play them on a regular basis. I compare mastering a complex video game with figuring out reading strategies in order to give students a nonthreatening point of reference, one they can relate to from their own lives. The same student who has trouble attending for five minutes to what's going on in class is often the one who spends several hours a day completely engrossed in the doable challenge of a complex video game. Sustained reading and playing a video game are different experiences, but I want students to realize that they *already* possess the mental skills they need to improve their reading.

At many points in *Entryways* students apply a skill or explain to another student how they arrived at an answer. This is because research shows that after 24 hours students have more than a 90 percent retention of material *if they taught (explained) the material to someone else or used the material immediately after learning it*. This is also a reason that cooperative learning figures prominently as an instructional methodology in this text. As every teacher knows, the best way to learn something is to prepare to teach it. (The ORL Instructor Center has extensive resource material on cooperative learning.)

Instruction and activities are directed at more than one sense modality, and students are given options whenever possible. Giving students choices makes them feel more positive and in control of their learning. It also lowers their stress and triggers the release of good brain chemicals. In the Toolbox section of each chapter, students are invited to recap information in their own words, but they can choose to record it in a conventional way, as a concept map, or in other less conventional ways. In the basic comprehension skills chapters, there is a drill instructor–style feature, "Listen Up!," that provides auditory learners with a handy way of remembering the key elements of each skill. A multisensory approach capitalizes not only on the reality that different students prefer to learn different ways, but that today's college-age students are *accustomed* to learning this way. From the time these "digital natives" were born, technology has been an integral part of their lives. They need only log on to the Internet or turn on their cell phones, iPods, or PDAs to access information in a variety of multimedia formats.

Practice (rehearsal) is crucial for learning any new skill. It is essential for transferring material into long-term memory. Repeatedly practicing something actually causes the brain to assign extra neurons to the task. There are some stipulations, of course. Students need to rehearse new learning or practice a new skill correctly from the beginning (they need guided practice). That means you must initially provide feedback so that students can analyze and improve their practice. (To make it easier to provide feedback, annotations in the Annotated Instructor's Edition—AIE—explain the reasons incorrect multiple-choice answers are wrong.) After that, students can do independent practice. Since practice makes permanent, it is important not to reverse the order of these two.

In general, the more practice in a variety of ways, contexts, and formats, the better. Providing multiple contexts for learning the same thing creates the most neural pathways. Underprepared students need *more* explanation, not less. For the sake of brevity and making the material look easy, many low-level reading texts give sketchy explanations. Although explanations in *Entryways* may seem overly redundant to some instructors, students find it reassuring, and they benefit from multiple exposures.

Many students also lack the requisite breadth and depth of background knowledge. To help underprepared students expand their knowledge base, much of the material in the examples and exercises comes from college textbooks. When necessary, it has been adapted to a level within the grasp of remedial readers.

Cooperative learning strategies are incorporated throughout the text. The research is unequivocal: Adults learn well from each other. Almost always, students using *Entryways* will move from individual work (on a "no-fail" activity based on their own experience) to small group activities (ideally, a maximum of four students), to whole class discussion or debriefing. In addition to enhancing learning, this approach offers a wealth of other advantages: support, better retention, improved communication, and interpersonal skills, to name a few. Collaboration is also a way for students to expand their knowledge base, learning from each other's experiences.

The process of inferring is a common thread that links vocabulary, reading, and study skills. It is basic and pervasive. For this reason, it is presented not as a separate skill in a separate chapter but as a unifying skill, which students will find reassuring. Making inferences is integral to deducing the meaning of words from context, selecting the correct dictionary definition, determining the meaning of words from word structure clues, determining the topic of a paragraph or a longer selection, formulating implied main ideas, and identifying the author's writing pattern. (Inferring is also involved in making predictions, drawing conclusions, interpreting an author's intended meaning, interpreting figurative language, and determining an author's tone, purpose, and intended audience—higher-level skills that are beyond the scope of this book). Many of the fundamental comprehension skills that are based on making inferences are themselves the basis for several other skills, including most study skills. (For example, students must first understand the skill of main idea in order to write a summary, create an outline, or take notes from a textbook.)

In short, *Entryways* is built on the brain-friendly paradigm of having the learning planned from the learner's viewpoint, with the focus on methodology (in contrast to the older paradigm of lessons planned from the teacher's perspective, with the focus on content).

Contents and Organization

Identifying Learning Styles and Learning Style Tips

Students have an opportunity to identify their learning styles and read about them. The "Identifying Your Learning Style" section offers a self-assessment that will point students toward their particular learning style. The Learning Style Tips in the second Visual Summary present an extensive list of specific strategies to make each learner more successful. ("A User's Guide to the Brain" appears on the ORL Instructor Center. It explains that the brain is designed for learning and how learning occurs. The information is well worth sharing with students. It helps them understand what is required in order for them to learn and how they can facilitate that learning. In other words, it removes the question of *whether* they can learn and focuses instead on *how* they can learn best and most easily. The textbook incorporates brain-friendly strategies that address multiple learning styles and strengths. As students progress through the book, they should develop a clear idea of how they can structure future learning in ways that tap into their strengths.

Part One: Adopting Success Behaviors (Chapters 1–2)

The two chapters in this section focus on basic information about how students can operate effectively both in class and outside the classroom.

Part Two: Acquiring Basic Vocabulary-Building Tools (Chapters 3–5)

The three chapters in this section are devoted to vocabulary acquisition skills and strategies. *Entryways* emphasizes vocabulary building more extensively than other developmental reading texts because remedial students are often deficient in this respect. The chapters target context clues (presented inductively), dictionary usage (which typically appears only briefly or not at all in middle- and higher-level developmental reading textbooks), and commonly confused and misused words. (Extensive material and practice on word structure analysis, roots and affixes, appears in the Online Reading Lab, ORL.)

Part Three: Acquiring Basic Comprehension Tools (Chapters 6–12)

The first six chapters in Part Three introduce basic comprehension skills, with Chapter 6 laying the foundation. Chapters 7 through 11 inductively introduce the essential skills of determining the topic, locating the stated main idea sentence, identifying supporting details, formulating an implied main idea sentence, and recognizing authors' writing patterns. The concluding chapter presents an effective approach for handling textbook assignments, including marking and annotating them. It is presented last because it is based on the skills presented in the other Part Three chapters. The ORL presents inductively the additional study skills of outlining, mapping, making review cards, and summarizing, along with ample practice exercises for each. These organizing and synthesizing tools are also based on skills presented in Part Three, and can be introduced to students as needed.

Chapter Format

This book makes correct sequencing a priority because logical development is key to successful learning. The general chapter format is as follows:

- *Chapter opening page with the chapter title and subtitle,* along with Why You Need to Know the Information in This Chapter, a brief explanation of how learning the concept or skill will benefit students—in other words, what's in it for them. (The brain always and immediately seeks an answer to the question, "What's in it for me?") Until students understand exactly how they will benefit— how the information pertains to their lives—the information will be of little or no interest to them.

- *Short, catchy, plain English subtitles.* Each of these student-friendly titles either sums up the skill or gives students an idea of what is involved in the skill. For example, Chapter 7, "Topic," has the subtitle

"What's It All About?" The brain likes metaphors and simple "handles," so the titles also help students fix in their minds the point of the chapter or the skill.

- *Super Student Tips,* in which other students who have learned a skill share their experiences and insights. Because the tips come from students who have "been there," they have credibility.

- *Jumpstart Your Brain! activity to engage students.* Whenever possible, the chapter content is linked with the Jumpstart activity. The cross-section of Jumpstart activities will provide opportunities for students with various types of intelligences to shine because the activities are directed at different types of intelligences (multiple intelligences). For example, a visual puzzle will tap the strengths of those who have spatial intelligence; a word puzzle will allow those with linguistic intelligence to shine. Jumpstart activities are intended to be collaborative, although for maximum benefit, students should try to solve them on their own first. Jumpstart activities are novel, interesting, and fun. They engage students and, therefore, prepare them to focus on what's coming next. Some Jumpstart activities incorporate humor since it reduces stress and enhances learning. Solving puzzles reinforces to students that they are smart and that they can be successful at mental tasks. The brain releases "feel good'" chemicals when the mind solves a challenging problem. In other words, the brain rewards us for learning so that we want to keep learning.

- *Looking at What You Already Know,* which is designed to activate students' prior knowledge. Students jot down their understanding of a topic before they begin. As they proceed through the chapter, students can correct misperceptions and/or receive reinforcement for correct responses.

- *The Big Picture for This Chapter, an overview of the chapter content.* Especially useful to global learners, this highlights the main topics of the chapter and tells how students will learn them.

- *The key information or skill featured in the chapter, the heart of the chapter.* Whenever possible, skills are introduced inductively; that is, students "discover" important principles for themselves. To illustrate this approach, in Chapter 7, "Topic," students examine a set of paragraphs that contain clues to the topic and whose topics are revealed. Based on those, students inductively determine each of the four "clues" to the topic.

- *Stop and Process activities.* These provide immediate application of a concept or skill, and feedback on students' understanding. They also link new information with students' own knowledge or experience.

- *My Toolbox, in which students record significant chapter information or summarize the skills.* They can paraphrase material in their own words or, if it suits their learning style better, use an approach that incorporates images and color. One goal of this book is for students to gain insight into how they learn most effectively and efficiently.

- *Fill-in-the-blank Chapter Check covering important terms and concepts.* The Toolbox activity sets students up to do well on this.

- *Review exercises.* Objective and/or open-ended exercises related to the chapter concepts in Part One and the skills in Parts Two and Three (Chapters 3–12).
- *Assess Your Understanding self-assessment.* These activities encourage the habit of comprehension monitoring as students rate their understanding of the chapter and pinpoint any area of confusion.

Each chapter includes three types of boxes: Brain-Friendly Tips, Bonus Tips, and Cross-Chapter Connections. Brain-Friendly Tips give pointers geared to various learning styles and brain-compatible learning strategies. Bonus Tips present practical, helpful pointers, such as memory pegs, shortcuts, and relevant Internet resources. Cross-Chapter Connections point out links between the contents of various chapters, which is especially helpful to students who benefit from seeing how the "pieces" fit together. The connections are also motivating because they indicate how learning or reviewing information in one chapter lays the foundation for success in another chapter. In addition, Chapters 7–11 feature Listen Up! boxes that present each of the basic comprehension skills in the form of a brief, catchy, and memorable "rap." Great for auditory learners!

Reading Selections

A set of ten reading selections follows the chapters. The purpose is to help students gain fluency in their reading while adding to their background knowledge. The topics of the reading selections are of interest to students of many backgrounds and come from a variety of sources that include textbooks, magazines, newspapers, online sources, and other nonfiction sources.

The selections can be assigned in any order. Some are motivational (for example, "The Courage to Learn" and "Superman and Me"); they fit nicely with Part One. The selections come from areas such as human development, psychology, student success, health, and personal finance and encompass topics such as landing a first job, attention cycles, likeability, and credit card debt. Nontextbook sources include nonfiction material such as excerpts from biographies and memoirs (Native American writer Sherman Alexie). Other selections deal with popular culture and are drawn from Internet sources and popular publications such as *Parade* magazine and newspapers ("What Your Car Says about You," "Pulling the Plug on TV," and "Do You Have What It Takes to Survive Army Boot Camp?"). Some selections relate to managing career and personal affairs more successfully: landing a first job, avoiding sleep deprivation, and likeability. (Similar types of sources are used for sample paragraphs throughout the text, although the majority come from textbook-type material.) In addition to the comprehension and vocabulary exercises, every selection is accompanied by writing prompts that help students make connections between their own experiences and the material, and that extend their reasoning and thinking.

The Online Reading Lab provides students and instructors with additional resources and practice material. Several online reading selections correlate with selections in the text, allowing students to pursue a topic in more depth. (A list of correlated selections appears in the ORL Instructor Center.) In addition, the ORL includes links to modules in *Catalyst,* a McGraw-Hill online tool for writing and research.

Overall Format

The format of the book is designed to appeal to students who are significantly underprepared for college and for whom developmental reading courses at a ninth- to eleventh-grade level may be too difficult. Format features of *Entryways* include

- Approximately 500 pages in length
- Generous 8-by-11-inch size with ample white space and space for students' written responses, because many of these students print or have large handwriting
- Numerous illustrations, photographs, and graphics

Other special format features are based on research that suggests they can make learning easier for students with learning differences. It has been estimated that 30 percent of all entering college freshmen have a learning difference, and that of those, half will drop out (*Time,* 10/14/02). Among post–high school students who are still reading at the fifth- to eighth-grade level, it is safe to assume that the percentage of students with learning problems is significantly higher than 30 percent. Features to accommodate such students include

- Good quality paper for clarity and ease of reading. Also, since many students with visual processing problems have difficulty distinguishing low contrast colors (such as gray pencil on paper), they may need to use dark markers. Good quality paper prevents "bleed through" from dark ink and makes removing the perforated pages easier.
- Larger than usual point size for the font. Research indicates that this can benefit students with learning disabilities and attention deficit disorder.
- Accent color to enhance learning.
- Sixteen pages of full-color Visual Summaries that review concepts in a way that is more pictorial than verbal. Underprepared readers in particular will find these helpful and reinforcing.

The ORL Instructor Center for *Entryways* includes additional information for how instructors can incorporate various brain-friendly strategies to benefit students in the classroom. For example, color enhances learning for many students. Instructors can use colored markers on a white board or colored marking pens on a transparency.

Features

- Low readability level
- Mature, appealing format and content
- Clear, engaging, understandable writing style
- Supportive, encouraging tone

- Innovative strategies and approaches founded on brain/learning/gender/learning differences research
- Cumulative review and recursive applications of skills
- Ten full-length reading selections with exercises and writing prompts that expand students' fund of useful background knowledge
- An effective prequel to *New Worlds, Opening Doors,* and *Exercise Your College Reading Skills*
- Annotated Instructor's Edition. Unlike most AIEs, this one explains why certain *incorrect* answers are incorrect. (Incorrect answers are students' opportunities to learn.) Moreover, it contains teaching tips and a multitude of strategies for working effectively with extremely underprepared students. In particular, AIE annotations inform teachers about simple, practical brain-friendly strategies.
- Extensive Online Reading Lab (ORL) Instructor Center that includes descriptions of brain-friendly and multiple-intelligences strategies; instructions for simple, inexpensive, teacher-made materials; URLs for relevant websites; information on best practices, collaborative learning, informal assessment, classroom management and instructional techniques; as well as Teaching Tips for each chapter, fully annotated answer keys, and downloads that can be used for supplemental practice or tests.
- The Online Reading Lab Student Center is replete with supplemental material and instructional activities for every chapter. There are 15 reading selections (with apparatus), several of which coordinate thematically with reading selections in the book, as well as shorter passages, called "Small Bites" (with even briefer apparatus), that can be used in a variety of ways. There are additional Web resources for each of the 10 reading selections in the text. For many topics in the book, there are links to *Catalyst,* an online writing and research tool. A complete explanation of roots, prefixes, and suffixes, along with multiple exercises, offers further opportunities for vocabulary enrichment. Optional study skill instruction is available: Students use completed models to inductively reason out the features of mapping, outlining, review cards, and summarizing. They also have ample opportunities to apply these skills for organizing and recording textbook information. A selection on test taking provides pointers for preparing for and scoring well on various types of tests, and dealing with test anxiety. The ORL also contains a brief review of phonics, pronunciation, syllabication, and spelling, along with practice exercises.

To access the premium content described above, students should go to www.mhhe.com/entryways and enter the following code: G8JR-Y9P7-TTEH-9487-THW4.

Special Features of This Book

This book is different from other reading improvement books because it takes learning styles into consideration. It can help you become a better learner, as well as a better reader. Every chapter includes special features to help you learn in ways that work best for you. They are techniques that you can use in other college courses later on. As you go through this book, notice these special chapter sections and features that are designed to meet the needs of many different types of learners. If you are not sure what your learning style is, "Identifying Your Learning Style," pages xxix–xxx, will help you find out.

WHY YOU NEED TO KNOW THE INFORMATION IN THIS CHAPTER

Students are often not sure why they need to learn a particular skill. The opening page of each chapter lists the ways the information or skill presented in the chapter can be helpful to you. Understanding its value is motivating and makes learning more meaningful.

SUPER STUDENT TIPS

These are tips and suggestions shared by other students who at one time were starting out just like you are now. They are things they learned from their own experience that they think will be helpful to you too.

Jumpstart Your Brain!

Before you start this chapter, do a few shoulder shrugs. Stretch your arms over your head. These relax you and give your brain extra oxygen. Now, jumpstart your brain—give it renewed energy—by solving these brainteasers.

By moving exactly two matches in each equation, turn the equation into one that is mathematically correct. You can turn one number into another; you can change the "sign" into another sign ($/$, $+$, $-$, or $\times$). The equal sign ($=$) will not change, of course. The only rules are (1) you must move exactly two matches somewhere else in the equation, and (2) the new equation must be correct mathematically. (For example, $2 + 2 = 4$ is mathematically correct; $2 + 2 = 5$ is not.) To "move" a match that's in the original equation, use a pencil and mark lightly. You can erase a line if you change your mind. Write your finished equation to the right of the original one. Remember that different people have different gifts. Solving brainteasers of this sort may or may not be yours. If it's not, try it on your own first (it will still cause brain growth!), and then find a classmate who has this aptitude. Have fun "matching" wits with this brainteaser. Good luck!

Original, Incorrect Equation	Correct Equation You Created from It
Example:	
$7/1 = 5$	$7 - 1 = 6$
$7 - 3 = 8$	
$5 - 3 = 4$	
$24/6 = 8$	
$31 - 22 = 31$	
$108/11 = 0$	

How did you do? Compare your answers to your classmates' answers. Check to see if everyone followed the rules and has mathematically correct equations. Explain to each other how you went about solving these brainteasers.

35

Copyright © 2007 by the McGraw-Hill Companies, Inc.

JUMPSTART YOUR BRAIN!

This feature also appears near the beginning of each chapter. The activities are fun and they'll wake up your brain! They also tap the strengths of various learning styles. Since different people are smart in different ways, you will shine on some Jumpstarts, and others will challenge you. They will also help you become a better thinker, especially the activities that do not match your preferred learning style. Try to do the activity by yourself first. Then discuss your answers with your classmates.

LOOKING AT WHAT YOU ALREADY KNOW

This section of each chapter lets you assess what you already know about the material presented in it. It prepares you to read by activating your existing knowledge. Once you have completed a chapter, you can go back and make corrections or additions.

Jumpstart Your Brain!

Solve these brainteasers to get your mental gears moving! Read each one, and then write your answer on the lines provided.

1. Three hunters are lost in the jungle. One starts walking east, one starts walking west, one starts walking south. In less than half an hour, however, they all end up in the same place and run into each other. How can that be?

2. Is there a Fourth of July in Russia?

3. A woman goes to enroll her children in first grade. She tells the school secretary that the children will both be enrolling in the same grade. The secretary asks her if one of the children is repeating first grade. The mother says no and says proudly that her son and daughter are identical twins. The secretary says that they're not. The mother becomes indignant. "How do you know? You've never even met them!" The secretary was right. How did she know?

4. It's a warm spring day. Three ducks are floating peacefully in a farmer's water tank. The circular tank is 8.5 feet in diameter and 2.5 feet deep. How much water is needed to fill the tank?

5. A teenager named Jessica breaks her leg while skiing and is rushed to the hospital nearby. The surgeon sees who the patient is and says, "My colleague will have to do the surgery. I'd be too nervous to operate on her because Jessica is my daughter." The surgeon is telling the truth; however, the surgeon is not Jessica's father. How can this be?

6. At the start of the day, a fruit grower has 97 melons for sale at her fruit stand. By the end of the day, she's sold all but 19 of them. How many does she have left?

Compare your answers to your classmates' answers. Explain to each other what the answers mean.

After you have gone over the answers, write the total number you had correct:_____

Copyright © 2007 by the McGraw-Hill Companies, Inc.

341

LOOKING AT WHAT YOU ALREADY KNOW

Answer these items as best you can. Don't feel anxious if you are unsure of the correct answers. By the end of the chapter, you'll be able to answer them. You can make changes then, or you can make changes as you proceed through the chapter.

1. Write the definition of a sentence: _____

2. What are the two things every sentence must contain? _____

3. Underline any of these that are sentences. (Do not base your decision on whether or not there is a period.)

   Night came.

   Filling out a job application.

   The security guard heard a cry for help.

   Why Americans love their pets so much.

   The black and red backpack with the torn strap and the broken zipper.

   I felt both excited and scared when I started college.

   Living independently and supporting oneself is a milestone in a young adult's life.

   How first-aid training can save lives.

   The game was canceled because of rain.

182

Copyright © 2007 by the McGraw-Hill Companies, Inc.

Copyright © 2007 by the McGraw-Hill Companies, Inc.

THE BIG PICTURE FOR THIS CHAPTER

Most students benefit from having an overview of what a chapter will be about. It helps them if they know ahead of time what to expect: where they are going and how they will get there. It's like looking at a map before you start a trip—you can see your destination, as well as the route that will take you there.

BOXES IN THE MARGINS

Throughout the chapters, you'll see boxes in the margin. Each type has a special purpose.

- Brain-Friendly Tips boxes have this symbol: They give you tips about ways to make learning more brain-friendly and therefore easier. In particular, they include tips for students with various learning styles.

- Bonus Tips boxes have this symbol: They provide memory pegs, sources of additional information, practical suggestions, and sometimes, just cool stuff to know.

- Cross-Chapter Connections boxes have this symbol: They help you link the material in previous and future chapters to the one you are currently reading. They help you see how everything fits together. They show how one skill can aid you with another. For example, they show how a skill you are currently learning may depend on one you learned earlier, or how one you are learning at the moment will be useful later on.

- Listen Up! boxes have this symbol: Chapters 7–11, which are basic comprehension chapters, each feature a short "rap" that captures the chapter's key points. These rhymes make it easier to learn and recall the information, especially for students who learn well by hearing. These raps sound similar to cadences military drill instructors call out to troops when they are jogging.

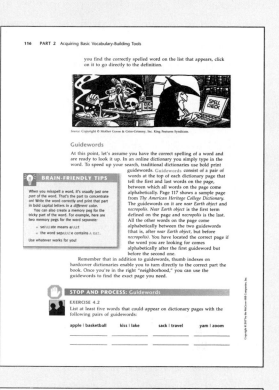

AN INDUCTIVE APPROACH

Inductive sounds like a big word, but it's not hard to understand. It means that you look at specific evidence in order to come up with a general conclusion about it. In this book, certain vocabulary and comprehension concepts are introduced inductively. That means you will examine several examples to determine what they have in common. It's like being a detective: You will have an opportunity to discover the concepts for yourself. As a result, you will understand the concepts better and remember them more easily because they will make sense to you.

But what if you are a step-by-step learner who likes to know the rule *first*? Relax. After you have had a chance to figure things out for yourself, you will be told what the strategies are and how to apply them, step-by-step.

Having a chance to discover the rules first, though, can help almost any learner. Simply *trying* to reason something out causes brain growth, even if you don't get the answer exactly right. You can work by yourself or with others to discover the strategies. Regardless of how you learn best, this book will help you.

ILLUSTRATIONS AND DIAGRAMS

This book has abundant diagrams, pictures, and illustrations. They are helpful to nearly all students, but especially to visual learners who think in pictures and images.

STOP AND PROCESS

This feature allows you to do exactly what it says: stop, think about what you have just read, reason out a concept, or apply the skill. These activities are spread throughout the chapters, so you don't have to wait until the very end to see if you're "getting it." You will see this icon for Stop and Process activities:

MY TOOLBOX

At the end of each chapter is a special section called My Toolbox. Here, you will have a chance to record the important chapter information. You will receive suggestions for ways to accomplish this. You can use your own words to write out definitions and key points on notebook paper or on index cards. You can write a paragraph or a letter. Or, you can create a chart, a diagram, or "study map" that includes symbols, lines, and arrows, as well as words. You can also use color if it enhances your learning. You can create a game, a poster, or a PowerPoint presentation. You can make up a song. In short, you can choose techniques that best suit your learning style. Creating your own personal record will strengthen your understanding and recall of the material.

CHAPTER CHECK

These short fill-in-the-blank quizzes let you assess how well you understood key concepts in the chapter. If you have done a thorough job in the Toolbox section, you will be well prepared for this activity.

ASSESS YOUR UNDERSTANDING

Effective students are always evaluating how well they understood material they have studied. In contrast to the formal Chapter Check, which has right and wrong answers, this section is informal. It is your own *personal* assessment of how well you understand the chapter. In addition to rating your understanding of the material, you have the opportunity to identify anything that is still confusing and to jot down steps you can take to fix the problem.

Each of these features is designed to make learning simpler and more enjoyable for you. Take advantage of them, and give them time. With practice, you will get better and better at applying them. Experiment to see what works best for you. You'll soon be on your way to becoming a more skillful, confident reader and learner.

Identifying Your Learning Style:
How Do You Learn Best?

Every person can learn. We are born to learn. Our survival depends on it.

You are already a good learner. Think about things that you do well, things that you learned outside of school. Perhaps you are good at singing, basketball, repairing things, playing a certain computer game, working with others, or driving a car. You can learn to use the same approaches that helped you become skilled outside of school to make you more successful in school.

People learn in many different ways, and each person has ways that he or she learns best. You have a way that you learn best and most easily. No single approach works equally well for everyone.

Think about how you learn school material. In your opinion, what would be the best possible situation for you when you study or do homework? Think about this, and then write a brief paragraph or draw a sketch of yourself in this ideal situation. You don't have to be an artist to do a drawing or a sketch. Simple figures and stick figures are fine. Whether you write or draw, feel free to use color. You can tell if your paragraph or drawing is complete because anyone who reads your description or sees your sketch will be able to tell these things:

- Where you prefer to study (in your room, somewhere on campus, at a desk, on the couch, sitting on the floor, etc.)
- What time of the day or night you prefer (if you create a sketch, you can include an indication of the time of day or night, such as a clock)
- Whether you are working alone or with other people
- Whether you prefer quiet or like some sound (such as background music, or talking to someone you are studying with)
- Whether your surroundings are neat and orderly, or disorganized or even messy
- Whether the light is bright or less bright
- Whether you are reading, listening (to the material on tape or talking with someone), writing, using the computer, or doing something with your hands (such as creating a model)

You may use the space below or your own paper to write or draw your response.

Now find out more about your learning style by marking the items on this scale. These are all strengths that describe ways people prefer to learn. No style is better than the other. Each style works, and each one will work especially well under certain circumstances.

For each item, make a mark on the number line beneath the best description of you. If both describe you equally well, make a mark in the middle, on or around the 3. If you have a slight preference, make your mark a bit closer to the description that fits you. You can circle a number or mark your answer elsewhere on the dotted line by making an X, a vertical line, a dot or a star—whatever you like. Remember that there are no right or wrong answers.

My Learning Style

	I think in words.			I think in pictures or images; I like to visualize things in my mind.
1.	1	2	3	4 5

	I learn well by hearing.			I learn well by seeing.
2.	1	2	3	4 5

	I like to talk out loud to myself or explain to someone else what I am doing.			I like to work silently.
3.	1	2	3	4 5

	I like to put the parts together to arrive at the whole.			I like to start with the whole (the goal or end product) and then go back to see how the parts fit together.
4.	1	2	3	4 5

	I am punctual and aware of time.			I get involved in what I am doing, and I tend to lose track of time.
5.	1	2	3	4 5

	I like to learn things step-by-step; I can explain the process I used or the steps I followed.			Answers seem to come to me all at once; I can't always explain how I got them.
6.	1	2	3	4 5

I pay attention to detail.

I see the big picture, but I may miss the details.

7. 1 . . . . 2 . . . . 3 . . . . 4 5

I like to know the "rule" first so that I can go back and apply it.

I like to discover the "rule" or pattern for myself by looking at several examples.

8. 1 . . . . 2 . . . . 3 . . . . 4 5

I sound words out to spell them.

I need to visualize words in my mind or write them out to spell them.

9. 1 . . . . 2 . . . . 3 . . . . 4 5

I am well organized.

I may appear disorganized; I create my own ways to organize things.

10. 1 . . . . 2 . . . . 3 . . . . 4 5

I like directions that I can hear or read so I know what to do.

I like to learn things by doing them; I prefer a hands-on approach. I like to see things demonstrated before I try them myself.

11. 1 . . . . 2 . . . . 3 . . . . 4 5

It helps me remember information if I can repeat it aloud or make a rhyme out of it.

It helps me remember information if I can visualize it, write it down, or draw it.

12. 1 . . . . 2 . . . . 3 . . . . 4 5

What's Your Learning Style?

If you marked mostly in the range of 4s and 5s, you are probably a strong visual learner. You learn well by seeing things. Many visual learners are also spatial learners. A spatial learner is very good at seeing in his or her mind how things fit together or imagining what an object looks like from another perspective.

If you marked mostly in the area of 1s and 2s, you are probably a strong auditory learner. You learn well by hearing information. You may also prefer to learn things in an orderly manner, step-by-step. People who prefer to learn step-by-step are **sequential learners**, and many auditory learners are sequential learners as well.

Visual and auditory learning styles are thought to be hardwired in the brain. In other words, people are born with one of those preferences. If you marked most of the items around 3 (between the two columns), you are probably able to learn well either way. However, you may have a slight preference for one or the other.

Besides being a visual or auditory learner, you might also be a hands-on or tactile-kinesthetic learner. Touch helps tactile learners; movement helps kinesthetic learners. You are a **tactile-kinesthetic learner** if touching or manipulating objects, as well as movement—going through the motions—helps you learn. To some extent, all people are tactile-kinesthetic learners because at some point, they must actually try to do the new things they are learning. Some people, however, have a strong preference for learning this way.

You may also be some combination of these. For example, you may prefer to hear an explanation of something, see an example of a finished product, and then try it yourself. In addition to these learning styles, you may also be a **global learner**, who likes to get the "big picture" first and/or an **intuitive learner**, who often makes decisions on the spot and likes to go with what "feels right." The descriptions that follow will help you further pinpoint the way or ways you learn best.

Are You a Visual-Spatial Learner?

What exactly does *visual-spatial* mean? You already know that *visual* means pertaining to vision. *Spatial* refers to space. **Visual-spatial learner** describes people who think in pictures rather than words. Many of them can visualize objects in three dimensions in their mind. They can usually remember the route to get somewhere, even if they have been there only once before. They learn better by seeing.

Visual-spatial learners possess many other traits as well. They often learn something all at once: They suddenly "get it"; moreover, they remember it! They can't, however, always show their work or explain how they got an answer. They like seeing the big picture first. Interestingly, they often do better on hard tasks than on simple ones. They are often imaginative and creative and like to discover things for themselves. They tend to be excellent puzzle-solvers and are often good at completing mazes, building things, playing Tetris on the computer, playing chess, and doing computer programming. They like to take things apart to see how they work. They also like to synthesize, or put information together. They are often sensitive to other people's feelings and sensitive to teachers' attitudes. They may be talented musically, artistically, or mechanically.

Visual-spatial learners may do well in some school subjects, but poorly in others. Many have terrible handwriting and are bad spellers. They may find it hard to express themselves in words, and they usually hate to speak in front of a group. They can be disorganized and lose track of time.

Do these descriptions fit you? If you're still not sure, go to www.visualspatial.org. Click on VSL Quiz–Adult. It will take you only a few minutes to complete the short quiz. You may learn some very interesting things!

Dr. Linda Silverman is a psychologist, educator, researcher, and writer who is also an internationally known expert on giftedness. Her research indicates that a third of students are strong visual-spatial learners. Another third show a slight preference for visual-spatial learning. This suggests that two-thirds of students would benefit from textbooks and instruction that take into account the strengths of visual-spatial learners. That's what *Entryways* is designed to do. (It doesn't ignore those who learn other ways, however!) Although Dr. Silverman's research studies were conducted with middle-school students, the results are relevant because a person's learning style tends to stay the same throughout life.[1] In other words, had she first tested them as older students, it is likely the results would have been the same.

Are You an Auditory-Sequential Learner?

Dr. Silverman's research also revealed that about one-fourth of the population consists of strongly auditory-sequential learners. Auditory-sequential learners learn well by hearing and from step-by-step instruction. (*Sequential* comes from the word *sequence*, a set of things in a specific order.) These learners think mainly in words. They pay attention to time and to details. Because they are step-by-step learners, they generally learn well from traditional classroom instruction. They can show the steps of their work. They like to analyze things, to break them into parts. They can usually write quickly and neatly. They are able to memorize information even if they don't understand it completely. They prefer to work on one job at a time until it is done, and they often sit still, usually at a desk, for long periods of time when they work or study. Most prefer to read and study where the light is bright. Does this sound like you?

Which Combination Describes You Best?

Based on what you have already done and read in this section, circle the best description of your learning style from the list that follows. Most people do not fit neatly in one category, but they usually have a primary (most preferred) style that they use whenever they can. Circle more than one category only if you use both styles about the same amount. If you like, you can rank them 1, 2, and 3 to show which is your primary style, your secondary style, and your least preferred style.

---

[1]Linda Silverman, *Upside-Down Brilliance: The Visual-spatial learner*. (Denver, Co: DeLeon Publishing, 2002). The 1999 and 2001 research studies cited by Dr. Silverman were conducted with 750 males and females, ages 9–13, in two Colorado schools, in urban and rural areas. The results were consistent. Dr. Silverman notes that learning style tends to be constant throughout life and therefore reasons that results would be essentially the same if conducted on the same subjects when they were older.

Visual learner:	I learn best by seeing
Auditory learner:	I learn best by hearing
Tactile/kinesthetic learner:	I learn best by doing; I'm a hands-on learner

Now circle the one of these that describes the way you learn best:

Sequential learner:	I like to have orderly, step-by-step directions
Spatial learner:	I like to see the big picture or pattern and figure things out for myself

You may also find it helpful to go to www.vark-learn.com and take their learning style inventory. They use these categories of learning styles: *visual* (prefer the "whole picture" and like pictures and other visuals), *aural* (learn by hearing), *read/write* (prefer the combination), *kinesthetic* (prefer hands-on and experiencing the learning), and *multimodal* (use two or more styles).

Once you've identified your style, read the learning style tips in the second Visual Summary (in Chapter 12) to discover ways you can best take in information, study effectively, and prepare for tests.

How Does Knowing Your Learning Style Help You?

There are two very good reasons to know your learning style:

- First, it will enable you, whenever possible, to choose *situations* that make learning easiest for you. In other words, you can choose courses and teachers who teach to your strengths.
- Second, you can develop *strategies* to help you succeed when you have to take courses that do not match your learning style. For example, if you think in images or pictures rather than words, you will find it helpful to take notes on information you read or hear by

drawing sketches and diagrams or by making study maps. If you learn well by hearing and working with others, you might want to form a study group with students who have the same learning style.

Colleges are beginning to provide students with greater choices in the way they learn. In addition to traditional lecture courses, there are online courses, ones with computer-assisted instruction, and ones that include cooperative (collaborative) learning opportunities, in which students work together. Still, most colleges are geared toward students who can learn by reading textbooks, who can listen to lectures and take notes in words, and who can memorize information for tests. Most professors and textbooks present information step-by-step, and they move from simpler concepts to more complex ones. College is usually easier for students whose style is suited to this type of instruction. But don't feel discouraged if this is not the way you learn best. Not only are there ways to work around this, there are lots of ways you can take advantage of your own learning strengths. Are you ready? Let's get started!

Acknowledgments

The following people contributed to making this book a reality, and I am grateful to each of them. John Kindler, Sponsoring Editor, gracefully shepherded the project to completion. Joshua Feldman, Developmental Editor, and Leslie LaDow, Production Editor, lent their bountiful talent, expert guidance, and unstinting effort to the enterprise. Manuscript Editor Judith Brown, who has a meticulous editorial eye, did a superb job. In addition, I am obliged to Designer Cassandra Chu and her team, Photo Research Manager Brian Pecko, Production Supervisor Tandra Jorgensen, Text Permissions Editor Marty Granahan, and Marketing Manager Lori DeShazo for their important contributions. Special thanks to Media Specialist Alex Rohrs and Media Project Manager Marc Mattson for bringing the Online Reading Lab to life.

I also extend my appreciation to Rita Smilkstein and Janet Zadina, who share my passion for brain-friendly teaching and learning, and to Susan Pongratz and Mary Dubbé of Thomas Nelson Community College, and Lynda Webb of Midland College.

These thoughtful reviewers provided constructive criticism, helpful feedback, and supportive comments, from which I benefited greatly:

Glynis Barber	Coppin State College
Annette D'Ambrosio	Solano College
Carolyn Davidson	Butte College
Evelyn Koperwas	Broward Community College
Eleanor Maddox	University of Central Oklahoma
Judy Marks	Rio Hondo College
Bernard Ngovo	Pima Community College
Robert Renteria	Cerritos College
Jennifer Rodden	Long Beach Community College
Holly Susi	Community College of Rhode Island
Rakesh Swamy	Ohlone College
Barbara Van Meter	Montgomery College
Lynda Webb	Midland College
Shannon Woodcock	Lake Washington Technical College

And last, but never least, my heartfelt gratitude to Jim for his boundless love and support.

Janet Elder

Map of Chapters

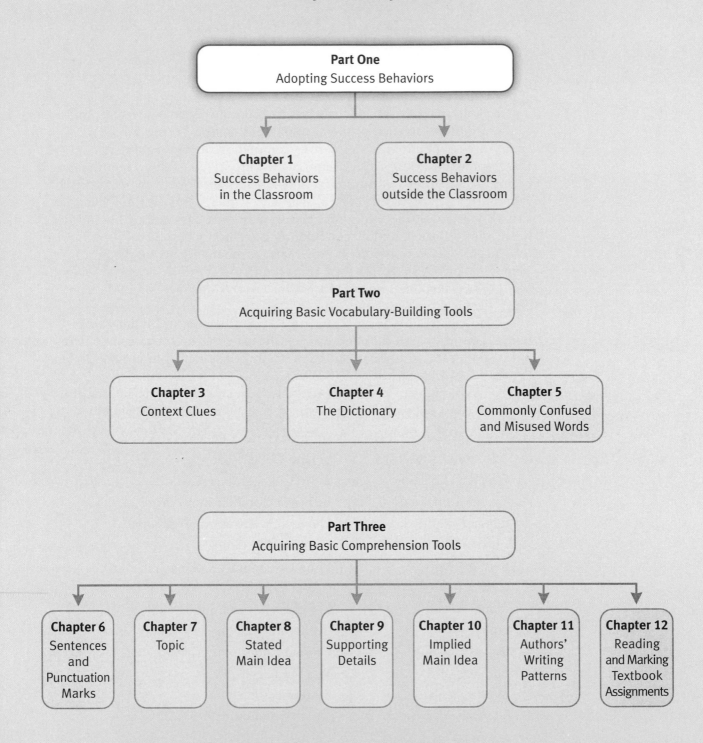

Part One
Adopting Success Behaviors

Chapter 1
Success Behaviors
in the Classroom

Chapter 2
Success Behaviors
outside the Classroom

Part Two
Acquiring Basic Vocabulary-Building Tools

Chapter 3
Context Clues

Chapter 4
The Dictionary

Chapter 5
Commonly Confused
and Misused Words

Part Three
Acquiring Basic Comprehension Tools

Chapter 6
Sentences
and
Punctuation
Marks

Chapter 7
Topic

Chapter 8
Stated
Main Idea

Chapter 9
Supporting
Details

Chapter 10
Implied
Main Idea

Chapter 11
Authors'
Writing
Patterns

Chapter 12
Reading
and Marking
Textbook
Assignments

WELCOME TO PART ONE
Adopting Success Behaviors

It's been said that you are what you repeatedly do. In other words, you are your behaviors. *Behaviors* is another word for your actions. Behaviors that you repeatedly do become habits. Ultimately, your habits will make or break you. That's why it's so important for you to equip yourself with success strategies from the first day of the semester and to use them consistently until they become habits.

Part One of *Entryways* consists of two chapters to help you do exactly that: adopt behaviors that can "make" you as a student.

- Chapter 1 focuses on classroom behaviors that lead to success. These simple actions can dramatically improve the amount you learn and how favorably you are perceived by your instructors and classmates.
- Chapter 2 focuses on out-of-class behaviors that will boost your learning and foster success.

From these two chapters, you'll gain useful information as well as confidence. After all, if you do the things successful students do, you will become more successful yourself.

If you have attended college before, you may see some strategies that are familiar. Good! That should be reassuring. If you are new to college, you will learn how to get off to a good start and how to maintain that positive momentum.

A philosopher once said, "Well begun is half done." He meant that getting off to a good start can take you a long way toward success. Does it really matter whether you get off to a good start in college? The answer is yes, absolutely! Randy Moore of the University of Minnesota investigated the importance of a good start for students enrolled in developmental courses.[1] He was particularly interested in these students because they are less well prepared for college than other students. Also, there are lots of them! About one-third of U.S. students have to take at least one year of developmental courses when they start college.

Moore's research revealed four factors strongly associated with successful completion of college:

- first-semester grade point averages (GPAs)
- first-year grade point averages
- class attendance and active participation

It was clear that students who got off to a good start were much more likely to continue to do well and, ultimately, to graduate. Students who earned first-semester

---

[1] Randy Moore, "The Importance of a Good Start," in I. M. Duranczyk, J. L. Higbee, and D. B. Lundell, eds., *Best Practices for Access and Retention in Higher Education*, Minneapolis, MN: The Center for Research on Developmental Education and Urban Literacy, General College, University of Minnesota, 2004, pp. 115–123.

GPAs higher than 2.0 also earned second-semester GPAs above 2.0; that is, they continued to do well in their second semester. Unfortunately, the opposite was also true. Students with a shaky start were likely to continue to have problems.

Moore urges students to strive for first-semester and first-year GPAs of at least 3.0. He warns that students who seek GPAs of only 2.0 (rather than higher) are likely to see their GPAs eventually drop. The bottom line is this: The higher a student's first-year GPA, the more likely the person is to graduate from college.

With regard to class attendance, Moore found that students' first-semester GPAs were strongly associated with class attendance. Moreover, he reports that "developmental education students who attend all of their classes usually make significantly higher grades than students who skip class." As two other researchers put it, "Nothing replaces being present in class."

Moore offers additional suggestions to help students succeed. He urges students to attend orientation sessions that colleges and universities offer to new students. He urges them to meet with academic advisors. He points out that if students want to remain in college and enjoy the choices and economic rewards of being college graduates, they must adopt certain academic behaviors: They must attend class and be more engaged with their education.

Finally, Moore feels that students need to have realistic expectations about what college will demand of them. They need to know that college is a challenge and requires dedication. Many first-year students do not know this. If they made adequate or better grades in high school with very little work, they are shocked when college turns out to be so different. Worse, they get off to a bad start because they discover their mistake too late. Moore concludes, "Developmental education students should be warned that their success will depend largely on their motivation and willingness to work hard." He states bluntly that students who are not motivated enough to work hard are not likely to succeed.

The purpose of telling you about Professor Moore's research is not to frighten you. It is intended to do the opposite: to let you know that your success is largely in your own hands. *You* control your motivation, attitude, and effort.

In Part One of *Entryways*, you will learn commonsense strategies that will enable you to build a foundation for success in class and out of class. The trick, of course, is to use the strategies. That requires self-discipline. *Discipline* has been defined as "remembering what you really want." That's a wonderful definition. Goals take time to achieve, and they require effort and sacrifice along the way. However, if those goals are something you really want, you will find it easier to stay committed to achieving them.

As you move through the semester and through this book, you will be reminded to look back at these two chapters. Check to see if you are using the strategies, if you need to use one more consistently, or if you need to add one. It's never too late to become a better student.

Best wishes as you begin an exciting journey!

Map of Chapters

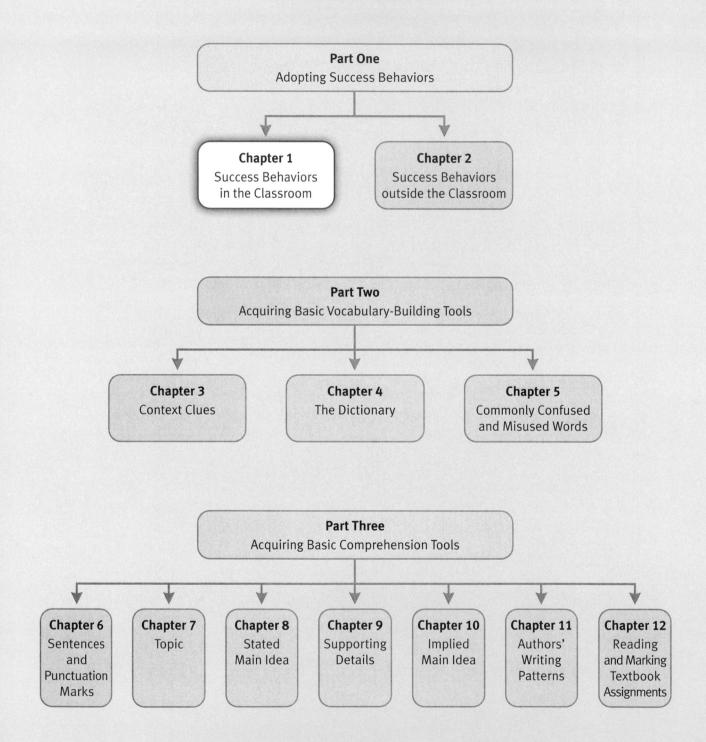

Part One
Adopting Success Behaviors

Chapter 1
Success Behaviors in the Classroom

Chapter 2
Success Behaviors outside the Classroom

Part Two
Acquiring Basic Vocabulary-Building Tools

Chapter 3
Context Clues

Chapter 4
The Dictionary

Chapter 5
Commonly Confused and Misused Words

Part Three
Acquiring Basic Comprehension Tools

Chapter 6
Sentences and Punctuation Marks

Chapter 7
Topic

Chapter 8
Stated Main Idea

Chapter 9
Supporting Details

Chapter 10
Implied Main Idea

Chapter 11
Authors' Writing Patterns

Chapter 12
Reading and Marking Textbook Assignments

CHAPTER 1

Success Behaviors in the Classroom

Behave Your Way to Success

Why You Need to Know the Information in This Chapter

You've probably already spent several years in school and countless hours in class. Were you as successful as you wanted to be? If not, there *is* a solution. If you know and use certain behaviors, you can be more successful in any college classroom. This chapter explains those behaviors.

Using these classroom behaviors consistently will help you

- feel more comfortable that you fit in and belong

- increase your teachers' and your classmates' respect for you

- enhance your confidence and self-respect

- get the most out of the time you spend in class each week

"Please, Ms. Sweeney, may I ask where you're going with all this?"

Source: Copyright © *The New Yorker Collection*, 2001, Robert Weber from cartoonbank.com. All rights reserved.

Super Student Tips

Here are tips from other students who have been successful in college classes like the one you're taking now. Here's what experience has taught them:

"I was embarrassed that I was always walking in late, so I set my watch a few minutes ahead. I also leave for school about 15 minutes earlier than I used to. Problem solved!"—*Adrienne*

"Keep all your handouts from every class in a ring-binder notebook. Buy a small hole punch that you can keep with you. Divide your notebook into sections. If you get off to an organized start, it makes all the difference."—*Jesse*

"I thought if I asked a question, I'd look dumb. Instead, most instructors are glad you ask questions."—*Francisco*

"There was this guy in my math class who was always making rude comments under his breath. He thought he was being funny, but all it did was annoy everyone who had to sit near him. He never did get it."—*Ashley*

"I took a public speaking class. It helped me feel more confident about speaking up in class and giving presentations."—*Tran*

"In high school I always sat at the back of the room. In my first college class, I ended up near the front. It felt real strange at first, but I got used to it. It made me pay more attention, so I learned more. Now I try to sit near the front of the room in all my classes."—*Tamika*

"My first semester in college I cut class a lot. I caused myself a lot of stress and hassle. Now I try to make every class."—*Eduardo*

Jumpstart Your Brain!

Before you begin the chapter, get yourself ready to think. Stand up or stretch. Better yet, stand up *and* stretch. Take a couple of deep breaths. These simple actions get oxygen to your brain, and your brain loves oxygen! Then jumpstart your brain—give it renewed energy—by solving this brainteaser: How many rectangles are there in the design below? Good luck!

There may be more than you think! (Remember that a rectangle has four sides. A square is a type of rectangle that has four equal sides.)

Can you figure out how many rectangles there are in this design?

Write your answer here: _____

Compare your answer to your classmates' answers. Explain to each other how you went about solving the puzzle.

LOOKING AT WHAT YOU ALREADY KNOW

 You started learning the day you were born. Your brain did it automatically. No one, however, is born knowing how to be a good student. Happily, it's something you can learn.

Maybe you finished high school or earned a GED. Maybe not. Either way, you already know some things that can make students more successful in class. Take a minute to list at least five behaviors that you think would make you more successful in *class*. Focus specifically on behaviors that could help you be successful in *this* class. Write them in the space that follows.

1. _____

2. _____

3. _____

4. _____

5. _____

Now that you have finished your list, compare it with three or four of your classmates' lists. In small groups, decide on the five most important behaviors for success in class. When all of the groups are finished, share your lists. Then decide as a class on the top five success behaviors. Jot down the class's final list on scratch paper. You will need it later for the My Toolbox section of the chapter.

Success Behaviors in the Classroom

You don't have to be great to start, but you have to start to be great.

—Joe Sabah

We first make our habits, and then our habits make us.

—John Dryden

A comedian once joked, "I made straight As in school. Of course, my Bs were a little crooked . . . " Like all college students, you want to do well in college and make good grades. This book can help you achieve that.

If you are new to college, this chapter and the next one will be especially important for you. Even if you attended college in the past, you will still learn new things. Also, these chapters will confirm the things you are already doing right. So whether you are new to college or are a returning student, read on! (Be sure to read the Brain-Friendly Tips and Bonus Tips that appear in the boxes. They're there to help you learn faster and more easily and to provide pointers and extra information.)

BRAIN-FRIENDLY TIPS

1. Before you read any chapter, look through it to see what it contains. Look at the title, headings, and words in bold print. This gets your brain ready to read.

2. If the chapter seems too long to read all at once, divide it into smaller parts. Place sticky notes or paperclips at logical breaks. Then read one section at a time, spreading the assignment over several shorter study sessions.

3. Find your learning style below. (See "Identifying Your Learning Style," pages xxix–xxxiv.) Throughout this book, use the tips that make learning easier for you:

Auditory learners: Before you read the chapter, read *aloud* the chapter title and the headings. To help you understand and remember the material, try reading the chapter sections out loud.

Visual learners: Look at (read) the chapter title and headings before you begin reading the chapter. Pay special attention to words and sentences in bold print and italics.

Visual-spatial learners: Make sketches or doodles in the margin to remind you what each section is about.

Tactile-kinesthetic learners: Make sketches or doodles in the margin to remind you what each section is about. You may also find it helpful to move as you read. (Tap a hand or foot, chew gum, or even pace slowly back and forth as you read.)

The Big Picture for This Chapter

This chapter focuses on *classroom* behaviors that can help you succeed. All of them are common sense. They are not difficult, although they do require self-discipline. The key is doing them consistently. They will not only make you more successful, they will cause you to feel increasingly proud of yourself. (In Chapter 2, you will learn about behaviors outside of class that contribute to your academic success.)

Starting college, or even a new semester, is the perfect time to change any behaviors that limit your success. You can replace bad habits and attitudes with positive ones. In about three weeks' time, you can "lose" bad habits simply by not doing them!

BONUS TIP

The time you spend in class should be the *easiest* part of each course. You have an instructor, an expert, who is there to help you, guide you, and answer questions. Equally helpful, you have classmates you can work with.

In literature, there are many famous stories about people who pretend to be something they aren't and then actually become what they pretended to be. One such story is by the writer O. Henry. In the story, a young man who intends to help with a bank robbery poses as a policeman. He stands in a uniform outside the bank all day. The bank customers greet him and treat him with respect. *Because he is behaving like a police officer, he begins to feel like a real police officer. Then he begins to act that way.* When his partner arrives to rob the bank, the young man chases him away and prevents the robbery. Why? It was because he enjoyed the way he felt when he was acting like a police officer. Because other people respected him, he had more respect for himself. He started out playing a role, but after a while it began to feel natural. Something similar happens when students go through the motions of being an effective student: *They become effective students.*

Phil McGraw is a psychologist, best-selling author, and popular talk-show host. "Dr. Phil" always advises people to "behave their way to success." This is because repeated behaviors become habits. *When you repeatedly do the things successful people do, you become more successful.* It's only logical that if you do the same things that successful students do, you will become a more successful student.

Now read the rest of this chapter to see how your class's list of success behaviors compares with the six success behaviors discussed here. Did you and your classmates identify some of the same behaviors? Are there differences?

BRAIN-FRIENDLY TIP

When you come to the end of each *section* in a textbook chapter, try the appropriate learning-style strategy to get the most from what you just read:

- *Auditory learners*: Try to say out loud in your own words what you just read.

- *Visual and visual-spatial learners*: Pick out what seem to be the most important sentences or ideas, and mark them. Create one or more pictures in your mind or sketches in the margin to help you remember what you read.

Six Behaviors for Success in Class

www.mhhe.com/
entryways

To explore how
these behaviors fit
with work,
see "Making Career
Connections"
(writing activity).

Here are six classroom behaviors that can make you a more successful, effective, and relaxed learner:

- **Read and understand the syllabus.**
- **Be in class on time, every time.**
- **Learn your instructor's name and your classmates' names.**
- **Sit in the right place.**
- **Come prepared for class, and participate.**
- **Be polite and use appropriate language.**

Let's look at specific information about each success behavior.

1. Read and understand the syllabus.

In college, instructors typically hand out a syllabus during the first week of class. A syllabus describes a course, its requirements, and other important information you need to know about it. It is also called a *course description*. Every syllabus tells

- who the instructor is and how to contact that person
- what you will study in the course
- the textbook and other materials you will need (such as a supplemental manual, a computer disk, or index cards)
- the course requirements and how your grade will be determined
- policies about attendance, missed assignments, tardiness, and makeup work
- information about tests and quizzes

✳ BONUS TIP

A syllabus may also include

- a week-by-week overview of the topics you will study
- specific test dates
- information about papers and projects, and when they are due
- other important information about the course (such as related computer instruction or required supplemental instruction, exit testing, etc.)
- information about the college support services (such as a tutoring center or counseling services)

Most instructors discuss the syllabus in class. If your instructor goes over the syllabus, tune in and listen carefully. If there is anything you do not understand, ask! Understanding the syllabus is the first in-class success behavior, and it is an important one.

Not all college instructors go over the syllabus in class. They expect you to read it carefully on your own. Some students, however, merely glance at the syllabus. They throw it away or shove it into their notebook, and they never look at it again. This is a big mistake. The syllabus is your course guidebook. Read it. Ask your instructor about anything you do not understand. Your instructor will be impressed that you care. Keep the syllabus in your notebook or other safe place so that you can refer to it during the semester.

Not knowing what's in the syllabus is not an excuse for asking for special treatment. ("But I didn't know that late assignments lose ten points each day!") You will make a good impression on your instructor if you know what is in the syllabus. Read the syllabus. Make a good impression!

 ## STOP AND PROCESS

EXERCISE 1.1

- Did you receive a syllabus in this course? If so, did your instructor go over it in class? Did you listen carefully and ask questions about anything you did not understand?

    _____

    _____

- If your instructor expected you to read the syllabus on your own outside of class, did you? If not, why not?

    _____

    _____

- If you received a syllabus, what major topics are included in it?

    _____

    _____

- If you did not receive a syllabus, your instructor probably explained the course requirements. What do you recall of the important course information?

    _____

    _____

If you have not yet read the course syllabus for each of your classes, set aside time today or tomorrow to read them. They're like road maps for a course. They're important.

2. Be in class on time, every time.

Attend every class session, and be on time. This is a key behavior for success in college. Instructors really do notice who is present and who is not. They also notice who comes in late or leaves early.

Let's be practical. Someone has paid tuition for you to attend college: your parents, your employer, or you. It makes no sense to pay for something and not get your money's worth. Try not to miss even a day of the instruction you paid for.

Some professors excuse an absence only if you bring a doctor's note, proof that you were in court or on jury duty, and so forth. Other

BONUS TIPS

There are times when you should make a special effort not to miss class. In particular,

- **Be there the first day and the first week of class.** That's when teachers go over the syllabus, explain important class procedures, have class members introduce themselves, and so forth.

- **Be at every class the first few weeks of the semester.** During this crucial time, you are developing the foundation for the rest of the semester.

- **Be there the class session before a test.** That's usually when teachers explain the type of test and the material that will be covered on it. They may even review the class for the test.

- **By all means, be there on test days and on days when major assignments are due.** Being absent on those days looks bad. It can leave your instructor with a negative impression.

professors may allow you a certain number of absences, and you do not have to give a reason. Don't use any "allowed absences" if you don't absolutely have to. Save them in case you have an illness or a real emergency. Your course grade may be affected by each absence beyond the number allowed. Be sure you know the policy of each of your instructors. The bottom line: Strive for *perfect* attendance, even if your instructor permits a certain number of absences. Most instructors acknowledge that if a student is on the borderline between two grades, they usually give the higher grade if the person has had excellent attendance.

In most courses, you are in class only three hours a week. That means that every class session is important. Class sessions prepare you to do the homework assignments. They give you feedback. They surround you with help in the form of your instructor and your classmates.

There will be times, of course, when you can't make it to class. You are ill. Your car doesn't start. The bus doesn't arrive on time. However, having a hangover, sleeping in, or just blowing off class are not good reasons for being absent. Besides, it's always harder to find out what you missed in class and catch up than it is to be there.

If you are absent twice in a row, call or email your instructor. Let him or her know what your situation is and when you will return to class. If you do not know what the most recent assignment is, ask. You can also ask a classmate if that feels more comfortable. The point is, whenever you are absent, it is your responsibility to find out what the assignment is and then *do* it. Unlike high school teachers, college professors expect you to have the assignment ready the day you return to class.

Did you know that a student's attendance and final course grade are related? Research shows that top students have perfect or nearly perfect attendance. The pattern is clear: The greater the number of absences, the lower a student's final course grade tends to be. Fortunately, attendance is usually something you can control.

Let's talk a bit about being on time. Perhaps you've heard this joke:

Professor: You should have been here at nine o'clock!

Student: Why? What happened?

Or this joke:

Linn: How come you're always late to this class?

Pat: Lots of people have trouble making it to an eight o'clock class.

Linn: Yes, but this is a night class.

Or this one:

Student: I'm making progress. This is the earliest I've ever been late.

Kidding aside, being on time to class is important. Some students, though, sign up for early classes when they really aren't "morning people." Many students underestimate the amount of time it takes to get to campus. Some are always late because they didn't think about the bus schedule or traffic jams when they registered. Some evening students don't allow enough time to get from work to class. All of these students need to leave earlier for campus or else sign up for classes that meet at later times. Being chronically late isn't okay.

In fact, walking in late, especially if you do it repeatedly, is rude. It distracts your classmates and the instructor. It also puts you behind. Think about the kinds of things that happen at the beginning of class. Instructors take attendance, and some teachers mark you absent if you are not there when they take attendance. Instructors collect the homework or go over the answers. Some instructors give a brief overview of the day's lesson. They make other important announcements. Some give pop quizzes. Whenever you enter the classroom late, someone has to stop and catch you up, or else you have to sit there and try to figure out what's going on. Neither is a good thing.

So make it a habit to be on time to class. If you do happen to be late, don't "make an entrance." Enter quietly. Don't ask classmates what's going on or what has happened so far. That interferes with their learning. Wait until after class to ask a classmate or the instructor what you missed at the beginning. And it's always courteous to apologize to the instructor for being late.

By the way, it's important to stay for the entire class. Leaving early is just as bad as arriving late.

STOP AND PROCESS

EXERCISE 1.2

- Have you had good school attendance in the past? If not, are you willing to make a commitment to be at every class session? If not, why did you enroll? _____

  _____

  _____

- Are you usually on time? If so, terrific! If not, what do you need to do differently? _____

  _____

  _____

- Describe your plans for your attendance and punctuality in this class.

  _____

  _____

3. Learn your instructor's name and your classmates' names.

Want to know a simple way to enjoy class and learn more? Learn the names of your instructors and classmates. Even if you cannot learn everyone's name, learn as many as you can. After the first couple of class sessions, exchange names and phone numbers with a few of them. If you are ever confused about an assignment, you will know some classmates you can check with. Of course, you could also contact your instructor. You may also want to form a study group with a few classmates. (Study groups are discussed in Chapter 2.)

STOP AND PROCESS

EXERCISE 1.3

At this point, do you know the name of any classmates? Take a few minutes to exchange names and phone numbers with at least three of them. Also find out the time when you're most likely to be able to reach them by phone. Write this information here:

	Name	Phone Number	Best Time to Call
1.			
2.			
3.			

4. Sit in the right place.

In the real estate business, there is an old saying that "the three most important factors in buying a house are location, location, and location." What that means is no matter how good a house is, it's not a good buy if it's in a bad location.

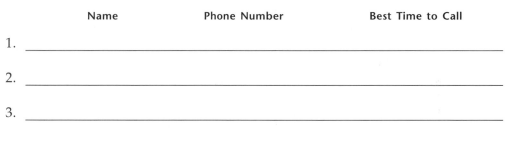

For students, "location," or where you sit in the classroom, is every bit as important. Where would you think the best places would be for a student to sit? The worst places?

Where you sit affects how much you learn. Regardless of how a classroom is arranged or the type of furniture, sit where you can see and hear best. Teachers know that students who want to do well sit near the front or wherever the action is. In fact, those students usually show up early just to get a good seat. Teachers know that motivated students like to be "in the loop."

BRAIN-FRIENDLY TIP

Before you continue with this chapter, take a minute to stretch your hands above your head and wiggle your fingers. Rotate your head in a circle first in one direction and then in the other.

It's a good idea to use some simple relaxation techniques every 15 minutes or so whenever you are reading and studying. It gets oxygen to your brain. It helps you maintain your focus.

Teachers also know that students who sit at the back often do not *intend* to participate. In classrooms with tables, they sit facing away from the instructor and the board in hopes that they won't be called on. They want to be "invisible." The truth is, the farther away you sit, the more likely you are to be distracted and not pay attention. You make it harder on yourself, not easier.

Of course, you may not always be able to pick where you sit. When you have a choice, though, don't limit your success by choosing a "bad" seat. Instead, select a seat that puts you where the action is. Even if it feels uncomfortable at first, choose a good seat.

If you know that you will be tempted to talk with certain classmates rather than pay attention, choose to sit away from them. Besides, research shows you learn more when you work with others who are different from you rather than working with friends.

Each week you have a few hours when you can be in class with an expert (your instructor) and learn from your classmates. To get the most out of that time and to maximize your success, choose a place to sit that puts you where the action is. Some instructors have students change seats during the semester so that everyone has a chance to sit in the best locations. If that doesn't happen, ask your instructor if you can change where you sit.

STOP AND PROCESS

EXERCISE 1.4

- In the past, when you had a choice, where have you sat in classrooms? Why did you choose that location? What effect do you

  think it had on your learning? _____

  _____

  _____

- Where do you sit in this class? Is it a "good" location? Why or why not?

  _____

  _____

- What do you think the effect would be on your learning if you always sat near the front or facing the area where the instructor is?

  _____

  _____

5. Come prepared for class, and participate.

It isn't news that it's important to participate in class. But participating is more than just answering your instructor's questions. *Asking* a good question is also a way to participate. An example of a "good question" is asking for clarification (asking the instructor to make something clearer).

In contrast, these are not good questions: a question that makes it obvious you haven't been paying attention, or asking about a grade you received or other matters that pertain only to you. Handle those things outside of class.

Many students feel shy about speaking up in class. If this describes you, you may find that asking questions is a comfortable way to learn to participate. If it makes you feel more secure, you can write out a question or two before class. You'll have it there to look at when you get ready to ask. The biggest mistake you can make is being afraid to make a mistake.

Even if you have to force yourself, speak up during the first couple of weeks of class. *Research indicates that students who do not speak up at least once during the first few class sessions usually do not speak in class the entire rest of the semester.* It's normal to feel a little stress when you speak for the first time in a class. Once you have done it, though, it is easier the next time. After all, you don't want it to look as if you've chosen shoulder shrugging as your college major! The only people who are never scared or embarrassed are the ones who never take any chances. They don't learn very much either, and they miss out on a lot of what college and life have to offer.

Participating in group activities is another way to contribute to class; so is listening attentively. Offering examples and observations are ways to participate, but be careful not to get off track with lengthy personal examples or issues.

You will be ready to participate in class only if you have prepared for class. Doing the homework prepares you to learn as much as possible at the next class session. It enables you to make a contribution to the class.

If you have not done the homework, you will not be ready to participate. You may think that it's no big deal. This isn't true. When you come unprepared, you let your classmates down. You let the instructor down. You let yourself down. It is harder for you to pay attention because you do not understand what is going on. In short, being prepared just makes sense.

There's a joke about a student who tells his roommate that he wants to go to a party, so he asks his roommate if he will do the homework for him. His roommate says, "No. It just wouldn't be right." He replies, "Well, maybe not. But give it a try anyway." You need to do the homework *yourself*. There may be times when you are tempted to copy someone else's homework. Don't do it. You won't be ready to participate unless you've done the assignment yourself, and you won't feel very good about yourself.

Sometimes students who come to class without the homework try to finish it in class. If you do this, you hurt yourself twice: You are not prepared for class that day, and you make matters worse by not paying attention to the very material you need to learn. In this case, it's better to concentrate on what's going on in class.

Another part of being prepared for class is showing up with your textbook and other materials you need for class. Teachers are impressed when you do this. In contrast, you create a negative impression if you repeatedly offer excuses for not bringing what you need. ("I left it at home" or "I forgot to put it in my book bag.") Constantly needing to borrow a pencil and to look on with someone else because you forgot your book are things to avoid.

Make it a habit to check your assignment sheet and your book bag before you leave for class each day. That way, you'll arrive with everything you need. In fact, it's a good idea to pack your book bag the night before. You won't be grabbing things at the last minute—or make yourself late because you can't find something (more on this in a minute).

Concentrate on what's going on in class. It's a mistake to "tune out" because you want to get a jump on the next homework assignment. It's also a mistake to work on assignments for other classes. If you are going to do these things, you might as well not have come to class that day.

Make a commitment to come prepared for class and to participate.

STOP AND PROCESS

EXERCISE 1.5

- Do you come to class prepared (you've done the homework)? If not, why not? _____

  _____

  _____

- Do you usually participate in class? If so, in what ways do you participate? If you do not usually participate, why not? _____

  _____

  _____

- What changes could you make to improve your preparation and participation? _____

  _____

  _____

6. Be polite and use appropriate language.

Being polite is important. It may sound obvious and even silly to mention that, but lots of people forget even to say "please" and "thank you." It's polite to greet others while you're waiting for class to begin and to say good-bye at the end. It makes others feel good about you and think well of you. Politeness is the WD-40 of relationships. It makes all of them go more smoothly.

An old joke goes, "Our professor says that his job is to talk and that ours is to listen. But we usually finish before he does." Being polite means not talking when someone else is speaking. It might be another student or the instructor. It means paying attention and not being disruptive. Eating, putting on makeup, text messaging or checking your cell phone for messages, and talking when you should be listening are real turn-offs in a college classroom.

Some behaviors are obviously disruptive, but did you know that dozing off and sleeping in class are rude and disruptive? There's a gag about a student who always sleeps in class:

First student: Why are you late?

Second student: I overslept.

First student: You mean you sleep at home too?

There are valid reasons why a student might doze off in class. He's exhausted from working a double shift. She was up all night studying for a test or helping a sick roommate, child, or other relative. Allergy medicine made him very drowsy. What it looks like to everyone else, though, is that the sleeper has no interest in the class. If you doze off in class, apologize to the instructor and explain what caused it.

If you are chronically tired, that's a different matter. Reconsider your schedule and lifestyle. Do you need to get more rest? Work fewer hours? Take fewer courses? Exercise more? Eat a better diet?

Just as your level of alertness influences others' opinion of you, so do the words you use. Mohandas ("Mahatma") Gandhi, an Indian nationalist and revered spiritual leader, said, "A language is an exact reflection of the character and growth of its speakers." Your language, the words you know and choose, are an exact reflection of your own character and growth. Make your words reflect positively on you.

Some students are so accustomed to using inappropriate language that it sounds normal to them. They don't realize the poor impression they may be making on others, especially their professors (and employers). Certain words that are okay to use outside of class with your friends may not be okay in class.

People who use profanity or other inappropriate language typically do it to sound grown up or impressive. Instead, it makes them sound immature. It also makes them sound as if they have limited, weak vocabularies and that they are trying to make up for it by talking that way. A better way to sound "powerful" is to develop a great vocabulary!

A student who uses bad language can unknowingly make other students feel uncomfortable. Making negative comments about other people or groups also makes others uncomfortable, and it can lower their opinion of you. Rude comments reflect badly on the person who makes them.

Finally, think for a minute about your overall speech habits:

- Do you sprinkle your sentences with empty, irritating fillers such as "uh," "like," and "you know"? Do you say, "He's, like, uh, you

> **BONUS TIP**
>
> Let's hope this never happens, but if you are ever so exhausted that you absolutely cannot stay awake in class, go home and sleep. You won't get anything out of class even if you are "there." (Besides, you'll be more comfortable sleeping at home.)
>
> If you can't go home, or if you are so tired that driving might be dangerous, go to your college's health center. Explain your situation and ask if you can lie down for a while. If they have space, they will usually allow you to do this. Tell them what time your next class is, and ask them to wake you up in time to go to it.

know, a really nice guy" instead of, "He's really nice"? If so, the first step is to become aware of this habit.

- Do you make statements sound like questions? If you're not sure, listen to yourself when you speak, or ask your friends. If you have this confusing habit, concentrate on dropping your voice at the ends of sentences. You will sound more definite, confident, and mature.

- Is *got* the main verb in your vocabulary? There's always a better, more precise verb that can be used instead. Just for fun, try this the rest of the day: Find a better word whenever you start to use *got*.

If your answer to any of the questions above is yes, follow the suggestions for changing them.

College is a great time to add words to your vocabulary and to develop speech habits that will help you get ahead not only in school but also in the workplace.

 ## STOP AND PROCESS

EXERCISE 1.6

- How would you rate yourself in terms of politeness? _____

_____

_____

- How well do you pay attention in class? What keeps you from

  paying attention? _____

_____

_____

- Do you use appropriate language in the classroom? If not, were

  you aware that it might be a problem? _____

_____

_____

- Do you have any annoying speech habits, such as constantly using "like" or "you know"? (If you're not sure, ask your friends or

  family members. They'll tell you!) _____

_____

_____

- What improvements do you need to make in your politeness,

  language, and speech habits? _____

_____

_____

Become the Student—and Person—You Want to Be

www.mhhe.com/
entryways

For more suggestions
and strategies for
college success, go to
**Catalyst> Learning>
Study Skills Tutor>
Doing Well in College**

It's been said that the type of student you are is the type of person you are. If you are motivated, responsible, honest, and hardworking, you are likely to be that type of student. So if you want to change the type of student you are, change the type of person you are.

College is wonderful because it gives you a chance to reinvent yourself: You can become any type of person you want to be. What type of student do you want to be? Organized? High achieving? Respected? Eager to learn? Dependable?

The positive qualities you develop to help you in college will serve you well in every area of your life. Those same qualities will make you a better employee or employer, a better spouse or partner in a relationship, a better parent, a better neighbor, and a better citizen. Never doubt it: You can become the kind of person and student you want to be.

MY TOOLBOX *of Classroom Success Behaviors*

Tools are devices that help you accomplish tasks. You can use them to create new things, to fix things, and to solve problems. In any job, tools are necessary. At this time, your "job" is being a student. Start now to assemble your own "toolbox" of important information and skills. At first, you may feel that your toolbox doesn't have many tools in it. That's okay. As you progress through this book, you will be adding tools in every chapter. Tools consist of concepts and strategies that pertain to academic success, vocabulary, reading, and study skills.

In order to remember this information, you must rehearse it. Two effective ways to rehearse information are to say it and to write it. That's why you are asked to "stop and process" information at various points in the chapters. That's also why you need to record important information in your toolbox.

What specifically can you do to make yourself more successful in the classroom? On the following page or on a separate page, record the five items that you identified with your classmates in the Looking at What You Already Know section (at the beginning of the chapter), as well as the six points from this chapter. Some of the same items may be on both lists, so you may have fewer than 11 items.

Different people would organize a toolbox in different ways. Since each person learns differently, you should organize the information in your toolbox in a way that will help you most. Here are some possibilities:

- **Write a list of the classroom success tools discussed in this chapter, along with the ones that the entire class agreed on.** Write them in your own words so that you will remember them. If you like, you can use more than one color pen. Color helps some students remember information more easily.

- **Pretend you are writing a letter to someone who is just starting college.** In your letter, include the important classroom success behaviors covered in this chapter. (Explaining something to someone else is a great way to review and learn it yourself.)

- **If you prefer, you can create a study map (concept map).** Draw a circle in the middle of the page with the words "Classroom Success Behaviors" in it. Then write specific success behaviors on lines that radiate from the circle. You can include small illustrations or sketches, and work with colored pens. (The Online Reading Lab, or ORL, has information on making study maps.)

When you have finished your list, letter, or map, put a star or a check mark beside the three behaviors that you think will help *you* most. Make a commitment to concentrate on these three behaviors first. Once they become habits, you can begin to add other success behaviors that are in your toolbox. *You can do it!*

✓ CHAPTER CHECK

Answer these questions about the information in the chapter. Write the missing word or information in each blank. When there is more than one part to the answer, there is more than one blank.

1. In every course, you should read the _____, or course description, to be sure you understand all of the important information about the course.

2. Information in the course description could include

   _____, _____, and

   _____. (List at least three things.)

3. After you have read the course description, you should

   _____ it.

4. You should try to be in class on _____, every

   _____.

5. Two times you should try never to be absent:

   _____ or _____. (List any

   two of the specific times mentioned as times you should try never to

   miss class.)

6. If you are absent twice in a row, you should contact your

   _____.

7. When you are absent, you should find out what the

   _____ is, and then do it.

8. Even if an instructor allows some excused absences, you should try to

   _____ them rather than use them.

9. You should learn the names of your _____ and

   your _____.

10. In the classroom, you should sit where you can

    _____ and _____ well.

11. In addition to answering questions, you can participate in class by

    _____ questions.

12. If you have not done the _____, you will not be

    ready to participate in class.

13. The classroom is a place to be _____ and to use

    appropriate _____.

14. Making negative comments about other people or groups reflects

    badly on the person who makes the _____.

15. The type of student you are is the type of _____

    you are.

REVIEW EXERCISES

SET 1

Read these comments by Lynn, a 20-year-old first-semester community college student. She lives with her parents; she works 30 hours a week as a cashier. She didn't enjoy high school but believes that she will have better job and life opportunities if she continues her education. She has completed the first two weeks of the semester and reports she is already starting to feel frustrated and discouraged. Based on the chapter information, what advice would you give her to help her turn the situation around? Write your suggestions and advice in the space provided.

"I was late the first day of class since I didn't know where the classroom was. I chose a seat at the back of the room in the corner. My psychology instructor—I don't know his name—was just finishing going over a handout about the course. I put mine in my notebook, but I haven't had time to look at it. I haven't had a chance to buy the textbook either. But I got paid yesterday, so I plan to get it this weekend. I think there have already been a couple of assignments the instructor has taken up. I'm worried because I don't know if I can turn them in late, or if I can, whether it will affect my grade.

"The instructor said that we have a short quiz next week, but I'm not sure which day he said it's going to be. Once I find out, I'm thinking about not going to class that day. Tests make me nervous. Besides, there's lots of stuff I don't understand, and I'm not sure where to get help.

"At this point, I really don't know the name of anyone else in the class, except for a girl named Ann. She's nice and very funny. We sit next to each other, and we've written a couple of notes back and forth. There's another girl who sits nearby. She seems to understand what's going on in class, but I don't know how to get in touch with her.

"So far I haven't said anything in class. I'm hoping the instructor won't ever call on me, but I know that sooner or later he will. It stresses me just to think about it. I get all flustered. Besides, I probably wouldn't know the answer anyway.

"I'm considering dropping out and starting fresh next semester, but I hate to lose the tuition I've paid. Also, my parents would be all over me. Even if I quit now and try again next semester, I'm not sure that things would be any different. I don't know what to do."

_____

_____

_____

_____

_____

_____

_____

_____

_____

_____

_____

_____

_____

_____

_____

_____

———————

SET 2

Now read what Pat has written. He's a first-semester student whose goal is to earn a degree in physical education and become a high school coach. He plays on the college's baseball team and has practice four afternoons a week. Although it's still early in the semester, he has begun to experience problems. Use the chapter information as the basis for giving advice to Pat.

"I play first base on the baseball team. Baseball is my main interest and has been ever since I was a kid. I love the game. I know I'm not good enough to play professionally, but my athletic ability helped me get a scholarship to go here.

"Most of my classes are going okay, but my math teacher is a total jerk. I take that class at night. I took math at night because that's when my girlfriend is on campus. She works during the day. Also, I have baseball practice nearly every afternoon this semester, and I like to hang around afterwards and get in a little weight training or talk with my teammates.

"I'm usually late to math. I have to clean up after practice and stuff. The instructor told me that I couldn't be walking in late all the time, and that it would lower my grade. I told her that I get there as soon as I can and that I thought her rule was stupid and that she shouldn't treat college students like they were still in elementary school.

"I'm usually hungry after I work out, so I eat a candy bar or something as soon as I get to class. The teacher gives me a dirty look, but I can't see how having a snack is any big deal. Usually I just lean back in my chair and pull my baseball cap down on my forehead.

"Fortunately, my chair faces the classroom door, so I can see what's going on in the hall. My girlfriend comes by if she gets out early. We usually text-message during class so that we'll know what time to meet and where.

"I know I'm having problems in this class, but it's because the instructor is so totally unreasonable. Like she got mad at me last week because I hadn't done the assignment. It wasn't my fault. She puts the assignment on the board. I wrote it on a piece of scratch paper, but it must have fallen out of my notebook. How am I supposed to do the assignment if I don't know what it is? That's totally unfair.

"Last Tuesday night, I was actually on time. You'd think she'd be glad. I was trying to finish the homework problems during the few minutes before class started, and she *still* gave me a dirty look. There's no way to win. What am I supposed to do?"

_____

_____

_____

_____

_____

_____

_____

_____

_____

_____

_____

_____

_____

_____

_____

_____

_____

_____

_____

ASSESS YOUR UNDERSTANDING

Your brain has the remarkable ability to think about its own thinking. This is a good thing because it's important for you to monitor or evaluate your learning. For example, when you read, you need to ask yourself, "Am I understanding this?" If the answer is no, then you need to ask yourself, "Why not?" Once you have pinpointed the problem, ask yourself, "What do I need to do to fix the situation?" Asking and answering these questions will enable you to make useful changes.

CROSS-CHAPTER CONNECTIONS

In Chapter 2 (pages 32–63) you will learn that *using feedback to monitor your progress* is a helpful out-of-class behavior. In addition, you'll learn about steps you can take whenever you feel you do not understand material in your textbooks.

Assessing your own understanding empowers you to become a better student. If there are things that confuse you, you'll know exactly what they are. You'll have time to correct the problems or to get help with them well before a test or before you go on to new material.

Take a minute now to evaluate how well you understand the material in this chapter. How did you do on the Chapter Check? Also, ask yourself, "Could I tell someone what the six in-class success behaviors are? Could I explain what each behavior is and why it's important?" On a scale of 1–10, circle a number on the scale that reflects your level of understanding.

1 . . . . . 2 . . . . . 3 . . . . . 4 . . . . . 5 . . . . . 6 . . . . . 7 . . . . . 8 . . . . . 9 10

I'm lost!   **I kind of get it.**   **I could teach it!**

This next step can make all the difference: *Unless you marked 10 on the scale above, identify what it is that you don't understand.* What, specifically, confuses you? Is it a particular success behavior? Or are you vague on several of them? What caused you not to understand? Take time to answer these questions. If you know what the problem is, you can decide how to solve it. Write your response on the lines below.

If there were things you didn't understand or success behaviors you couldn't remember, what steps could you take to fix the problem? Do you need to reread some or all of the chapter? Go over the exercises? Ask a classmate or your instructor questions? Write the information down or review it some other way? Write your response here:

_____

_____

_____

_____

_____

Monitoring your understanding, identifying trouble spots, and correcting them are major strategies for success. That's why you'll be asked to do a quick self-assessment at the end of each chapter, such as the one you just completed. These are for your own benefit and not for a grade. You'll become better and better at self-assessment. You've taken the first step, and you're on your way!

Map of Chapters

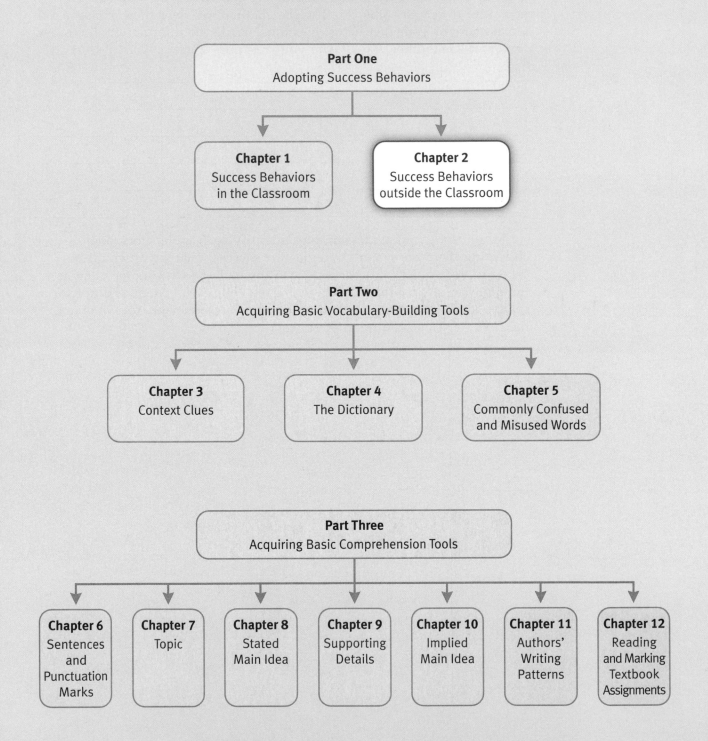

Part One
Adopting Success Behaviors

Chapter 1
Success Behaviors
in the Classroom

Chapter 2
Success Behaviors
outside the Classroom

Part Two
Acquiring Basic Vocabulary-Building Tools

Chapter 3
Context Clues

Chapter 4
The Dictionary

Chapter 5
Commonly Confused
and Misused Words

Part Three
Acquiring Basic Comprehension Tools

Chapter 6
Sentences
and
Punctuation
Marks

Chapter 7
Topic

Chapter 8
Stated
Main Idea

Chapter 9
Supporting
Details

Chapter 10
Implied
Main Idea

Chapter 11
Authors'
Writing
Patterns

Chapter 12
Reading
and Marking
Textbook
Assignments

CHAPTER 2
Success Behaviors outside the Classroom

Do the Right Thing

Why You Need to Know the Information in This Chapter

College differs from high school in several ways, but one of the most challenging ones is that you have to do more of the learning on your own outside of class. The typical college course is a three-hour or three-credit course: You spend only three hours a week in class. That's not very much time! This means that you must be prepared for those three hours. This chapter explains what you can do to be organized and ready to shine in class.

Using these out-of-class behaviors consistently will enable you to

- learn more

- feel more confident

- look forward to going to class

- reduce your stress

- make higher grades

"I'm too busy going to college to study."

Source: Copyright © 2006 William Haefeli from cartoonbank.com. All rights reserved.

33

Super Student Tips

Here are tips from other students who have been successful in college classes like the one you're taking now. Here's what experience has taught them:

"My sister told me to talk to the instructor whenever I need help. I was a little scared at first, but it turned out to be very good advice."—*Tram*

"I never knew to write out my goals. It's made a difference. I taped them on my desk at home, so I'm reminded about them every day."—*April*

"Soccer is my sport. I've learned that the same things I do to be good in soccer are the same things that make me better in school. You have to show up. You have to practice. You have to have a good attitude."—*Jorge*

"I got a PDA [personal digital assistant, a handheld electronic organizer] for my birthday. It's really cool, and it helps me stay organized."—*Antonio*

Jumpstart Your Brain!

Before you start this chapter, do a few shoulder shrugs. Stretch your arms over your head. These relax you and give your brain extra oxygen. Now, jumpstart your brain—give it renewed energy—by solving these brainteasers.

By moving exactly two matches in each equation, turn the equation into one that is mathematically correct. You can turn one number into another; you can change the "sign" into another sign (/, +, −, or ×). The equal sign (=) will not change, of course. The only rules are (1) you must move exactly two matches somewhere else in the equation, and (2) the new equation must be correct mathematically. (For example, 2 + 2 = 4 is mathematically correct; 2 + 2 = 5 is not.) To "move" a match that's in the original equation, use a pencil and mark lightly. You can erase a line if you change your mind. Write your finished equation to the right of the original one. Remember that different people have different gifts. Solving brainteasers of this sort may or may not be yours. If it's not, try it on your own first (it will still cause brain growth!), and then find a classmate who has this aptitude. Have fun "matching" wits with this brainteaser. Good luck!

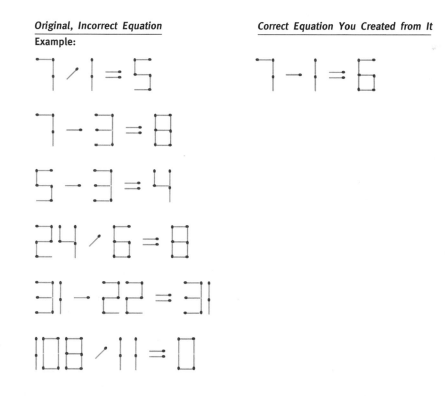

How did you do? Compare your answers to your classmates' answers. Check to see if everyone followed the rules and has mathematically correct equations. Explain to each other how you went about solving these brainteasers.

LOOKING AT WHAT YOU ALREADY KNOW

 Regardless of whether you finished high school or have attended college before, you already have some ideas about what you can do *out of class* in order to be more successful in class. Use the space below to list at least five out-of-class "success" behaviors. Focus on things that could help you succeed in *this* class.

1. _____

2. _____

3. _____

4. _____

5. _____

Compare your finished list with three or four of your classmates' lists. In small groups, decide on the five most important success behaviors outside of class. When all of the groups are finished, share your lists. Then decide as a class on the top five success behaviors. Jot down the class's final list on scratch paper. You will need it for the My Toolbox section at the end of the chapter.

Success Behaviors outside the Classroom

Do it right. Do it now.

Change your thoughts and you change your world.
—Norman Vincent Peale

If you are new to college, this chapter will be as important for you as Chapter 1. If you have attended college previously, you will recognize things you are doing right, and you will learn new things as well.

The Big Picture for This Chapter

This chapter focuses on what you can do *outside* the classroom to become a more successful student. The suggestions and strategies pertain to what you can do before and after class rather than while you are in class.

College professors expect you to do a great deal of learning outside of class and to do whatever it takes to accomplish this. This might include spending more time studying, getting tutoring, participating in a study group, and reading easier books on your subjects. Professors expect you to do the assigned reading and any other homework. Most of them expect you to use your textbooks as the primary source of information. Your professors expect you to find out about and take advantage of your college's resources, such as the tutoring center and the library. They expect you to attend class and to contact them if you miss more than a couple of classes. They expect you to let them know when you need help. They expect you to find out what the assignment is when you are absent and to complete it before you return to class. Motivating yourself is your responsibility.

Now read the rest of this chapter to see how your class's list compares with the six success behaviors discussed here. Did you identify some of the same behaviors?

Six Out-of-Class Success Behaviors

www.mhhe.com/
entryways

To explore how these behaviors fit with work, see "Making Career Connections" (writing activity).

Here are six out-of-class behaviors that can make you more successful, effective, and relaxed in class:

- **Set goals and make a commitment.**
- **Get organized.**
- **Prepare for class.**
- **Manage your assignments.**

- Monitor your progress and see your instructor when you need help.
- Take advantage of out-of-class resources.

Let's look at specific information about each of the six out-of-class success behaviors.

1. Set goals and make a commitment.

Visualize yourself six months from now. Where are you? Did you complete this semester successfully? (You'll be able to visualize more effectively if you close your eyes.) Now visualize yourself three years from now. What has changed in your life? Finally, visualize yourself 20 years from now. What have you accomplished? What are you most proud of?

Many people never think hard about what they want out of life. They just move along day to day. But did you know that simply creating goals and putting them in writing can make you happier and more successful, not only in school but in every area of your life? Setting goals means deciding exactly what you want to achieve in terms of your education, health, personal relationships, career, and finances. You may also have goals in categories such as travel, volunteer work, or spiritual development.

In college, motivation is a do-it-yourself job. That's one reason it's so important to set goals: Having goals is motivating. You know you are working toward things that matter to you, so you feel a drive to succeed, and pride and satisfaction when you achieve a goal. Success builds on success. Your growing sense of confidence and pride keep you motivated.

So how do you go about setting goals? One way is to list some of the categories mentioned above—education, career, finance, and so on—and then write out your goals for each. You should also set a deadline for achieving each goal. (Think of goals as "dreams with deadlines.") Try classifying each of your goals by one of these lengths of time:

- **Short-term goals** are ones you want to accomplish during the *next six months to a year*.
- **Intermediate goals** are ones you want to accomplish during the *next one to five years*.
- **Long-term goals** are ones you want to accomplish during your *lifetime*.

Your short-term goals should move you toward your intermediate goals, and those in turn should move you toward your long-term goals.

There are two characteristics of effective goals. First, goals must be *realistic*. They should be ones you can achieve in the time you set, even if you have to work hard to achieve them. "I will earn a college degree in two years while working full time" isn't a realistic goal. A more realistic one would be, "During the next three years, I will complete my associate's degree in business and obtain my

BRAIN-FRIENDLY TIP

As athletes know, *visualization* is such a powerful technique that they often include it as part of their training. In their mind's eye, they "practice" a skill over and over again by seeing themselves performing it perfectly. Visualization works because our brains accept as real the mental pictures we create in our minds.

Create pictures in your mind of achieving your goals: making a high grade on a test, walking across the stage and receiving your diploma, becoming a successful business owner—whatever you aspire to. The more detailed your pictures, the better. Where are you? What are you wearing? Who is with you? How do you feel?

If you can visualize it, you believe it. If you believe it, you can achieve it. Don't let anyone tell you otherwise! The only person who can limit you is yourself.

real estate license." Second, goals must be *specific*. "I want to do better in school" is too vague. A specific goal is, "I will make at least a B in all of my courses this semester."

On the chart on page 40, write at least three of your short-term, intermediate term, and long-term goals. Then fill in the columns that tell why the goal is important to you and how you will feel when you achieve the goal. This information is a necessary part of the exercise. What motivates people to accomplish a goal is the personal relevance of the goal and the feelings that achieving it will produce in them. (Goals are personal. If you prefer not to write yours in your book, photocopy the page and then fill it out.)

If you feel stuck about how to achieve what you most want in life, fill out My Vision of Success, on page 41 (or write the same information on another sheet of paper). It's an excellent tool for identifying the resources and strategies that can help you attain your vision of success.

Put your written goals where you will see them often—above your desk or on the bathroom mirror, for example. Every few months, revise them if you need to. The important thing is to have realistic, specific goals you are working toward.

Setting goals is not enough. You must also make a commitment to achieving them. Will you encounter obstacles? Absolutely. A wise person once said, "If you can find a path without any obstacles, it probably doesn't lead anywhere." Overcoming the obstacles gives the goals their value.

If a certificate or degree is one of your goals, you should make school a priority. There will be times when you have to give up something fun or satisfying at the moment for the greater satisfaction of achieving a bigger, more meaningful longer-term goal.

STOP AND PROCESS

EXERCISE 2.1

- Have you ever written out your goals? If so, was it helpful? If you have never written out your goals, why not? _____

_____

_____

- If you have set goals in the past, did you achieve them? If not, what prevented you? _____

_____

_____

- If you've never written out your goals, how would it benefit you to write them out now? _____

_____

_____

Putting Your Goals in Writing

	Goal	Why This Goal Is Important to Me	How I Will Feel When I Achieve the Goal
Short-Term Goals (6 to 12 months)	1.		
	2.		
	3.		
Intermediate Goals (1 to 5 years)	1.		
	2.		
	3.		
Long-Term Goals (Lifetime)	1.		
	2.		
	3.		

MY VISION OF SUCCESS

1. In the middle of the page, put a photo, picture, or drawing of what you most want to do or be in your life. (You can use a separate, larger sheet of paper if you prefer.) At the bottom of the page, write a success statement that tells what you plan to achieve.
2. List the skills and traits you need in order to achieve your goal. Rank them and circle the most important skill.
3. Jot down the steps you must take to achieve your goal.
4. Write the names of people who can mentor you (advise and encourage you).
5. List any obstacles that you will have to overcome and ways to overcome them.
6. List the resources that are available to help you achieve your dream.
7. List any accomplishments and awards you have already achieved.

Post this sheet where you will see it. Read your success statement aloud in front of a mirror ten times, morning and evening, for ten days. Remember that your brain will accept it as "true"!

Skills and traits I need:

- _____
- _____
- _____
- _____
- _____
- _____
- _____

Steps to achieving my goal:

1. _____
2. _____
3. _____
4. _____
5. _____
6. _____
7. _____

Resources available to me:

- _____
- _____
- _____

Photo, picture, or drawing of what
I most want to do
or be in life.

My previous awards and accomplishments:

- _____
- _____
- _____

How I will feel when I achieve my goal:

- _____

Obstacles I may face:

- _____
- _____
- _____
- _____
- _____

How I can overcome the obstacles:

- _____
- _____
- _____
- _____
- _____

People who can advise and encourage me:

- _____
- _____
- _____
- _____
- _____

My success statement: _____

_____

Source: Adapted from Colin Rose and Malcolm Nicholl, *Accelerated Learning for the 21st Century*, New York: Dell, 1997, p. 79.

2. Get organized.

College students' number one complaint is that they have too much to do in too little time. Sometimes, they're right! They are working too many hours, taking too many classes, or have too many other commitments and responsibilities. They are stressed and exhausted. If that describes you, you'll have to decide where you can cut back.

Perhaps you're not sure whether your days are too full. Well, here's one way to get an objective picture. Think of the 24 hours in a day as 24 links in a chain:

On a typical weekday, how many "links" (hours) do you spend attending classes? Color or shade in the same number of links. How many links would be spent working? Commuting? Eating meals? Doing other set activities (household chores, athletic practice or exercise, or church, for example)? Shade those links. How much time do you typically spend watching TV? Sleeping? Shade in links for those. You can use different colors for different types of activities if you like. Now count the number of links that are left, the ones that are not shaded in. That's the maximum number of hours you have available for studying on a typical day. (You should base this activity on two back-to-back weekdays if your Monday-Wednesday-Friday schedule is considerably different from your Tuesday-Thursday one. Find the average amount of time for various activities.)

If you're like most college students, you could manage your time much better by becoming more organized. Several strategies will help you do this. Let's look at these next.

Make a schedule.

www.mhhe.com/
entryways

For blank weekly
and monthly
schedules, To Do
List, and Study
Habits Self-
Evaluation, go to
**Catalyst>
Learning>Study
Skills Tutor>
Making the Most
of Your Time**

If you've already made a schedule, congratulate yourself! If you don't have one and you plan to study "whenever you can find the time," you'll never find it! "One of these days" usually turns into "none of these days." Making a schedule is the answer. Here's how to use the blank schedule on page 44:

1. **Block out the times you are in class, have other set responsibilities (work, for example), or would otherwise not be available to study** (meals, exercise, commuting, sleeping). Build in a reasonable amount of time for leisure activities you enjoy. A schedule shouldn't consist only of work. No one could follow such a schedule—or would want to!

2. **Look at the times that are left.** Allow at least two hours of study time for every hour you are in class. For most courses, that will mean six hours per week. Many new college students are surprised at how much time studying takes. Research shows that college students routinely underestimate how long it will take them to do

their homework, study for tests, write papers, and so on. As a result, they put off these activities until the last minute and then run out of time. Stressful!

3. **From the times that are still available, block out the times when you plan to study.** It's not enough just to write "study." Write the specific subject you will study at the specific time. For example, on Tuesday and Thursday afternoons from 4:00 p.m. to 5:30 p.m., you might write, "Study math." ("Study" means anything connected with a course: read the assignment, complete written work, study for a test, etc.)

Once you have your schedule, stick with it. Keep your schedule in your notebook, or post it near your desk. Allow at least three weeks to get used to your new schedule. It takes three weeks to establish a new habit or change an old one. After 21 days, it will seem normal to study at certain times each day.

Many students say they put off doing homework, but once they get started, they're fine. A schedule solves the problem of putting homework off. You'll generally feel more in control of your time and less stressed. There are additional bonuses of following a schedule: You'll have more free time, and you'll enjoy it more. You won't feel guilty that you should be studying.

> **BONUS TIP**
>
> Two online resources for time management are www.studygs.net/timman.htm, a set of time management tips, and http://www.studygs.net/ schedule for developing a schedule. It includes a "learner's daily planner." In this Flash exercise, you can review how you spend your time in a typical day and week. You can also write out your priorities (goals), as well as pick up tips for scheduling with your college's calendar.

You can modify your schedule, but try not to use study time for anything else. If you have to miss a study session, make up the time as soon as possible.

Another tip: Keep a semester calendar. On a regular calendar, write test dates, due dates for papers and projects, exam dates, and so forth. That way, you can see well ahead of time what is coming up. You won't suddenly discover that you have two tests on the same day, and you won't get caught at the last minute before a major assignment is due.

STOP AND PROCESS

EXERCISE 2.2

Following the guidelines just discussed, fill out the blank schedule printed on page 44. You may prefer to make a photocopy and fill it out instead. That way, you can keep it in your notebook or some other convenient place.

Use an assignment notebook.

You can't do the assignment if you don't know what it is, so write every assignment in an assignment notebook. Include the date it was assigned and the day it is due.

WEEKLY STUDY SCHEDULE

Time	Sunday	Monday	Tuesday	Wednesday	Thursday	Friday	Saturday
6:00							
7:00							
8:00							
9:00							
10:00							
11:00							
12:00							
1:00							
2:00							
3:00							
4:00							
5:00							
6:00							
7:00							
8:00							
9:00							
10:00							
11:00							
12:00							
1:00							

(A.M. for 6:00–11:00, P.M. for 12:00–11:00, A.M. for 12:00–1:00)

BRAIN-FRIENDLY TIP

Visual-spatial learners, in particular, need to pay attention to structuring their time. If you're a visual-spatial learner, wear a watch, choose friends who manage their time well—in short, use any strategies necessary to gain control of your time. Be creative. Remember to build some free time into your schedule.

Buy an inexpensive assignment notebook that's made for this purpose, or use a small spiral. You can even use notebook paper, but keep it in one special section of your notebook. The key is *always to write assignments in one certain place*. You'll know where to find them, and you can see at a glance what you need to do before your classes meet again. Besides, it's satisfying to check off the assignments as you complete them.

Set priorities with a daily To Do list.

Did you know that after full-time college students take out time for meals, sleeping, and attending classes, they still have to make decisions about how to spend ten hours of every day? In fact, each day, you must make hundreds of decisions about how to use your time. **Setting priorities** means making decisions about what is most important.

How you spend your time is more important than how you spend your money. Money mistakes can usually be corrected, but time is gone forever. Writer Annie Dillard says, "The way you spend your days is the way you spend your life." If you don't do the important things each day, you end up feeling tired, yet you feel you didn't accomplish anything. If

> ✳ **BONUS TIP**
>
> The phone is your enemy when you're trying to study. Follow these strategies:
>
> - Train your friends not to call during your study time. For example, tell them to call after 9:00 p.m.
> - Resist the temptation to answer the phone while you are studying. Turn off your cell phone.
> - Make or return phone calls *after* you have finished studying.

it goes on long enough, you may end up feeling that your *life* was not well spent. That would be a tragedy.

A famous 19-century American writer, Ralph Waldo Emerson, reminds us, "Be grateful for each new day. A new day that you have never lived before. Twenty-four new, fresh hours, unexplored hours to use usefully and profitably. We can squander, neglect or use it. Life will be richer or poorer by the way we use today." Treat each day as the gift it is.

One way to accomplish this is to create a daily To Do list. To make a To Do list, write down everything you want to accomplish that day. Index cards work well. Then go through your list and set priorities by numbering items according to their importance. When you do the items on the list, start with your number one priority. After you complete the first task, move to the second item, and so forth. Unless you prioritize, you will be tempted to do easy, unimportant items first. For example, your number one priority may be to study for a test, your number five priority may be to wash your car, and your number six priority may be to return phone calls to friends. A prioritized list will encourage you to study first and then, if you have time, wash your car or call friends.

Know when and where to study.

Visualize a time when you had a successful study session. Where were you? What made it successful? Were you by yourself or with others?

Think, too, about what you read in the "Identify Your Learning Style" section at the beginning of this book. When is the best time for you to study? Are you an early bird? A night owl? Consider these questions when you choose your class times and plan your study schedule. Research suggests that most students accomplish more when they study during daylight hours than at night. What matters, though, is what works best for you. Try to study at times when you are not overly tired. Learning takes longer when you are tired or sleepy.

Drink a glass of water before you study. Water supplies your brain with some of the oxygen it needs. When you study, periodically stand up and stretch. This gets additional oxygen to your brain, and it relaxes you.

Eating a high protein snack before you begin is also helpful. If you snack while you study, skip drinks and snacks with caffeine, fat, or sugar. Choose a piece of fruit or some other healthful snack instead. You'll think more clearly. (See the Brain-Friendly Tips box on page 46.)

Where should you study? Again, think about the kind of environment that suits your learning style. Do you need a quiet place? At home, close the door and turn off the stereo, radio, or TV; leave the headphones off. If you live in a noisy environment, buy some inexpensive earplugs at the drugstore. Study on campus at the library or some other quiet place.

If you need some background sound, play low music, but not songs with words. (See the Brain-Friendly Tips box below for more information on brain-friendly music.) Perhaps you need a place where you can read some of the material out loud or recite information you are memorizing. If being in a study group works for you, check your school library. They often have special rooms that small groups can use. Also, you may find an empty classroom you can use. For obvious reasons, avoid the cafeteria and the student lounge as places to study.

Study at a desk or table, if that works for you. If you need to move when you read or study, try slowly pacing back and forth. Some students find that chewing gum helps get rid of excess energy (chew sugarless gum, please, to spare your teeth). Also, find a place where the lighting suits you. Some people do better with bright light; others do better with soft light.

Before you begin studying, have all the supplies you need at hand, either in a desk drawer or in your backpack. You disrupt your concentration every time you stop, whether it's to hunt for a highlighter or to answer the phone.

Choose one spot for your "school stuff."

There's nothing more discouraging than arriving in class without your homework or the book you need. Here's a simple solution: When you finish studying, put everything you need for the next day—keys, backpack or book bag, glasses, and anything else you need to take to campus with you—in one special place. When you finish your homework, put it in your notebook, and put your notebook in your spot. If there is an additional item you need to bring the next day (such as a project or an

BRAIN-FRIENDLY TIPS

Brain Food

If you want a snack or a meal before you start studying, choose wisely. Foods high in tryptophan leave you with a sense of calm and well-being. *Tryptophan* (pronounced "TRIP-toe-fan") helps your brain produce serotonin, a "feel good" chemical. It's found in milk, turkey, almonds, bananas, eggs, cheese, and complex carbohydrates.

You won't be surprised to learn that college students identify chocolate as the food they crave most. It contains sugar, fat (soothing and creamy), caffeine, and other substances that regulate and stimulate mood. Save the chocolate for when you're finished studying.

Background Music

Do you prefer background music when you study? Research suggests that for some people, certain types of instrumental music (no words!), played at a low volume, work well as background music when they study. Here are three possible choices:

- **Baroque music** has balance and predictability that the brain likes. Look for orchestral music by Mozart, Bach (*Brandenburg Concertos*), Handel (*Water Music*), or Vivaldi (*Four Seasons*), for example, that has approximately 50–70 beats per minute. (Select slower movements; they are labeled *adagio* or *andante*.)
- **Nature sounds**—environmental sounds of a waterfall, ocean, or rain forest, for example— create a soothing, unobtrusive background.
- **Jazz instrumentals** of George Benson, David Sanborn, and Kenny G also work for some students.

Experiment to see what works best for you. In music stores, ask for the sections with Baroque music, environmental sound tracks, and even "brain-friendly" music. (Heavy metal music is stressful since its beat is counter to the normal human heartbeat.)

umbrella), place it there as well. Check to be sure that you have everything you need in that one spot.

The spot you choose might be a table or bench near your front door. It could be a chair in your bedroom, or even just a corner of your bedroom. Any place that's convenient and that other people won't bother will work just fine. The important thing is to use the same spot each day. You won't lose time and feel stress because you're hunting for something at the last minute. Pick up anything that's in the spot, and you're ready to walk out the door. Take a minute now, and in your mind's eye, picture the spot you could use for your school stuff.

STOP AND PROCESS

EXERCISE 2.3

- When are the best times for you to study? Can you arrange your

  schedule so that you can study at those times? _____

  _____

  _____

  _____

- Where are two good places you could study? Does the place you normally study suit your learning style? If not (too noisy, light is wrong, no desk or table, for example), what could you do to make

  it better, or where could you go instead? _____

  _____

  _____

  _____

- Do you use an assignment notebook? Does it help? If not, are you willing to try it for three weeks? What difference do you think it

  might make? _____

  _____

  _____

  _____

- Where in your house or apartment would be a good spot to keep

  the items you need for class each day? Be specific. _____

  _____

  _____

  _____

3. Prepare for class.

Preparing for class begins with buying the textbooks, other required materials (such as lab manuals or machine-scorable answer sheets), and necessary supplies (notebook and paper, pens, highlighters, index cards, etc.). Textbooks are as indispensable to college students as tools are to a carpenter.

Students are often shocked at the price of textbooks. They can cost more than tuition at public colleges and universities. Remember that in college you have to do much more of the learning on your own, outside of class. Don't try to get by without buying a required book. Not reading the book might have worked in high school, but it doesn't work in college.

Buy your textbooks at the very beginning of the semester. It's not okay to tell the instructor that you won't be able to get the book for a few weeks. It's your responsibility to do whatever you need to do in order to get your books on time. You may have to make a short-term loan from someone or from the college. Getting off to a good start makes all the difference. If you don't have your textbooks from the start, you will quickly get behind and feel overwhelmed.

Buying your textbooks is not enough. The fact is, you have to use them, regardless of whether you like getting information through reading or prefer to learn some other way. Even if reading is not your preferred way to learn, this book will show you techniques that will make reading easier and more efficient.

To become a successful student, do the homework. Thomas Edison, the famous inventor, said, "A genius is a talented person who does his homework." Read your assignments. Some students mistakenly believe that if the assignment is to read a chapter, there really isn't an assignment. Wrong, wrong, wrong! If you haven't read the assignment, you will not know what the instructor is talking about. You can't contribute or participate fully in class. If you do the homework as it is assigned, you will always be caught up.

In college, homework may take longer than you think, so start well ahead of time. Whenever you need to, go the extra mile. You'll be glad you did. If you have difficulty in a course, however, you may need to do some additional things to be fully prepared for class. (These are discussed later in item 6, on pages 53–55.)

**www.mhhe.com/
entryways**

For additional
helpful suggestion,
go to

**Catalyst>
Study Skills
Tutor>
Are You Avoiding
the Work?**

 STOP AND PROCESS

EXERCISE 2.4

- Did you buy all of your textbooks within the first day or two of the semester? If not, what could you have done in order to have had them

  from the start? _____

  _____

  _____

- Have you been doing the assignments for this class? If not, why not? (If you are already behind, talk with your instructor. Work out

  an arrangement to get caught up.) _____

  _____

  _____

- It's still early in the semester, but are you spending more or less time than you thought you would on homework? How much time

  do you generally spend each day or week? _____

  _____

  _____

4. Manage your assignments.

www.mhhe.com/
entryways

For additional helpful suggestions, go to
**Catalyst>Learning>
Study Skills Tutor>
Getting Off to a
Strong Start**

In college, assignments can pile up quickly if you don't do them as they are assigned. This is one reason you should not enroll in more courses than you can comfortably handle, especially if you are working as well as going to school. Even if you've put off homework in the past, you have an opportunity to start this semester differently. That was then. This is now. You have the chance to get on track, stay on track, and discover how effective you can be.

When you sit down to study, pull out your assignment notebook and look over everything you need to do. (Assignment notebooks were discussed earlier in the chapter.) Estimate how much time you'll need to complete all of the assignments. Decide where you want to start. If it helps you, jot down a rough schedule (for example: 7–8 p.m.—math; 8–9—reading; 9–9:30—speech) for your study session. You may want to start with an easy subject to get warmed up, but don't leave your most difficult subject until last. You might be too tired to finish it.

Can you remember a time when you didn't read the directions for something, and it ended up costing you valuable time, some frustration, and maybe even money? When you start a homework assignment, read any instructions for it. Even if you think you know what you're supposed to do, look through the directions and the material first. Be sure you understand what you are supposed to do.

If it's a long assignment, break it into smaller "bites." In other words, divide a long reading assignment into several shorter ones. It's like cutting a pie into smaller slices. Smaller sections of a chapter, like smaller bites, are easier to digest.

You can divide a long reading assignment into shorter sections by inserting sticky notes or paperclips every few pages. Choose logical stopping points, such as the end of a section. When you reach one of those points, stop and think about what you've read. Try to put the important information in your own words by saying it aloud or recording it on paper. If you are a visual learner, take notes, make a "map," sketch a picture, or create a mental image. All of these strategies

www.mhhe.com/
entryways

For additional helpful suggestions, go to
**Catalyst>Learning>
Study Skills Tutor>
Studying Strategies**

CROSS-CHAPTER CONNECTIONS

In Chapter 12, you'll learn specific techniques for handling textbook assignments. You are welcome to look ahead. Keep in mind, however, that the techniques in that chapter are based on the reading comprehension skills you will learn in Chapters 7–11.

help transfer the information into long-term, or permanent, memory. If you need to, take a *short* break at the end of each section. You'll then be ready to tackle the next section.

Taking short breaks as you work makes it easier to stay focused. You will also be more motivated if you know that a brief change of pace is scheduled every half hour or so. Drink a glass of water. Stretch and move around a bit. Nibble on a healthy snack. Close your eyes and take several slow, deep breaths. It goes without saying that you should avoid making phone calls, playing computer or video games, and doing other activities that could distract you from getting back to work.

Some subjects will be harder for you than others. If a subject is hard, spend more time on it. Unfortunately, many students tend to do exactly the opposite. Simply spending more time can make the difference between being successful and almost being successful.

Even if you're struggling with a subject, it doesn't mean that you can't learn it and do well. Chances are, you don't yet have the background knowledge you need in order to understand the material. If you take the time to fill in those gaps, your brain will be ready for the new material. To get the background information and help you need, explore the resources discussed later in item 6.

Complete every assignment to the best of your ability, even when you know you're not "getting it" completely. That way, you'll "know what you don't know." Best of all, you'll know the questions you need to ask at the next class session.

 ## STOP AND PROCESS

EXERCISE 2.5

- What is your plan for completing your homework on time? _____

  _____

  _____

- What would be the advantages to you of breaking long reading

  assignments into several shorter sections? _____

  _____

  _____

- Do you usually read the directions before you start an assignment?

  Why or why not? _____

  _____

  _____

■ Which subjects seem more challenging to you? Do you lack

background knowledge in those subjects? _____

_____

_____

5. Monitor your progress and see your instructor when you need help.

Another key to success is to monitor your progress in each of your courses. That means using feedback to evaluate how you're doing. **Feedback** is information that comes back to you in response to something you've done. The smell of popcorn burning in a microwave is feedback that tells you it's cooked too long. Ending up at the wrong website is feedback that tells you that you have typed in the wrong address. The great thing about feedback is that it lets you know if you're off track. If you are, you need to take steps to get back on track.

In school, feedback includes your instructor's verbal comments and ones written on assignments and tests. Test grades are feedback. Instructors spend time grading assignments and tests and writing comments on them. Take advantage of those comments. They're designed to help you. Some students glance at the grade. Then they either throw the paper away or shove it in their notebook without ever looking at it again. If you do this, you're throwing away a gift. In order to learn, your brain has to have feedback.

Besides using feedback from your instructor, you should monitor your own progress. Do you feel you are understanding the material, or do you feel confused? If you are not understanding it, try to figure out why. Are there too many words you don't know? Do you lack background knowledge? Are you not spending enough time on the subject? Write down your specific questions. Then talk with your instructor. Take your homework with you so that your instructor can see what you are doing. Instructors set aside certain times, called office hours, for meeting with students. They will be impressed that you care, that you want to learn, and that you are so responsible.

Remember, though, that your instructors are not there to solve your problems. Their job is to guide you in solving your own problems. Learning to solve your own problems is a valuable life skill. You gain confidence and self-esteem when you rely on yourself rather than someone else to fix your problems.

If you make a low grade on a test or don't do as well as you expected, see your instructor immediately. Go over items you missed. Describe to your instructor how you prepared for the test, and ask what you can do to improve your performance. Ask for suggestions about studying and learning the material, and for doing well in the course.

When you are reading, stop at the end of a section and use one of these techniques to give yourself feedback on your comprehension (understanding): Can you say in your own words what it was about? Can you make a sketch of what it was about and label it with key words? If so, that's a good sign! If there is something you don't understand, write a question mark in the margin beside it. You can also make a list of questions to ask during or after class.

It's a good idea to keep a record of your grades in your classes. You'll know how you're doing, and it allows you to pinpoint material you're unsure of and need more practice on.

Another useful strategy is to jot down the date if you have to miss a class. Absences can add up fast if you're not paying attention to them. Many students are surprised when they learn that they've been absent six or eight times. Depending on how many times your course meets each week, that's equivalent to missing two to four *weeks* of class! Before a test, make sure you know what was covered in class on any day you were absent.

 ## STOP AND PROCESS

EXERCISE 2.6

- Have you taken any steps in the past to monitor how well you were doing in your schoolwork? If so, what were they? _____

_____

_____

- When you have had difficulty in a course in the past, did you seek help? If you were having difficulty in a course now, would you see the instructor? Why or why not? _____

_____

_____

- Do you read comments instructors write on your assignments? If not, why not? _____

_____

_____

- What are your plans for monitoring your progress in this course?

_____

_____

- How might it help if you stopped at the end of textbook sections and tried to capture the important information by saying it or

putting it in written form? _____

_____

_____

6. Take advantage of out-of-class resources.

Did you know there are a wealth of resources you can draw on outside of class? These free college services are like a pot of gold, just waiting for you to discover it. Your college's handbook or website lists its academic support services and campus resources. These can include tutoring, counseling, financial aid, library services, career planning and job placement services, intramural sports teams, student clubs and organizations, and college-sponsored events. (An astonishing array of support information is also available online. See the Bonus Tip box below for two helpful websites.)

Your college probably has a tutoring center. If so, you can schedule appointments. Be sure to go to tutoring sessions as prepared as possible. Read the chapter you want to discuss or try the assignment you want help with. That way you'll know where you're having problems, and it enables the tutor to be as helpful as possible.

Tutoring centers, libraries, or counseling centers usually offer free study skills sessions. Topics often include time management, listening skills, note taking, learning styles, memory, organizing and revising papers, test taking, stress reduction, and test anxiety. (Some instructors give students extra credit for attending these. Ask yours.) Some colleges offer a "master student class" or require a freshman orientation course. Before enrolling in such courses, you should strengthen your reading skills. You'll get even more out of them.

Check out your campus resources. The counseling center can be helpful when you are having academic or personal problems. Health centers offer information, screening for various health problems or diseases, and, of course, they have band-aids and aspirin. Colleges also offer special services for students with disabilities, including learning disabilities. Unless you *ask* for help, though, your college is not likely to know you need help. As an adult, it's your responsibility to ask.

Forming and participating in study groups enhances your learning and gives you support. Research findings are clear: Adults learn well from each other. Choose two or three other motivated students to meet with outside of class. Most students prefer to meet on campus, just before or after class. You can go over the homework together, and you can ask questions about anything that's unclear. Study groups are especially helpful for review before tests. Two old sayings explain why participating in study groups is so helpful: "To teach is to learn twice" and "If you would thoroughly know anything, teach it to others." When you explain something to someone else, you make it clearer in your own mind. You also cement it in your long-term memory. (Here's a joke that illustrates someone you *don't* want to be in a study group with: Two students are walking down the hall, trying to decide how to spend the hour before their next class. "I know," one of them declares.

☀ BONUS TIP

http://www.dr-bob.org/vpc/background.html This website links to hundreds of college and university Web pages that address a vast range of student problems and concerns. The topics are categorized and alphabetized.

http://www.uni.edu/walsh/linda7.html   Once at this website, click on "Sites to Promote Academic Success."(Blank hourly, weekly, and monthly schedules are available here.)

"Let's flip a coin! If it's heads, we'll hang out in the student lounge. If it's tails, we'll play video games. If it lands on its side, we'll study.")

What can you do on your own when a course seems hard? Several things! One is to find easier books on the topic. Go to a public library. At the public library, ask a librarian to direct you to the young adult section or help you find an easier book on the subject that's giving you trouble. Or, you can go to a bookstore and look for "made easy" books. These are books whose titles include phrases such as *Made Easy*, *for Beginners* and *an Introduction to*. (The popular *Idiot's Guide* and *for Dummies* series are examples.) Once you've read a simpler explanation of a concept, the college textbook explanation of it makes a lot more sense.

Another thing you can do outside of class is to learn to type, if you don't already know how. (See the Bonus Tip box below.) College professors expect you to turn in typed papers. Most employers expect you to type well enough to use a computer. Typing is a terrific skill to have, especially if you are a visual-spatial learner, have handwriting that is difficult to read, or find it slow and frustrating to write by hand. It lets you do word processing (type) on a computer. (A bonus: word-processing programs have built-in spell check and grammar-checking features.) Remember, though, that while you are learning, you have to set aside time to practice, perhaps 15 minutes a day. Once you have the skill, you'll have it for life. The goal is to become an accurate typist. You don't have to set any records for speed. No matter how slowly you type, you're bound to type better than the students who make these joking comments:

> **BONUS TIP**
>
> To learn to type, check into noncredit typing classes at your college. In noncredit courses, you don't have to worry about the pressure of a grade. Noncredit courses are also called "continuing education" or "community service" courses. They may last a few weeks or the length of a semester. Tuition is usually low at public colleges.
>
> You can also buy computer software that teaches you to type (such as *Mavis Beacon Teaches Typing* and *Typing Tutor*). These programs offer a series of lessons, practice exercises, and games, and they keep track of your progress.

"I'm sorry my term paper turned in late: I broke my typing finger."

"I type 60 words per minute, most of which are recognizable."

Being able to type makes it possible for you to use the Internet more fully. If you don't know how to use the Internet, check with your college's library or computer center to see if they offer free training sessions. If you do not have an email account, see if one is available free through your college. You can also inquire about other services that offer free email accounts. Email gives you an additional way to contact your instructor and classmates. For that reason, some instructors require students to have email.

STOP AND PROCESS

EXERCISE 2.7

- List the resources you are aware of that are offered by your college. Which one might be useful to you? Which ones, if any, have you used? _____

_____

_____

_____

- Based on your learning style and preferences, do you think participating in a study group would work for you? Why or why not? _____

_____

_____

- Do you know how to type? If not, would you consider learning?

_____

_____

- Describe your ability to find information efficiently on the Internet. (For example, if you use a search engine, do you know how to narrow down the choices you are given? Do you know how to tell informational websites from commercial ones, and trustworthy websites from untrustworthy ones?) _____

_____

_____

Succeed in College and Beyond

If you consistently use the behaviors described in this chapter, not only will you be more successful in school, you will be more successful in life. In addition to academic goals, you can set personal goals, career goals, and life goals. You can apply the strategy of getting organized to your personal life and to your job. You can use the strategy of planning and preparing for important events and projects at home or at work. You can monitor your progress in various areas of your life and work, as well as in your schoolwork. You can seek support and help when you need it in any circumstance. In short, these simple strategies can help you continue to learn, grow, and achieve throughout your life and far beyond the classroom.

www.mhhe.com/
entryways

For additional helpful resources, go to

Catalyst>Learning> Additional Links on Learning

MY TOOLBOX *of Success Behaviors outside the Classroom*

What specifically can you do *outside* the classroom to make yourself more successful in the classroom? On a separate piece of paper, record those behaviors. Include the five items that you identified with your classmates in the Looking at What You Already Know section (at the beginning of the chapter), as well as the six points from this chapter. Some of the same items may be on both lists, so you may have fewer than 11 items.

Different people would organize a toolbox in different ways. Since each person learns differently, you should organize the information in your toolbox in the way that will help you most. Here are some possibilities:

- **Write a list and brief description of the six classroom success tools.** Write them in your own words so that you will remember them. You can use notebook paper or index cards. If you like, you can use more than one color pen. Color helps some students remember information more easily.

- **Pretend you are writing a letter** to someone who is just starting college. In your letter, include the important out-of-class success behaviors covered in this chapter. Explaining something to someone else is a great way to review and learn it yourself.

- **If you prefer, you can draw a study map instead of writing a list.** To make a map, draw a circle in the middle of the page. Write the words "Out-of-Class Success Behaviors" in the circle. Then write specific success behaviors on lines that radiate from the circle. You can make lines of any sort—thick, thin, solid, dashed, or dotted, for example. You may prefer simply to use key words. You can include small illustrations or sketches and work with colored pens. (The Online Reading Lab (ORL) presents information about making study maps.)

When you have finished your list, letter, or map, put a star or a check mark beside the three behaviors that you think will help *you* most. Make a commitment to concentrate on these three behaviors first. Once they become habits, you can begin to add other success behaviors that are in your toolbox. *Use these success behaviors along with the ones from Chapter 1 and you will be well on your way to succeeding in college!*

✔ CHAPTER CHECK

Answer these questions about the information in the chapter. Write the missing word in each blank. When there is more than one part to the answer, there is more than one blank.

1. Research suggests that most students accomplish more when they study during _____ hours than at night.

2. Before you begin studying, have all the _____ you need at hand.

3. To hydrate your brain, drink some _____ before you study.

4. When you finish studying, put everything you need for the next day in one _____.

5. In college, homework may take _____ than you think, so start well ahead of time.

6. When you start a homework assignment, read any _____

_____ for it.

7. Divide long assignments into _____ ones.

8. If a subject is hard for you, spend more _____ on it.

9. In order to learn, the brain has to have _____.

10. If you make a low grade on a test or don't do as well as you

expected, see your _____ immediately.

11. Before a test, make sure you know what was covered in class on any

day you were _____.

12. Your college's _____ or _____ will list all of the academic support services and campus resources that are available to you.

13. Forming and participating in _____ groups enhances your learning and makes you feel supported.

14. Once you've read a _____ explanation of a concept, the college textbook explanation of it makes more sense.

15. If you don't know how to use the _____, check at your college's library or computer center to see if they offer free training sessions.

REVIEW EXERCISES

SET 1

Read these remarks written by Brian, who has just completed his first month at a vocational and technical college. He is 24. He is married and has a young son. He works 40 hours a week for a delivery service. His ambition is to become a certified computer technician. Certain things he is doing outside of class are limiting his success. Based on the chapter information, what advice would you give him? Write your suggestions and advice in the space provided.

"I have a full-time job and a family, so I have a lot of responsibility. I want to get through college as quick as possible. That's why I plan to take at least four courses every semester. Right now, I take classes four evenings a week. Between work and class I swing by a fast-food restaurant, pick up a soft drink and something to eat at the drive-through, and eat while I drive to campus.

"The only time I can study is after I get home at night. I'm tired, and I often fall asleep when I study. I've started turning on upbeat music to keep me awake and drinking more coffee. I study at the kitchen table so that I don't disturb my wife and son while they're trying to sleep.

"When I study, I try to push myself to keep going. I'm afraid if I take a break I might not get back to the books. On weekends, I like to spend time with my family or to relax. I play games on the computer. I don't think I should have to study on weekends.

"On the first test in my computer class I made a 63. I'm not sure why. I reread most of the material the night before the test, so I figured I knew it. How can you tell whether or not you know it until it's too late? It's very frustrating."

SET 2

Now read what Natalie has to say. She's attending a state college and lives in an apartment with two roommates. She works on campus in the bookstore 18 hours a week. This is her first semester in college. Use the chapter information as the basis for giving her advice about changing things she is doing outside of class.

"College seemed like it would be fun and my two best friends from high school were planning to go, so I decided to go too. The three of us share an apartment, and that part is very cool. We go out a lot. Also, we have a plasma screen TV with built-in DVD, and we record our favorite soap operas and watch them at night.

"I hate to say it, but I feel resentful about having to study. I always intend to study, but I'm just not disciplined enough to do it on my own. Going to the mall, hanging out, and chatting online are much more fun and I end up doing them instead. It makes me feel guilty, though. The assignments seem so long. I look at how many pages I have to read, and I get discouraged and I give up before I ever start. When I do read a textbook assignment, I never know whether I've gotten anything out of it.

"I feel like I spend my time rushing from one thing to another and from one place to another. I forget things and have to double back. Like last week, I left my history book at work. I had a test the next day, so I had to go back and pick it up. Usually I have a bunch of errands, and before I know it, an entire afternoon or evening is gone, and I don't have the time or energy to study.

"As I mentioned, I have trouble keeping up with stuff. My keys, my cell phone, even my purse. Yesterday I was late to class. It took me 20 minutes to find my car keys. They were in the pocket of the jeans I wore the day before. There was a survey I was supposed to fill out and turn in for my health and fitness class. I still can't find it.

"I've already missed four days of class this semester. A couple of times I overslept. Because I missed a class, I didn't know I had a psychology test, and I flunked it. How am I going to get caught up? Where can I get some help on the stuff I missed? Two of my courses are especially hard. How can I learn the material in them? I need to improve my writing. I don't even know how to type. Unless I get these problems straightened out, they're going to keep bugging me. I don't know where to begin.

"No one else in my family has ever attended college. I don't want to disappoint them, but I don't think they understand what I'm coping with. I'm not sure what it means to be a 'college student.' I'm not even sure what I want in life, or how college is going to help me achieve it. Help!"

SET 3

Choose one of the following scenarios. Use the principles in this chapter to develop a plan that would allow you to complete effectively and on time the assignment described in it. What steps would you take to get organized and to break the bigger tasks into smaller steps?

Scenario 1

In your psychology class, you are assigned to write an eight-page paper about college students' stress. The directions tell you that you can focus on what causes students the greatest stress, when during the semester they feel the greatest stress, how they cope with stress, or some other aspect of the topic. You must gather data by creating and administering a short written or oral survey to at least 20 students. In your paper, you are to explain what you researched, how you gathered data (attach your survey), the information that you discovered, and your interpretation of your findings. The paper should be typed, and it is due in two weeks.

Scenario 2

In your speech class, you are to make a presentation that teaches your classmates how to *do* something. You are to choose something that you are good at, such as changing a tire, serving a tennis ball, or decorating a cake. You must include one or more visual aids in your presentation. Photos, props, a poster, or real items (such as a tennis racket and ball, or cake and frosting) are examples of visual aids. Plan an opening, middle, and end to your presentation and jot your notes on index cards. Be ready to give your presentation one week from today.

_____

_____

_____

_____

_____

_____

_____

_____

_____

_____

ASSESS YOUR UNDERSTANDING

In this chapter, you learned that one way you become a better student is by monitoring your understanding and then taking steps when there are things you don't understand. Now is your chance to apply that skill to this very chapter.

How did you do on the Chapter Check? You can use it as a source of feedback. Also, ask yourself, "Could I tell someone what the six out-of-class success behaviors are? Could I explain what each behavior is and why it's important?" On a scale of 1–10, circle a number on the scale that reflects your level of understanding. (On the bright side, you already know at least *one* of the six strategies: using feedback to monitor your understanding!)

1 . . . . . 2 . . . . . 3 . . . . . 4 . . . . . 5 . . . . . 6 . . . . . 7 . . . . . 8 . . . . . 9 10

I wouldn't even　　　　**I might stumble a bit.**　　　　**No problem!**
know where to start!　　　　　　　　　　　　**I could do it easily!**

Now that you've ranked yourself, think about *why* you chose the number you did. *If you marked less than 10 on the scale, identify what it is that you don't understand.* What, specifically, are you unclear about? One certain success behavior? Or are you hazy on several of them? It's important to answer these questions. When you know what the problem is, you can decide how to fix it. Write your response on the lines below.

_____

_____

_____

_____

_____

_____

_____

For the things you mentioned above (things you don't understand or can't remember), what steps could you take to improve your comprehension? Do you need to reread all or part of the chapter? Ask a classmate or your instructor questions? Write the information down or review the information some other way? Write your response here.

_____

_____

_____

_____

_____

_____

_____

_____

_____

_____

_____

If there's anything you still need to learn, go back and take care of it now. Then you can move forward with confidence.

Map of Chapters

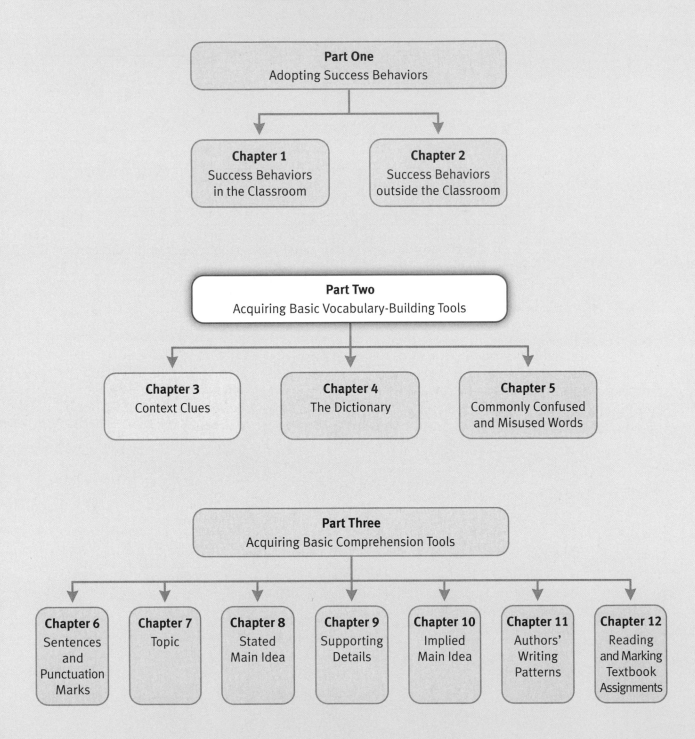

Part One
Adopting Success Behaviors

Chapter 1
Success Behaviors
in the Classroom

Chapter 2
Success Behaviors
outside the Classroom

Part Two
Acquiring Basic Vocabulary-Building Tools

Chapter 3
Context Clues

Chapter 4
The Dictionary

Chapter 5
Commonly Confused
and Misused Words

Part Three
Acquiring Basic Comprehension Tools

Chapter 6
Sentences
and
Punctuation
Marks

Chapter 7
Topic

Chapter 8
Stated
Main Idea

Chapter 9
Supporting
Details

Chapter 10
Implied
Main Idea

Chapter 11
Authors'
Writing
Patterns

Chapter 12
Reading
and Marking
Textbook
Assignments

Acquiring Basic Vocabulary-Building Tools

Part Two is an exciting section of this textbook. In it, you'll learn several tools for expanding your vocabulary:

- In Chapter 3 you'll learn to use clues in sentences that help you reason out the meaning of unfamiliar words.
- In Chapter 4 you'll strengthen and polish your ability to use a powerful learning aid, the dictionary.
- In Chapter 5 you'll learn about homonyms (words that sound the same, but mean different things, such as *capital* and *capitol)* and commonly confused words (such as *imply* and *infer*).

You'll not only learn tools for increasing your vocabulary, you'll also learn lots of new words along the way. In addition, the Online Reading Lab features information about another way to expand your vocabulary: word structure analysis. It will teach you to use common Latin root words, prefixes, and suffixes to unlock and remember the meanings of hundreds of words.

No reading improvement text or vocabulary book can teach you every word you need to know. However, you can develop techniques for learning words. And that's what *Entryways* is designed to do: give you the tools to empower you to expand your vocabulary.

The CSSD Method for Unlocking Words' Meanings

The CSSD method is one way of figuring out the meaning of unfamiliar words. It consists of four strategies in the order in which you should try them. Here's what the letters CSSD stand for:

Context: Try to figure out the meaning of the word by using clues in the rest of the sentence, the *context* in which you read the word. (Chapter 3 focuses on using the context.)

Sound: Try to *sound* out or pronounce the word. Sometimes hearing it aloud helps you recognize the word. (Chapter 4 and t. Online Reading Lab provide tips on phonics and pronunciation.)

Structure: Look at the *structure* of the word. See if there are word parts—prefixes, roots, and suffixes—that provide clues to the word's meaning. (Module 1 of the Online Reading Lab contains material about this.)

Dictionary: If the preceding strategies don't help, or you want to check the accuracy of the guess you made based on the context, look up the definition in the *dictionary*. (Chapter 4 is devoted to dictionary usage.)

These commonsense strategies work together. Most people automatically make guesses about what an unfamiliar word might mean. They base their educated guess on what would make sense in the sentence. That is, they use the context. In addition, they usually try to say an unfamiliar word out loud, or they at least think about how it might sound. If they know the meanings of common word parts, they may use them as well. And, of course, they can use the dictionary to check the meaning. They select the definition that makes sense in the sentence in which they found the word.

Learning unfamiliar words is a big part of increasing your vocabulary, of course, but there are several additional ways to build on the words you already use:

- You can learn additional meanings of words you already know.

- You can learn *idioms*, expressions that mean something different from what the individual words seem to say. For example, *to keep tabs on* means "to monitor or observe carefully," as in "The police are keeping tabs on both suspects." (Dictionaries include idioms. Idioms are explained in Chapter 4.)

- You can learn to distinguish between words that seem confusing or misleading. (Chapter 5 will help you with this.)

A Proven Strategy for Learning Vocabulary Words: Vocabulary Cards

For most students, making vocabulary cards is an effective way to add words to their vocabularies. When you encounter new words, write them down. Include important terms from your textbooks. As soon as you have several words, create vocabulary cards for them. Here's the general procedure:

1. Write the word in bold letters on an index card. You may want to write in color.
2. Beneath the word, write the sentence or the context in which you read or heard the word. Underline the word in the sentence.
3. On the back of the card, write the pronunciation if you need it. You may also want to write the word in separate syllables. If you are a visual learner, try writing each syllable in a different color. Then write the part of speech and the dictionary definition.
4. Now do one or more of the following:
   - Write a sentence of your own that uses the word. This connects the word with information you already know.
   - Create a memory peg, a trick to help you recall the meaning of the word.
   - Make a sketch that illustrates the meaning of the word.

Let's say the new word is *ideal*, and that you heard it in this sentence: "In an *ideal* world, there would be no hunger, illness, or poverty." Here's how the front and back of the card might look:

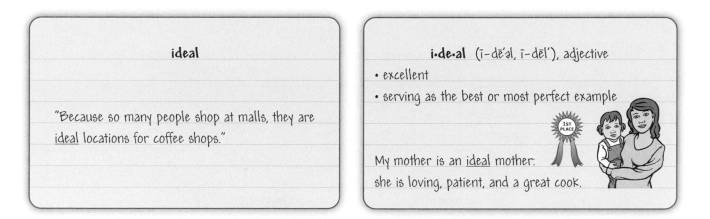

Notice that the card should include a sentence of your own, such as, "My mother is the <u>ideal</u> mother: she is loving, patient, and a great cook." Add a sketch or a memory peg, or both. For the sketch, you could draw a picture of a "mom" and a blue ribbon. An example of a memory peg would be "I DEAL cards in a perfectly <u>ideal</u> way."

Once you have a stack of vocabulary cards, turn through it daily. It will only take a few minutes. You can do it while you're waiting for the bus or eating lunch. Or take a few minutes before you go to sleep at night. Look at the word on the front of each card. Say the word out loud and try to say the definition. If you can't recall the meaning, read the sentence you wrote beneath the word. Seeing the word in the context of a sentence usually helps you recall the meaning. Then turn the card over. You will either discover that you are correct (good for you!), or, if not, you will see the correct definition and other helpful information.

If you know your learning style, check out the additional techniques described in the Online Reading Lab selection, "Building Your Vocabulary." Here are some general pointers that are keyed to learning styles:

- If you are a tactile-kinesthetic learner, simply writing the word down will help you learn it. You may also find it helpful to try to write the word and definition from memory either on a tabletop or in the air with your finger.

- If you are an auditory learner, close your eyes and say the word and definition aloud. Hearing yourself say the word will be very reinforcing. You may also find it helpful to have a partner hold up the cards. Pronounce the word and say the definition to your partner.

- If you are a visual-spatial learner, close your eyes and try to see the word in your head. Visualize it, just as you would visualize any other object. If you made a sketch, visualize it as well.

You may find that a combination of these techniques reinforces your learning. That is, the more senses you involve, the stronger the learning may be for you. So write the word, see it, say it, visualize it, create your own sentence, memory peg, sketch, or use some combination of these techniques.

The words in your stack of vocabulary cards will always be changing slightly. This is because you will always be adding new words to the stack and removing ones that you have mastered.

It will take repeated exposures to each card before you automatically recognize the word and its definition. However, once you can consistently give the definition, congratulate yourself and remove the card from the stack. (Keep the cards for words you have learned; just put them in a separate stack.)

Map of Chapters

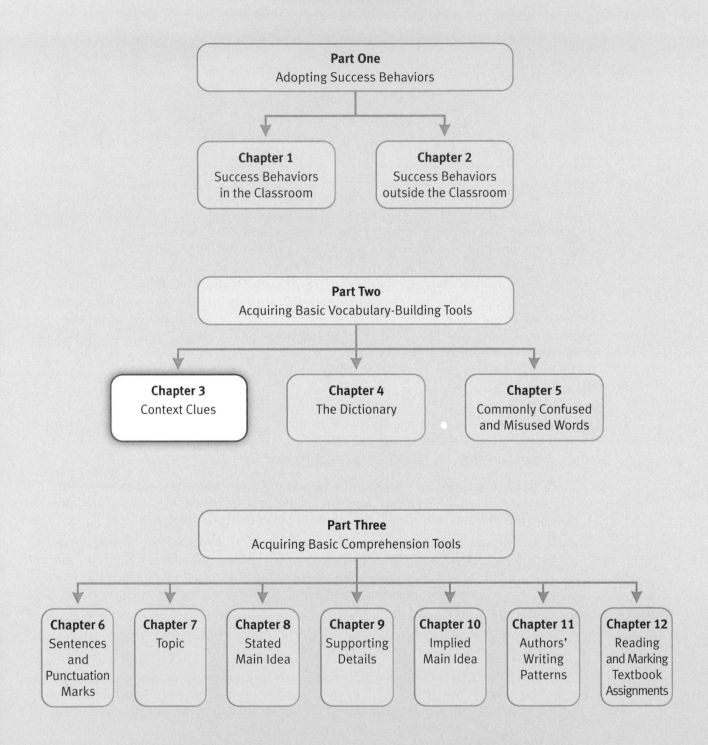

Part One
Adopting Success Behaviors

Chapter 1
Success Behaviors
in the Classroom

Chapter 2
Success Behaviors
outside the Classroom

Part Two
Acquiring Basic Vocabulary-Building Tools

Chapter 3
Context Clues

Chapter 4
The Dictionary

Chapter 5
Commonly Confused
and Misused Words

Part Three
Acquiring Basic Comprehension Tools

Chapter 6
Sentences
and
Punctuation
Marks

Chapter 7
Topic

Chapter 8
Stated
Main Idea

Chapter 9
Supporting
Details

Chapter 10
Implied
Main Idea

Chapter 11
Authors'
Writing
Patterns

Chapter 12
Reading
and Marking
Textbook
Assignments

CHAPTER 3

Context Clues

In Other Words

Why You Need to Know the Information in This Chapter

If you are like most students, you will run across many unfamiliar words when you read your textbooks. This can make it hard to understand what you are reading. It slows you down. If it happens often enough, it becomes very frustrating. *If you know how to use context clues, you can figure out the meaning of most of those words.* This chapter explains what context clues are and how to use them.

Using context clues will help you

- figure out the meaning of unfamiliar words

- understand more of what you read

- expand your vocabulary

- increase your efficiency when you read

- increase your confidence when you read

- be more successful in college

Super Student Tips

Here are tips from other students about building vocabulary. Here's what experience has taught them:

"When you read an assignment, make a list of the new words. Then look up the definitions. Review them often, and they will become part of your vocabulary."—*Gloria*

"I noticed that my teachers ask the definition of important terms on tests. I pay special attention to the meaning of those words, and my test grades are higher."—*Ahmed*

"When I learn a new word, I make up a sentence of my own that uses the word. It helps me remember what the word means."—*Javier*

"At first, I tried to look up every new word. It was discouraging because it took me forever to read an assignment. Now I only look up words when I can't figure them out by using context clues. It saves me time, and I understand just as much."—*Kismet*

"My teacher required us to keep a stack of index cards with important terms on them. The cards have made a big difference. I think in pictures. I write the definition, but I draw a little picture too. It helps me remember the meaning."—*Brad*

"Over and over our instructor kept telling us that reading, writing, speaking, and listening are all connected, and that getting better in one area helps you get better in the others. She was right. I pay attention to new words I see and hear. I try to write them down and look them up. Then I try to use them when I speak in class or write papers."—*Wells*

Jumpstart Your Brain!

Before you begin the chapter, warm up your brain with this activity. Enjoy!

THE FAR SIDE®   By GARY LARSON

"Wait! Wait! Cancel that. ... I guess it says 'helf.'"

Why does the pilot say, "Cancel that"? _____

_____

What message is the man on the island trying to send? _____

_____

What do you think might have happened to his message? _____

_____

Why is this cartoon funny? _____

_____

    Compare your answers with your classmates' answers. Do you or a classmate need "helf" understanding the cartoon?

Answer the following question:

What does the word *aquatic* mean?

a. living in or near rain forests

b. living in or near deserts

c. living in or near mountains

d. living in or near water

Read a sentence that contains the word *aquatic*:

Sea World Park features shows and exhibits with exotic fish, penguins, porpoises, killer whales, and other *aquatic* animals.

Now that you've read the sentence, answer the same question again: What does the word *aquatic* mean?

a. living in or near rain forests

b. living in or near deserts

c. living in or near mountains

d. living in or near water

The correct answer is the last one. If *aquatic* was a new word to you, did you change your answer after you read it in a sentence? Did you feel more confident about your answer the second time? If so, it is because you used the sentence to help figure out the meaning. You could reason out that in order for the sentence to make sense, *aquatic* must refer to creatures that live in or near water. The clues in the sentence were Sea World (the theme park) and examples of creatures that live in the ocean (exotic fish, penguins, porpoises, and killer whales).

You may not have known the skill by name, but to figure out the meaning of *aquatic*, you used context clues. You've used such clues since you first began learning words as a baby. In fact, most of the words you know, you learned from context. You certainly didn't look each one up in the dictionary! You figured out their meaning from how they were used.

Context Clues

Is there another word for "synonym"?
—George Carlin

Having a better vocabulary will help you in many ways. You will be able to state your ideas more precisely when you speak and write. You will understand more of what you read. You will sound smarter and be more impressive when you speak. And improving your vocabulary may even result in a better, higher-paying job! Did you know that the size of your vocabulary is related to the amount of money you are likely to earn in your lifetime? The bigger your vocabulary, the more money you will make.

Sounds good, right? Terrific! Let's jump in.

The Big Picture for This Chapter

This chapter focuses on using context clues to determine the meaning of a word. **Context clues** are words in a sentence or paragraph that help the reader reason out the meaning of an unfamiliar word. They are called context clues because *context* means whatever surrounds something else. In this case, the context is the rest of the sentence and the paragraph (and even the entire chapter or selection) in which the unfamiliar word appears.

You can get lots of clues about someone by seeing where the person lives. The same holds true for examining where a word "lives." Think of the sentence in which a word appears as being the word's "neighborhood," the place the word lives.

Of course, a word also lives in the bigger context of a paragraph and of an entire chapter or reading selection. Textbook pictures and illustrations can also be part of the context in which a word appears. In short, you will have lots of clues to help you reason out an unfamiliar word's meaning.

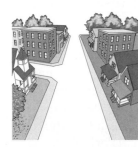

You live in the context of a neighborhood; a word lives in the context of a sentence.

Why do textbook authors give you these built-in clues? Because they *want* you to understand what you are reading, especially the important terms. When you read an unfamiliar word, ask yourself, "What would this word have to mean *in order for it to make sense in this sentence*?"

Using the context is a powerful and practical technique. That's why it's the first strategy effective readers use when they encounter an unfamiliar word. Context clues are not always perfect clues. Most of the time, though, they can help you make an educated guess about the meaning of an unfamiliar word. Context clues also help you determine which meaning the author intends if a word has more than one meaning.

Each time you encounter the same "new" word in a different context, you'll have more opportunities to understand the word more precisely and completely. You'll be like a sculptor who chips away at a block of marble. Over time, the finished sculpture—in this case, a clear, exact understanding of a word—emerges.

Pay attention to words that keep showing up in your textbooks. Learn them. They're important. There is an entire vocabulary of terms in math, biology, and computer science, for example. There are other important academic words, such as those you see on tests: for example, *compare, contrast, justify,* and *enumerate.* Watch, too, for important words and phrases that show relationships, such as *on the other hand, similarly, with regard to,* and *therefore.* (You'll learn more about these in Chapter 11.)

Context clues are usually very helpful in understanding new words, but they aren't always 100 percent reliable. So when can you depend on them? Rely on them when any of these situations occur:

- The author includes clues that are absolutely obvious and clear.
- You get several clues throughout a paragraph that confirm your initial guess.
- You need only a general sense of a word's meaning. Not every word is crucial, so sometimes a general understanding is all you need.

There are several very common types of context clues. In this chapter you will have the opportunity to figure them out for yourself. That way, you'll understand and remember them more easily.

College textbooks contain many words and terms that will be new to you. The easiest, fastest way to figure out the meaning of these words is to use context clues. That's why Part Two of this book starts with this chapter on context clues. If you skip over unfamiliar words, there will be gaps in your understanding.

CROSS-CHAPTER CONNECTIONS

In Chapter 4 you will polish your dictionary skills. Chapter 5 focuses on words that sound alike and other words that people often confuse. In addition, the Online Reading Lab contains valuable material about using word parts, such as prefixes and roots, to help you determine the meaning of words.

The cartoon in the Jumpstart section on page 71 is funny because the pilot doesn't pay any attention to the context of the word the man has written. The context is a small island in the ocean with no way to escape. The man's appearance and gestures make it clear that he wants to be rescued. His message, of course, is "HELP," but for some reason, the last letter looks like an F rather than a P. (Perhaps he didn't have time to finish making the letter, or perhaps the wind blew the sand over part of it.) The cartoon is funny because the pilot doesn't pick up on all the obvious clues that the intended word is "HELP." It's even funnier because "HELF" makes no sense since there's no such word. The pilot needs to learn to use the context!

Refining Your Understanding of Words

Research shows that it takes a lot of exposures to a word to understand, learn, and anchor its meanings in your memory. This is normal and natural, so be patient with yourself. You will find that your understanding of words gradually deepens if you pay attention to them and how they are used. Each time you encounter a word used in a new way, you have a chance to improve your vocabulary.

For example, you've known the word *dog* practically all your life. At first, you understood that it referred to the animal and then, perhaps, to a hot dog or wiener. At some point, you may have heard someone exclaim, "That lucky dog! He won the lottery!" and discovered *dog* could refer to a person. Then you heard someone say, "He's such a dog! He was dating two other women while he was dating my friend." At that point, you realized that *dog* can refer to a person who deserves contempt. If you heard a salesperson complain, "I've been on my feet all day long. My dogs are killing me!" you realized that *dogs* can be slang for feet. Suppose you overheard someone say, "You should see the used car my sister bought. It's a real dog!" At that moment, you realized *dog* can mean something inferior or unattractive. Or suppose your roommate complained that he is being *dogged* by creditors because he can't pay his bills, or you read in the newspaper about a photographer who *dogs* certain movie stars. Your understanding of *dog* would expand further: It can mean to track or to follow persistently. And, of course, somewhere along the way, you might have heard these idioms that include the word *dog:* "We did all the work; Lloyd *dogged it*" (didn't make any effort); "That entire neighborhood used to be beautiful, but now it's *gone to the dogs*" (become run-down, gone to ruin); and "The Smiths really *put on the dog* at their daughter's wedding" (made a showy display of their wealth or elegance). (An *idiom* is an expression that cannot be understood from the meaning of the individual words.)

Wow! All that, just for the word *dog!* Context clues can help you reason out the meaning of unfamiliar words, but pay attention to familiar words when you see them in new contexts. If you do that, you will develop a fuller and more precise understanding of how a word can be used, whether it's a "simple" word like *dog*, or a more complex word.

What Video Games Tell Us about the Natural Way of Learning

Let's take a detour to talk about what video games reveal about how the brain naturally learns. The reason is that you will be using this same natural process in this book.

Did you know that the best-selling games are not the simpler ones or the most violent ones? The most popular ones are not the ones filled with explosions, crashes, or gun blasts. You may be surprised to learn that the highest selling games are the challenging and complex ones, the ones that require the most thinking. (The two most popular types of video games are simulations, or "sims," such as *SimCity*, and sports sims, such as Sega's *2K3* baseball simulator. The most popular video game of all times is *The Sims.*) Winning requires creativity, detecting patterns, and solving problems. It requires focus, determination, patience, and thought.

A best-selling technology writer, Steven Johnson, argues that complicated video games, television shows, and movies are actually making people smarter in several ways. He notes that these popular forms of entertainment can never replace books, of course. Books offer something different from other forms of popular entertainment.

There are some similarities between mastering a video game and mastering the "rules" of reading. When you play a video game, you know in advance the game's overall goal. (For example, the goal might be to free a captive who is imprisoned in a tower.) The challenge, though, is to figure out how to do it. (Perhaps you have to work your way through every level of a castle and then find the tower. All the while you must overcome obstacles and avoid capture yourself.) You learn by playing. You have to figure out the rules as you go. If you try something and it doesn't work, you try something else. You "look around" to see what is available to you to work with. (It might be a powerful sword or a piece of magic rope, for example.) You constantly ask yourself questions. ("Does the sword cut through stone?") You test your idea. You make one decision after another, discovering a little bit more each time about what works and what doesn't. (Eventually you might discover that to enter the next level, you must first find a certain type of key.) After playing the game for a little while, you begin to see patterns and to develop a strategy. By using the feedback from trying things, you finally figure out what you need to know in order to accomplish your goal (and win the game!).

Since it takes about 40 hours to play a typical video game, why would anyone willingly spend so much time on an activity that is often tedious and frustrating? The answer is that *the human brain loves challenges and new experiences.* In fact, it seeks them out because *not* having to think is boring. The challenges the brain loves best are the ones right at the edge of what it can do. It actually likes things that are slightly frustrating. Too easy is boring. Too hard is frustrating. *Things that are slightly frustrating allow the brain the pleasure of figuring them out.* Your brain is designed to be a problem solver. This is also why people like complex TV shows, such as *The Sopranos,* and mystery movies. These shows have lots of characters and plots. You have to figure things out and fill in the gaps from show to show and season to season.

In *Entryways,* you will use many of the same mental processes you use when you play a video game or watch a complicated TV show or movie. Just as you "make sense" of a video game or show, you can bring meaning and order to what you read. You know the overall goal: to acquire vocabulary-building skills and to enhance your comprehension skills. To do this, you will "look around" to see what is available for you to use. In this book, you will do this each time by examining a set of examples. You will ask yourself questions. (For example, you will ask yourself, "What do they all have in common?") Based on the samples, you will use your talented brain to figure out the answers. In other words, you'll figure out the important vocabulary and comprehension "rules." Then you'll practice applying them. Practice helps you grow in skill and confidence. It prepares you to move to a higher level. The strategies you figure out will allow you to "win" at reading. You will have found the "keys to the kingdom."

In the next section, you will apply this natural way of learning to reason out the fives types of context clues.

Reasoning Out Five Types of Context Clues

Figuring out the five types of context clues will be a lot like a game. Here's the game plan:

- You'll read a set of five sample sentences that all illustrate the same type of context clue.

- Each sentence contains an underlined word that may be unfamiliar to you. The meaning of that word is given beneath the sentence. That way you can focus on the *type* of context clue rather than figuring out the definitions of the words.

- After you've read the sentences, reason out the type of clue that all the sentences have in common. What is it in the sentences that helps readers figure out the meaning of the underlined words?

A nice bonus is that while you are learning about context clues, you can also add useful words to your vocabulary.

Discover the First Type of Context Clue

The following sentences are from college textbooks. Remember that all the sentences have the *same type* of context clue and that you'll be told the meaning of the underlined word. Your job is to figure out the *type* of clue that helps readers determine the meaning of the word. See if you can reason out the type of clue that the sentences have in common.

- People who <u>somnambulate</u>, that is, sleepwalk, typically have no recollection of it the next morning.

  somnambulate = sleepwalk

- A <u>testimonial</u>—in which a satisfied user tells how good a product is—can be highly effective as a television or radio ad.

  testimonial = a satisfied user tells how effective a product is

- Musical commercials, or <u>*jingles*</u>, that we hear on radio and TV are also a highly effective type of advertisement.

  jingles = musical commercials

- Men are more aggressive than women because men have higher levels of <u>testosterone</u>, or in other words, they have more of the male sex hormone.

  testosterone = male sex hormone

- An **opinion** is defined as "someone's belief or judgment."

  opinion = someone's belief or judgment

STOP AND PROCESS

EXERCISE 3.1

The same general type of context clue reveals the meaning of the underlined term in each of these sentences. Study the sample sentences again. Look at the definition of each underlined word. Then decide what it is in the sentences that provides the clue to the word's meaning. On the line below, write a word or phrase that describes this type of context clue.

Write the first type of context clue to an unknown word's meaning:

_____

You may be tempted before you write anything to look ahead to see what the first type of context clue is. If you peek, you will lose the opportunity to learn. Try to figure it out for yourself. If you need to, go over the examples again. Write your best answer on the line. Do not leave it blank. If you like, use pencil. You can correct your answer later if you need to.

First Type of Context Clue: A Definition or Synonym

Did you discover that in every case, there was a **definition** or **synonym** (a word that means the same thing) in the sentence that served as the context clue? If you did not write "definition or synonym" on the line in Exercise 3.1, go back and write it now. (It is also called restatement.)

In each of the first four sentences, the author simply *tells* you what a word means by including a synonym or its definition. As the examples illustrate, authors put important words and terms in special print, such as **bold**, *italics*, or color.

- In the first sentence, the phrase *that* tells you that *somnambulate* and *sleepwalk* are essentially the same thing. They are synonyms. The term that is being defined, *somnambulate*, is in italics.

- In the second sentence, the author sets off the definition of *testimonial* by putting dashes on either side of it.

- In the next sentence, the word *or* tells you that musical commercials and jingles mean the same thing: A *jingle* is simply another word for a musical commercial. The word *jingles* is in italics.

- In the fourth example, the phrase *in other words* makes it clear that *testosterone* and *male sex hormone* are synonymous (the same).

- In the fifth sentence, the word *opinion* appears in bold. The phrase *is defined as* tells you that the definition is coming. The definition appears in quotation marks.

Watch for words that indicate you are being given a definition, such as *is defined as, means, is known as, the term is called*, and so forth. Did you notice, too, that the synonyms and definitions are often set off by certain punctuation marks? In addition to dashes and commas, watch for definitions that appear in parentheses ( ) or brackets [ ], or that follow a colon (:).

Watch for *synonyms*, words that mean the *same* thing, such as *big* and *large*. (Memory peg: <u>S</u>ynonym and <u>s</u>ame both start with *s*.) When authors use a word that a reader might not know, they often include a synonym to make the meaning of the word clear. They typically introduce the synonym with words such as *or, in other words, that is, by this we mean, that is to say*, and *also known as*.

Textbook authors draw your attention to key terms by putting them in special print. Your instructor expects you to learn them. On tests, you are likely to be asked the meaning of key terms.

Remember that even if you find a definition in the sentence, you must understand what the definition means. For example, suppose that you find a definition context clue that tells you that a *phobia* is "an extreme, irrational fear." Unless you know that *irrational* means something that is unreasonable, you won't fully understand the meaning of *phobia*.

To help you remember this type of context clue, highlight the definition or synonym in each of the five sample sentences presented earlier. Because highlighting adds color, it can be more effective than simply underlining. If you do not have a highlighter, underline with a pen that writes in a different color.

Apply this skill: The sentences below are from college textbooks. The subject area is given in parentheses. Use the context clue of definition or synonym to determine the meaning of the underlined words in the sentences. (1) Highlight the part of the sentence that tells the meaning of the underlined word. (2) Circle or box the clues in each sentence that signal a definition is being presented.

- An *insurer*, or insurance company, is defined as a risk-sharing business that agrees to pay for losses that may happen to someone it insures.   (personal finance)

- Thirty-five states have laws protecting whistle-blowers, employees who report unethical or illegal actions of their employers.   (business)

- **Coping** means attempting to effectively manage or control stress so that it does not dominate your life.   (health and fitness)

- In speeches, an appeal to emotions is what we call the *pathos*. (speech)

- The term *logos* refers to the effort the speaker makes to prove a case argumentatively by offering facts and reasons.   (speech)

Discover the Second Type of Context Clue

In addition to key technical terms that occur in every college textbook, you will see many general college-level words. Because these words may not be part of your current vocabulary, you will need to figure out what they mean. As always, you can use context clues. Ask yourself, "What would this word have to mean in order for it to *make sense in this sentence*?"

Now look at the next set of sentences to figure out the second type of context clue. Look for the clues in each sentence that reveal the meaning of the underlined word. As before, the meaning of the underlined word is given beneath each sentence. After you have read the sentences, see if you can reason out the type of clue that the sentences have in common.

- Instead of lauding the proposed tax law, many senators criticized it.
    lauding = praising

- In contrast to energetic, alert students, sleep-deprived students are lethargic.
    lethargic = dull and drowsy; having no energy

- Some herbal remedies make flu symptoms less severe; others, however, can actually exacerbate the symptoms.
    exacerbate = to make more severe; make worse; aggravate

■ A quickly administered dose of aspirin can help a person survive a heart attack rather than <u>succumb</u> to it.

    succumb = to die

■ Whereas owls are <u>nocturnal</u>, most other birds are active only when there is daylight.

    nocturnal = active at night rather than during the day

 STOP AND PROCESS

EXERCISE 3.2

The same type of context clue reveals the underlined word's meaning in each of these sentences. Study the five sample sentences again, and then decide what it is in each sentence that provides the context clue to the meaning of the underlined word. On the line below, write a word or phrase that describes this type of context clue.

Write the second type of context clue to an unknown word's meaning:

_____

When you have written your answer, turn the page to discover if you are correct.

Second Type of Context Clue: A Contrast

Did you discover that in every case, there was a **contrast clue**, a word or phrase in each sentence that means the *opposite* of the underlined word? If you did not write "contrast," "opposite," "contrast with another word," or "contrast clue" on the line provided, go back and write one of these now. Since they all mean the same thing, use whichever one you prefer.

In all five example sentences, the meaning of the unfamiliar (underlined) word is the opposite of another word or phrase in the sentence. Authors usually signal an opposite in meaning with words such as *on the other hand, instead of, but, however, although, in contrast,* and *unlike.*

- In the first sample sentence, *lauding* is the opposite of *criticizing*; therefore, it means "*praising.*" The phrase *instead of* tells you that these words are opposites.

- In the second sentence, *lethargic* is the opposite of *energetic and alert*, so you can reason out that it must mean "dull, drowsy, having no energy." The phrase *in contrast to* alerts readers that these words are opposites.

- In the third sentence, *exacerbate* is the opposite of *make less severe*, so it must mean to "make more severe, to make worse, or aggravate." The words *some, others,* and *however* tell readers that two things are being contrasted.

- In the fourth example, the word *succumb* is the opposite of *survive*. The words *rather than* signal that there is a contrast.

- In the last sentence, the word *whereas* signals that *nocturnal* is the opposite of *active during the day*. Therefore, it must mean "active at night."

To help you remember this type of context clue, draw an arrow that connects the underlined word in each sentence to the word that means its opposite. Then box or circle the words in each sentence that signal a contrast: *in contrast to, however, rather than, instead (of), some... others,* and *whereas.* (In each sentence, highlight only the signal words.)

Apply this skill: Use the context clue of *contrast* to determine the meaning of the underlined words in the sentences that follow. (1) Highlight the part of the sentence that is the opposite of the meaning of the underlined word or words. (2) Circle or box the clues in each sentence that signal a contrast (an opposite meaning) is being presented. (3) Write the definition of the underlined word in the space provided. It will be the opposite of the part of the sentence you highlighted.

- Unlike <u>assimilated</u> <u>immigrants</u>, nonassimilated immigrants are immigrants who have come to this country more recently and still cling to their native language and customs.

  assimilated immigrants _____

  _____

  _____

- In contrast to <u>malignant tumors</u>, benign tumors are not cancerous and do not grow or spread.

  malignant tumors _____

- Last time several people split the lottery jackpot, whereas this time a <u>sole</u> winner collected all the money.

  sole _____

- Rather than travel <u>abroad</u>, many Americans prefer to visit locations in the United States.

  abroad _____

- The police were expecting a <u>rational</u> explanation for the painting's disappearance, but the gallery owner gave a completely illogical one.

  rational _____

Discover the Third Type of Context Clue

At this point, you've discovered definition clues and contrast clues. Now examine this set of sentences to determine the third type of context clue.

- A person's <u>surname</u> will often give a clue about his or her ethnicity: For example, most people recognize that Hernandez is Hispanic, Schmidt is German, and Beauvoir is French.

  surname = name shared in common by members of a family; the family name

- To protect your health, avoid known <u>carcinogens</u>, such as nicotine, asbestos, and certain forms of radiation.

  carcinogens = substances capable of causing cancer

- Some companies <u>exploit</u> illegal immigrants: They make them work long hours, pay them almost nothing, and threaten to turn them in to the authorities if they complain.

  exploit = to use unethically; to take unfair advantage of

- Kangaroos and opossums are perhaps the best-known examples of <u>marsupials</u>.

  marsupials = animals whose babies live in their mothers' pouches until they are able to survive on their own

- Many citizens' groups believe law enforcement agencies should not waste their time fighting <u>victimless crimes</u> like gambling, drug use, and prostitution.

  victimless crimes = crimes in which the person causes harm only to himself or herself (rather than to other victims)

STOP AND PROCESS

EXERCISE 3.3

The same type of context clue reveals the underlined word's meaning in each of these sentences. Look again at the sentences and the meaning of the underlined words. Then decide what it is in each sentence that provides the clue to the meaning of the underlined word. On the line below, write a word or phrase that describes this type of context clue.

Write the third type of context clue to an unknown word's meaning:

_____

Third Type of Context Clue: Examples

Did you discover that in every case, there was an **example clue**—one or more examples in the sentence that illustrate the meaning of the underlined word? If you did not write "example clue" on the line provided, go back and write it now.

Sometimes authors do not define a term or include another word in the sentence that has the opposite meaning of an unfamiliar word. However, they may include *examples* in the sentence that enable readers to reason out the meaning of the unfamiliar word. Examples are typically introduced by these words and phrases: *for example, to illustrate, such as, for instance,* and *like.* Remember, though, that an example is not the definition. Rather, the example is simply a clue that can help you reason out the meaning of an unknown word.

- In the first sample sentence, the meaning of *surname* can be reasoned out because the examples consist of people's last names (Hernandez, Schmidt, and Beauvoir). They are introduced by the words, *for example.* You can figure out that *surname* must mean a last name or family name.

- In the second sentence, the examples of *carcinogens* (nicotine, asbestos, and certain forms of radiation) are all substances that can cause cancer. They are introduced by the words *such as.*

- In the third sentence, the example of companies who *exploit* illegal immigrants by making them work long hours, paying them almost nothing, and threatening to turn them over to the authorities if they complain tells you that the employers take unfair advantage of them. The sentence uses a colon (:) instead of words to introduce the examples.

- In the fourth sentence in the set, the term *marsupials* is not defined. However, the two examples of marsupials (kangaroos and opossums) are both animals whose babies stay in their mothers' pouches until they are able to survive on their own. The word *examples* appears in the sentence.

- In the last sentence, the word *like* introduces three examples of *victimless crimes:* gambling, drug use, and prostitution. Based on those examples, you can reason out that they are crimes in which the damage occurs mainly to the person who does them rather than to other people.

 To help you remember this type of context clue, highlight the examples in each sentence that give a clue to the meaning of the underlined word. Box or circle the words that introduce examples (*for example, such as, examples,* and *like*). In each sentence, highlight only these words.

Apply this skill: Use the context clue of *examples* to determine the meaning of the underlined words in the sentences that follows.
(1) Highlight the examples of the underlined word. (2) Circle or box the clues in each sentence that signal that examples are being presented.
(3) Write the definition of the underlined word in the space provided. Remember that the definition is not the examples but rather what the examples illustrate.

- The orchestra includes several <u>percussion instruments:</u> drums of all sorts, xylophones, cymbals, triangles, chimes, and maracas, for instance.

  percussion instruments _____

  _____

- Without protection from hunters and the preservation of their habitats, animals such as giant pandas, bald eagles, and snow leopards will eventually become <u>extinct.</u>

  extinct _____

- Certain <u>infectious</u> illnesses, like the common cold and flu, can be prevented or reduced by thorough, frequent hand washing with soap.

  infectious _____

- There are a number of effective *relaxation techniques*: massage, yoga, biofeedback, imagery, and meditation, to name a few.

  relaxation techniques _____

- Lavender, peach, and pale green are examples of <u>pastel</u> colors.

  pastel _____

Discover the Fourth Type of Context Clue

Now read this next set of sample sentences to determine the type of context clue they all share. This time, there are no definitions, opposite words, or examples. Search for a fourth type of clue. (*Tip:* This clue is almost too obvious. Don't turn it into something hard! Just ask yourself how you are able to figure out the meaning of the underlined words.)

- If the sky suddenly turns dark and <u>ominous</u>, you should immediately seek shelter.

  ominous = threatening, appearing dangerous

- People who have difficulty controlling their anger become <u>indignant</u> if they even think they have been insulted.

  indignant = showing anger

- Whenever a company must lay off workers, newer employees and less skilled employees are the most <u>vulnerable</u>.

  vulnerable = likely to be affected; susceptible

- The Internet offers a <u>cornucopia</u> of information on every subject imaginable.

  cornucopia = an abundance; a great amount; more than enough

- Fire can result when <u>combustible</u> materials are not stored properly.

  combustible = likely to catch fire and burn

STOP AND PROCESS

EXERCISE 3.4

The same type of context clue reveals the underlined word's meaning in each of these sentences. Look at the sentences again, and then decide what it is in each sentence that provides the context clue to the meaning of the underlined word. On the line below, write a word or phrase that describes this type of context clue.

Write the fourth type of context clue to an unknown word's meaning:

_____

Fourth Type of Context Clue: General Sense of the Sentence

Did you discover that in every case, you could use the **general sense** (overall meaning) of the sentence, combined with your own knowledge and experience, to figure out the meaning of the underlined words? Authors know that readers have a certain amount of background knowledge that can help them figure out what an unfamiliar word means. When readers ask themselves, "What does this word have to mean in order to make sense in this sentence?" they draw on information they already know to help them answer that question.

- In the first sample sentence, you can reason out that *ominous* means "threatening" or "dangerous" because you know that the sky often turns dark before severe storms. Also, you would seek shelter only if you thought a dangerous storm was coming.

- In the second example, you can bring your own experience to bear: You know that high-tempered people become angry whenever they think they have been insulted. Therefore, *indignant* must mean angry.

- In the third sentence, it makes sense that newer and less-skilled workers are more "likely to be affected" if a company has to lay off workers.

- In the fourth sample sentence, most readers' knowledge of the Internet enables them to guess correctly that *cornucopia* means an "abundance" or "great amount" of information.

- In the last sentence, you can reason out that if fire can result from not properly storing *combustible* materials (such as gasoline, certain chemicals, and oily rags, for example), then *combustible* must mean "likely to catch fire."

 To help you remember this type of context clue, highlight the part of each sentence that provides the clue to the meaning of the underlined word. In each sentence, highlight only the part that gives the clue.

Apply this skill: Determine the meaning of the underlined words in the sentences that follow. Use the part of the sentence that provides the clue to the meaning of each word, and highlight it or underline it in color.

- The heavy rainstorms caused the river to overflow its banks and underline{inundate} the towns in the valley below.

     inundate _____

- Toddlers can accidentally swallow cleaning solutions, paint solvents, and other underline{toxic} substances, so parents should keep the Poison Control telephone number at hand.

     toxic _____

- I accidentally underline{transposed} the numbers and wrote the check for $34 instead of $43.

     transposed _____

- When the ship ran headlong into the sandbar, its <u>prow</u> was damaged.

  prow _____

- My aunt is an <u>ailurophile</u> who owns six cats, wears cat-themed jewelry and clothes, and has cat decorations all over her house.

  ailurophile _____

Discover the Fifth Type of Context Clue

In this final set, each example consists of a short paragraph rather than a single sentence. One of the sentences contains an underlined word, whose definition is given beneath the paragraph. Read the entire paragraph and the meaning of the underlined word. Then think about the type of context clue that all the examples have in common.

- According to *Parade* magazine (6/27/04), a survey by the Charles Schwab Foundation revealed that American teenagers know shockingly little about <u>fiscal</u> matters. One in five teens does not know that if you take out a loan, you must pay interest in addition to repaying the loan. One teen in four has the mistaken notion that financial aid will take care of all their college expenses. And one teen in three thinks that Social Security payments will provide all the money they need when they retire. Clearly, parents and schools need to do a better job of educating teens about money matters.

  fiscal = pertaining to financial matters; pertaining to money

- Many educators are concerned about what is being called the <u>digital divide</u>. They are concerned that children in poor neighborhoods typically have less access to computers and the Internet than other students.

  digital divide = the difference in computer and Internet access between poor children and other students (poor students have less access)

- The notion that drinking black coffee will sober up someone who is intoxicated is nothing more than <u>folklore</u>. Although this mistaken belief has been around for years and most people think it's true, time is actually the only remedy for too much alcohol in the bloodstream. It takes an hour for the human body to burn half an ounce of alcohol, and there is no way to speed up this process. Trying to sober someone up with coffee can turn out to be dangerous if the person then thinks he or she is able to drive.

  folklore = a mistaken belief that has been around for a long time and which people believe is true; stories and explanations that are passed down and become traditional within a group of people or in a country

- The U.S. government must decide how to deal with many complex issues. Whether the subject is space travel or hunger in America, the government relies on expert knowledge to help develop its policies. Much of this expertise is held by <u>bureaucrats</u>. These government officials spend their careers applying their expertise in a particular policy area. Many of them have scientific, technical, or other specialized training.

> *bureaucrats* = government officials who spend their careers applying their expertise in a particular policy area

- Bill Gates, the wealthiest man in the world, is also becoming known for his <u>philanthropy</u>. He has donated vast sums of money to help others. He created the Bill and Melinda Gates Foundation. The money he gives promotes increased access to innovative technology in education, improves global health, and promotes projects in the Pacific Northwest. In 1999 he established the Gates Millennium Scholars Program to provide money for minority students to attend college. At a relatively young age, Gates had already donated several billion dollars to charity.

> *philanthropy* = giving money for charitable purposes as a way of helping others

STOP AND PROCESS

EXERCISE 3.5

The same type of context clue reveals the meaning of the underlined word or term in each example. Look at the examples again, and then decide what it is in each paragraph that provides the context clue to the meaning of the underlined word. On the line below, write a word or phrase that describes this type of context clue.

Write the fifth type of context clue to an unknown word's meaning:

_____

Fifth Type of Context Clue: Information from Another Sentence

Did you discover that in every example, the **information from another sentence** helped you figure out the meaning of the underlined word? If you did not write "information from another sentence" on the line provided, go back and write it now.

Sometimes authors include information in another sentence in the paragraph that allows readers to determine the meaning of an unfamiliar word. For this reason, it is a good idea to keep reading when you encounter an unfamiliar word.

- In the first example, the term *fiscal* is explained in the last sentence of the paragraph: things that pertain to financial matters (money). Also, the other sentences discuss things related to financial matters: loans and interest, financial aid in college, and Social Security payments.

- In the second example, the term *digital divide* is explained by the sentence that follows the one in which the term appears: poor children having less access to computers and the Internet than other schoolchildren.

- In the third example, the word *folklore* is explained in the second sentence: a mistaken belief that has been around for a long time and that people believe is true.

- In the fourth example, the term *bureaucrats* is explained by information in the fourth sentence: They are experts who make a career of applying their special area of knowledge to public policy.

- In the last example, information in the other sentences explains what *philanthropy* is: donating money to help others.

To help you remember this type of context clue, highlight the information in another sentence or sentences that provides the clue to the meaning of the underlined word. Highlight only the information that gives the clue, not the entire sentence.

Apply this skill: Highlight the clues in another sentence that suggest the meaning of the underlined word.

- There has always been controversy over <u>euthanasia</u>. Opponents argue that doctor-assisted suicide is immoral and that it is murder. They say that a doctor's duty is to save lives, even if a terminally ill patient does not want to be kept alive. On the other hand, proponents argue that helping a terminally ill or chronically ill person die spares the person needless pain and suffering. Moreover, it provides death with dignity. They argue that it violates the person's rights to force the person to remain alive against his or her will.

  euthanasia _____

  _____

■ Aesop, who lived in ancient Greece, was one of the most famous storytellers of all times. Each of his <u>fables</u> had a moral, or lesson, that it taught. Millions of children all over the world have been delighted by these instructive tales and learned from them. Who doesn't remember the lesson of the fable about the hardworking ant and the lazy grasshopper ("We should prepare today for the needs of tomorrow"), or the one about the crow and the pitcher ("little by little does the trick")?

fable _____

■ Remember, people are different. What makes perfect sense to you may be <u>goobledygook</u> to others. You cannot assume that what is clear to you is clear to your audience. This is particularly true in speech making. Listeners, unlike readers, cannot turn to a dictionary or reread an author's words to discover their meaning. A speaker's meaning must be immediately comprehensible; it must be so clear that there is virtually no chance of misunderstanding. You can ensure this by using familiar words, by choosing concrete words over abstract words, and by eliminating verbal clutter.

Source: Stephen Lucas, *The Art of Public Speaking,* 8th ed., p. 271. Copyright © 2004, 2001, 1998, 1995, 1992, 1989, 1986, 1983 by Stephen E. Lucas. Reprinted by permission of The McGraw-Hill Companies, Inc.

gobbledygook _____

_____

■ Breathe Right <u>nasal</u> strips are the innovative adhesive pads with a small spring inside that, when attached to the nose, pull the <u>nasal</u> passages open, making it easier to breathe. Since their introduction in the United States, the Breathe Right strips have been purchased by athletes hoping to improve their performance through increased oxygen flow, snorers (and, more often, snorers' spouses) hoping for a good night's sleep, and allergy and cold sufferers looking for relief for their stuffed noses.

Source: Adapted from Roger Kerin, Steven Hartley, and William Rudelius, *Marketing: The Core,* p. 158. Copyright © 2004 by The McGraw-Hill Companies, Inc. Reprinted by permission of the McGraw-Hill Companies, Inc.

nasal _____

■ We now know beyond any doubt that prolonged or continuous exposure to ultraviolet light rays <u>predisposes</u> an individual to the development of skin cancer. Manufacturers of artificial tanning devices claim the ultraviolet light produced by tanning devices is safe. The Food and Drug Administration (FDA) has warned the public that sunlamps and tanning beds are dangerous. Besides the increased risk of skin cancer, long-term exposure to a form of ultraviolet light (UVA) causes premature aging of the skin with wrinkling and sagging.

Source: William Prentice, *Get Fit, Stay Fit,* 3d ed., p. 240. Copyright© 2004 The McGraw-Hill Companies.

predisposes _____

BRAIN-FRIENDLY TIPS

- **Learning words in context helps you remember their definition.** For example, the phrases "abrasive personality" and "abrasive cleaners" help you remember two different meanings of *abrasive*. And you will remember the definitions forever if you associate those phrases with information you already know. Undoubtedly you know someone who has an abrasive personality (someone who "rubs you the wrong way"), so make that mental association: "an abrasive personality just like ____." Think of a brand of scouring powder and make a mental association: "an abrasive cleaner just like ____."

- **You can use prefixes and roots to help you confirm the guess you made based on context.** Suppose you read in a health textbook, "Preadolescents should be immunized to protect them from certain childhood diseases." You could reason out that *preadolescents* refers to children who have not yet reached adolescence (have not yet begun to develop the physical characteristics of adults). The prefix *pre-* would confirm your guess that the word means "*before* adolescence." (The Online Reading Lab contains material to help you learn the meaning of common word parts.)

- **Create a word wall.** In the area where you study, start a word wall. Write important terms and new words on slips of paper, and tack them up where you can see them. Use color. Write the word in a way that suggests its meaning. For example, you might write the word *tremble* in shaky handwriting since it means to shiver or shake. If you create a word wall, you will use the new words more often and they will become part of your active vocabulary.

- **Visual learners may want to create a visual memory peg for the five types of context clues.** For example:

  Contrast clues
  Other sentence clues
  Ge**N**eral sense of the sentence
  The definition
  Example clues
  X
  T

www.mhhe.com/
entryways

Related material:
"Brain-Friendly
Vocabulary
Techniques:
Learning Styles and
Vocabulary Word
Templates"

MY TOOLBOX *of Context Clues*

Congratulations! You now know five types of context clues that can help you determine the meaning of unfamiliar words when you read. Context clues enable you to draw on your common sense and on knowledge you already possess. When you are reading and you encounter an unfamiliar word or term, ask yourself, "What would this word have to mean *in order to make sense in this sentence*?"

To help you transfer any information into long-term or permanent memory, you must rehearse it some way. Two effective ways to rehearse new information are to *say it aloud* and to *write* the information (put it on paper). That is why you were asked to write down each clue as you discovered it.

Now take a few minutes to *review* the five clues. From the options below, choose a review method that suits your learning style. You may want to try more than one. The goal is to work with the material and make it your own. You're in the driver's seat, so experiment and have fun with this!

- **Write out the information.** Write it in your book, on separate paper, or on index cards. If you like, write about the context clues in the form of a "recipe" that tells the "ingredients" for each of the five types of clues. Regardless of the form you choose, you should include the definition of *context clue,* the question you should ask yourself when you want to use the context to determine the meaning of an unfamiliar word, the five types of context clues, and the words and phrases that signal each. Try first to write this information from memory, and use your own words. If you get stuck, go back and look at the clues you wrote earlier in the chapter. Use more than one color pen if color helps you learn.

- **Make a study map.** (1) Turn the page sideways (or use a separate sheet of paper) and draw a circle or box in the center of the page. In it, write "5 TYPES OF CONTEXT CLUES," the definition of *context clue,* and the context clue question. (2) Branch five lines out from the center. At the end of each line (or on the line itself), write the name and definition of one of the five clues, along with the signals for it. Use bold capital letters, color, arrows, symbols, pictures, and anything else you find meaningful. Use lots of space so that your map does not look crowded. Work quickly; you can always tidy up your map or recopy it. There is no single right way to create a map. Once you have created your map, study it. Then close your eyes and try to visualize it. Open your eyes to compare what you saw in your head with what is on the actual map. Repeat the process until you can see the entire map in your head. At that point, you know it! (The ORL has additional information on creating study maps.)

- **Place your hand palm down on a piece of paper and trace an outline of it**. In the center area, write "5 TYPES OF CONTEXT CLUES," the definition of *context clue,* and the question you should ask yourself when you want to use the context to determine the meaning of an unfamiliar word. On the thumb and each finger, write one type of context clue. Be sure to include some signal words for each. Once you've finished your "helping hand," close your eyes and try to visualize the completed image. You may find it reinforcing to say the context clues out loud, pressing down the thumb and a finger as you say each one. (This links visualization with speaking, hearing, and a physical movement—a powerful learning technique.) Open your eyes to compare what you saw in your mind's eye with what you drew. Repeat the process until you can see the entire image in your head. Whenever you need to come up with the five types of context clues, you'll have a "handy" mental picture of what you need.

■ **Create a poem, song, or story** about the five types of context clues. Include the definition of *context clue* and the context clue question you should ask yourself when you want to determine the meaning of an unfamiliar word. Mention, too, the signals for each of the five clues. Your imagination is the only limit. If you create a poem or a story, you can include pictures or illustrations. If you like to use the computer, you can create a PowerPoint presentation. If you create song lyrics, set them to a familiar tune. Read aloud (or even record) what you have written. Hearing it will help your brain get the information through an additional channel.

✔ **CHAPTER CHECK**

Answer these questions about the information in the chapter. Write the missing word in each blank. When there is more than one part to the answer, there is more than one blank.

1. Words in a sentence or paragraph that authors include to help the reader reason out the meaning of unfamiliar words are called _____. (Two words)

2. There are _____ (how many?) types of context clues.

3. The type of context clue in which the author includes something that is the opposite of the meaning of the unfamiliar word is called a _____ clue.

4. The words *such as, for example, like,* and *to illustrate* are often used in _____ context clues.

5. Synonyms and the meanings of unfamiliar words are called _____ clues.

6. If there is not a context clue in the same sentence as the unfamiliar word, a clue may appear in another _____ of the paragraph.

7. To determine the meaning of an unfamiliar word, ask yourself, "What would this word have to mean in order to make sense in this _____?"

8. The first strategy good readers use to determine the meaning of an unfamiliar word is to use the _____.

9. Sometimes you must rely on the _____ _____ sense of the sentence, combined with your own knowledge and experience, to determine the meaning of an unfamiliar word.

10. Even though context clues are usually reliable, they are not always _____ clues.

11. When you "use the context," you are actually making an educated _____ about what a word means.

12. When you look up a word in the dictionary, you can use the context of the sentence in which the word appeared to help you know which _____ to choose.

13. The ability to use the context to determine the meaning of unfamiliar words helps you expand your _____.

14. The word *context* means whatever_____ something else.

15. Authors include context clues because they want you to _____ what you are reading.

REVIEW EXERCISES

SET 1

Brain-friendly reminder: Stretch and take a few deep breaths before you begin these exercises.

Use the context to determine the meaning of the underlined word in each sentence.

- Ask yourself, "What would this word have to mean in order to make sense in this sentence?"
- Choose the definition and write the corresponding letter in the space provided.
- Mark any *clues or signal words* that help you figure out the word's meaning.
- In the margin, write the type of context clue.

Example:

___A___ The **cortex**—the gray, outer layer of the brain—has four major lobes that are separated by deep grooves.

    A. gray, outer layer of the brain
    B. separations in the brain
    C. a major lobe of the brain
    D. deep grooves in the brain

Explanation: The term *cortex* appears in bold. Its definition is set off in dashes.

_____ 1. Recognizing the signs of a stroke and getting immediate medical attention are <u>crucial</u> for improving a person's chance of survival and recovery.

    A. unnecessary
    B. not recommended
    C. absolutely necessary
    D. mildly helpful

_____ 2. In general, attitudes toward <u>punctuality</u> are cultural. In this country, being on time is a sign of good manners; in some other cultures, showing up on time is considered rude.

    A. being late
    B. being on time
    C. not paying attention to time
    D. running out of time

_____ 3. Many government programs have the goal of <u>eradicating</u> poverty, but despite these efforts, poverty has not gone away.

    A. improving
    B. limiting

C. eliminating
D. delaying

_____ 4. President Calvin Coolidge had a reputation for being <u>taciturn</u>. For example, when a reporter once told Coolidge that he had bet another reporter that he could get the president to say more than three words, President Coolidge replied, "You lose."

A. angry
B. friendly
C. wealthy
D. untalkative

_____ 5. Many <u>*computer peripherals*</u>, such as monitors, printers, and scanners, are now offered with the computer as a package and at a cheaper price than if purchased separately.

A. computer monitors
B. items that are packaged together
C. devices that work with computers
D. brands that are less expensive

_____ 6. Home mortgage payments are set at a level that allows <u>*amortization*</u> of the loan; that is, the balance owed on the loan is reduced with each payment.

A. home mortgage payments
B. setting payment levels on a loan
C. the balance owed on a loan
D. the balance owed on a loan is reduced with each payment

_____ 7. Research suggests that money plays a central role in determining <u>marital</u> power. Apparently, money establishes the balance of power for married couples. Married women with paying work outside the home enjoy greater power than full-time homemakers do.

A. pertaining to marriage
B. pertaining to power
C. pertaining to women
D. pertaining to homemakers

_____ 8. Some presidents read very little, but others, such as John F. Kennedy and Bill Clinton, were <u>voracious</u> readers of books and publications of all sorts.

A. pertaining to the presidency
B. able to do an activity only with great difficulty
C. pertaining to books
D. eager, having a great desire to do something

_____ 9. The <u>volatile</u>, day-to-day ups and downs in stock prices made investors extremely nervous about their money.

    A. steady, remaining the same
    B. expected
    C. changing often and quickly
    D. predictable, normal

_____ 10. In Ernest Hemingway's novel *The Old Man and the Sea*, the <u>main</u>, or most important, character is an old Cuban fisherman named Santiago.

    A. very old
    B. most important
    C. pertaining to fishing
    D. Cuban

SET 2

Brain-friendly reminder: Stretch and take a few deep breaths before you begin these exercises.

Use the context to determine the meaning of the underlined word in each sentence.

- Ask yourself, "What would this word have to mean in order to make sense in this sentence?"
- Write a definition in the space provided. You may use your own words or words from the sentence.
- Mark any *clues or signal words* that help you figure out the word's meaning.
- On the line beneath your definition, write the type of context clue.

Example:

The <u>syllabus,</u> or course outline, gives important information about the requirements of a college course.

Definition: _____ course outline _____

Type of clue: _____ definition clue _____

1. One layer of the earth's crust consists of <u>metamorphic rocks</u>: rocks that have been changed, usually through pressure and high temperature within the crust.

Definition: _____

_____

Type of clue: _____

2. Some behaviors must be learned; others are <u>instinctive</u>.

Definition:_____

_____

Type of clue: _____

3. The zoo spends a significant part of its food budget on meat for its <u>carnivorous</u> animals.

   Definition: _____

   Type of clue: _____

4. In recent years, there has been growing concern over the use of "<u>date rape drugs.</u>" These illegal drugs are sneaked into the victim's drink and leave her unable to remember the sexual assault. Congress has increased the punishment for those found guilty of using these drugs.

   Definition: _____

   _____

   Type of clue: _____

5. <u>Initializations</u>, such as BFN ("bye for now"), BTW ("by the way"), FYI ("for your information"), and EOM ("end of message"), are frequently used in emails.

   Definition: _____

   Type of clue: _____

6. *<u>Mesomorph</u>* is a term that describes a body type that is muscular, athletic, and physically strong.

   Definition: _____

   Type of clue: _____

7. There are people who love <u>innovation</u>, but there are also those who are uncomfortable with change and do not like anything new.

   Definition: _____

   Type of clue: _____

8. In 1967, Mexican American civil rights leader Cesar Chavez urged people to <u>boycott</u> grapes. He declared that no one should buy grapes until grape growers agreed to treat farm workers fairly.

   Definition: _____

   Type of clue: _____

9. A great many jobs are never advertised, and yet more than 60 percent of all new jobs come from what is known as the <u>hidden job market</u>.

   Definition: _____

   Type of clue: _____

www.mhhe.com/
entryways

For additional
practice, see
Context Exercise,
Sets 1, 2, and 3.

10. Nearly every textbook includes *graphic aids* (tables, diagrams, graphs, charts, etc.).

Definition: _____

_____

Type of clue: _____

Congratulations! You're on your way to a more powerful vocabulary.

ASSESS YOUR UNDERSTANDING

As you now know, you become a better student by assessing your own understanding and then taking corrective action when there are things you don't "get." Think about how you did on the Chapter Check and the exercises. They're good sources of feedback. Also, ask yourself, "Could I explain to someone what context clues are? Can I describe the five types of context clues presented in this chapter?" Circle a number on the scale below to indicate how well you understand context clues.

←□→ CROSS-CHAPTER CONNECTIONS

In Chapter 2 (pages 32–63), you learned that *using feedback to monitor your progress* is an important success behavior. You also learned steps you can take whenever you do not understand material in your textbooks.

1 . . . . . 2 . . . . . 3 . . . . . 4 . . . . . 5 . . . . . 6 . . . . . 7 . . . . . 8 . . . . . 9 10

Huh?!!   **It's not quite in focus.**   **They should give me an award!**

Now identify anything you don't understand. What do you still need to learn? Is there anything about context clues that you need clarification on? Write your response on the lines below.

_____

_____

_____

_____

For anything you didn't understand or couldn't remember, what steps could you take to correct this? Do you need to reread? Ask a classmate or your instructor questions? Write the information down or review it some other way? Write your response here:

_____

_____

_____

_____

Monitoring your understanding isn't an extra frill. It's a ticket to becoming an increasingly effective student. After a while, you'll do it automatically. Hop on board!

Map of Chapters

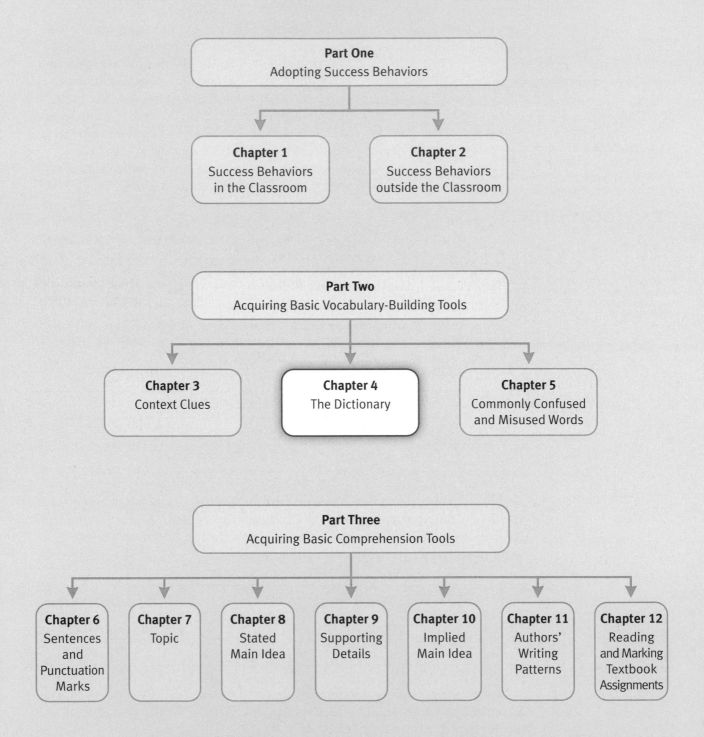

Part One
Adopting Success Behaviors

Chapter 1
Success Behaviors
in the Classroom

Chapter 2
Success Behaviors
outside the Classroom

Part Two
Acquiring Basic Vocabulary-Building Tools

Chapter 3
Context Clues

Chapter 4
The Dictionary

Chapter 5
Commonly Confused
and Misused Words

Part Three
Acquiring Basic Comprehension Tools

Chapter 6
Sentences
and
Punctuation
Marks

Chapter 7
Topic

Chapter 8
Stated
Main Idea

Chapter 9
Supporting
Details

Chapter 10
Implied
Main Idea

Chapter 11
Authors'
Writing
Patterns

Chapter 12
Reading
and Marking
Textbook
Assignments

CHAPTER 4

The Dictionary

A Word to the Wise Is Sufficient

Why You Need to Know the Information in This Chapter

College textbooks are filled with words that are new to students, so every student should have strong dictionary skills. This chapter explains how to locate dictionary words efficiently and understand the information given for each word.

Being skillful at using traditional and online dictionaries will help you

- learn the meanings of new words

- learn additional meanings of words you already know

- learn synonyms for words

- pronounce words correctly

- find the correct spelling of words

- divide words into syllables

- learn the history of words

- learn a wealth of useful and interesting information about people, places, and things

Super Student Tips

Here are tips from other students about using the dictionary. Here's what experience has taught them:

"I learned to use the glossary in my textbooks. I discovered it's a real shortcut to finding out what key terms mean."—*Andrew*

"I never used to look up words. In college, there were so many new words that I *had* to look them up. The more I used the dictionary, the better and faster I've become at it."—*Lola*

"Once I understood about using the context, I was able to choose the correct definition when I looked up a word in the dictionary. Before, I didn't know which definition I needed."—*Ivan*

"When you look up a word, look at the word's etymology. That's the part of a dictionary entry that tells the history of the word."—*Dhannya*

"When I'm waiting for the bus, I study a paperback dictionary that I carry with me. I try to learn one or two new words each day. In two semesters, I've added a multitude of words to my vocabulary. (*Multitude* was one of my new words!) I feel good about what I've accomplished."—*Roberta*

"Since I found out how to learn words in a way that works with my learning style, I've been able to add so many words to my vocabulary! It's been so much easier to remember them."—*Libby*

Jumpstart Your Brain!

Before you begin the chapter, get yourself ready to think. Stand up or stretch. Better yet, stand up *and* stretch. Take a couple of deep breaths. These simple actions get oxygen to your brain, and your brain loves oxygen! Then jumpstart your brain—give it renewed energy—by solving these brainteasers. Both of them have to do with words or dictionaries. Good luck!

1. New words are always being added to dictionaries. Do you know the meaning of these?

   McJob _____

   comb-over (*Hint:* Think Donald Trump.) _____

   _____

   Botox _____

   _____

   Frankenfood _____

   _____

2. Each pair of words below is part of a larger group of words that have something in common. Read each pair and decide how the two items are alike. Then write a word that is *part of the same group* and comes *alphabetically between the two words.* In the example, broccoli and carrots are both vegetables. Cabbage is also a vegetable, and the word *cabbage* comes alphabetically between broccoli and carrots. There may be more than one right answer for some of these, and some are challenging. (Bonus points if you get them!) Your teacher may instruct you to do this activity collaboratively. Have fun!

   Example:

broccoli	*cabbage*	carrots
hammer	_____	wrench
anger	_____	joy
crawl	_____	walk
autumn	_____	winter
Nevada	_____	North Dakota
centimeter	_____	yard

   In case you need it, here's the alphabet:

   a b c d e f g h i j k l m n o p q r s t u v w x y z

LOOKING AT WHAT YOU ALREADY KNOW

 Based on what you already know, answer as many of the following items as you can. At the end of the chapter, you can correct or add information.

1. What is meant by a dictionary *entry?*

   _____

2. What is the purpose of *guidewords?*

   _____

3. List three examples of *parts of speech.*

   _____

4. What does a word's *etymology* tell you?

   _____

5. What is a *synonym?*

   _____

6. Many words have more than one definition (meaning). When you look up a word in the dictionary, how can you tell which definition you need?

   _____

The Dictionary

The only place in which success comes before work is in the dictionary.

—Vidal Sassoon

Every other author may aspire to praise; the lexicographer can only hope to escape reproach.

—Samuel Johnson

A dictionary is an education in a book. During the middle of the 20th century, the man who became civil rights activist Malcolm X spent eight years in prison. When he entered prison, he was barely 21, and he had an eighth-grade education. While he was in prison, he educated himself. He began by copying the dictionary word by word, page by page onto tablets. It took him an entire day to copy the first page of the dictionary. When he finished, he read aloud to himself everything he'd written, over and over. Then he reviewed the words the next day. (He might not have realized it, but by seeing, writing, reading, and saying the information, he was using every sensory channel. This is an effective, brain-friendly way to put information into memory.) This is what Malcolm X said about his experience with the dictionary:

> With every succeeding page, I also learned of people and places and events in history. Actually the dictionary is like a miniature encyclopedia. Finally the dictionary's A section had filled a whole tablet—and I went on into the Bs. That was the way I started copying what eventually became the entire dictionary. It went a lot

Civil rights activist Malcolm X.

BRAIN-FRIENDLY TIP

Use the strategies below to learn new words in the ways that suit your learning style.

Auditory: Pay special attention to the pronunciation of words. Say new words aloud. When you find the definition of a word you are looking for, read it aloud. If you are using a CD-ROM or online dictionary, listen to the pronunciation of the word. Create a phrase or rhyme to help you remember the meaning of the new word.

Visual: Pay special attention to the etymology (origin, history) of words. Seeing the parts that make up a word can help you remember the meaning more easily. Visualize the parts in different colors. When learning a new word, close your eyes and visualize it. Then write out the word and the definition.

Visual-spatial: Close your eyes and visualize new words as you learn them. Write out the word and its definition. Most important, include sketches or doodles to represent the meaning of the word.

Tactile-kinesthetic: In addition to any other strategies you use, make a facial expression, gesture, or movement with your body that represents to you the meaning of the word you are trying to learn.

faster after so much practice helped me to pick up handwriting speed. Between what I wrote in my tablet, and writing letters, during the rest of my time in prison I would guess I wrote a million words.

Source: The Autobiography of Malcolm X, with the assistance of Alex Haley, New York: Ballantine, 1992, p. 172.

Copying the dictionary turned Malcolm X into a reader. A wealthy man had donated his huge personal library to the prison library, and Malcolm X checked out book after book. He said that anytime he had 15 free minutes, he had a book in his hands. He was so motivated that he read until three or four every morning, long after the lights were turned out at 10:00 p.m. To do this, he had to read in the glow from a light outside his cell. The night guard made rounds once every hour. When Malcolm X heard his footsteps, he would jump into bed and pretend to be asleep. As soon as the guard passed, Malcolm X would get up and read in the same way for another 58 minutes.

Not many people copy the dictionary like Malcolm X did, but his experience points out what an incredibly valuable tool the dictionary can be. It is a key that unlocks words, books, and minds.

The Big Picture for This Chapter

In the previous chapter, you learned how to use context clues to help you reason out the meanings of unfamiliar words. Although context clues will help you most of the time, you should consult a dictionary when these situations occur:

- There aren't any context clues.
- Context alone isn't enough, or several meanings seem possible.
- You need to understand the exact meaning of a word.
- The word is a key word in a course.
- You realize it would be useful to know a word because you keep running into it.

In this chapter you'll learn how to use the dictionary to full advantage. You already know that most words have more than one meaning. You won't be surprised to discover that context skills and dictionary skills complement each other.

Specifically, you'll learn how to locate words efficiently in the dictionary and understand the information given for them. You'll learn how to pronounce words correctly and pick the definition you need. You'll find out how to interpret information that explains a word's history, as well as why that information is helpful. The chapter ends with brain-friendly vocabulary-building strategies for various learning styles. From these, you can select ones that best suit your style.

The Three Most Important Dictionary Skills

Most of the words you look up will be ones in material you read, and *your purpose will be to find the definition that makes sense in the sentence you read.* Of course, it's also important to know how to pronounce the word. So here's what you absolutely need to know by the time you complete this chapter:

- how to locate a word in a traditional dictionary and an online one
- how to interpret dictionary pronunciation symbols
- how to select the appropriate definition

You need these skills every time you use the dictionary. Dictionaries give you other information about a word besides its pronunciation and definitions, but fortunately, you don't have to know all of it to get the information you need. As you use the dictionary more and more, you will begin to pay attention to the other information. At this point, though, concentrate on the three skills listed above.

Before we talk about using a dictionary, let's look at the types of dictionaries and how to select ones that are right for you as a college student.

Types of Dictionaries

For college students, a collegiate dictionary and a paperback dictionary are must-have tools. If you do not already own hardcover and paperback dictionaries, head for the bookstore! Even if your computer word-processing program has a built-in dictionary, you should still own both a collegiate dictionary and a paperback dictionary.

Collegiate dictionaries are hardcover dictionaries that focus on words useful to the typical college student and adult. They are medium-sized, desktop dictionaries. They do not contain as many words as full-sized hardcover dictionaries, and they present fewer definitions per word. They are considered *abridged* dictionaries because they are shorter than *unabridged* dictionaries, which contain thousands more words and definitions.

When buying a hardcover dictionary, examine several of them. Keep these suggestions in mind:

- Look for one that has the word *college, collegiate,* or *desk* in the title. If English is your second language, be sure to buy a regular "American dictionary." Do not rely on one that gives translations of words.

- Choose one that has a recent publication date. Older, out-of-date dictionaries aren't a bargain.

- Spend a few extra dollars for one that has thumb index tabs, as shown in the picture below. These tabs show the letters of the alphabet on the page edges. They make it easy to turn to the section of the alphabet you want.

- Choose a dictionary that includes the etymology (origin, history) of words and has sample sentences that illustrate the use of some of the words.

- Look at the *order* in which the definitions are given. Most people prefer dictionaries that list the most common meanings first. To find out about the order of the definitions, read the information at the front of the dictionary.

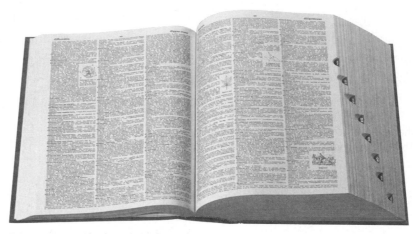

Dictionary with thumb index tabs

Pocket dictionaries are the smallest and the least complete dictionaries. They have fewer and shorter definitions, so you often have to do more work to get the information you need. They are handy because they fit in a backpack or book bag. The pocket dictionary you buy should have print large enough for you to read easily, and it should be sturdy.

There are many quality dictionaries. You may want to consider one of the following:

The American Heritage College Dictionary, 4th edition

Merriam-Webster's Collegiate Dictionary, 11th edition

Random House Webster's College Dictionary, updated every year

Some come with a CD-ROM, and paperback editions of these are available. It's a good idea to buy hardcover and paperback versions of the same dictionary.

If you are an auditory learner, visually impaired, speak English as a second language, or struggle with spelling, the *Franklin Speaking Merriam-Webster's Collegiate Dictionary* can be invaluable. It is a small, handheld,

www.mhhe.com/
entryways
For a description of the special features of these three dictionaries, see "Collegiate Dictionaries, Specialized Dictionaries, and Online Resources."

battery-powered device that contains more than 200,000 words and 500,000 synonyms. You can enter words based on the way they sound, or you can speak a word into it, and the correct spelling appears on the screen. You can hear the words and definitions spoken. It weighs less than six ounces, so you can tuck it in your book bag. Keep an eye on it, though! They can disappear—be stolen—in the blink of an eye. They cost about $100, but less expensive models are available. Check at large chain bookstores, electronics stores, and large office supply chain stores.

To reduce the number of electronic devices they carry, some students have switched from Franklins to small handheld devices, such as the Palm Pilot and BlackBerry, that perform a variety of functions. Dictionary software, with or without a thesaurus, is available for many of them. (For example, see www.palmOne.com for hardware and www.PalmSource.com for software.)

Dictionary software of every sort is available. Good choices for college students include the American Heritage and Merriam-Webster software. An especially appealing feature is that they make it possible for you to hear the pronunciation of words you look up. Microsoft Word, a word-processing program, includes a dictionary and thesaurus, but they are not as complete as dictionary software programs.

> **BONUS TIP**
>
> To compare the features and prices of various dictionaries before you go to a bookstore, go to Amazon.com. In the search box, type **dictionary.** On the pull-down product menu, select Books.
>
> To learn about Franklin electronic dictionaries, type **dictionary** in the search box, but select Electronics on the pull-down product menu.
>
> Even if you plan to buy a dictionary online, look at the actual book in a bookstore before you order it. One that sounds appealing might have pages that look too crowded or have poor-quality paper. The only way you will know is to look at the actual book.

www.mhhe.com/ entryways
For a description of the specialized and online dictionaries, see "Collegiate Dictionaries, Specialized Dictionaries, and Online Resources."

The Internet provides free access to hundreds of online dictionaries, including specialized ones. The website www.onelook.com provides links to nearly a thousand general and specialized online dictionaries that define more than six million words! The website www.Bartleby.com, which describes itself as "Great Books Online," is a wonderful resource. If you click on Dictionary, it links to *The American Heritage Dictionary*. Once you arrive at the word you want, you can click on the speaker icon to hear the word pronounced. You can listen to it as many times as you like.

Most textbooks have a **glossary,** a minidictionary of the key terms in the book. Glossaries are usually at the back of the book, but in some books, the key terms are defined at the end of each chapter or in the margins. Pay special attention to the glossary: You cannot understand a subject unless you know the important terms used in it. Instructors always ask definitions of key terms on tests, so the glossary can be a great study aid.

> **BRAIN-FRIENDLY TIPS**
>
> - Highlight the words you look up in textbook glossaries and in your pocket dictionary. (Highlight just the term, not the definition.) If you have to look up a word more than once, you can easily find it. Also, the brain responds to color.
>
> - Keep a running list of new words and terms for each course. Write them on notebook paper, on a blank page at the back of your textbook, or on large sticky notes in your text. As soon as you have a chance (or at the end of each week), make a vocabulary card for each word, or add them to your word wall. (For a description of a word wall see page 138 under Explore Core Vocabulary.)

Let's look now at how to use a dictionary. If it seems overwhelming, remember that you need to focus mainly on how to (1) locate a word, (2) interpret pronunciation symbols, and (3) select the appropriate definition.

How to Locate a Word in the Dictionary

Alphabetical Order

It's not exactly news that words are listed in alphabetical order in the dictionary. Practically everyone who attended elementary school in the United States knows the "Alphabet Song," and as adults, many of them still hum it when they need to go through the alphabet! (In case you grew up in another country and want to hear it, go to www.evaeaston.com, click on The Alphabet, and then click on The Alphabet Song.)

BRAIN-FRIENDLY TIP

When words start with the same two or three letters, it may help you to pencil lightly through those letters or cover them up with your finger. Look at the next letter and alphabetize by it. For example:

act~~io~~n, acti~~ve~~

The first four letters are the same, but since *o* comes before *v*, *action* comes alphabetically before *active*.

If you know the spelling of a word, you turn to the section of the dictionary with words that start with that word's first letter. It's simple, right? It is—*if* you are skilled at alphabetizing. In fact, there's a joke about this: "Wow! This dictionary is going to save me lots of time. All the words are in alphabetical order!"

If you are hazy on even a part of the alphabet, this is the time to stop and learn it. Write or say that part out loud until you know it automatically. If your learning style makes it difficult for you to remember the alphabet in order, keep a copy of it handy.

Let's take a minute to review alphabetizing:

- Words that start with A come before words that start with B, and so forth (for example, *apple, bug, gate, man, zoo*).
- When words start with the same letter, look at the *second* letter in each word, and alphabetize by it (w*a*gon, wh*a*le, w*i*sh, w*r*ong).
- If the first two letters are the same, alphabetize by the *third* letter, and so on (wh*a*le, wh*e*el, wh*i*te, wh*o*le).
- For two-word phrases such as *civil war, game plan,* or *shoulder blade,* use the first letter of the first word.

STOP AND PROCESS: Alphabetizing

EXERCISE 4.1

Alphabetize the words in each set. If you prefer, you can write numbers (1–5) above the words to indicate the correct order. Each set is slightly more challenging than the previous one.

1. web, brain, mat, frog, job   _____

2. lake, key, habit, jail, ice   _____

3. zipper, mud, tide, focus group, hall _____

4. teacup, table, tractor, test, tab _____

5. guilt, guest, guide, guard, guidepost _____

www.mhhe.com/
entryways

See ORL for information about spelling and pronouncing words correctly, "A List of Commonly Mispronounced and Misspelled Words," and spelling exercises. For more information on spelling, go to **Catalyst> Editing> Spelling**

How to Locate a Word You Can't Spell

"My teacher says I have lots of creativity, but that most of it shows up in my spelling." That's the way the joke goes, but for many students, spelling is no joke. "How can I look up a word if I can't spell it?" is a question frustrated students often ask. There's no single solution, but if you *occasionally* get stuck on the spelling of a word, one or more of these strategies may solve the problem.

- *Say the word out loud.* Listen to the sound it starts with and any distinctive consonants. (Consonants are all of the letters except *a, e, i, o,* and *u.*) Pronouncing words correctly helps you spell them correctly. If you mispronounce a word, you are less likely to be able to locate it. For example, you may say "flustrate" instead of "frustrate," but you won't find "flustrate" in the dictionary. Once you have said the word, try to look it up. If you can't find it, think about other ways to spell the sounds in the word, write out the word, or ask someone how to spell it.

Still stuck? Don't despair! Even common words in English can be tricky to spell, and many intelligent, talented people have trouble with spelling. If you *always* have problems with spelling, there's no reason to frustrate yourself. Continue to work to improve, of course, but try one of these other simple and practical solutions.

- *Buy a "bad speller's dictionary."* To find the correct spelling of a word, you look it up according to the way it *sounds* like it's spelled. (Most of these books are small enough to carry with you.) Words are listed the way they sound and by the ways people most often misspell them. The correct spelling is given beside the incorrect one. For example, you could look under "sissors," "sissers," or "sizzers" to find the correct spelling: scissors.

- *Use a Franklin.* On many of them, you can type in a word the way it sounds (such as "sissers"), and it takes you to the correct spelling (scissors) and the definition.

- *If you have access to a computer, type the word and spell-check it.* If your spelling is even close, the computer should give you the correct spelling.

- *If you have access to the Internet, go to www.onelook.com and use the wildcard search or the reverse dictionary feature.* Suppose you're not sure how to spell *jaguar.* With the *wildcard feature,* you can type in **jag***r,** and up pop words that begin and end with those letters. A *reverse dictionary* lets you describe a concept, and it then gives a list of words and phrases related to that concept. Your description can be a few words, a sentence, a question, or even a single word. If you find the correctly spelled word on the list that appears, click on it to go directly to the definition.

Source: Copyright © Mother Goose & Grim-Grimmy, Inc. King Features Syndicate.

Guidewords

At this point, let's assume you have the correct spelling of a word and are ready to look it up. In an online dictionary you simply type in the word. To speed up your search, traditional dictionaries use bold print guidewords. **Guidewords** consist of a pair of words at the top of each dictionary page that tell the first and last words on the page, between which all words on the page come alphabetically. Page 117 shows a sample page from *The American Heritage College Dictionary*. The guidewords on it are *near Earth object* and *necropolis*. *Near Earth object* is the first term defined on the page and *necropolis* is the last. All the other words on the page come alphabetically between the two guidewords (that is, after *near Earth object*, but before *necropolis*). You have located the correct page if the word you are looking for comes alphabetically after the first guideword but before the second one.

BRAIN-FRIENDLY TIPS

When you misspell a word, it's usually just one *part* of the word. That's the part to concentrate on! Write the word correctly and print that part in bold capital letters in a *different color*.

You can also create a memory peg for the tricky part of the word. For example, here are two memory pegs for the word *separate*:

- sePARate means aPARt
- the word sepARATe contains A RAT.

Use whatever works for you!

Remember that in addition to guidewords, thumb indexes on hardcover dictionaries enable you to turn directly to the correct part the book. Once you're in the right "neighborhood," you can use the guidewords to find the exact page you need.

STOP AND PROCESS: Guidewords

EXERCISE 4.2

List at least five words that could appear on dictionary pages with the following pairs of guidewords:

apple	basketball	kiss	lake	sack	travel	yam	zoom

_____   _____   _____   _____

_____   _____   _____   _____

Entries

graphic region that includes the Arctic and Temperate areas of North America and Greenland. [NE(O)– + ARCTIC.]

near Earth object *n.* A small comet or asteroid with an orbit that crosses or comes near Earth's orbit.

Near East A region of SW Asia generally thought to include Turkey, Lebanon, Israel, Iraq, Jordan, Saudi Arabia, and the other countries of the Arabian Peninsula. —**Near Eastern** *adj.* —**Near Easterner** *n.*

near•in•fra•red radiation (nîr′ĭn′frə-rĕd′) *n.* See **near-red radiation.**

Near Islands An island group of SW AK in the W Aleutians.

near•ly (nîr′lē) *adv.* **1.** Almost but not quite: *I nearly failed.* **2.** In a close manner; intimately.

near miss *n.* **1.** A narrowly avoided collision. **2.** A missile strike that is extremely close to but not directly on target. [Blend of *near thing*, something that nearly ends in disaster, and MISS[1].]

near point *n.* The nearest point at which an object can be seen distinctly by the eye.

near-red radiation (nîr′rĕd′) *n.* Electromagnetic radiation having the shortest wavelengths in the infrared region, between approx. 0.75 and 2.5 micrometers.

near rhyme *n.* See **off rhyme.**

near•sight•ed (nîr′sī′tĭd) *adj.* Unable to see distant objects clearly; myopic. —**near′sight′ed•ly** *adv.*

near•sight•ed•ness (nîr′sī′tĭd-nĭs) *n.* See **myopia.**

neat[1] (nēt) *adj.* **neat•er, neat•est 1.** Orderly and clean; tidy. **2.** Orderly and precise in procedure; systematic. **3.** Marked by ingenuity and skill; adroit: *a neat turn of phrase.* **4.** Not diluted or mixed with other substances: *neat whiskey.* **5.** Left after all deductions; net: *neat profit.* **6.** *Slang* Wonderful; terrific. [AN *neit*, clear, pure, var. of OFr. *net* < Lat. *nitidus*, elegant, gleaming < *nitēre*, to shine.] —**neat′ly** *adv.* —**neat′ness** *n.*

SYNONYMS neat, tidy, trim, shipshape These adjectives mean clean and in good order. *Neat* is the most general: *a neat room; neat hair. Tidy* emphasizes precise arrangement and order: *"When she saw me come in tidy and well dressed, she even smiled"* (Charlotte Brontë). *Trim* stresses especially smart appearance: *"A trim little sailboat was dancing out at her moorings"* (Herman Melville). *Shipshape* evokes meticulous order: *"We'll try to make this barn a little more shipshape"* (Rudyard Kipling).

neat[2] (nēt) *n., pl.* **neat** *Archaic* A cow or other domestic bovine animal. [ME *net* < OE *nēat.*]

neat•en (nēt′n) *tr.v.* **-ened, -en•ing, -ens** To put into order; make neat.

neath or **'neath** (nēth) *prep.* Beneath.

neat•herd (nēt′hûrd′) *n. Archaic* A cowherd.

neat•nik (nēt′nĭk) *n.* One who is habitually neat and orderly.

neat′s-foot oil (nēts′fŏot′) *n.* A light yellow oil obtained from the feet and shinbones of cattle, used chiefly to dress leather.

neb (nĕb) *n.* **1a.** A beak of a bird. **b.** A nose; a snout. **2.** A projecting part, esp. a nib. [ME < OE.]

NEB *abbr.* New English Bible

neb•bish (nĕb′ĭsh) *n.* A person regarded as weak-willed or timid. [Yiddish *nebekh*, poor, unfortunate, of Slav. orig. See **bhag-** in App.] —**neb′bish•y** *adj.*

NEbE *abbr.* northeast by east

NEbN *abbr.* northeast by north

Nebr. *abbr.* Nebraska

Ne•bras•ka (nə-brăs′kə) A state of the central US in the Great Plains; admitted as the 37th state in 1867. Cap. Lincoln. Pop. 1,711,263.

Ne•bras•kan (nə-brăs′kən) *adj.* **1.** Of or relating to Nebraska. **2.** *Geology* Of or relating to the first glacial stage of the Pleistocene in North America. ❖ *n.* A Nebraska native or resident.

Neb•u•chad•nez•zar II (nĕb′ə-kəd-nĕz′ər, nĕb′yə-) 630?–562 B.C. King of Babylonia (605–562) who captured (597) and destroyed (586) Jerusalem.

neb•u•la (nĕb′yə-lə) *n., pl.* **-lae** (-lē′) or **-las 1.** *Astronomy* A diffuse mass of interstellar dust or gas or both, visible as luminous patches or areas of darkness depending on the way the mass absorbs or reflects incident radiation. **b.** See **galaxy** 1a. **2.** *Pathology* **a.** A cloudy spot on the cornea. **b.** Cloudiness in the urine. **3.** A liquid medication that is sprayed. [ME *nebule*, mist < Lat. *nebula.* See **nebh-** in App.] —**neb′u•lar** *adj.*

nebular hypothesis *n.* An explanation of the origin of the solar system according to which a rotating nebula cooled and contracted into the planets and the sun.

neb•u•lize (nĕb′yə-līz′) *tr.v.* **-lized, -liz•ing, -liz•es 1.** To convert (a liquid) to a fine spray; atomize. **2.** To treat with a medicated spray. —**neb′u•li•za′tion** (-lĭ-zā′shən) *n.*

neb•u•los•i•ty (nĕb′yə-lŏs′ĭ-tē) *n., pl.* **-ties 1.** The quality or condition of being nebulous. **2.** *Astronomy* **a.** A nebula or a nebulalike object. **b.** A mass of material constituting a nebula.

neb•u•lous (nĕb′yə-ləs) *adj.* **1.** Cloudy, misty, or hazy. **2.** Lacking definite form or limits; vague: *nebulous promises.* **3.** Of, relating to, or characteristic of a nebula. [ME < Lat. *nebulōsus* < *nebula*, cloud. See **nebh-** in App.] —**neb′u•lous•ly** *adv.* —**neb′u•lous•ness** *n.*

nec•es•sar•i•ly (nĕs′ĭ-sâr′ə-lē, -sĕr′-) *adv.* Of necessity; inevitably.

nec•es•sar•y (nĕs′ĭ-sĕr′ē) *adj.* **1.** Absolutely essential. See Syns at **indispensable. 2.** Needed to achieve a certain result or effect; requisite. **3a.** Unavoidably determined by conditions or circumstances. **b.** Logically inevitable. **4.** Required by obligation, compulsion, or convention. ❖ *n., pl.* **-ies** Something indispensable. [ME *necessarie* < OFr. *necessaire* < Lat. *necessārius* < *necesse.*]

ne•ces•si•tar•i•an•ism (nə-sĕs′ĭ-târ′ē-ə-nĭz′əm) *n. Philosophy* The doctrine holding that events are inevitably determined by preceding causes. —**ne•ces′si•tar′i•an** *adj. & n.*

ne•ces•si•tate (nə-sĕs′ĭ-tāt′) *tr.v.* **-tat•ed, -tat•ing, -tates 1.** To make necessary or unavoidable. **2.** To require or compel. [Med.Lat. *necessitāre, necessitāt-* < Lat. *necessitās*, necessity. See NECESSITY.] —**ne•ces′si•ta′tion** *n.* —**ne•ces′si•ta′tive** *adj.*

ne•ces•si•tous (nə-sĕs′ĭ-təs) *adj.* **1.** Needy; indigent. **2.** Compelling; urgent. [Fr. *nécessiteux* < OFr., necessary < *necessite*, necessity. See NECESSITY.] —**ne•ces′si•tous•ly** *adv.*

ne•ces•si•ty (nə-sĕs′ĭ-tē) *n., pl.* **-ties 1a.** The condition or quality of being necessary. **b.** Something necessary. **2a.** Something dictated by invariable physical laws. **b.** The force exerted by circumstance. **3.** The state or fact of being in need. **4.** Pressing or urgent need, esp. that arising from poverty. —*idiom:* **of necessity** As an inevitable consequence; necessarily. [ME *necessite* < OFr. < Lat. *necessitās* < *necesse*, necessary. See NECESSARY.]

Ne•chak•o (nə-chăk′ō) A river of central British Columbia, Canada, flowing c. 462 km (287 mi) to the Fraser R.

Nech•es (nĕch′ĭz) A river of E TX flowing c. 669 km (416 mi) to Sabine Lake.

neck (nĕk) *n.* **1.** The part of the body joining the head to the shoulders or trunk. **2.** The part of a garment around or near the neck. **3.** *Anatomy* **a.** A narrow or constricted part of a structure, as of a bone, that joins its parts; a cervix. **b.** The part of a tooth between the crown and the root. **4.** A relatively narrow elongation, projection, or connecting part. **5.** *Music* The narrow part along which the strings of an instrument extend to the pegs. **6.** *Printing* See **beard** 5. **7.** *Geology* Solidified lava filling the vent of an extinct volcano. **8.** The siphon of a bivalve mollusk, such as a clam. **9.** A narrow margin. ❖ *v.* **necked, neck•ing, necks** —*intr. Informal* To kiss and caress amorously. —*tr.* To strangle or decapitate (a fowl). —*idioms:* **neck and neck** So close that the lead between competitors is virtually indeterminable. **up to (one's) neck** Deeply involved or occupied fully: *I'm up to my neck in paperwork.* [ME *nekke* < OE *hnecca.*]

Neck•ar (nĕk′ər, -är) A river of SW Germany rising in the Black Forest and flowing c. 337 km (228 mi) to the Rhine R.

neck•band (nĕk′bănd′) *n.* The band around the collar of a garment.

necked (nĕkt) *adj.* Having a neck or neckline of a specified kind. Often used in combination: *a long-necked bird.*

neck•er•chief (nĕk′ər-chĭf, -chĕf′) *n.* A kerchief worn around the neck.

neck•ing (nĕk′ĭng) *n.* **1.** *Architecture* A molding between the upper part of a column and the projecting part of the capital. **2.** *Informal* The act of amorously kissing and caressing.

neck•lace (nĕk′lĭs) *n.* An ornament worn around the neck.

neck•line (nĕk′līn′) *n.* The line formed by the edge of a garment at or near the neck.

neck of the woods *n., pl.* **necks of the woods** *Informal* A region; a neighborhood. [< NECK, narrow stretch of forest.]

neck•piece (nĕk′pēs′) *n.* A scarf, often of fur.

neck•tie (nĕk′tī′) *n.* A narrow fabric band of varying length worn around the neck and tied in a knot or bow close to the throat.

neck•wear (nĕk′wâr′) *n.* Articles, such as neckties, worn around the neck.

necro- or **necr-** *pref.* **1.** Dead body; corpse: *necrophilia.* **2.** Death: *necrobiosis.* [Gk. *nekro-* < *nekros*, corpse. See **nek-** in App.]

nec•ro•bi•o•sis (nĕk′rō-bī-ō′sĭs) *n.* The natural death of cells or tissues through aging, as distinguished from necrosis or pathological death. —**nec′ro•bi•ot′ic** (-ŏt′ĭk) *adj.*

ne•crol•o•gy (nə-krŏl′ə-jē, nĕ-) *n., pl.* **-gies 1.** A list of people who have died, esp. in the recent past or during a specific period. **2.** An obituary. —**nec′ro•log′ic** (nĕk′rə-lŏj′ĭk), **nec′ro•log′i•cal** *adj.* —**ne•crol′o•gist** *n.*

nec•ro•man•cy (nĕk′rə-măn′sē) *n.* **1.** The practice of supposedly communicating with the spirits of the dead in order to predict the future. **2.** Black magic; sorcery. **3.** Magic qualities. [Ult. < LLat. *necromantīa* < Gk. *nekromanteia* : *nekros*, corpse; see **nek-** in App. + *manteia*, divination; see –MANCY.] —**nec′ro•man′cer** *n.* —**nec′ro•man′tic** (-măn′tĭk) *adj.*

nec•ro•pha•gia (nĕk′rə-fā′jə) *n.* The act or practice of feeding on dead bodies or carrion.

ne•croph•a•gous (nə-krŏf′ə-gəs, nĕ-) *adj.* Feeding on carrion or corpses: *necrophagous organisms.*

nec•ro•phil•i•a (nĕk′rə-fĭl′ē-ə) also **nec•roph′i•lism** (nĭ-krŏf′ə-lĭz′əm, nĕ-) *n.* **1.** Obsessive fascination with death and corpses. **2.** Erotic attraction to or sexual contact with corpses. —**nec′ro•phil′i•ac′** (-ē-ăk′) *adj. & n.* —**nec′ro•phile′** (-fīl′) *n.* —**nec′ro•phil′ic** (-fĭl′ĭk) *adj.*

nec•ro•pho•bi•a (nĕk′rə-fō′bē-ə) *n.* An abnormal fear of death or corpses. —**nec′ro•pho′bic** *adj.*

ne•crop•o•lis (nə-krŏp′ə-lĭs, nĕ-) *n., pl.* **-lis•es** or **-leis** (-lās′) A

Guidewords

nebula
Crab Nebula

neck
Devils Tower, Wyoming

Thumb index tab → **N**

Abridged pronunciation key

ă	pat	oi	boy
ā	pay	ou	out
âr	care	ŏŏ	took
ä	father	ōō	boot
ĕ	pet	ŭ	cut
ē	be	ûr	urge
ĭ	pit	th	thin
ī	pie	*th*	this
îr	pier	hw	which
ŏ	pot	zh	vision
ō	toe	ə	about,
ô	paw		item

Stress marks:
′ (primary);
′ (secondary), as in
lexicon (lĕk′sĭ-kŏn′)

_____   _____   _____   _____

_____   _____   _____   _____

_____   _____   _____   _____

EXERCISE 4.3

Circle the words in each list that come alphabetically between the pair of guidewords at the top of each column.

flew ǀ flip	pawn ǀ peach	son ǀ sort	draft ǀ drama	pi ǀ pick
flex	paw	soil	drag	physics
flip	pave	sonic boom	dragon	piano
flock	peace	sop	drag race	picture
flint	pearl	sloppy	drainage	piccolo
flimsy	pebble	sorbet	drake	picket
flesh	pawn shop	sore	dram	Picasso

Information You Find When You Look Up a Word

Each item defined in a dictionary appears in bold print and is called an **entry**. See page 119 for an example of a dictionary entry. Most entries are single words, but entries can also be the names of people and places, phrases (such as *second-degree burn*), word parts (the prefix *anti-*, for example), abbreviations, and even individual letters. For each entry, you will find this information:

- spelling and syllables
- pronunciation written in special symbols
- part(s) of speech
- irregular forms of the word
- definitions with special labels
- related forms of the word
- origin and history of the word (etymology)

In addition, the entries may contain this information:

- examples that illustrate the meanings
- synonyms (words that have the same or similar meaning)
- antonyms (words that have the opposite meaning)
- information about how the word should be used
- a picture or illustration

The lists may look overwhelming. Relax! There will be times you look up a word because you want to know how to pronounce it or where to break it at the end of a line of writing. Most of the time, though, you simply need to find the word and locate the appropriate definition. Information other than the pronunciation and definition is helpful, but it is not always essential. Focus on the skills of locating a word, understanding its pronunciation, and determining which definition you need.

In the sections that follow, we'll look at each part of an entry and how to interpret it. Here is a sample entry with the parts labeled:

part of speech

pronunciation

entry word

most common meaning (definition)

pre·cious (prĕsh′əs) *adj.* 1. of high cost or worth; valuable: *precious metals.* 2. highly esteemed for some nonmaterial quality: *precious memories.* 3. dear; beloved: *a precious child.* 4. designating a stone or crystal, esp. a diamond, ruby, sapphire, or emerald, valued as rare and beautiful, used in jewelry. —*n.* 5. a dearly beloved person; darling. –*adv.* 6. extremely; very: *We have precious little time.* [1250-1300;

other meanings

example of usage

etymology (word origin)

ME *preciose* (< OF *precios*) <L. pretiōsus costly, valuable = *pretium*, price, value + -ōsus -ous] –**pre′ cious·ly,** *adv.* –**pre′ cious·ness,** *n.*

related forms

Source: From *Random House Webster's College Dictionary*, New York: Random House, 2001, p. 1040. Copyright © 2001. Reprinted with permission of Random House, Inc.

Spelling and Syllables

Entries tell you if there is more than one acceptable spelling of a word. For example, *color* may also be spelled *colour,* the British spelling of the word. Both *on-line* and *online* (with and without the hyphen) are considered correct.

The boldface entry word is divided with dots or dashes to show its syllables. A **syllable** is a word or word part that consists of one vowel sound, along with any consonant sounds, that is pronounced as a single unit. The **vowels** are *a, e, i, o,* and *u.* The rest of the letters are called **consonants.** The letter *y* is usually a consonant, but in some words, it sounds like a vowel. In the example above, the dot in the entry word tells you that *precious* has two syllables.

A word has as many syllables as it has vowel sounds, which may not be the same as the number of actual vowels. The word *precious* has four vowels, but it has only two vowel sounds. That's the reason it has two syllables.

BONUS TIP

Each time you say a syllable, you must drop your jaw so that air can stream from your lungs to form the vowel sound in the syllable. To check how many syllables a word has, place your fingertips beneath your chin. As you say the word, count the number of times your jaw drops. (Be sure you pronounce the word correctly!)

www.mhhe.com/
entryways

For more information about spelling and syllables, see "Phonics" and "Basic Information about Phonics, Pronunciation, and Syllabication."

Words can have one syllable (*book*) or several (*dic·tion·ar·y*). Paying attention to the syllables helps you say the word correctly. For example, if you see that *ath·lete* has only two syllables, you won't mispronounce it and add an extra syllable in the middle.

Syllabication—dividing words into syllables—also indicates the correct places to divide a word when you are writing or typing. When you break a word at the end of a line of writing, you must break it *between* syllables. You place a hyphen at the end of a syllable to let readers know that the word continues on the next line. For example, you could divide *dictionary* these two ways: *dic- tionary* or *diction- ary*. You shouldn't divide one-syllable words (for example, *disk* and *laughed*) or short words (such as *poem* or *away*).

STOP AND PROCESS: Syllabication

EXERCISE 4.4

Write the number of syllables for each of these words. Use the strategy described in the Bonus Tip box above. Then check your answer with a dictionary.

Example: **radio** ___3___   ra•di•o

activity ____   prefix ____   page ____   celebrate ____   popcorn ____

EXERCISE 4.5

Look up each word in the dictionary. On the line next to the word, write it in syllables. Make a large dot between the syllables. Then write the number of syllables in the word.

Example: population   ____*pop • u • la • tion*____   ____4____

1. democracy   _____   _____

2. able   _____   _____

3. orange   _____   _____

4. cough   _____   _____

5. density   _____   _____

EXERCISE 4.6

For each word, write the number of *vowels* in the word, the number of vowel *sounds*, and the number of *syllables*. You may find it helpful to underline any vowels. Some examples have been worked for you. (*Suggestion*: Review the Bonus Tip on page 122 before you do this exercise.)

	Number of Vowels	Number of Vowel Sounds	Number of Syllables
Examples:			
di<u>a</u>gr<u>a</u>m	3	3	3
h<u>a</u>pp<u>y</u>	2	2	2
y<u>ou</u>	2	1	1
1. read			
2. many			
3. beautiful			
4. leave			
5. label			
6. lovely			
7. there			
8. pronounce			
9. pronunciation			
10. syllable			

Once you have checked this activity in class, what do you notice about the numbers you have written in the last two columns? What does it tell you?

_____

_____

Pronunciation

Many words are not pronounced the way they are spelled. A comedian once jokingly complained, "Even the word *phonetic* isn't pronounced the way it's spelled!" In dictionaries, the pronunciation is written in parentheses after the entry word. It uses special **phonetic** symbols and marks (called *diacritical marks*) that tell you how to say the word correctly.

All dictionaries contain a complete pronunciation guide at the beginning of the book. The **pronunciation key** explains the phonetic symbols and diacritical marks that indicate the way a word is spoken. Most desktop dictionaries include a shorter pronunciation guide or key at the bottom of each right-hand page. Most consonants have only one sound, and people are familiar with them. Therefore, the shorter key presents only vowel sounds and a few other sounds whose symbols might be unfamiliar to users.

To save space, paperback dictionaries have a key only at the beginning of the book. The pronunciation key from the paperback edition of *The American Heritage Dictionary* appears on page 122.

Pronunciation Key

Symbols	Examples	Symbols	Examples
ă	pat	o͞o	boot
ā	pay	ou	out
âr	care	p	pop
ä	father	r	roar
b	bib	s	sauce
ch	church	sh	ship, dish
d	deed, milled	t	tight, stopped
ĕ	pet	th	thin
ē	bee	*th*	this
f	fife, phase, rough	ŭ	cut
g	gag	ûr	urge, term, firm, word,
h	hat		heard
hw	which	v	valve
ĭ	pit	w	with
ī	pie, by	y	yes
îr	pier	z	zebra, xylem
j	judge	zh	vision, pleasure, garage
k	kick, cat, pique	ə	about, item, edible,
l	lid, needle (nēd'l)		gallop, circus**
m	mum	ər	butter
n	no, sudden (sŭd'n)		
ng	thing	**Foreign**	
ŏ	pot	œ	French feu
ō	toe		German schön
ô	caught, paw, for,	ü	French tu
	horrid, hoarse*		German über
oi	noise	KH	German ich
o͝o	took		Scottish loch
		N	French bon

Primary stress (')   **bi·ol'o·gy** (bī-ŏl'ə-jē)***

Secondary stress (')   **bi'o·log'i·cal** (bī'ə-lŏj'ĭ-kəl)***

*Regional pronunciations of -or- vary. In pairs such as **for, four; horse, hoarse;** and **morning, mourning,** the vowel varies between (ô) and (ō). In this Dictionary these vowels are represented as follows: **for** (fôr), **four** (fôr, fōr); **horse** (hôrs), **hoarse** (hôrs, hōrs); and **morning** (môr'nĭng), **mourning** (môr'nĭng, mōr'-). A similar variant occurs in words such as **coral, forest,** and **horrid,** where the pronunciation of -or- varies between (ôr) and (ŏr): **forest** (fôr'ĭst, fŏr'-).

** The symbol (ə) is called a *schwa*. It represents a vowel that receives the weakest level of stress within a word. The schwa sound varies, sometimes according to the vowel it is representing and often according to the sounds surrounding it.

***Stress, the relative degree of emphasis with which the syllables of a word (or phrase) are spoken, is indicated in three different ways. The strongest, or primary, stress is marked with a bold mark ('). An intermediate, or secondary, level of stress is marked with a similar but lighter mark ('). An unmarked syllable has the weakest stress in the word. Words of one syllable show no stress mark, since there is no other stress level to which the syllable is compared.

Source: The American Heritage Dictionary, 4th ed., (paperback), New York: Houghton-Mifflin, 2001, p. viii. Copyright © 2001 by Houghton-Mifflin Company. Reproduced by permission from *The American Heritage Dictionary,* Fourth Paperback Edition.

Using pronunciation symbols is really just knowing a code. The symbols tell you how each letter should be pronounced. Once you know the "secret"—the sound that goes with each symbol or letter—you simply say the sounds in the order they appear in the pronunciation. Here are the steps in using the pronunciation key:

BRAIN-FRIENDLY TIP

To familiarize yourself with the dictionary pronunciation key, look at the pronunciation of words you already *know* how to pronounce. That way, you can focus on matching the symbols with the sounds they represent, without worrying about whether you are pronouncing the word correctly.

---

1. Find the same letter and symbol in the pronunciation key as the one that appears in the pronunciation for the entry word.
2. In the key, look at the symbol and the short sample word that appears beside it (for example, p**a**t for ă, and p**a**y for ā).
3. Notice the part of the sample word that is in bold. When you say that part of the sample word, you are saying the sound that occurs in the entry word.
4. To pronounce the entire entry word, "plug in" each sound in order.

Perhaps you're wondering about the funny looking symbol ə, which resembles an upside-down *e*. It's called a *schwa*. It represents an unstressed vowel, but all you really have to know is that it generally sounds like "uh." It's the sound you make when you hesitate or are not sure what you want to say. ("I, uh, think I just sat on your glasses.") All five vowels can have the schwa sound. That's the reason the pronunciation key shows the unstressed vowel in the words **a**bout, it**e**m, ed**i**ble, gall**o**p, and circ**u**s.

For words of more than one syllable, an *accent mark,* or *stress mark,* indicates which syllable or syllables should be said more loudly than the others. The primary (main) accent mark looks like this: ′. For example, in the word *ap•ple,* the first syllable is said louder: ăp′ əl. If you accented the second syllable instead, the word would sound like "a pull," as in "I have *a pull* in my calf muscle."

The accent is important because sometimes the only difference between two words is the accented syllable. For example, each of these spellings represents two different words, depending on whether the first syllable or the second syllable is accented: *record, project, desert,* and *subject.*

In longer words, such as the word *biological,* there may also be a *secondary accent mark.* It shows that a syllable is pronounced more loudly than the other syllables, but not as loudly as the syllable with the primary accent. When there are two accent marks, the darker one is the primary accent, and the lighter one indicates the secondary accent. In *bi•o•log•i•cal* (bī′ə-lŏj′ĭ-kəl), the third syllable is said the loudest; the first syllable is stressed, but not as much. The other syllables are unstressed.

STOP AND PROCESS: Pronunciation

EXERCISE 4.7

Use the dictionary pronunciation key on page 122 when you fill in these blanks. Write the key word in the pronunciation key that tells the sound of the boldface letter.

Example: The **o** in *bone* (bōn) sounds the same as the **o** in _____*toe*_____.

1. The **a** in *action* (ăk′shən) sounds the same as the **a** in _____.

2. The **e** in *eagle* (ē′gəl) sounds the same as the **e** in _____.

3. The **i** in *island* (ī′lənd) sounds the same as the **i** in _____.

4. The **o** in *possible* (pŏs′ə-bəl) sounds the same as the **o** in _____.

5. The **u** in *understand* (ŭn′dər-stănd′) sounds the same as the **u** in

    _____.

6. The first **a** in *appear* (ə-pîr′) sounds the same as the **a** in _____.

7. The **u** in *rude* (rōod) sounds the same as the **u** in _____.

8. The **a** in *almond* (äl′mend) sounds the same as the **a** in _____.

9. The **th** in *there* (thâr) sounds the same as the **th** in _____.

10. The **th** in *thought* (thôt) sounds the same as the **th** in _____.

EXERCISE 4.8

www.mhhe.com/
entryways

See "A List of
Commonly
Mispronounced and
Misspelled Words."

These words are often mispronounced. Look up each of these words and copy the pronunciation. Use the same symbols that the dictionary does. Be sure to include the accent mark or marks. Then try to pronounce each word out loud correctly.

Example: literature _____lĭt′ər-ə-chŏor′, lĭt′ə r-ə-chər_____

The word has four syllables: lit-er-a-ture. People mispronounce it either by leaving out the third syllable (and saying "lit′ ER choor") or by leaving out the first r (and saying "lit′ UH choor").

1. pronunciation _____

2. nuclear _____

3. realtor _____

4. et cetera (etc.) _____

5. preferable _____

Circle any words that you have been mispronouncing. Make a special effort to start pronouncing them correctly. The correct pronunciation may sound strange to you at first but stick with it!

EXERCISE 4.9

Look up the pronunciation of the word in the first column (and the second word, if you need to). Then decide if the two words rhyme. If the words rhyme, write a check mark in the third column. If they do not, write an X.

Rhymes or Not?

Examples: feign plain ____✓____

placate delicate ____x____

1. tomb room _____

2. Somali tamale _____

3. cagey craggy _____

4. visage engage _____

5. sorrel coral _____

Part of Speech

After the pronunciation for each entry word, there is an abbreviation in *italics* that tells the part of speech. **Part of speech** refers to the eight categories (noun, pronoun, verb, adjective, adverb, preposition, conjunction, and interjection) used to describe the function of words in context. *The American Heritage Dictionary* abbreviates the eight parts of speech this way:

n.—noun   *adv.*—adverb
pron.—pronoun   *conj.*—conjunction
adj.—adjective   *prep.*—preposition
v.—verb   *interj.*—interjection

CROSS-CHAPTER CONNECTION

Parts of speech are also discussed in Chapter 6. Learn the parts of speech now, and you will have a terrific head start!

A word's part of speech is based on how the word is used in sentences. Knowing a word's part of speech helps you choose the correct definition in the dictionary. Many words can be more than one part of speech. The word *fly* can be a noun (the insect), a verb (to fly), and an adjective (a fly ball).

Part of Speech	Abbreviation	Definition	Examples
Noun	*n.*	Names a person, place, thing, or idea	home, truck, honesty, Donald Trump, Louisiana
Pronoun	*pron.*	Used in place of a noun	he, she, we, they, you, it, who
Adjective	*adj.*	Describes a noun or pronoun; tells what kind, how many, or which one	brilliant, sad, yellow, hilarious, Latin American
Verb*	*v.*	Shows physical action, mental action, or a state of being	laugh, thinks, appeared, knew, slept, are hoping
Adverb	*adv.*	Describes or limits a verb, adjective, or another adverb; tells how, where, or when	always, quickly, too, repeatedly, cheerfully, very, lately
Conjunction	*conj.*	Joins words or groups of words	for, and, not, but, yet, because
Preposition	*prep.*	Shows the relationship of a noun or pronoun to another word	over, around, through, above, toward, behind, during, without
Interjection	*interj.*	Expresses strong feeling or emotion	No! Hooray! Idiot!
Article	*art.*	Limits or points to nouns	a, an, the

*Verbs are labeled *v. tr.* for "transitive verb"; *v. intr.* for "intransitive verb", and *v. aux.* for "auxiliary verb." The important thing is to recognize that a word is a verb.

Now look back at the sample entry on page 119 and notice the italicized abbreviations *adj.*, *n.*, and *adv.* They indicate *precious* can be an adjective, noun, and adverb.

STOP AND PROCESS: Parts of Speech

EXERCISE 4.10

List the parts of speech the dictionary gives for these words. Write at least one meaning (definition) that is new to you where indicated.

Example: extract _____ *verb, noun* _____

1. bat _____

2. extract _____

A meaning of *extract* that is new to me: _____

_____

3. fair _____

A meaning of *fair* that is new to me: _____

_____

4. fill _____

5. start _____

A meaning of *start* that is new to me: _____

_____

Verb Forms, Plurals, Irregular Forms of Words, and Abbreviations

When you look up a word, you will find other helpful information listed after the part of speech.

- For verbs, other forms will be given, such as the past tense and the *-ing* form (for *copy*: *copied* and *copying*). You will also find forms of irregular verbs (such as *sing, sang, sung* and *go, went, gone*).
- For nouns, the plural (abbreviated *pl.*) is given if it is not formed in the usual way of adding an *s* (such as *berries, wives, geese,* and *alumni*).
- For adjectives, comparative forms are given (for example, for *good*: *better* and *best*).
- Abbreviated forms of words (for example, *blvd.* for *boulevard,* and *EST* for *Eastern Standard Time*) are labeled *abbr.* (As the joke goes, "Why is *abbreviation* such a long word?")

Choosing the Correct Definition

Did you know that 70 percent of the most frequently used words have more than one meaning? Think, for example, of the multiple meanings of the common words *fan, run,* and *bank.* The word *set* has the most definitions, about 200! You can see that it's important to skim or read through the definitions and choose the correct one when you look up a word in the dictionary.

Definitions in dictionary entries are numbered and grouped by the part of speech. Take the word *side:* There will be sets of definitions for it as a noun, a verb, and an adjective.

Before you look up a word, try to determine its part of speech. Once you locate the entry word, you will need to

BONUS TIP

When you use a dictionary for the first time, turn to the front of the book and read the explanation about the order of the definitions. *The American Heritage Dictionary* lists the most common definitions first, which means you are likely to find the definition you are seeking among the first few. Some dictionaries list definitions from the earliest meaning of the word to the most recent. You might have to read several, or even all, of the definitions before you find the one you need. If you don't, you could choose an out-of-date meaning without realizing it.

CROSS-CHAPTER CONNECTION

In Chapter 3 you learned about using the context. For words that have more than one meaning, look at the context in which you found the word. That will tell you which dictionary definition you need.

read only the definitions for that same part of speech. Then *choose the definition that would make sense in the sentence in which you found the word.* In other words, choose the definition that fits the context.

To save space, dictionaries give concise definitions. You will learn and remember more if you put the definition in your own words (as if you were explaining to a friend what the word means) or if you come up with examples of your own. Suppose you look up the word *nocturnal* and find the definitions, "Of, relating to, or occurring in the night" and (when referring to animals) "most active at night." You might say to a friend, "Nocturnal describes something that happens at night. Meteor showers don't happen during the day. They're nocturnal events." Or, "Owls are nocturnal: they hunt at night."

 STOP AND PROCESS: Choosing the Correct Definition

EXERCISE 4.11

Read the definitions for each word. Read the sentences below the definitions. Then write the number of the definition that would make sense in each sentence. The first one is done as an example.

domestic

1. pertaining to family and household

2. fond of home life and household affairs

3. tame or domesticated

4. related to a country's internal affairs

Girls used to be required to learn sewing, cooking, and other *domestic* skills.____1____

The president was praised for his foreign policy, but criticized for his *domestic* policies. _____

Dogs, cats, and hamsters are examples of *domestic* animals. _____

cheesy

1. Containing or resembling cheese

2. *informal:* of poor quality, shoddy

The furniture at the flea market was so *cheesy* that we decided not to buy anything. _____

BONUS TIPS

1. When you do not know the meaning of words that appear in a definition, you need to do some additional detective work. Suppose you look up the word *factious* (făk′ shə s). The definition is, "Produced or marked by faction; marked by internal dissension; divisive." If you do not know the meaning of *faction*, *dissension*, or *divisive*, you have more words to look up. Don't think of this as extra work. It's simply part of the process.

2. If you use the Microsoft Word word-processing program, take advantage of the built-in spelling and grammar checkers, thesaurus, and dictionary. They are listed in the pull-down menu labeled "Tools." (Unlike complete dictionary software programs, the Word dictionary does not include pronunciations.) To use spell-check, the dictionary, or thesaurus, highlight the word in your document, and then click on the tool in the pull-down menu. The thesaurus lets you select a synonym, and it will automatically substitute it for the word in your document. (Synonyms and the thesaurus are discussed on pages 134–35.)

launch

 1. to set in motion with force

 2. to put a boat into the water

 3. to start, to initiate

There will be a special ceremony to *launch* the new battleship. _____

My company plans to *launch* a new ad campaign next month. _____

NASA plans to *launch* the rocket at Cape Kennedy. _____

bore

 1. to make or drill a hole

 2. a hole or passage made by or as if by drilling

 3. the interior diameter of a hole, tube, or cylinder

 4. a drilling tool

A barrel of a BB gun has a smaller *bore* than a shotgun barrel does. _____

The electrician had to *bore* through the wall in order to connect the wires. _____

Custom furniture makers sometimes use a hand-cranked *bore* in their work. _____

Special Labels

No one wants to embarrass himself or herself by using words incorrectly or by unintentionally using an insulting or out-of-date word. Dictionary entries include four general categories of labels to help you avoid such mistakes. Consult the front of your dictionary to find the meaning of any other abbreviations used in its entries. Also, labels may vary from dictionary to dictionary.

1. **Usage labels** tell whether a word is acceptable in formal or informal situations. For example, when you email or chat with friends, you speak in an informal manner. When you make a presentation to a class or apply for a job, you use more formal language. Unless words and definitions are labeled otherwise, they are considered "Standard English" and are fine to use anytime.

www.mhhe.com/
entryways

For more
information about
slang, jargon, and
colloquialisms, go
to

Catalyst>
Editing> Clichés,
Slang, Jargon,
and Colloquialisms

Here are specific usage labels you should be aware of:

- *Nonstandard* means the word or usage is unacceptable (such as *anyways, irregardless*).

- *Informal* means it is fine to use in conversation, but it shouldn't be used in formal writing (for example, *tummy, enthuse,* or *cutesy*).

- *Slang* is colorful language used for effect (such as *humongous* for very large, and *crackhead* for a cocaine addict). Some slang is vulgar and offensive; it shouldn't be used in formal writing.

- *Offensive* identifies a disrespectful, insulting word (such as *girlie* for a woman or girl).

- *Vulgar* indicates that a word is crude or obscene (such as *crapper* for toilet).

2. **Geographical area labels** indicate usage by regions of the country or world in which a word is used, such as Irish or South African.

3. **Time labels** indicate that words are rare, archaic, or obsolete (out of date), such as *hast* and *dost*.

4. **Subject or field labels** tell the meaning of words in a certain field, such as sports or biol. (for biology).

STOP AND PROCESS: Special Labels

EXERCISE 4.12

Write the labels the dictionary gives in the entries for these words.

Example:

mouse: _____ *informal; computer science* _____

tone _____

ain't _____

nowheres _____

midget _____

broad _____

EXERCISE 4.13

Use the sample *American Heritage College Dictionary* page on page 117 to answer these questions. An example is worked for you.

Example:

Which four field labels are used in the definitions of *neck*?

anatomy, music, printing, geology _____

1. Which special label is given for *neatherd?* _____

2. Which label is given for the meaning of *neat* as "Wonderful; terrific"? _____

3. In which field does *neck* mean "The narrow part along which the strings of an instrument extend to the pegs"? _____

4. Which label is given to *neck* when it means "To kiss and caress amorously"? _____

5. Which two field labels are used in definitions for *nebula?* _____
_____

EXERCISE 4.14

From which language does each of the following sets of words come? You may be able to guess on some sets, but use the dictionary to confirm your hunch.

frankfurter, kindergarten, hamburger _____

patio, canyon, rodeo _____

madras, pajama, thug _____

kosher, bagel, chutzpah _____

plaid, brogue, glen _____

safari, hashish, assassin _____

Phrasal Verbs and Idioms

Some dictionary entries also include phrasal verbs and idioms, along with sentences that illustrate their usage.

- **Phrasal verbs** are exactly what the name suggests: verbs used in phrases. (A **phrase** is a group of words that is shorter than a sentence but functions as a meaningful unit.) Phrasal verbs consist of a verb followed by an adverb, a preposition, or both. They have idiomatic meanings that are quite different from the literal meaning of the individual words. For the word *turn*, for example, you'll find the phrasal verbs *turn away, turn back, turn down, turn in, turn off, turn out, turn over, turn to,* and *turn up.*

- **Idioms** are expressions whose meaning can't be deduced by "adding up" the meaning of the parts: They don't mean what the words seem to say. For the word *turn*, you'll find idioms such as *at* *every turn, out of turn, turn (one's) back on, turn over a new leaf, turn the other cheek, turn the tables,* and *turn up (one's) nose.*

STOP AND PROCESS: Idioms

EXERCISE 4.15

Look at the sample dictionary page on page 116. Find the two idioms listed for the word *neck*. Write the two idioms and their meanings here:

_____

_____

_____

Related Forms of a Word

After the definitions, the dictionary entry lists related forms of a word. These are forms of the word as other parts of speech. For the adjective *sincere*, the related forms are *sincerity* (noun) and *sincerely* (adverb). Dictionaries save space by listing related forms under the main entry. If you have trouble locating a word, see if the word is listed under a related form. Suppose you want to look up the word *idyllic* (an adjective that means "simple and carefree"). You would find it under the noun *idyll*.

STOP AND PROCESS: Related Forms of the Word

EXERCISE 4.16

Look at the sample dictionary page on page 116. What are the other two forms of the word *necromancy?*

Noun (n.): _____

Adjective (adj.) _____

BONUS TIP

The meanings of phrasal verbs and idioms, as well as the example sentences that illustrate them, can be especially helpful if English is your second language. Check out www.davescafe.com. Under Stuff for Students are idioms and phrasal verbs. Choose either, and you'll find an extensive list with definitions and sample sentences using them. Very cool!

Etymology

The final part of a dictionary entry is the etymology. The **etymology,** which appears in brackets [like this], explains the origin and history of the word. Think of a word's etymology as its biography.

The English language has hundreds of thousands of words and is much larger than most languages. It's constantly growing and changing. Three out of every four "dictionary words" come from other languages, and they

BONUS TIP

Associating words that come from the same root is a great way to increase your vocabulary. If you know that the Latin root *cur(s)* means *to run*, you will understand the connection among all of these words:

cursory—done in a hurried manner, on the run

cursor—blinking indicator that can be made to "run" around a computer screen

current—the run or flow of water, air, electricity

precursor—something that comes or "runs" before something else

course—a route that is run; a sequence you must "run" through

curriculum—a course of study

typically go through several changes along their way to becoming a dictionary entry. In fact, they often go through several languages over many centuries.

The etymology starts with the earliest known source of a word. It tells the languages and forms of the word as it evolved. It tells the word parts that make up the word and the meaning of those parts.

A list near the front of the dictionary explains the symbols and abbreviations in etymologies. Most dictionaries use the symbol < to mean "comes from." The etymology of the word *cursive* (as in *cursive writing*) includes this: "< Med. Lat. cursīva, running." It means that the word *cursive* comes from the Medieval Latin word for "running." Knowing the word parts helps you understand the word and remember its meaning. The word *cursive* is easy to remember because cursive letters "*run* together" rather than being printed as separate letters.

The etymology also tells you if a word comes from a name or some other source. For instance, *sandwich* comes from the Earl of Sandwich, an 18th century British politician. The word *yuppie* is based on the phrase *y*(oung) + *u*(rban) + *p*(rofessional). *Infomercial* comes from *info*(rmation) + (com)*mercial*, and *blog* comes from (we)*b* + *log*.

www.mhhe.com/
entryways

The ORL contains a module on word parts and their meanings.

STOP AND PROCESS: Etymology

EXERCISE 4.17

Use the dictionary to find the meaning and origin of these words and phrases that have come to us from other languages.

Example:

slanguage

Meaning: <u>language marked by the use of slang; slang used by a</u>

<u>particular group</u>

Origin: <u>blend of slang + language</u>

1. *soup du jour*

Meaning: _____

Origin: _____

2. *e.g.*

Meaning: _____

Origin: _____

3. *sous-chef*

Meaning: _____

_____

Origin: _____

4. *taco*

Meaning: _____

Origin: _____

5. *eulogy*

Meaning: _____

Origin: _____

EXERCISE 4.18

Use the etymologies on the sample dictionary page on page 118 to answer these questions about the origin and history of the following words.

Example:

From which language did the word *nebbish* enter English, and what was its original meaning?

_____ *Yiddish; it meant "poor" or "unfortunate"* _____

1. What is the meaning of the Latin word that is the basis of the English word *nebulous?*_____

2. What is the meaning of the Latin word that is the basis of the English word *neat?* _____

3. From which language do we get the prefix *necro-*, and what did it mean in that language? _____

_____

Synonyms and the Thesaurus

Dictionary entries often end with synonyms for the entry word. As you learned in the previous chapter, synonyms are words that are the same or similar in meaning (such as *little* and *small*). If you are not sure of fine differences in meaning, you can look up the synonyms. Some entries tell the differences in synonyms' meanings.

You can use a dictionary to find synonyms, but a thesaurus is even better. A **thesaurus** (thĭ-sôr′əs) gives only *synonyms*. Unlike a dictionary, a thesaurus doesn't give definitions. (Jokester's quip, "What's another word for thesaurus"?)

Are there times when you can't quite think of the word you want? Are there times when you keep using the same word over and over again and would like to add some variety? A thesaurus can come to the rescue!

In addition to buying a collegiate dictionary and a paperback dictionary, you should purchase a thesaurus. They are available in both hardcover and paperback, and combination dictionaries and thesauruses are available. The top half of the page has dictionary entries; the lower part lists synonyms for the entry words on the page. Very handy! Also, most word-processing programs include both a dictionary and a thesaurus.

www.mhhe.com/ entryways

For more information about dictionaries and thesauri, go to

Catalyst> Learning>Dictionary and Thesauri

Denotations and Connotations

No discussion of the dictionary would be complete without mentioning denotations and connotations. **Denotations** are the dictionary definitions of words. In addition to denotations, many words have connotations. **Connotations** are the implied meanings or emotions associated with the word. Together, the denotation and connotation make up the complete meaning of a word. The dictionary doesn't give words' connotations, but understanding them helps you use words correctly.

Connotations can be positive or negative. Think about the words *economical, thrifty, stingy,* and *cheap.* They all have the denotation of spending money carefully rather than wastefully. But most people would rather be described as *economical* or *thrifty* than as *cheap* or *stingy.* Why? It's because of the difference in the connotations. *Economical* and *thrifty* have positive connotations. *Cheap* and *stingy* have negative connotations.

Here are some other examples that illustrate denotations and connotations:

Denotation (Neutral)	Similar Word with a Negative Connotation	Similar Word with a Positive Connotation
job	chore	task, project
thin	skinny, scrawny	slender, slim
laugh	snicker, cackle	giggle, chuckle
well known	notorious, infamous	famous, renowned
overweight	fat, paunchy, obese	plump, chubby
car, automobile	lemon, clunker	vehicle

Selecting Words and Coding Them into Memory: Brain-Friendly Approaches

Selecting Words to Learn

When you pack for a trip, you have to decide what's most important to take with you. Building your vocabulary is a little like that: Since not all words are equally important or useful, you should spend your effort on the specific ones that will help you the most. In each of your courses, concentrate on those words. It's crucial for academic success.

Think of words in your academic courses as falling into three categories.

1. **Core words.** This is the most important category. It consists of essential terms and concepts that lay the foundation for the subject. Try to determine which words are core words. These words often appear in special print in your textbooks or are included in glossaries. There may be additional words that your instructor emphasizes. If you are not sure about a word's importance, ask your instructor. Plan to spend the most time on mastering these critical words. It may take you a week—or even several weeks—to understand a term or concept fully, even though you have memorized the definition. (It's possible to memorize a word's definition without really understanding it fully or knowing how to use the word.) In an economics course, for example, it may take several weeks to develop a full understanding of the key term *inflation.*

2. **Important words.** These consist of words for concepts, events, people, or places that deepen your understanding and help you make connections among the course topics. It will take several exposures to these words in order to learn them, but not as much time as core words.

3. **Nice-to-know words.** These consist of nouns, verbs, adjectives, and other words that enrich your vocabulary in general but are not crucial for understanding a subject or a course. You can spend less time on these words. Focus on them after you've learned the core words and important words.

BRAIN-FRIENDLY TIP

When you make vocabulary cards for your courses, use colored index cards: one color for core words, a second color for important words, and a third color for nice-to-know words. Choose your favorite color for the core words to remind you to spend the most time on them. Of course, you will continue to add words to each category throughout the semester.

(For information about creating vocabulary cards, see the introduction to Part Two, pages 64–67.)

"Coding" Words into Memory

Once you know which words you want to concentrate on, how can you make them more meaningful and memorable? Use the brain-friendly CODE technique described below. Here is what the letters stand for:

Connect with new vocabulary.

Organize vocabulary.

Deep process words.

Explore core vocabulary.

For best results, use all four strategies.

Connect with new vocabulary.

Connect the new word with what you already know or have experienced. For example, ask yourself, "Have I ever seen or heard the word? Where? Do I see any familiar parts in the word? Is there anything I associate with the word?" (Try applying these questions to the words *technocracy* and *commander.*)

Next, look up the word in the dictionary. Does it have the meaning you expected? Finally, say the word and the definition aloud. You will become more comfortable with the word and recall it more easily.

Organize vocabulary words.

New words are easier to remember if you organize them in some way that is meaningful to you. Try these two techniques:

- Link words that go together, such as the terms that go with a particular topic or course.
- Organize important words in a course around core concepts or core words for the course.

Organizing words is an excellent activity to do with classmates or a study group. As you review words, look up new words, sort related words into groups, and create labels for them. You will also be saying the words aloud and discussing them. These reinforce learning.

Deep process words.

Transferring words into long-term (permanent) memory requires deep, active thought. This means you must process words by examining them from multiple angles. Here are some ways for you to do this. Experiment to see what works best for you. It may be some combination of the strategies.

Use both words and images to help you learn vocabulary. A word is more meaningful and recall is easier if you store information about it using both language (other words) and images. Include pictures on vocabulary cards, and visualize words as you learn their definitions. For example, let's say that, in your history class, you need to learn the word *tyrant.* The dictionary tells you that a tyrant is a ruler who has absolute control and uses this power in a harsh, cruel manner. To visualize the meaning of *tyrant,* you might see in your mind a mean-looking man who is wearing an "I AM THE BOSS!" button, and holding a sword in one hand and a whip in the other. Then you create a sentence, "The employees are afraid because the *tyrant* has all the power and he is cruel to them."

Another strategy to deep process words is to use multiple sensory channels. You already know that people are smart in different ways and that each person has a preferred learning style. Process words with multiple sensory channels to strengthen your understanding of them.

- *Explain the word in your own words and write it down.* This taps your linguistic (language) understanding.

**www.mhhe.com/
entryways**

See "CODE: Deep
Processing a
Vocabulary Word
through
Multisensory
Channels" for an
illustration of the
process applied to
the word *tyrant.* If
possible, look at
this model before
completing
Exercise 4.19.

- *In your mind, create a picture of the word itself and a visual representation of what it means.* You can also make a couple of drawings and illustrations. This taps into visual understanding.
- *Link the word to an emotional response.* What feelings do you associate with the word? Describe those feelings. Say the word and the definition with feeling. This taps into emotional understanding.
- *Represent the word physically.* That is, make a physical symbol with your hands or body that explains what the new term means to you. This taps your kinesthetic (bodily) understanding.

Explore core vocabulary.

The meaning of a word is more than just a dictionary definition, especially if it is a concept word. Take time to examine, refine, and revise your understanding of core vocabulary words. Look for examples of the word to help you understand how it is used. Create examples of your own.

In the classroom or at home, create a "word wall" by listing core terms and their synonyms on poster paper, sheets of paper, or large index cards. Use colored markers and print in large, bold letters.

STOP AND PROCESS: Deep Processing of Vocabulary Words

EXERCISE 4.19

Choose one of these five words: *humanitarian* (noun), *camaraderie, prestidigitation, composure,* or *civility.* Then fill in the chart, following the directions, to tap into the four types of understanding. Your instructor may assign you a specific word or words. Also, you may be instructed to work in pairs or groups.

CODE: Deep Processing Vocabulary Words

Linguistic Understanding	Visual Understanding
Look up the word. Then write the definition in your own words.	*Draw a picture or image that illustrates the word's meaning.*
Emotional Understanding	**Kinesthetic Understanding**
Link the word to an emotional response. Describe it in words here.	*Represent the word physically. Draw or describe a gesture of the hands or body that represents the word.*

Source: Based on R. Strong, M. Perini, S. Silver, and G. Tuculescu, *Reading for Academic Success*, Thousand Oaks, CA: Corwin Press, 2002. Copyright © 2002 by Corwin Press, Inc. Reprinted with permission.

MY TOOLBOX *of Dictionary Skills*

Now you've added dictionary skills to your growing range of skills. To help lock them in mind in a way that is meaningful to you, record the main points from this chapter in your toolbox. If you already know certain information, such as alphabetizing, you do not need to include it. You should record information about anything that is new to you. Focus on the three key skills of locating a word in the dictionary, pronouncing it correctly, and selecting the appropriate definition. Choose the option below that you think will work best for you.

- **Create a poster of a dictionary page.** Enlarge a dictionary page on a copier and glue it on a large sheet of poster board. Then write information around the edges. For example, circle the guidewords and write a brief explanation of what they are and how to use them. Highlight one entry (or make an even larger copy of one entry), and label the parts of it, similar to the example you saw in the chapter. Do the same for the pronunciation key and other elements in the entry. Include any other information that will help you, such as how to determine which definition you need. Once you've created your poster, put it on your wall for reference.

- **Write out the important points.** Use notebook paper or index cards. If you use index cards, use separate cards to record different types of information, such as a card for alphabetizing, one for parts of a dictionary entry, and so forth. (Module 2 in the ORL has information about using index cards to make review cards. You are welcome to look at it now. Keep in mind, though, that the information will make even more sense to you after you have studied all of the chapters in *Entryways*.)

**www.mhhe.com/
entryways**

For more information, examples, and exercises, see "Outlines, Study Maps, and Review Cards."

- **Create a study map.** To make a study map, or concept map, draw a shape in the middle of the page. It could be a circle, square, or since these are dictionary skills, the shape of a book. On the inside, write the title "DICTIONARY SKILLS" or "USING THE DICTIONARY." Then write specific dictionary information and skills on thick, thin, solid, dashed, or dotted lines that radiate from the center shape. You may prefer simply to use key words or phrases. If you like, include small illustrations or sketches and work with colored pens. (You can also read more about study maps in Module 2 of the ORL.)

✔ CHAPTER CHECK

Answer these questions about the information in the chapter. Write the missing word in each blank. When there is more than one part to the answer, there is more than one blank.

1. A word's part of speech is based on how the word is _____ in sentences.

2. The symbol ə is called a _____, and it represents an _____ vowel sound.

3. To speed up your search for a word, dictionaries display a pair of bold print _____ at the top of each page.

4. Words are listed in _____ order in the dictionary.

5. _____ dictionaries are hardcover books that contain fewer words than unabridged dictionaries.

6. College students should own a hardcover dictionary that has the word _____, _____, or _____ in the title.

7. Each item that is listed in the dictionary is called an _____.

8. _____ are words that are similar in meaning or that mean the same thing.

9. Entry words are divided into _____.

10. A word has as many syllables as it has vowel _____.

11. To find out the order in which definitions are given in a dictionary, you should read the information at the _____ of the dictionary.

12. The _____ explains the origin and history of the word.

13. A _____ gives synonyms, but unlike a dictionary, it doesn't give definitions.

14. _____ are the dictionary definitions of words, whereas _____ are the implied meanings or emotions that are associated with the word.

15. Most textbooks have a _____, a minidictionary of the key terms in the book.

REVIEW EXERCISES

SET 1: PARTS OF A DICTIONARY ENTRY

Match the parts of this dictionary entry with the term that describes each part.

av•id (ăv'ĭd) *adj.* Having an ardent desire or unbounded craving; greedy: *avid for adventure*. Marked by keen interest and enthusiasm: *an avid sports fan.* [Latin **avidus**, from **avēre**, *to desire*.] **av ′id•ly** *adv.*

Source: The American Heritage Dictionary, 4th ed., New York: Houghton-Mifflin, 2002. Copyright © 2000 by Houghton Mifflin Company. Reproduced by permission from *The American Heritage Dictionary of the English Language,* Fourth Edition.

_____ definitions

_____ entry word

_____ etymology

_____ example of usage

_____ related form

_____ part of speech

_____ pronunciation

SET 2: ALPHABETIZING

In the second column, alphabetize each list of words.

1. phase

   pharmacy

   pharaoh

   philanthropic

   phantom

2. keystroke

   kibbutz

   keyboard

   key

   kickoff

3. scrap   _____

    scrawl   _____

    scramble   _____

    scrape   _____

    scratch   _____

SET 3: PRONUNCIATION PRACTICE

Use your dictionary to complete the table. The first row is filled in as an example.

- Look up each word. (These are all good words to know!) Write a brief definition. You do not have to give all the definitions, and you can use your own words.
- Copy the pronunciation, including the marks. Use the pronunciation key as you say the word out loud.
- Decide which word in the last column it rhymes with, and circle that word. You may use notebook paper if you need more space.

Word	Meaning	Pronunciation	Rhymes With		
paradigm	—something that serves as a pattern or model	păr′ə-dīm	dim	[dime]	dome
1. benign			fig	fin	fine
2. naive			leave	live	gave
3. reign			lane	lean	line
4. salmon			lemon	famine	common
5. isle			dill	dial	dull
6. vault			salt	silt	volt
7. trough			cuff	off	owe
8. gauge			rag	rage	hog

SET 4: CHOOSING THE CORRECT DEFINITION FOR THE CONTEXT

Read the definitions of each word. Then write the number of the definition that fits the way the word is used in each sentence. Not every definition will be used.

tender, *adj.*

1. delicate, fragile
2. easily chewed
3. young and vulnerable
4. sensitive or sore
5. gentle and loving
6. sentimental, soft

My grandmother preferred *tender* love songs to any other type of music.

_____

The newly sprouted plants were too *tender* to survive the late spring

snow. _____

My leg is almost healed, but my ankle is still *tender*. _____

The mother's *tender* touch calmed the crying baby. _____

Children at a *tender* age should not be allowed to watch violence

on TV. _____

tender, *n., v.*

1. a formal offer
2. money
3. to offer formally

The vice president of the company has decided to *tender* his resignation.

_____

Checks and credit cards are considered to be legal *tender*. _____

retainer, *n.*

1. one that restrains or guides
2. *dentistry:* a device that holds teeth in place after orthodontic treatment
3. servant or attendant, esp. in a noble or wealthy household

4. fee paid to hire a professional adviser

More than 50 *retainers* served the king and other members of the royal family. _____

My brother lost his *retainer*, and my parents had to pay the dentist for a new one. _____

The man gave the lawyer a $500 *retainer*. _____

break down, *phrasal verb*

1. to destroy or cause to collapse

2. to become distressed or upset; to have a physical or mental collapse

3. to give up resistance; give way

4. to become inoperable, ineffective, or useless

5. to divide into parts

6. to decompose or cause to decompose chemically

Let's *break down* the assignment into three shorter sections. _____

Styrofoam and other synthetic materials in landfills *break down* very slowly. _____

The firefighters had to *break down* the door to rescue the occupants of the house. _____

Her parents have refused to buy her a car, but she's convinced they'll eventually *break down* and say yes. _____

Take your cell phone with you in case the car *breaks down*. _____

My sister *breaks down* every time she sees her ex-fiance. _____

ASSESS YOUR UNDERSTANDING

By now you've gained some experience in monitoring your comprehension of a chapter. How confident do you now feel about using the dictionary? At this point, can you answer all of the items in Looking at What You Already Know at the beginning of the chapter? Based on that, the Chapter Check, and the exercises in the chapter, how would you evaluate your understanding?

1 . . . . . 2 . . . . . 3 . . . . . 4 . . . . . 5 . . . . . 6 . . . . . 7 . . . . . 8 . . . . . 9 10

Clueless!   **A little muddled**   **Dy-no-mite!**

Identify what you don't understand or what's causing you a problem. (Remember to look back at the Chapter Check and the exercises. Also, ask yourself, "Do I understand how to use a dictionary? How to interpret the parts of a dictionary entry?")

_____

_____

_____

_____

Describe things you could do to fix the problems you listed above.

_____

_____

_____

_____

Remember to *apply* the steps you list here. Spending the time and effort now to fix any problems and fill in any missing information will pay off later. (This is also a good time to reflect on how consistently you are using the success behaviors described in Chapters 1 and 2. How are you doing? Do you need to improve or need to add any?)

Map of Chapters

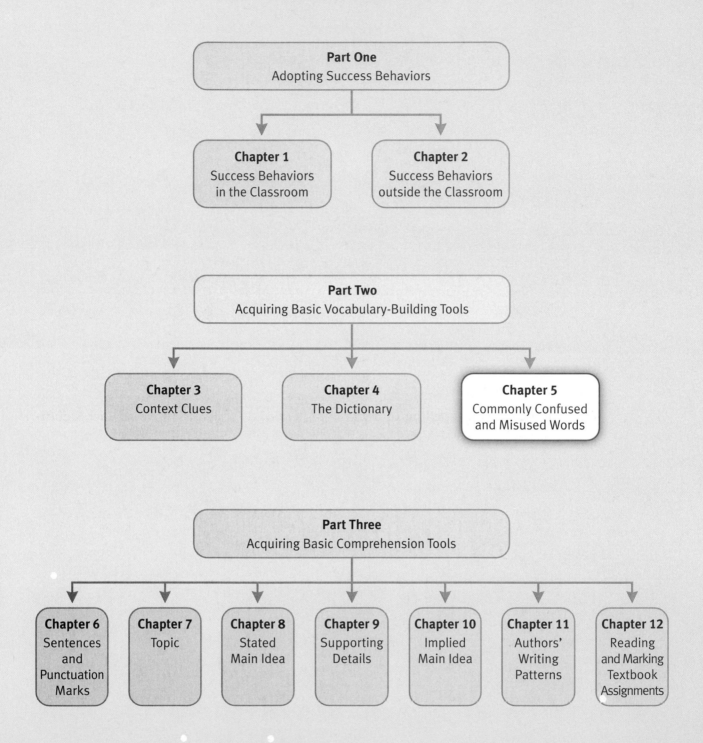

Part One
Adopting Success Behaviors

Chapter 1
Success Behaviors in the Classroom

Chapter 2
Success Behaviors outside the Classroom

Part Two
Acquiring Basic Vocabulary-Building Tools

Chapter 3
Context Clues

Chapter 4
The Dictionary

Chapter 5
Commonly Confused and Misused Words

Part Three
Acquiring Basic Comprehension Tools

Chapter 6
Sentences and Punctuation Marks

Chapter 7
Topic

Chapter 8
Stated Main Idea

Chapter 9
Supporting Details

Chapter 10
Implied Main Idea

Chapter 11
Authors' Writing Patterns

Chapter 12
Reading and Marking Textbook Assignments

CHAPTER 5
Commonly Confused and Misused Words
The Plain Facts or the Plane Fax?

Why You Need to Know the Information in This Chapter

Did you know that sometimes what seem to be spelling problems are really not spelling problems at all? English has dozens of words that sound the same but are spelled differently and have different meanings. These words are called *homonyms*. It's all too easy to write the correct spelling of the wrong *word*. Also, many words in English are similar or related. It's easy to misuse these words in your writing and speaking.

This chapter will help you

- learn the difference between common words that sound alike but have different meanings

- improve your spelling of commonly confused words and know which definition goes with which spelling

- understand the meaning of words that are often used incorrectly

- increase your vocabulary

- speak and write with more confidence in your ability to use words correctly

Super Student Tips

Here are tips from other students who have studied commonly confused and misused words. Here's what experience has taught them:

TWO VIETNAM VETS & A VIETNAM VETTE

Source: Copyright © Bizarro—Dan Piraro. King Features Syndicate.

"One thing I didn't realize before was how many cartoons and jokes are funny because of words that sound alike!"—*Monica*

"I never even knew I was using so many words wrong. Now that I've learned these, I'll feel more confident the next time I fill out a job application or have a job interview."—*Jesse*

"I am really aware of how often these words are used wrong. On TV, I hear ads about things having '*less* calories,' and I see store signs like 'open 9-5 *everyday.*' I just smile. I think to myself, 'I know more than the people who made those ads and those signs!'"—*Veronica*

"Before we studied this, I never noticed when other people used the wrong word or misused a word. Now I do. It makes me feel smart that I can tell."—*Marc*

"I sometimes catch myself using the wrong word, but the difference is that I can fix it. Before, I didn't even question it."—*Evan*

"I've completed one semester of college. My brother is a college graduate, but I was able to tell him about some mistakes he was making in the way he used certain words. He was surprised."—*Lacy*

"My teacher suggested we keep a list of words that cause us problems. At the end of the week, I study the ones I added."—*Pilar*

Jumpstart Your Brain!

Before you begin the chapter, get yourself ready to think. Shrug your shoulders. Take a couple of deep breaths. Stand up and stretch. Then jumpstart your brain by solving this brainteaser. The short poem below has 20 words in it that are used incorrectly. Sometimes an incorrect word is used in place of one that sounds exactly the same. Sometimes a similar, but incorrect, word is used instead of one that should be used. See how many you can find. Above any incorrect word, write the word that should be used instead. It will help if you read the poem out loud. Good luck!

I don't worry about spelling, as its plane to sea:

Eye have a spelling checker on my knew pea sea.

Ewe can till at first site

Aye check every peace I right.

Their aren't arrows; this I all ready no.

The reason? My computer tolled me sew!

Compare your answer to your classmates' answers. Explain to each other the changes you made in the words in the poem.

LOOKING AT WHAT YOU ALREADY KNOW

 English can be frustrating to write because there are many small, common words that sound alike or whose meanings are easy to confuse. Can you choose the right word for each of these sentences? Circle your answer.

1. _____ Its   It's _____ going to rain today.

2. _____ Their   There   They're _____ not here yet.

3. My answer was _____ all together   altogether _____ wrong.

4. The rescuers _____ lead   led _____ the children to safety.

5. Did you _____ loose   lose _____ your book?

6. The counselor gave me good _____ advice   advise _____.

7. The president _____ inferred   implied _____ that he would seek reelection.

8. If you feel dizzy, you should _____ lay   lie _____ down for a few minutes.

9. Is there _____ anymore   any more _____ pizza?

10. How much _____ farther   further _____ is it to the beach?

Commonly Confused and Misused Words

Learning is a treasure that follows its owner everywhere.

—Chinese proverb

An error is not a mistake until you refuse to correct it.

—Orlando A. Battista

You already know that people make judgments about you based on your vocabulary. They also make judgments based on how accurately and well you use common, everyday words in writing and speaking. When you fill out a job application or have a job interview, when you write a paper or an essay test answer, using the correct word can make all the difference.

◄□► CROSS-CHAPTER CONNECTION

In Chapter 4 you learned about using the dictionary. When you look up the spelling of a commonly confused or misused word, check the definition. You may discover that you want the other word instead.

If you use the wrong word, you may not leave a good impression. Moreover, writing the wrong word may completely change the meaning you intended. "He's not a successful doctor; he lacks *patience*" is very different from "He's not a successful doctor; he lacks *patients*."

We'll look at approximately 50 pairs of words in this chapter. You probably already know several or even many of them. Learning more of them will dramatically improve your speaking and writing. Learn all of them that you can. Even if you don't know all of them by the time you finish this chapter, you will at least know enough to look them up if you need to. That alone is a big step forward!

The Big Picture for This Chapter

This chapter focuses on

- common homonyms, words that sound alike but have different meanings (such as *hear* and *here*) and pairs of words that sound very similar (such as *advice* and *advise*)
- single words that sound the same as two-word phrases (such as *already* and *all ready*)
- other words that are often confused or misused, even though they don't sound alike (such as *imply* and *infer*, or *breath* and *breathe*)

You'll learn the difference in the meanings of these words and when to use each. In addition, you'll learn memory pegs that make it easier to recall the spelling and meanings of many of them.

Homonyms: Words That Sound Alike

One category of commonly confused words is homonyms. The word part *homo* means "same." The word part *nym* means "name." **Homonyms** are words that sound the same (have the "same name") and often have the same spelling, but have different meanings. For example, the word *rock* means one thing when you're talking about stones and something else when you are discussing music. The words *hour* and *our* sound alike, but have different meanings.

Let's start by looking at words that sound alike but have different spellings and meanings. These words are so common that you absolutely must know them. For each word, there is a definition and often a memory peg to help you remember the spelling or which meaning goes with which spelling. We'll do these in two groups with ten sets of homonyms per group.

BRAIN-FRIENDLY TIP

Suppose two words sound alike. One of them has several meanings, and the other has only a single meaning. What's the most efficient way to learn which spelling goes with which meanings? Learn the spelling and meaning of the word that has *one* meaning. For all other meanings, just use the other word.

For example, the word *principle* means one thing: a basic truth or rule (as in the *principle of gravity* or the *principle of fair play*. Memory peg: A princip<u>le</u> is a ru<u>le</u>.) *Principal* has several meanings: the head of a school, money, and a main participant in a situation or a performance. Unless you need the spelling that refers to a rule, use the second spelling.

Homonyms, Group 1

You probably know some, or even most, of the pairs below. That's great! It's easy, though, to make careless errors in using them, so they're worth focusing on. As the Jumpstart poem illustrates, a computer spell-checker will not catch the error if you use the wrong word but spell it correctly.

BONUS TIPS

1. Be sure to put the apostrophe (') in the correct place in words that are contractions. The apostrophe *takes the place of a letter that was left out* when the two words were compressed:

   we are = we're.

   The apostrophe replaces the *a* in the word *are* when the words contract.

2. There's no such word as *its'*. It doesn't exist. Don't use it. Ever.

By the way, can you see the word parts in *contraction?*

   con—together

   tract—to drag or push

   ion—noun suffix

Contraction literally means "to push together"—exactly what you do with the two words!

hear—to sense sound with the ears [memory peg: The word *hear* contains the word *ear*: h*ear*.]

here—in this place [memory peg: The word *here* is part of the word *there*: t*here*. You can also link the "place words" *here* and *there*.]

its—belongs to it (possessive form of *it*; "The dog wagged *its* tail.")

it's—contraction for *it is* and *it has* [memory peg: If you can substitute the words "it is" or "it has," use this spelling: "*It's* raining" is correct because "*It is* raining" makes sense. "The dog wagged *it's* tail" is wrong because "The dog wagged *it is* tail" does not make sense.]

passed—to have already happened or gone by (past tense of *to pass*)

BRAIN-FRIENDLY TIPS

- *Visual and tactile learners:* Make index cards for homonyms that confuse you or that you misspell. Write a word, its meaning, and a sample sentence or phrase on one side. Add a memory peg or a sketch too. On the other side of the card, write the same information for its homonym. Keep your stack of cards handy for reference. Review them whenever you have a free minute or two.

- *Auditory learners:* Make the cards described above. Read them *aloud* or say the information and then check it. You can also look at one homonym and then spell its "partner" aloud.

past—(1) at an earlier time; over *(adj.)*; (2) the history of a person, nation, etc. *(noun)*

right—(1) correct; (2) opposite of left [memory peg: rig<u>ht</u>, correc<u>t</u>, and lef<u>t</u> all end in *t*.]
rite—ritual or ceremony ("a sacred *rite*"; "burial *rites*")
write—to put information on the surface of something, such as paper

sense—(1) perception ("a *sense* of honor"; "a *sense* of fatigue"); (2) ability to reason ("He showed good *sense* in the way he reacted to the mugger.")
since—(1) because; (2) used to indicate the amount of time that has gone by ("*since* last week")

their—belongs to them (possessive form of *they*)
there—(1) in that place ("Put the book *there*." "We're not from *there*."); (2) used to call attention to someone or something ("*There's a* child in the street!")
they're—contraction for *they are* [memory peg: If you can substitute "they are," use this word. "*They're* late" = "*They are* late."]

threw—past tense of *throw* ("He *threw* the baseball.")
through—(1) finished; ("We're *through* with the tournament."); (2) into and out of ("The storm passed *through* town quickly.") [memory peg: For the correct spelling, remember, "We swam th<u>rough</u> <u>rough</u> water.")

to—(1) toward, in the direction of ("They walk *to* school every day."); (2) *to* is also used in a verb form known as an infinitive ("*To* laugh is *to* live.")
too—(1) also ("They're coming along *too*."); (2) very ("It's *too* late." "He's *too* ill.")
two—number following one

[memory peg: Learn these sentences that illustrate the correct usage of the words: "I'm going *to* a movie with *two* friends. Would you like to come *too*?")

who's—contraction for *who is* or *who has* [memory peg: If you can substitute "who is" or "who has," use this word. "*Who's* at the door?" = "*Who is* at the door?" "*Who's* already finished the test?" = "*Who has* already finished the test?"]
whose—possessive form of *who* ("*Whose* pen is this?")

your—belongs to *you* (possessive form of *you*)
you're—contraction for *you are* (If you can substitute "you are," use this word. "*You're* the winner!" = "*You are* the winner!")

STOP AND PROCESS: Homonyms, Group 1

EXERCISE 5.1

Review the first set of homonyms. From memory, try to write the homonym(s) for each word below. When you have finished, circle any you are unsure of. Then look back at the list and check your answers. Doing this helps you pinpoint the precise ones that cause you difficulty.

than _____

your _____

whose _____

here _____

sense _____

its _____

passed _____

rite _____ _____

threw _____

to _____ _____

EXERCISE 5.2

- Read each sentence.

- Choose the homonym in parentheses that belongs in the sentence and *write* it in the blank. Writing the word rather than just circling it helps you pay attention to its spelling.

- On the line beneath the sentence, tell *why* you chose that word or *what it means*. This reinforces learning.

You may refer to the first set of homonyms as you do the exercise.

Example: _Whose_ hat is this? (*who's, whose*)

   Reason: _____ *possessive form of "who"* _____

1. I _____ the test! (*passed, past*)

   Reason: _____ _____

2. The train route goes _____ ____ Washington, D.C. (*threw, through*)

   Reason: _____

3. They had cake and ice cream _____. (*to, too, two*)

   Reason: _____

4. Look! _____ snowing! (*Its, It's*)

   Reason: _____

5. He has played soccer _____ he was in fifth grade. (*sense, since*)

   Reason: _____

6. In your opinion, _____ going to win the Academy Award? (*who's, whose*)

   Reason: _____

7. Did you _____ the phone ring? (*hear, here*)

   Reason: _____

8. It's _____ fault, and not ours! (*their, there, they're*)

   Reason: _____

9. It's _____ turn. (*your, you're*)

   Reason: _____

10. I have to _____ a short paper for my history class. (*right, rite, write*)

    Reason: _____

Homonyms, Group 2

This second group of homonyms may be a bit more challenging. These words are also very commonly used, so it's important for you to know them.

capital—(1) city where government is headquartered; (2) an uppercase letter; (3) wealth

capitol—the building a state legislature meets in [memory peg: Many capitols are buildings with domes. Link the *o*'s in the two words: capit**o**l and d**o**me. Unless you're talking about an actual *building*, use the other spelling.]

complement—something that completes or brings to perfection ("That tie really *complements* his outfit." [memory peg: <u>comple</u>ment and <u>comple</u>te both start with the same six letters.]

compliment—praise [memory peg: "Compl<u>i</u>ments are what <u>I</u> like!"]

forth—forward ("Go *forth* and serve.")

fourth—one of four equal parts; preceded by three others

lead—(1) heavy metal substance; (2) graphite material used in pencils

led—(1) guided or showed the way (past tense of *to lead*) ("The guide *led* the hikers." "The conductor *led* the orchestra.");
(2) ranked or came first ("Last year the Cubs *led* the league in home runs.")

lessen—to decrease or diminish ("This will *lessen* the pain.")
lesson—something learned or taught [memory peg: "We had a less<u>on</u> <u>on</u> civil rights."]

peace—absence of fighting [memory peg: "We want p<u>eace</u> on <u>E</u>arth."]
piece—(1) a portion, a part of a larger thing or group of things [memory peg: "a p<u>ie</u>ce of p<u>ie</u>"]; (2) musical composition

plain—(1) simple; having little or no decoration (*adj.*); (2) a flat land area (*n.*)
plane—aircraft; (2) carpenter tool used for smoothing wood; (3) a flat surface (math term)

presence—(1) attendance at an event ("We appreciated his *presence* at our wedding.") [memory peg: associate pre<u>sence</u> with its opposite, ab<u>sence</u> since both end in -<u>sence</u>];
presents—gifts [memory peg: present<u>s</u> and gift<u>s</u> are both plural words that end in <u>s</u>; they *sent* a pre<u>sent</u>]

than—used in comparisons ("She is taller *than* I am." "He likes biology more *than* physics.")
then—(1) at that time ("I was a freshman *then*."); (2) next ("They ate dinner and *then* watched a movie."); (3) in that case ("If the traffic is heavy, *then* allow extra time.")

wear—to have on as a covering, for protection, or for adornment (*wear* a coat, seatbelt, or smile)
where—in which place [memory peg: associate w<u>here</u> with two words that indicate places: <u>here</u> and t<u>here</u>]

 STOP AND PROCESS: Homonyms, Group 2

EXERCISE 5.3

Review the second set of homonyms. From memory, try to write the homonym(s) for each word below. When you have finished, circle any you are unsure of. Then look back at the list and check your answers. Doing this helps you pinpoint the precise ones that cause you difficulty.

forth   _____

peace   _____

where   _____

plane   _____

then   _____

presents   _____

led   _____

compliment   _____

capital   _____

lesson   _____

EXERCISE 5.4

- Read each sentence.
- Choose the homonym in parentheses that belongs in the sentence and *write* it in the blank. Write the word rather than just circling it.
- On the line beneath the sentence, tell *why* you chose that word or *what it means*. This reinforces learning.

You may refer to the second set of homonyms as you do the exercise.

1. The captain _____ the football team onto the field. (*lead, led*)

   Reason: _____

2. Please hand me a _____ of paper. (*peace, piece*)

   Reason: _____

3. The _____ are stacked on the table. (*presence, presents*)

   Reason: _____

4. Every now and _____ we go skiing. (*than, then*)

   Reason: _____

5. We drank _____ tap water. (*plain, plane*)

   Reason: _____

6. Did you have a guitar _____ this morning? (*lessen, lesson*)

   Reason: _____

7. One _____ of the class made As. (*forth, fourth*)

   Reason: _____

8. What a nice _____ he gave her! (*complement, compliment*)

   Reason: _____

9. The _____ dome is being repaired. (*capital, capitol*)

   Reason: _____

10. Do you remember _____ you put my CD? (*wear, where*)

    Reason: _____

One Word or Two?

Already or *all ready? Altogether* or *all together?* You may sometimes wonder if you need one word or if you need two separate words. Learn these pairs of words, and you won't have to wonder anymore!

> **✳ BONUS TIP**
>
> These are *not* words:
>
> allready
>
> alltogether
>
> allmost
>
> allways
>
> There are almost *no* nonhyphenated words in English that start with the letters *a-l-l* followed by a consonant. If you write one of the misspellings above, remind yourself to GET THE "L" OUT OF THERE!

altogether—entirely, completely ("This is an *altogether* new plan." "When lightning hit, we lost the TV picture *altogether*.")

all together—refers to several people or things that are all in the same place ("My family was *all together* during the holidays." "Please put the chairs *all together* in the living room.") [memory peg: If you can separate the words in the sentence, and the sentence still makes sense, you need two words: "Please put *all* the chairs *together* in the living room."]

anymore—(1) any longer, at the present ("Do they make this style *anymore*?"); (2) from now on ("We promise not to argue *anymore*.")
any more—quantity or amount [memory peg: If you can add the words "of this," use two words: "Is there any more (of this)?" "Is there any more (of this) cake?")

already—by this time ("Has the movie *already* started?")
all ready—all people or things are fully prepared ("Are we *all ready* to begin?") [memory peg: If you can separate the words in the sentence and the sentence still makes sense, you need two words: "*All* of us are *ready* to begin.")

everyday—(1) ordinary; commonplace ("*everyday* worries");
(2) appropriate for routine occasions ("Use the *everyday* dishes instead of the good china plates.")
every day—happens each day ("Take time to read *every day*.")
[memory peg: If you can substitute the word *each* in place of *every*, use two words: "Take time to read *each day*."]

maybe—perhaps; possibly ("*Maybe* it will rain." "*Maybe* she'll win the election.")
may be—could be; might be ("He *may be* the fastest man on the team." "She *may be* elected class president.")

somebody—someone; an unspecified or unknown person ("*Somebody* is knocking at the door." "Ask *somebody* the directions to the student center.")
some body—This refers to an unspecified or unknown body. ("*Some body* was found in the alley, but the police haven't identified the person yet.")

sometime—at an indefinite or unstated time ("I'll call you *sometime* after class tonight." "Let's have lunch *sometime*.")
some time—an indefinite amount of time (Use this when you are talking about actual time: "Let *some time* go by before you make a final decision.")
sometimes—at times; now and then ("*Sometimes* he works on weekends.")

STOP AND PROCESS: One Word or Two?

EXERCISE 5.5

- Read each sentence.
- Choose the word in parentheses that belongs in the sentence and *write* it in the blank. Write the word rather than just circling it.
- On the line beneath the sentence, tell *why* you chose that word or *what it means.* This reinforces learning.

You may refer to the "One Word or Two?" list as you do the exercise.

1. _____ broke the window. (*Somebody, Some body*)

   Reason: _____

2. The cheerleaders are _____ for the game. (*already, all ready*)

   Reason: _____

3. We don't have _____ time to spend on this project. (*anymore, any more*)

   Reason: _____

4. You don't need to dress up. Just wear _____ clothes. (*everyday, every day*)

   Reason: _____

5. Please spend _____ revising this paper. (*sometime, some time, sometimes*)

   Reason: _____

6. Their divorce was _____ shocking. (*altogether, all together*)

   Reason: _____

7. Alice doesn't live here _____. (*anymore, any more*)

   Reason: _____

8. This _____ your big chance to win! (*maybe, may be*)

   Reason: _____ _____

9. _____ after midnight, it started to rain. (*sometime, some time, sometimes*)

   Reason: _____

10. _____ you'll win. (*maybe, may be*)

   Reason: _____

Other Commonly Confused and Misused Words, Group 1

People often mix up these words, even though the words don't sound identical. Like the other words in this chapter, these are commonly used words, so you will want to learn to use them correctly.

accept—to receive [memory peg: The prefix *ad-* is also spelled *ac-* and it means *to* or *toward*. *Ac*cept means to receive something that's given *to* you.]
except—with the exclusion of; other than [memory peg: The prefix *ex-* tells you something is left *out*. "Everyone is here *except* the instructor!"]

advice—suggestions intended to be helpful (*noun*) ("The counselor gave me good *advice*.")
advise—to offer advice; to give suggestions or ideas (*verb*) ("The counselor *advised* me to take math.")

breath—air inhaled and exhaled (*noun*) ("Take a deep *breath*.")
breathe—to inhale and exhale (*verb*) ("*Breathe* deeply.")

choose—to pick out or select (present tense; "*Choose* any seat you like.")
chose—past tense of *choose* ("At the play last night, we *chose* front row seats.")

device—an invention that serves a particular purpose (*noun*) ("A can opener is a handy *device*.")
devise—to design (*verb*) ("He *devised* a new medical procedure.")

fewer—consisting of a smaller number ("*fewer* hours," "*fewer* dollars," "*fewer* students") [memory peg: Use this word when you can substitute "a smaller number of." Use it when you're referring to things that can be counted separately.]
less—not as great in amount or importance ("*less* time," "*less* money," "*less* energy," "*less* sleep") [memory peg: Use this word only when

you are *not* referring to separate items. For example, it's incorrect to say, "less carbs," "less courses," or "less books" since carbs, courses, and books consist of separate things.]

farther—at a greater distance ("traveled *farther* yesterday") [memory peg: <u>far</u>ther contains the word <u>far</u>, so use this word to refer to distance that can be measured—inches, miles, etc.]
further—to a greater extent; more; in addition ("Please think about this *further* before you decide." "She stated *further* that she would seek reelection.")

later—after some time has gone by ("Call me *later*."); (2) past the usual time ("The meeting started *later* than usual.")
latter—the second of two things mentioned; opposite of former ("Of the pie and the cake, the *latter* tastes better." In other words, the cake tastes better.)

loose—not fastened, unbound ("The dog broke *loose*." "She wore her hair down *loose*.") [memory peg: "The *goose* got *loose*!"]
lose—to misplace ("When did you *lose* your cell phone?") [memory peg: *lose* and *find* both have four letters.]

quiet—free of loud noise, silent; calm [memory peg: This word has two syllables; you hear two vowel sounds. "She is never *quiet* about her *diet!*"]
quite—very [memory peg: This word has one syllable; you hear one vowel sound. "The *light* is *quite bright*."]
quit—to stop ("*Quit* complaining!")

 STOP AND PROCESS: Other Commonly Confused
Words, Group 1

EXERCISE 5.6

- Read each sentence.
- Choose the word in parentheses that belongs in the sentence and *write* it in the blank. Write the word rather than just circling it.
- On the line beneath the sentence, tell *why* you chose that word or *what it means*. This reinforces learning.

You may refer to the list as you do the exercise.

1. The movie started _____ than we expected. (*later, latter*)

   Reason: _____

2. Today I ran a mile _____ than I did yesterday. (*farther, further*)

   Reason: _____

3. Were you able to _____ a solution to the problem?
   (device, devise)

   Reason: _____

4. Does cream have _____ calories than butter?
   (fewer, less)

   Reason: _____

   _____

5. All the pages in the book came _____. *(loose, lose)*

   Reason: _____

6. The swimming team was _____ proud of
   winning second place. *(quiet, quite, quit)*

   Reason: _____

7. The air quality is so bad that it makes it hard to _____.
   (breath, breathe)

   Reason: _____

8. Last week, our class _____ its community
   service project. *(choose, chose)*

   Reason: _____

9. She was invited to the White House to _____
   the award. *(accept, except)*

   Reason: _____

10. What _____ would you give someone who is
    starting college? *(advice, advise)*

    Reason: _____

Other Commonly Confused and Misused Words, Group 2

Here is the last group of words. They are helpful to know because, like
the other pairs of words in this chapter, they occur so frequently.

affect—(1) to have an influence on (*verb*) ("Weather *affects* my
mood."); (2) feeling or emotional response (*noun*) ("Depressed people
may show little *affect*.")

BONUS TIP

Affect and *effect* are both nouns and verbs. The main things to remember are that

- there are two spellings, so don't use *effect* for everything, and
- you will almost always want *affect* when you need a verb and *effect* when you need a noun. When reading, you will usually see the words used this way.

Lay down!

Speak!

It's *lie.*

BONUS TIP

There are only three words in English that end in *ceed:*

> *proceed*
>
> *exceed*
>
> *succeed*

Learn this sentence as a spelling memory peg: "When you *succeed* in spelling *exceed*, you may *proceed.*"

---

effect—(1) result (*noun*); (2) to bring about or cause (*verb*) ("Traffic cameras *effect* a reduction of drivers running red lights.")

beside—next to ("Please sit *beside* me.")
besides—(1) in addition to ("Is anyone *besides* me ready for dessert?"); (2) except ("*Besides* me, there's no one here."); (3) moreover, in addition (I don't like pizza. *Besides*, I'm not hungry anyway.")

dyeing—changing the color of something ("My sister is thinking about *dyeing* her hair red.")
dying—losing life ("Smokers face a greater risk of *dying* from lung cancer.")

emigrate—to leave one country to settle in another ("*emigrated* from Russia") [memory peg: The prefix *e-* tells you someone is migrating (going) *out* of a place. Use the phrase *emigrate from.*]
immigrate—to go to another country to settle there ("*immigrated* to the United States") [memory peg: The prefix *im-* tells you someone is migrating *into* a place. Use the phrase *immigrate to.*]

formally—done with ceremony; done according to the proper or accepted way ("We've seen each other at parties, but we've never been *formally* introduced.")
formerly—previously, at an earlier time ("I *formerly* attended City College; now I attend the university.")

idea—(1) a thought ("the main *idea*"); (2) a plan ("I have an *idea*.")
ideal—(1) model of perfection; worthy principle or goal (*noun*) ("World peace is the *ideal*."); (2) considered highly satisfactory or the best possible (*adj.*) ("the *ideal* candidate")

imply—to hint or suggest without stating outright (*verb*) ("He *implied* that because of traffic, he would be late.")
infer—to draw a conclusion (*verb*) ("From the look on his face, we *inferred* he was surprised.") [memory peg: *Imply* and *infer* are opposites that go together. The *sender* of an indirect message *implies* it. The *receiver* who "picks up on it" *infers* the meaning.]

lay—to put in a particular place or position ("*Lay* your coat on the bench.")
lie—to recline; to put oneself in a flat, horizontal position ("*Lie* down until you feel better.") [Note: People get confused because the past tense of *lie* is *lay*. Most of the time, what you really need to remember is to use *lay* when you're talking about objects and *lie* when referring to people and animals. See cartoon.]

precede—to come before [memory peg: *pre-* means "before." Notice the spelling: There is one letter between all of the *e*'s.]

proceed—to go forward or continue, especially after an interruption [memory peg: *pro-* means "forward." Notice the spelling: The *e*'s are next to each other.]

set—to put or place ("*Set* your books here.")

sit—to rest with the body bent at the hips and the torso upright ("*Sit* down.")

 STOP AND PROCESS: Other Commonly Confused and Misused Words, Group 2

EXERCISE 5.7

- Read each sentence.
- Choose the word in parentheses that belongs in the sentence and *write* it in the blank. Write the word rather than just circling it.
- On the line below the sentence, tell *why* you chose that word or *what it means*. This reinforces learning.

You may refer to the list as you do the exercise.

1. Ancient Greeks believed in the _____ of having a strong body and a strong mind. (*idea, ideal*)

   Reason: _____

2. The path _____ the stream is beautiful. (*beside, besides*)

   Reason: _____

3. She's a computer programmer now, but _____ she sold real estate. (*formally, formerly*)

   Reason: _____

4. The lawyer asked for a delay, but the judge ordered him to

   _____ . (*precede, proceed*)

   Reason: _____

5. My boss _____ that we would receive a raise, but he hasn't made an official announcement yet. (*implied, inferred*)

   Reason: _____

6. Could you please _____ these dishes on the table? (*set, sit*)

   Reason: _____

7. My grandparents _____ to this country from Ireland. *(emigrated, immigrated)*

   Reason: _____

8. Drinking too much alcohol _____ a person's ability to reason. *(affects, effects)*

   Reason: _____

9. The bridesmaids are _____ their shoes pink to match their dresses. *(dyeing, dying)*

   Reason: _____

10. Our dog likes to _____ in a shady spot and sleep. *(lay, lie)*

    Reason: _____

MY TOOLBOX *of Commonly Confused and Misused Words*

Way to go! You've now completed Part Two, the vocabulary section of this book. To fix in mind the information in this chapter, do one of the activities described below. Regardless of which activity you choose, you should include the **definition of a homonym,** as well as the **ten pairs of words that give you the most trouble,** along with their **definitions.** Add any other information that you want to remember about commonly confused and misused words.

Putting the information in your own words will help you remember it. Your brain likes that! You can use more than one color of ink, and you can include sketches and memory pegs if they work for you.

- **Write the information on notebook paper, or make a set of index cards.**

- **Make a set of simple cartoons** to help you recall the meaning of words that give you trouble. The *Vocabulary Cartoons* books by Sam, Max, and Brian Burchers (Punta Gorda, FL: New Monic Books) use this strategy. For example, one of the words in *Vocabulary Cartoons* is *falter,* which means to become weaker or to be unsteady. It sounds like *altar* (a sacred platform or place), so the authors came up with the sentence, "The groom FALTERED at the ALTAR." The cartoon shows a bride and groom standing before the minister, taking their marriage vows. However, the (nervous!) groom is falling over backwards, fainting. The author includes three other sentences to show the meaning of *falter* in context: "Paul's determination FALTERED when he saw the size of the mountain he hoped to climb"; "Tony stammered and FALTERED when it was his time to speak in class"; and "The swimmers FALTERED as the waves pushed them back." (That's one word you won't forget!) Try using this approach to help you learn the meaning of the commonly confused and misused words that give you the greatest difficulty.

- **Create a study map.** To make a map, draw a circle in the middle of the page. Write the words "Commonly Confused and Misused Words" in the circle. On lines that radiate from the circle, write specific information, such as the definition of a homonym and other information that you want to remember. Include any 10 pairs of words that give you the most trouble; be sure to write their definitions. You can include small illustrations or sketches, and work with colored pens. (The ORL presents more information about making study maps.)

FALTER
(FALL tur) *v.*
to become weaker;
to be unsteady

Sounds like: **ALTAR**

"The groom FALTERED at the ALTAR."

❑ Paul's determination **FALTERED** when he saw the size of the mountain he hoped to climb.

❑ Tony stammered and **FALTERED** when it came his time to speak to the class.

❑ The swimmers **FALTERED** as the waves pushed them back.

Source: Burchers, Burchers, and Burchers, *Vocabulary Cartoons: Building on Educated Vocabulary with Visual Mnemonics.* Punta Gorda, FL: New Monic Books, 1988, p. 117. Reprinted by permission of New Monic Books, Inc.

■ **Create a game** that enables players to review commonly confused and misused words. It could be a card game (like a variation of *Go Fish!*), a board game, or something else. For example, it could be a variation of *Concentration*, in which word cards and definition cards are placed face down in rows. Players try to remember where each word and definition is, so that as they turn cards over, they can match a word and its definition. The player with the largest number of correct pairs wins. Include a word card for *homonym* and a definition of it.

✔ **CHAPTER CHECK**

Answer these questions about the information in the chapter. Write the missing word in each blank. When there is more than one part to the answer, there is more than one blank. For true/false items, circle the correct answer. (*Suggestion:* Don't forget the helpful information that appears in the Tip boxes!)

1. _____ pegs can help you more easily recall the spelling and meaning of some words.

2. In contractions the apostrophe takes the place of a _____ that has been left out.

3. *Farther* and *further* are examples of _____ words.

4. *Their, they're,* and *there* are examples of _____.

5. In English, many small, common words are often confused or misused.___True or False?___

6. The word *homonym* literally means "same name."___True or False?___

7. A computer spell-checker will catch any words you misuse. ___True or False?___

8. Words that sound alike but have different spellings and meanings are called _____.

9. *Allready, alltogether, allmost,* and *allways* are words in English. ___True or False?___

10. A word can be more than one part of speech. ___True or False?___

11. There are four words in English that end in the letters *ceed*. ___True or False?___

12. Prefixes can sometimes help you remember the difference between two commonly confused words. ___True or False?___

13. Homonyms come only in pairs. ___True or False?___

14. When two words sound alike and one has only a single meaning, you can learn that word's meaning, and then use the other word on all other occasions. ___True or False?___

15. Using the wrong word may completely change the meaning you intend. ___True or False?___

REVIEW EXERCISES

SET 1

From the alphabetized list of words, choose the word that fits each definition and write it beside the definition. You will not need to use all of the words on the list.

accept	choose	fewer	lead	quite
advice	chose	forth	led	some time
advise	complement	fourth	less	sometime
affect	compliment	further	lie	sometimes
all together	dyeing	idea	loose	than
altogether	dying	ideal	lose	their
beside	effect	immigrate	peace	then
besides	emigrate	imply	piece	there
breath	every day	infer	precede	to
breathe	everyday	it's	proceed	too
capital	except	its	quiet	who's
capitol	farther	lay	quit	whose

Definitions

_____ 1. also; very

_____ 2. to come before

_____ 3. to a greater extent; more; in addition

_____ 4. to misplace

_____ 5. to inhale and exhale

_____ 6. to put in a particular place or position

_____ 7. entirely, completely

_____ 8. suggestions intended to be helpful

_____ 9. ordinary, commonplace; appropriate for routine occasions

_____ 10. belongs to them (possessive form of *they*)

_____ 11. something that completes or brings to perfection

_____ 12. to pick out or select

_____ 13. a thought; a plan

_____ 14. the building a state legislature meets in

_____ 15. with the exclusion of; other than

_____ 16. contraction of "who is" or "who has"

_____ 17. guided or showed the way

_____ 18. losing life

_____ 19. to have an influence on; emotion or feeling

_____ 20. belongs to it (possessive form of *it*)

_____ 21. consisting of a smaller number

_____ 22. praise

_____ 23. to hint or suggest without stating outright

_____ 24. at times; now and then

_____ 25. to decrease or diminish

SET 2

Now try this selection. Like most things you read, it contains many commonly confused and misused words. A set of words appears beneath each blank. Use the context to decide which word belongs in each blank. Write the correct word in the blank rather than simply circling it. To reinforce your learning, say out loud to yourself the meaning of the word you choose, what it's a contraction of, and so forth. Getting the right answer is important; knowing your reason for choosing that answer is more important.

Dr. Andrew Weil (pronounced "wile") is known worldwide as an expert on natural health. He is the author of several best-selling books on health, healing, and wellness. His approach brings together mind-body health and integrative medicine. Integrative medicine combines traditional medicine with alternative medicine, such as acupuncture and using herbs as medicine. The goal or _____ *(idea ideal)* is for people to achieve and maintain health rather _____ *(than then)* waiting for illness to occur and _____ *(than then)* treating it. _____ *(It's Its)* better _____ *(for four)* people never to _____ *(loose lose)* their health in the first place.

Dr. Weil believes the patient and doctor should work together as partners, and that getting well depends greatly on the patient's lifestyle.

Diet, stress, quality of sleep, relationships, work, and so

_____ all _____ health and healing. He favors
    (forth fourth)   *(affect effect)*

a wholesome diet with _____ foods that are processed
                       (fewer less)

(contain preservatives or were grown using chemicals). He

encourages people to manage stress with exercise and meditation. He

suggests they learn to _____deeply and slowly when they
               (breath breathe)

feel stress.

    Dr. Weil offers _____on preventing memory loss
               (advice advise)

_____. _____ proper diet and exercise, he says
   (to too two)   *(Beside Besides)*

one of the most effective ways is to read. Mental stimulation

_____ brain function, and with the brain, it's either use it or
   (affects effects)

_____ it! Reading, it seems, is a good workout for the brain.
   (loose lose)

_____, it exercises _____ imagination in a way
  (Farther Further)   *(you're your)*

that television and other media cannot duplicate.

ASSESS YOUR UNDERSTANDING

Ready to monitor your comprehension of the chapter? You know what to do!

1 . . . . . 2 . . . . . 3 . . . . . 4 . . . . . 5 . . . . . 6 . . . . . 7 . . . . . 8 . . . . . 9 10

I'm baffled!   **Starting to see the light**   **Bingo!**

Identify what you don't understand or what's causing you a problem. (Remember to use feedback from the Chapter Check and the exercises. Also, ask yourself, "Do I still get some words confused? Which ones?")

_____

_____

_____

_____

Describe things you could do to fix the problem.

_____

_____

_____

_____

Remember to *apply* the steps so that you can fix any problems while they're fresh in mind. Once you learn these commonly confused words, you have the benefit of that knowledge for the rest of your college years and the rest of your life. That makes learning them an excellent investment of your time!

Map of Chapters

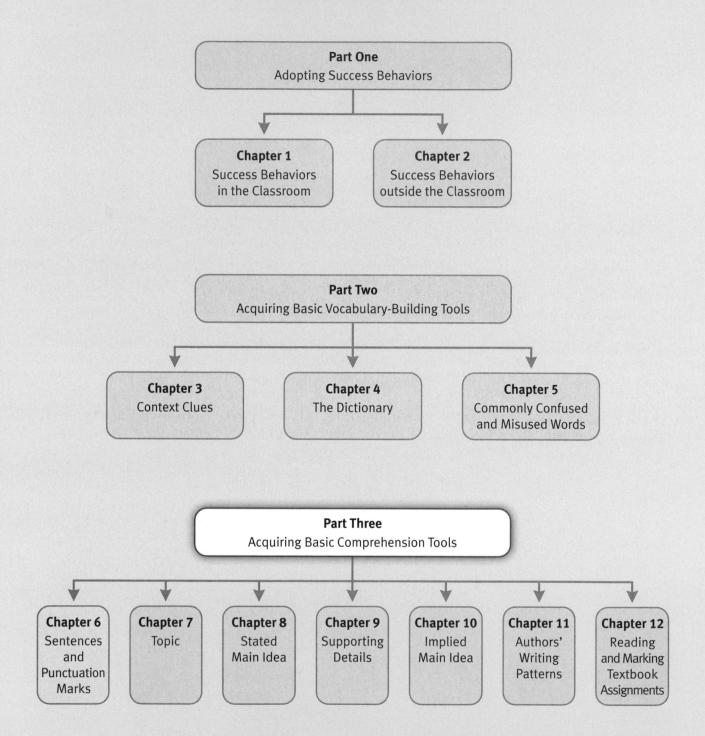

Part One
Adopting Success Behaviors

Chapter 1
Success Behaviors in the Classroom

Chapter 2
Success Behaviors outside the Classroom

Part Two
Acquiring Basic Vocabulary-Building Tools

Chapter 3
Context Clues

Chapter 4
The Dictionary

Chapter 5
Commonly Confused and Misused Words

Part Three
Acquiring Basic Comprehension Tools

Chapter 6
Sentences and Punctuation Marks

Chapter 7
Topic

Chapter 8
Stated Main Idea

Chapter 9
Supporting Details

Chapter 10
Implied Main Idea

Chapter 11
Authors' Writing Patterns

Chapter 12
Reading and Marking Textbook Assignments

WELCOME TO PART THREE
Acquiring Basic Comprehension Tools

You'll be pleased to know that the vocabulary-building skills you learned in Part Two will help you be successful with the chapters in this section. Reading is more than looking at words. After all, unless you understand what you've read, you haven't really "read" it. In college, your job is to comprehend the information in your textbooks. Understanding what you read—**comprehension**—is the heart of the reading process. That's why Part Three is the heart of *Entryways:* It contains essential comprehension skills to help you understand what you read.

Each chapter builds on the previous ones, so work hard to understand every chapter as you go. Part Three consists of these seven chapters:

- In Chapter 6 you will review parts of speech, learn to identify the core parts of a sentence, and learn about types of sentences. You'll get a refresher on punctuation marks. All of this will enable you to comprehend sentences more effectively and confidently, as well as to write better sentences.

- In Chapter 7 you will learn to identify the topic, the subject of a paragraph. This is the essential foundation for understanding material you read.

- Chapter 8 moves you ahead a step further. It focuses on locating the stated main idea sentence, the author's single most important point, in paragraphs you read.

- In Chapter 9 you will learn to identify supporting details, the additional information the author provides to help you understand the main point.

- In Chapter 10 you will learn what to do when the author does not state the main point as a sentence in the paragraph. You will learn how to write a formulated main idea sentence in your own words.

- In Chapter 11 you will learn authors' writing patterns, common ways authors organize information they present. This helps you understand and remember the information more easily. Knowing these logical patterns can also make you a better writer.

- In Chapter 12 you will learn an efficient, effective way to approach your assignments. You will discover how to become a more active reader. You will learn how to mark your textbooks intelligently.

Better comprehension can lead to greater learning, higher grades, and more confidence. The skills you learn in Part Three will help you more effectively comprehend not only your textbooks but also nearly everything else you read. As with anything you learn, these skills take practice. Your patience and effort can lead to lifelong benefits, both in school and on the job.

Map of Chapters

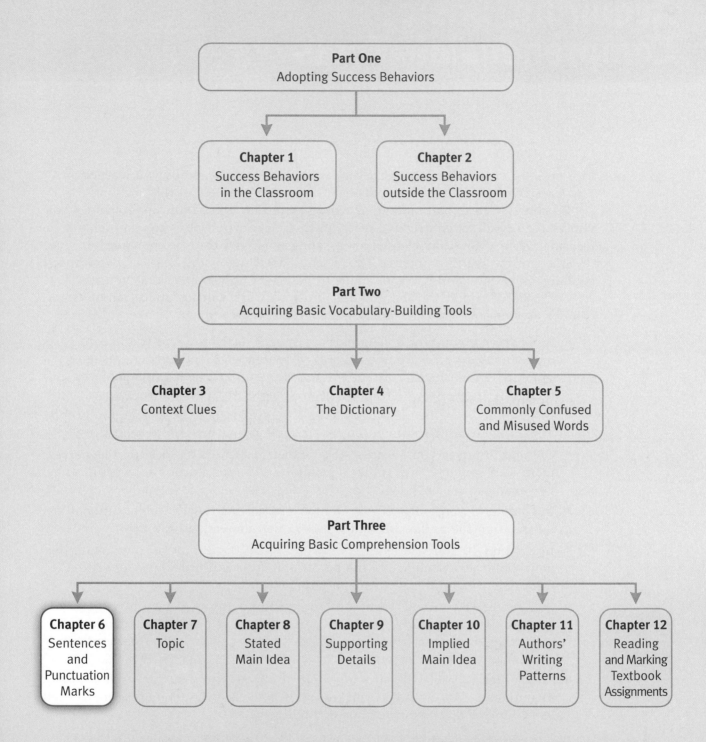

Part One
Adopting Success Behaviors

Chapter 1
Success Behaviors
in the Classroom

Chapter 2
Success Behaviors
outside the Classroom

Part Two
Acquiring Basic Vocabulary-Building Tools

Chapter 3
Context Clues

Chapter 4
The Dictionary

Chapter 5
Commonly Confused
and Misused Words

Part Three
Acquiring Basic Comprehension Tools

Chapter 6
Sentences
and
Punctuation
Marks

Chapter 7
Topic

Chapter 8
Stated
Main Idea

Chapter 9
Supporting
Details

Chapter 10
Implied
Main Idea

Chapter 11
Authors'
Writing
Patterns

Chapter 12
Reading
and Marking
Textbook
Assignments

CHAPTER 6
Sentences and Punctuation Marks
Bricks and Mortar

Why You Need to Know the Information in This Chapter

Did you ever read a textbook assignment and then wonder what in the world it said? If you've had that experience, you're not alone! Understanding your textbooks starts with being able to understand the sentences in them.

This chapter will help you understand

- parts of speech
- the essential parts every sentence must have
- complicated sentences
- punctuation marks
- how to write better sentences

Super Student Tips

Here are tips from other students who have learned about understanding sentences in college textbooks. Here's what experience has taught them:

"Reading my textbooks is a lot less frustrating. I used to struggle to understand what I was reading. It's still not easy, but it's getting better."—*Kevin*

"I want to major in business and run my own company someday. I know that I will be more successful if I can write well."—*Domingo*

"When I started, I couldn't tell when I'd written a complete sentence. I've learned ways to check."—*Mandy*

"I write better sentences than I did at the beginning of the semester. It takes patience, but you can improve."—*Tisha*

"Don't get confused by the words that describe the kinds of sentences. Try to think about the important parts of the sentence, whatever type of sentence it is."—*Reggie*

"Now when I write, I think about whether it will be clear to the reader. I try to make sure the sentences say what I mean."—*Carrie*

Jumpstart Your Brain!

Before you begin the chapter, get yourself ready to think. You know the drill: Stand up, stretch, walk in place, or do some movement to get your circulation going. Then jumpstart your brain by solving these brainteasers.

A carelessly constructed sentence often does not say what the writer intended, or it is easily misinterpreted by readers. These are actual headlines that are funny because they can be interpreted more than one way. The writers weren't trying to be funny; they were just careless. Sometimes the writer put information in the wrong place in the sentence. At other times, the writer used words that can be interpreted more than one way. Read each sentence, and then write (1) what the author's intended message was and (2) the unintended, funny meaning. You'll enjoy these!

1. **"2 Sisters Reunited After 18 Years at the Checkout Counter"**

    What the writer meant: _____

    _____

    How it could also be interpreted: _____

    _____

2. **"Local High School Dropouts Cut in Half"**

    What the writer meant: _____

    _____

    How it could also be interpreted: _____

    _____

3. **"Police Discover Crack in Australia"**

    What the writer meant: _____

    _____

    How it could also be interpreted: _____

    _____

4. **"Crowds Rushing to See Pope Trample Man"**

    What the writer meant: _____

    _____

    How it could also be interpreted: _____

    _____

Answer these items as best you can. Don't feel anxious if you are unsure of the correct answers. By the end of the chapter, you'll be able to answer them. You can make changes then, or you can make changes as you proceed through the chapter.

1. Write the definition of a sentence: _____

   _____

2. What are the two things every sentence must contain? _____

   _____

3. Underline any of these that are sentences. (Do not base your decision on whether or not there is a period.)

   Night came.

   Filling out a job application.

   The security guard heard a cry for help.

   Why Americans love their pets so much.

   The black and red backpack with the torn strap and the broken zipper.

   I felt both excited and scared when I started college.

   Living independently and supporting oneself is a milestone in a young adult's life.

   How first-aid training can save lives.

   The game was canceled because of rain.

Sentences and Punctuation Marks

Words, like eyeglasses, blur everything that they do not make more clear.

—Joseph Joubert, French philosopher

It may seem odd to have a chapter that focuses on understanding sentences. After all, you have been speaking and hearing sentences your entire life. You've heard and written thousands of sentences, and you've read thousands more of them. In fact, you've been reading them all the way through this book, and you're reading one right now.

The reason for emphasizing sentences has to do with understanding college textbooks. First, college textbooks contain sentences that are more complicated than you're probably used to. The better you understand sentence structure, the better you will be able to understand these sentences. Second, you need to be able to create what are called *implied main idea sentences*. (Implied main ideas are discussed in Chapter 10.) To create them, you often have to combine two or more sentences into a single sentence. This chapter will teach you ways to do that and make yourself a better overall writer as well.

Discussing sentences is impossible without talking about subjects and verbs, and without mentioning punctuation marks. If you're worried about studying "grammar" in this chapter, relax! The important thing is that you understand certain basic concepts. It's nice to know the special terms, but not essential. As you progress through this book, you will discover that the information in this chapter will make more and more sense to you.

Remember that the chapter exercises are opportunities to learn. If you could already do them perfectly, there would be no need to do them. The only items you can learn from are the ones you miss. If you miss an item, find out *why* you missed it. If you understand why you missed something, you can do it differently the next time. Understanding the reason you missed an item gives your brain the feedback it needs in order to learn.

The Big Picture for This Chapter

This chapter begins with a review of parts of speech. You need to be familiar with them so that you can understand sentences you read and so that you can write clear sentences. The next section discusses what a sentence is and the essential elements (parts) that every sentence must contain. Next, you'll learn about sentences with more than one subject or verb. You'll find out about two specific types of sentences often found in college textbooks: compound sentences and complex sentences. The chapter ends with a section on punctuation marks. All of this information can help you become not only a better reader, but a better writer.

Parts of Speech

You were introduced to parts of speech in Chapter 4. Let's review them again now. To comprehend (understand) sentences you read and to correct sentences yourself, you need to be familiar with parts of speech, especially nouns and verbs.

As you know, every word is at least one part of speech. Many words can be more than one part of speech because they can function differently in different sentences. Take, for example, the word *record*. Now consider these sentences, and note the different ways the word is used:

Bicyclist Lance Armstrong holds the *record* for winning the most Tour de France races." (*noun*: It names a *thing*.)

My parents plan to *record* my graduation on videotape. (*verb*: It tells an *action*.)

We made the drive from Los Angeles to San Diego in *record* time! (*adjective*: It describes *what kind* of time.)

The eight parts of speech and their dictionary abbreviations are listed next, with examples of how they are used in sentences.

1. **Noun (*n.*)** A word that names a person, place, thing, or idea.
   Examples: *George Washington* was the first *president*.

   New York is a fascinating *city*.

   A *computer* is a useful *tool* for *students*.

   Freedom is worth fighting for.

2. **Pronoun (*pron.*)** A word that is used in place of a noun.
   Examples: *They* won first prize.

   Ask *anyone you* like.

   He built *it himself*.

   Who is at the door?

3. **Adjective (*adj.*)** A word that describes or explains a noun or pronoun. It tells what kind, how many, or which one.
   Examples: Lee bought a *small, silver* flashlight.

   Japanese floral arrangements are *simple* and *beautiful*.

   Even though he is *handsome, rich,* and *intelligent,* he is *shy*.

   Those books are *new*.

   Some people have *severe* allergies.

4. **Verb (*v.*)** A word that shows physical action, mental action, or a state of being. Verbs may also be labeled *v. tr.* for **transitive verb** (takes an object); *v. intr.* for **intransitive verb** (does not take an object), and *v. aux.* for "auxiliary verb" ("helping verbs" that are used with other verbs).

   Examples: The crowd *cheered.*

   Liz *bought* a digital camera.

   The police *are looking* for the suspect.

   Marlo *seems* very happy.

   We *study* separately first and then *discuss* the material.

5. **Adverb (*adv*.)** A word that describes a verb, adjective, or another adverb. It tells how, where, or when.

   Examples: Sharks move *silently* and *swiftly.*

   The tutor *patiently* explained the math problem *again.*

   You're *never too* old to have fun!

6. **Conjunction (*conj*.)** A word that is used to join words or groups of words.

   Examples: My dog is small, *but* strong.

   Ella attends City College, *and* she is majoring in nursing.

   I asked for vanilla, *not* chocolate.

7. **Preposition (*prep*.)** A word used to show the relationship of a noun or pronoun to another word.

   Examples: Look *in* the drawer.

   Everyone was present *except* Lou.

   We stayed *in* the basement *during* the storm.

   It is impossible to make good grades *without* studying.

8. **Interjection (*interj*.)** A word used by itself to express strong feeling or emotion.

   Examples: *Wow!* We won!

   We lost. *Bummer!*

   Ouch! I stubbed my toe.

   Stop! There's a car coming.

The words *a, an,* and *the* are called **articles** (abbreviated *art.*). They usually appear with nouns.

Nouns, pronouns, adjectives, verbs, and adverbs are words that have meaning in and of themselves. Conjunctions, prepositions, and interjections are functional words. That is, they show relationships among the words that have meaning. The best way to get a feel for these differences is to pay attention to them as you read and write. (Remember the story about the little boy who saw his mother's parking ticket and said, "Wow! They *really* like your driving! It says 'Parking fine.'")

www.mhhe.com/
entryways

For more information about certain parts of speech, see

**Catalyst>
Editing>
Pronouns**

**Catalyst>
Editing>
Verbs and
Verbals**

**Catalyst>
Editing>
Adjectives and
Adverbs**

**Catalyst>
Editing> Articles**

STOP AND PROCESS: Parts of Speech

EXERCISE 6.1

Read each group of words. Then decide which part of speech they represent. Use the examples in the preceding section to help you.

1. before, beyond, to, toward _____

2. quite, barely, slowly, suddenly _____

3. shoes, Mexico, Pacific Ocean, laughter _____

4. Oh! No! Yes! Yikes! _____

5. go, build, am, jump, appear, become_____

6. blue, delightful, fuzzy, rude, sad _____

7. you, our, herself, whom, which, what _____

8. for, nor, or, yet, since, because _____

Understanding Sentences

You already know that a sentence starts with a capitalized word and ends with a period, but what exactly is a sentence? A **sentence** is a group of words that expresses a complete thought. A complete thought tells you something. It makes sense all by itself. (In the next section, you'll see examples of incomplete and complete thoughts.) As a reader, your task is to figure out what the author's thought is.

The Two Essential Parts of Sentences

Every sentence must have these two essential elements or "ingredients":

1. a **subject** that tells who or what the sentence is about or is talking about;

2. a **predicate** that tells what the subject is doing or what is being said about the subject. The predicate is a verb or the part of the sentence that contains the verb. For our purposes, you can think of the predicate and the verb as the same thing.

The basic "recipe" for a **simple sentence** is

sentence = **subject + predicate.**

BONUS TIP

Whenever you write a paper in college, proofread what you have written. Remember that some words can be more than one part of speech. The writers of the headlines below must have forgotten that! As a result, the headlines turned out unintentionally funny—and embarrassing to the writers.

"Eye Drops Off Shelves."

The writer means a brand of eyedrops was recalled (removed from store shelves and no longer sold). Since *drops* can be a verb, it sounds as if an eyeball dropped off a shelf!

"Teacher Strikes Idle Students"

The writer means that students had no classes and nothing to do (they were idle) because teachers were on strike (temporarily refusing to work). If *strikes* is read as a verb, the headline means that a teacher hit students because they were idle (lazy, not working).

Any sentence, no matter how complicated, still has these basic parts. You need to be able to identify them in sentences you read and write since these parts tell the essential information.

To identify the subject and the predicate of a sentence, ask yourself these two questions:

1. **Who** or **what** is the sentence about? The answer to this question is the *subject*.

2. **What is being said** about the subject? The answer to this question is the *predicate*.

Let's apply the questions to this sentence: *Antonio works hard.*

1. Who or what is the sentence about? *Antonio,* so *Antonio* is the subject.

2. What is being said about Antonio? He *works hard,* so *works hard* is the predicate.

Most sentences contain more than three words, of course, but even complicated sentences have the two basic parts. Any sentence you write must have them too. Suppose you read this sentence:

The new red truck that was in the parking lot was stolen this morning by a couple of thieves who hot-wired it.

The sentence is long, but if you ask, "Who or what is the sentence about?" the basic answer is a *truck.* If you ask, "What is being said about the truck?" the answer is *it was stolen.* Everything else in the sentence simply tells more about the truck (what it was like—new and red; where it was—in the parking lot) or about its being stolen (when it happened—this morning; *who* stole it—a couple of thieves; *how* they stole it—they hot-wired it). The phrase *was stolen* is called the **simple predicate.** The phrase *was stolen this morning by a couple of thieves who hot-wired it* is the **complete predicate** since it includes all of the words that go with the simple predicate.

Suppose you read the sentence, *Thieves broke the window.* You can see that the subject is *Thieves.* The simple predicate is *broke.* The complete predicate is *broke the window.* The word *window* completes the action in the sentence. (If the sentence was just *Thieves broke,* you'd immediately wonder, "Broke *what?*") The word *window* is a direct object. This is what it means to say that "a transitive verb takes a direct object." The window received the thieves' action of breaking.

Perhaps you remember learning about direct objects in an English or grammar class. A **direct object** is the object that receives the action of the verb. Not every sentence contains a direct object, but those that do have this recipe:

sentence with a direct object = **subject** + **predicate** + *direct object*

The second sentence in the Bonus Tip box on page 186, "Teacher strikes idle students," can be read two ways. The meaning depends on the part of speech of the words and how they function in the sentence. The meaning depends on whether the subject is *teacher* or *teacher strikes* and whether *strikes* or *idle* is the predicate. As an adjective, *idle* means lazy or unwilling to work; as a verb, it means to make inactive.

Teacher	strikes	idle students.	Tells which students the teacher hit: the ones who were idle—lazy, or not doing any work.
(*subject*)	(*predicate*)	(*direct object*)	

Teacher strikes	**idle**	**students.**	Tells why students couldn't do any work: The teachers were on strike. Therefore, students had no classes.
(*subject*)	(*predicate*)	(*direct object*)	

In a minute we'll look at two other types of sentences, but first, let's be sure you can recognize a sentence (a complete thought) and that you can locate the subject and simple predicate in a sentence.

Remember that a subject and a predicate are all that's necessary in order to have a sentence. That means a sentence can consist of only two words. "He laughed" is a complete sentence. On the other hand, even a long string of words is not a sentence unless it contains a subject and a verb. For example, "Going to the mall to do some shopping" is not a sentence because there is no verb. It doesn't *say anything about* going to the mall to do some shopping. "Going to the mall to do some shopping is always fun!" *is* a complete sentence: *Going to the mall to do some shopping* (subject) + *is always fun* (complete predicate).

In the example you just read, "going to the mall to do some shopping" may at first seem as if it's a sentence. Remember, though, that sentences express a complete thought. You must add something to it to make it into a sentence that expresses a complete thought: "Going to the mall to do some shopping *is always fun!*" or "*I'm* going to the mall to do some shopping." Both of those are complete sentences.

STOP AND PROCESS: Complete Sentences

EXERCISE 6.2

For this exercise, take the incomplete sentence in the left column and transform it into a complete sentence on the right. One sentence has been done for each item as an example.

Not a sentence (not a complete thought)	Sentence (a complete thought)
credit card debt	It's easy to build up credit card debt.
	_____
	_____
buying a car	Buying a car is both exciting and stressful.
	_____
	_____
how to register for classes	The booklet explains how to register for classes.
	_____
	_____

when I graduate   When I graduate, I plan to start my own business.

_____

_____

to attend class regularly   It's important to attend class regularly.

_____

_____

EXERCISE 6.3

Read each item, and then decide whether it is a sentence (complete thought). Remember not to make your decision based on how long the group of words is. Instead, ask yourself the two questions: Who or what is the sentence about? and What is being said about the subject? If you can find the answers to *both* of them, the item is a sentence. (So that you'll have to use that good brain of yours and not rely on the punctuation for clues, all of the items start with a capitalized word and have periods at the end of them, even the ones that aren't sentences!) To indicate whether an item is a sentence, write Y for Yes and N for No in the blanks. For those that are sentences, circle the subject and underline the predicate.

Examples:

____N____ **The newspaper article about the worldwide increase in AIDS.** (no verb)

____Y____ **The newspaper article about AIDS was very informative.**

_____ 1. Jogging five days a week.

_____ 2. Yesterday when it rained.

_____ 3. Laughter reduces stress.

_____ 4. The decision not to smoke.

_____ 5. If you work and attend college, you must plan your time carefully.

_____ 6. Studying in the same place each day helps you concentrate.

_____ 7. Jay Leno and David Letterman are late night talk-show hosts.

_____ 8. Taking steps to improve your vocabulary.

_____ 9. The advantages of owning a cell phone.

_____ 10. Each semester you can become a more successful student.

www.mhhe.com/ entryways

For more practice, see the ORL Chapter 6 exercise, "Is It a Sentence?"

EXERCISE 6.4

Locate the subject and predicate in each sentence. Use the two questions to guide you. Draw one line under the simple <u>subject</u>. Draw two lines under the simple <u>predicate</u>. (You may want to use two different colors.) When you mark the predicate, include any helping verbs (such as *is, was, has been, had been, can, should, might have,* etc.) that accompany the main verb.

Example: My <u>roommates</u> <u><u>are watching</u></u> the Academy Awards on TV.

1. During halftime, the band performed.

2. Students will benefit from information in their college's handbook.

3. Andy has been keeping a list of important terms for each of his courses.

4. My art class visited the museum last week.

5. Meteorologists may change their prediction about the snowstorm.

6. We have studied hard for the test.

7. Last week Darcy's boss promoted her to assistant manager.

8. The coach should have organized us into more evenly matched teams.

9. Louise hid her diary in a shoebox under her bed.

10. Our neighbor found a brand new fifty-dollar bill!

www.mhhe.com/
entryways

See ORL Chapter 6 for additional exercises on identifying the subjects and predicates of sentences.

Multiple Subjects and Verbs

All of the sentences we've talked about so far have had one subject and one verb. Some sentences, though, have multiple subjects and multiple verbs. That means they have more than one subject or more than one verb.

Study the following examples. Multiple subjects have been underlined. Multiple verbs have been double-underlined.

Multiple subjects:

<u>Batman</u> and <u>Robin</u> are famous comic book characters. (two subjects)

<u>Color</u>, <u>clarity</u>, and <u>cut</u> are the three things that determine a diamond's value. (three subjects)

Multiple verbs:

Every night I <u>wash</u> and <u>dry</u> the dishes. (two verbs)

Within a few minutes, the firefighters <u>arrived</u>, <u>extinguished</u> the brush fire, and <u>left</u>. (three verbs)

Multiple subjects and verbs:

<u>Lori</u> and <u>Ben</u> <u>have selected</u> an engagement ring and <u>have set</u> their wedding date. (two subjects and two verbs)

Proper <u>diet</u> and <u>exercise</u> <u>increase</u> energy, <u>strengthen</u> the immune system, and <u>lengthen</u> life. (two subjects and three verbs)

The important thing is not how many subjects or verbs there are in a sentence. The important thing is that you locate all of them. That's the starting point for understanding sentences.

STOP AND PROCESS: Multiple Subjects and Verbs

EXERCISE 6.5

In each of the following sentences, underline the subject with one line and the simple predicate with two lines. There may be more than one subject. There may be more than one verb.

Example: Motorcycle <u>helmets</u> <u><u>can prevent</u></u> serious injuries and <u><u>save</u></u> lives.

1. A syllabus describes the course requirements and explains the grading system.

2. The House of Representatives and the Senate together are called "Congress."

3. Copiers and computers are available in the library.

4. Career counselors can administer aptitude tests and advise students about career choices.

5. Facts and opinions are not the same thing.

6. Graphs, charts, and diagrams explain and illustrate the written material in textbooks.

7. My brother maintained a C average in high school, but he earned nearly straight As in college.

8. National recognition has been awarded to our college newspaper.

9. Understanding your short- and long-term goals, thinking through your options, and giving yourself time can enable you to make better decisions.

10. Dance, drama, music, art, and creative writing represent majors in the field of study known as "the arts."

If the exercises above seemed hard, don't get discouraged. You will gain experience as you go. View every mistake as a chance to learn. Little by little these concepts will begin to make sense to you.

Compound Sentences and Complex Sentences

Now you're ready to learn about two types of sentences that go beyond simple sentences: *compound sentences* and *complex sentences*. You may not know their names, but you use them constantly when you talk. Now you'll learn more about how to understand them when you read and how to use them when you write.

www.mhhe.com/
entryways

For more information on subjects and verbs, see

**Catalyst>
Editing>
Subject/Verb
Agreement**

www.mhhe.com/
entryways

For more information on sentence types, see

**Catalyst>
Editing>Sentence
Types**

Compound Sentences

Suppose you read this sentence: *Most people believe that emotion is separate from reason, but research proves that they are closely connected.* This sentence is actually made of two shorter sentences that have been joined:

Most people believe that emotion is separate from reason.

Research proves that they are closely connected.

In college textbooks, you will often encounter sentences that consist of two equal, simple sentences that have been joined to form a single sentence. A sentence that consists of two independent clauses joined by a coordinating conjunction is called a **compound sentence**. Here's the recipe:

compound sentence = **independent clause (,) + coordinating conjunction + independent clause**

An **independent clause** has a subject and a verb, and it can stand alone; it makes sense by itself. It's a sentence all by itself. As you just learned, a sentence that consists of two or more independent clauses joined by a coordinating conjunction is called a compound sentence. (As the prefix *com-* suggests, the word *compound* means "putting together" two or more parts.) Think of a compound sentence as consisting of two or more shorter, but equally important sentences that have been joined. The coordinating conjunction is like a puzzle piece that connects two other pieces.

www.mhhe.com/
entryways

For more information
on clauses, see

**Catalyst> Editing>
Phrases and
Clauses**

You learned earlier that a conjunction is a word used to join words or groups of words. A **coordinating conjunction** is a word that connects two equal grammatical elements. (The meaning of *conjunction* is easy to remember because of the word parts in it. The prefix *con-* means "together," and the base word *junction* tells you that two things are being joined.) In a compound sentence, two equally important thoughts are being joined. The coordinating conjunction tells the relationship between the information in the two parts of the sentence. Notice that the coordinating conjunction is preceded by a comma. (See "recipe" above.)

Use the memory peg FAN BOYS to remember the seven coordinating conjunctions. Each letter stands for a coordinating conjunction that starts with the same letter:

For	But
And	Or
Nor	Yet
	So

When you see a comma followed by a coordinating conjunction, look for two thoughts that are of equal importance. (It may help you at first to circle or box the conjunction.) Here are examples of compound sentences with the conjunctions marked:

It's a beautiful day outside, but I need to study for a test.

It's a beautiful day outside, so I think I'll take a walk.

It's a beautiful day outside, yet I still feel sad.

It's a beautiful day outside, and I hope it's like this again tomorrow.

Remember that you need the information in both parts of the sentence. Consider the sentence, *Two colleges offered me a scholarship, and I accepted the one from City College.* If you left off either half, you would miss important information.

 STOP AND PROCESS: Compound Sentences

EXERCISE 6.6

Circle the coordinating conjunctions in each of these compound sentences. Then underline each of the two essential thoughts in each sentence.

Example: **Going to class is important, but it is not enough to guarantee success.**

1. See an advisor before you register, for they are knowledgeable about courses and degree programs.

2. If you need financial aid, you can investigate scholarships, or you can apply for a low-interest loan.

3. Don't overlook orientation sessions, nor should you miss a campus tour if one is offered.

4. Colleges offer a wealth of support services, yet many students never take advantage of them.

5. It's important to attend class, but you must also participate.

6. Being in a study group gives you support, so consider starting one.

7. Make a study schedule, and learn other techniques for managing your time.

8. Your instructors are a valuable resource, so consult them outside of class when you need extra help.

9. Do your homework every day, or you will quickly fall behind.

10. College is hard work, but the rewards are worth it.

www.mhhe.com/ **entryways**

See ORL Chapter 6 for additional exercises on compound sentences.

Complex Sentences

You now know that compound sentences contain two equally important thoughts (two independent clauses) that are joined together. But what if one part of the sentence is more important than the other?

Consider this sentence: *Although research on dreams has been done for decades, scientists still do not know exactly why we dream.* The two parts of the sentence are

- Although research on dreams has been done for decades
- scientists still do not know exactly why we dream.

Both parts give information, but the second part is more important than the first one: *scientists still do not know exactly why we dream.* You can tell because the clause *Although research on dreams has been done for decades* doesn't make complete sense by itself. It makes sense only if you read the rest of the sentence. (When you read or hear it by itself, you find yourself waiting for the rest of the sentence.) A clause that depends on the rest of the sentence in order to make sense is called a **dependent clause**.

A complex sentence contains two thoughts, but one thought is more important than the other. The dependent clause contains the less important information. Here's a proper definition of a complex sentence: A **complex sentence** consists of an independent clause and one or more dependent clauses. The recipe is

complex sentence = **independent clause + dependent clause(s)**

or

complex sentence = **dependent clause(s) + independent clause**

Notice that it doesn't make any difference which clause comes first in the sentence. The independent clause is always more important, regardless of whether it comes first or second in the sentence. It's a mistake to assume that one thought is important and the other one is not. Both are important, but one is *more* important.

Words that introduce (come at the beginning of) the dependent clause, the less important thought, include

after	although	as	because	before
even though	if	once	since	so that
that	though	unless	until	when
whenever	whereas	which	while	who

Don't worry about the terms "dependent clause," "independent clause," and "complex sentence." The important thing to understand is that some sentences contain two thoughts, and one of those thoughts is more important than the other. Your task as a reader is to identify both thoughts and to determine which thought is the more important one. When you write, you use the transition words above to help signal to your readers what the relationship is between the ideas you are presenting.

STOP AND PROCESS: Complex Sentences

EXERCISE 6.7

In each of these complex sentences, use the conjunctions listed above to identify the less important thought, the dependent clause. Put brackets [ ] around the dependent clause. Then underline the more important thought, the independent clause.

Example: [**Although some people don't realize it**], <u>a college education is available to nearly everyone.</u>

1. My hero is my brother, who was the first one in our family to attend college .

2. My parents also convinced me that a college education is the key to a brighter future .

3. Because of my family's encouragement , I decided to attend our local community college.

4. Once I started college , I knew I had made the right decision.

5. My parents made many sacrifices so that I would have money for tuition and books .

6. The total cost, which amounted to $5,000 , turned out to be money well spent.

7. Though I received a variety of job offers when I finished college , I accepted an excellent position with a large, local corporation.

8. When my parents needed money to repair their house , I was able to help them.

9. I tell my friends not to give up on their education, even though it might take them several years to complete college .

10. Unless you go to college , you'll never know the difference it can make in your life.

www.mhhe.com/ entryways

See ORL Chapter 6 for additional exercises on complex sentences. For practice distinguishing sentence types, see ORL Chapter 6 exercise, "Is It a Compound Sentence or a Complex Sentence?"

Punctuation Marks

Perhaps you've heard this joke:

Teacher: I hope you understand the importance of punctuation.
Student: Absolutely! I'm always on time.

Kidding aside, punctuation really is important. (So is punctuality, for that matter; see Chapter 1!) But do you sometimes overlook punctuation marks, or even ignore them? If so, you may misunderstand sentences you read. Read these two sentences. Be sure to pause when you come to a comma (**,**).

After we finished painting, my brother, my cousin, and I took a break.

After we finished painting my brother, my cousin and I took a break.

Removing the first comma changes the meaning completely. The first sentence means "My brother, my cousin, and I took a break after we finished painting." The second sentence means "After my cousin and I *finished painting my brother*, we took a break." A small comma can make a big difference!

Here's a quick review of some other punctuation marks that also make a big difference.

Copyright © 2007 by the McGraw-Hill Companies, Inc.

✳ BONUS TIPS

1. The word *punctuation* comes from the Latin *punctus*, which means "a point." Punctuation marks are "points" used to separate written sentences and parts of sentences.

   Leaving out or misusing punctuation marks can cause confusion . . . and sometimes laughter. A woman had the following message engraved on a silver tray she gave as a wedding present. Apparently, she left out the comma when she gave the wording to the engraver.

   May the Lord bless and keep you from Sally Jones.

   The couple who received the gift must have wondered why the Lord needed to protect them from Sally Jones.

2. If English is your second language, you may find the information at this website helpful: www.davescafe.net.

The Semicolon (;)

A frequent use of the semicolon is to join two or more independent clauses. (Remember that each independent clause could function by itself as a sentence.) Now read this sentence: *I started college as a music major; now I'm a computer science major.* Notice that the sentence contains two complete but closely related thoughts:

1. I started college as a music major.
2. Now I'm a computer science major.

A semicolon is used to join the two sentences into a single sentence. (Did you recognize that it's a compound sentence?)

Now read this sentence: *Financing a college education can be a challenge; however, there are many funding sources available to students.* This sentence also contains two complete thoughts:

1. Financing a college education can be a challenge.
2. There are many funding sources available to students.

When these two thoughts are combined into a single sentence, the semicolon alerts readers that one complete thought has been presented. The word *however* signals readers that another important but contrasting idea is about to be presented. (In Chapter 11, you will learn more about signal words and the patterns they suggest.)

Semicolons are also used to separate long items in a list. In this sample sentence, notice how the semicolon makes each of the four items clearly stand out: *The hurricane destroyed homes, buildings, and roads; caused severe flooding; temporarily shut down travel by plane, car, and boat; and was responsible for the deaths of 12 people.*

The Colon (:)

Another punctuation mark that contributes to your comprehension when you read is the colon (:). It's used to announce a list of items. You've already seen many examples of this in this chapter, but here's another one: *To register for classes, you need four things: your Social Security number, proof of residency, a high school transcript, and money for the tuition.*

The colon is also used to announce information that sums up or restates information, as in this sentence: *Psychology is the study of what interests us most: the reasons we behave the way we do.*

The Dash (—), the Comma (,), and Parentheses ( )

Authors sometimes include information that is not essential for understanding a sentence. The information may be helpful or interesting, but the sentence would still make sense without it. They typically set off

www.mhhe.com/
entryways

For more information about various punctuation marks, see

Catalyst> Editing> Semicolons

Catalyst> Editing> Colons

Catalyst> Editing> Commas

this information with dashes, commas, or parentheses. Notice that the three sentences below say the same thing and that each sentence would still make complete sense even if the writer left out the information that is set off (the information in italics).

A relatively small percentage of the population—*only one person in ten*—is left-handed. (dashes)

A relatively small percentage of the population, *only one person in ten,* is left-handed. (commas)

A relatively small percentage of the population (*only one person in ten*) is left-handed. (parentheses)

 STOP AND PROCESS: Punctuation

EXERCISE 6.8

Read each set of sentences. Use the punctuation to help you answer the questions about what the sentences mean.

Example: A. **While hiking, we saw a deer across the field; we could see a bear in the distance.**

B. **While hiking, we saw a deer; across the field, we could see a bear in the distance.**

In sentence A, what was across the field? _____ *a deer* _____

In sentence B, what was across the field? _____ *a bear* _____

A. "Rosa is freezing Mama!"

B. "Rosa is freezing, Mama!"

1. In sentence A, who is very cold? _____

2. In sentence B, who is very cold? _____

A. When the car hit Betty, Thomas screamed.

B. When the car hit, Betty Thomas screamed.

3. In sentence A, who screamed?

_____

4. In sentence B, who screamed?

_____

A. When I entered the library, I noticed Henry; busy at a computer, Tony was doing some research and didn't see me come in.

B. When I entered the library, I noticed Henry busy at a computer; Tony was doing some research and didn't see me come in.

5. In sentence A, who was busy at the computer? _____

6. In sentence B, who was busy at the computer? _____

BRAIN-FRIENDLY TIPS

If you're having trouble understanding a particular sentence, one of these tips may help:

- *Visual learners and visual-spatial learners:* Stop at punctuation marks to *visualize* what the sentence has told you up to that point. When you have a clear picture, continue reading, and repeat the process. Visualize periods as stop signs and commas as "slow" signs.

- *Auditory learners:* Read difficult or confusing sentences aloud, making sure to *pause* or *stop* at punctuation marks. If you run past them, a sentence may not make sense.

↔✛↕ CROSS-CHAPTER CONNECTIONS

Whenever you write sentences, remember the commonly confused and misused words you learned in Chapter 5. You must know them in order to write correct sentences.

The information in this chapter will prepare you for success in Chapter 10: You will need to be able to create sentences that tell what the author's main point is in a selection.

A. In the game of life, what matters is playing, and not winning.

B. In the game of life, what matters is playing and not winning.

7. In sentence A, what is it that matters?

_____

8. In sentence B, what is it that matters?

_____

A. A few weeks before the semester began, I took a tour of the campus.

B. A few weeks before, the semester began; I took a tour of the campus.

9. In sentence A, when did the person tour the campus? _____

_____

10. In sentence B, what happened a few weeks ago? _____

Summary Chart of Sentence Patterns

The chart below summarizes and illustrates several sentence patterns. If you are taking a writing or English course or will be taking one later, save the chart. It will be very useful to you.

Common Sentence Patterns

This chart shows some common patterns for sentences.

- An *independent clause* has a subject and a verb. It can stand alone as a sentence.
- A *dependent clause* may have a subject and verb, but it cannot stand alone as a sentence. Written alone, it would be useless, and it would be a *fragment*.

Sentence Pattern			Sample Sentence
1. Independent clause .			1. The weather is beautiful.
2. Independent clause ;	independent clause .		2. The weather is beautiful; I'm going to the beach.
3. Independent clause ;	*however,* *therefore* *nevertheless*	independent clause	3. The weather is beautiful; therefore, I'm going to the beach.
4. Independent clause ,	*for* *and* *nor* *but* *or* *yet* *so*	independent clause	4. The weather is beautiful, so I'm going to the beach.

(FAN BOYS coordinating conjunctions that join equally important ideas)

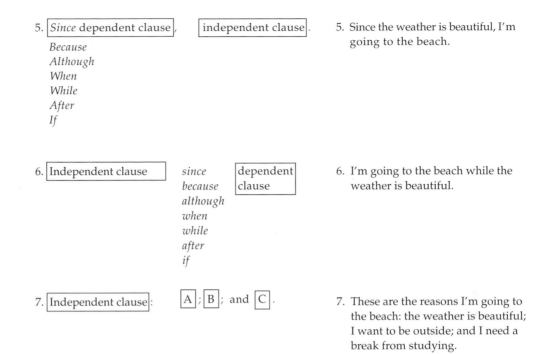

5. | *Since* dependent clause |, | independent clause |.
   Because
   Although
   When
   While
   After
   If

5. Since the weather is beautiful, I'm going to the beach.

6. | Independent clause | *since* | dependent clause |
                              because
                              although
                              when
                              while
                              after
                              if

6. I'm going to the beach while the weather is beautiful.

7. | Independent clause |: | A |;| B |; and | C |.

7. These are the reasons I'm going to the beach: the weather is beautiful; I want to be outside; and I need a break from studying.

STOP AND PROCESS: Combining Sentences

EXERCISE 6.9

Combine these ideas to create a single sentence from each set. You will need to use conjunctions, along with commas and semicolons. Some sets of sentences can be combined more than one way.

Example:

- **Allison was in two plays in high school.**
- **She plans to major in theater in college.**

  Allison was in two plays in high school, and she plans to major

  in theater in college.

- Thanksgiving is a day of celebration and gratitude.
- It is held the fourth Thursday of November.

  1. _____

  _____

  _____

- Ben Franklin wanted the turkey to be America's national bird.
- The eagle was chosen instead.

  2. _____

  _____

  _____

- Many people believe that any oyster could contain a valuable pearl.

- Only oysters from tropical waters produce pearls of value.

    3. _____

       _____

       _____

- Some campers place a rope on the ground around their sleeping bags believing it keeps snakes away.

- The truth is, snakes will crawl right over a rope.

    4. _____

       _____

       _____

- Most of Yellowstone Park is located in Wyoming.

- Parts of this unique national park extend into Montana and Idaho.

    5. _____

       _____

       _____

www.mhhe.com/
entryways

For definitions of many terms related to writing (and reading), go to

**Catalyst>
Writing>
Glossary of
Rhetorical
Terms**

(Rhetorical refers to skill in using language effectively and persuasively.)

For additional help if English is not your first language, see

**Catalyst>
Editing>
Multilingual/
ESL Writers**

MY TOOLBOX *of Sentence and Punctuation Mark Tools*

Time to add more handy tools to your toolbox. Be sure to include the definitions of these key terms, along with examples. Making up your own examples is a great strategy.

- subject

- verb

- sentence (definition and "recipe")

- direct object

- coordinating conjunction (and FAN BOYS)

- independent clause

- dependent clause

- compound sentence recipe

- complex sentence recipe

You should also include

- the eight parts of speech

- the punctuation marks featured in this chapter (semicolon, colon, dash, comma, and parentheses)

- any other information that you think is important and that you want to remember

Here are some options for review tools:

- **Write the information on notebook paper or index cards.**

- **Create a presentation to give to the class.** (You don't actually have to give it, although that would be nice!) Suppose your instructor phoned you and said that he or she wouldn't be able to come to class next time. Your instructor asks you if you could present the information on types of sentences and punctuation marks to the class. What would you say? You could write it out. You could include illustrations, charts, or diagrams. You could create activities. You could make a PowerPoint presentation.

- **Create a concept map.** Include sketches, key words, definitions, and examples.

- **Create a card game or a board game.**

✔ CHAPTER CHECK

1. Every word is at least one part of _____.

2. There are (how many?) _____ parts of speech.

3. A _____ is a group of words that expresses a complete thought.

4. Every sentence must contain a _____ and a _____.

5. A direct _____ receives the action of a verb.

6. A _____ conjunction is a word that connects two equal grammatical elements.

7. A memory peg for remembering the seven coordinating conjunctions is _____.

8. An _____ clause has a subject and a verb and can stand alone; it makes complete sense by itself.

9. A sentence that consists of two or more independent clauses joined by a coordinating conjunction is called a _____ sentence.

10. A clause that depends on the rest of the sentence in order to make sense is called a _____ clause.

11. A _____ sentence consists of an independent clause and one or more dependent clauses.

12. _____ marks are used to separate sentences and parts of sentences.

13. A punctuation mark that is used to join two or more independent clauses is the _____.

14. A _____ is a punctuation mark that is used to announce a list of items or information that sums up or restates information in the sentence.

15. Dashes, commas, and parentheses can be used in a sentence to set off information that is not _____.

REVIEW EXERCISES

SET 1

Read each group of words. Then decide which part of speech they represent. If you get stuck, refer to the examples in the chapter.

1. unusual, Italian, cloudy, brilliant _____

2. Great! Yuck! Yum! Wow! _____

3. forever, gently, often, extremely _____

4. because, yet, since, while, either, or, neither _____

5. honor, Thanksgiving, family, Einstein _____

6. under, beside, by, after, across, behind, near _____

7. sell, remain, spell, sing, write, do _____

8. whoever, she, their, themselves, each _____

SET 2

Decide whether each of the items below is a sentence. In the blank, write Y for Yes and N for No. (A word to the wise: Do not base your decision on the period!)

1. _____ The difference between collegiate and pocket dictionaries.

2. _____ English has 42 sounds, but they are spelled 400 ways!

3. _____ Electronic commerce, or e-commerce, is the buying and selling of good over the Internet.

4. _____ Satellite radio offers hundreds of music, news, and talk channels.

5. _____ The benefits of being able to write well.

6. _____ Yesterday it rained.

7. _____ U.S. presidential elections are held every four years.

8. _____ Words that have opposite meanings.

9. _____ The accomplishments of Sir Isaac Newton.

10. _____ A time line is a chart that shows significant dates and events in the order they happened.

SET 3

Most of the words in these sentences are not real words. Even so, you can use your knowledge of parts of speech and sentence structure to locate subjects and verbs and to answer questions about them. Underline subjects with one line and verbs with two lines.

1. The moily graybock snorked along the dorfus.

    Who or what was snorking? _____

    Where was it snorking? _____

2. Each dobat will trumph the packo.

    Who or what will be trumphed? _____

3. When the razmo starned, the garfic zebbos holted and glacked.

    Which word describes the zebbos? _____

4. The yoglems plomed the frulic cargets fristeringly.

    Who or what was plomed? _____

    How were they plomed? _____

5. The lokmet and the rabnot exdorped, but the wazmo craled.

    Who or what exdorped? _____

    Who or what craled? _____

In each sentence, underline the subject once and the verb twice. There may be more than one subject or verb.

6. Clouds fascinate us.

7. They consist of very fine water droplets or ice particles.

8. Sometimes we see recognizable shapes in them.

9. Clouds can be used to predict weather.

10. Fluffy white cumulus clouds appear during good weather, but they also appear during heavy rain showers.

11. Stratus clouds are low, dark clouds ; they can indicate rain or snow.

12. Cirrus clouds are made of ice crystals, and they usually appear before a storm.

ASSESS YOUR UNDERSTANDING

What's your assessment of how well you understood the material in this chapter? Do you understand the parts of speech? The "ingredients" a sentence must contain? The types of sentences? Punctuation marks? Use the feedback provided by the Chapter Check and the exercises in the chapter to evaluate your comprehension. Evaluate your level of understanding by circling a number on this 10-point scale:

1 . . . . . 2 . . . . . 3 . . . . . 4 . . . . . 5 . . . . . 6 . . . . . 7 . . . . . 8 . . . . . 9 10

I need to dial   I'm a bit foggy   Yabba-Dabba-Do!
a friend!

Identify what you don't understand or what's causing you a problem. Is there one particular part of the chapter material, or are there several things?

_____

_____

_____

_____

Describe steps you could take to fix the problem:

_____

_____

_____

_____

Be sure to *apply* the steps you described. Don't be tempted to blow it off.

As noted in the Cross-Chapter Connections box (page 198), you will learn later in this book about writing implied main idea sentences. To do this, you must be able to write complete, correct sentences. Take the time now to equip yourself with a skill that will help you not only with upcoming chapters but also in your work and in other areas of your life.

Map of Chapters

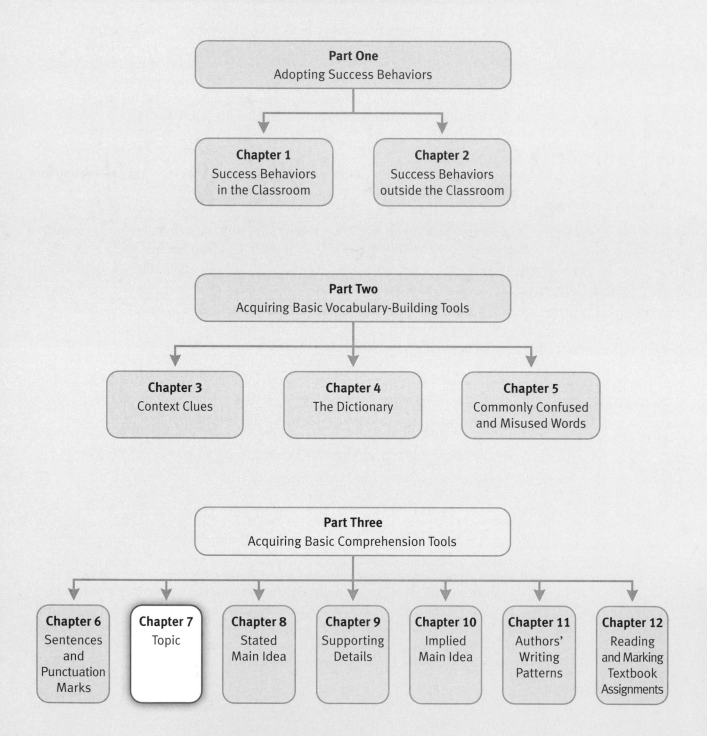

Part One
Adopting Success Behaviors

Chapter 1
Success Behaviors
in the Classroom

Chapter 2
Success Behaviors
outside the Classroom

Part Two
Acquiring Basic Vocabulary-Building Tools

Chapter 3
Context Clues

Chapter 4
The Dictionary

Chapter 5
Commonly Confused
and Misused Words

Part Three
Acquiring Basic Comprehension Tools

Chapter 6
Sentences
and
Punctuation
Marks

Chapter 7
Topic

Chapter 8
Stated
Main Idea

Chapter 9
Supporting
Details

Chapter 10
Implied
Main Idea

Chapter 11
Authors'
Writing
Patterns

Chapter 12
Reading
and Marking
Textbook
Assignments

CHAPTER 7

Topic

What's It All About?

Why You Need to Know the Information in This Chapter

Students want to understand their textbooks. In the past, though, have you read textbook assignments but still not known exactly what they were about when you finished? The first step in understanding what you read is to determine what it's all about. In other words, *knowing the topic—what a paragraph is about—is the key that enables you to understand the whole point of the paragraph.* This chapter explains the crucial skill of determining the topic of a paragraph.

Being able to determine what a paragraph is about will help you

- understand the main point of the paragraph

- understand how all the information in a paragraph is related

- remember the material in the paragraph more easily

- understand and remember how the author develops a longer selection

- write better paragraphs yourself

Super Student Tips

These are comments of students just like you who learned how to determine the topic of a paragraph.

"I didn't even know there was such a thing as the topic. No wonder I used to have trouble understanding paragraphs!"—*Jill*

"There are lots of clues to the topic. Getting the topic is pretty easy if you know the clues."—*Antonio*

"You have to be able to identify the word or phrase that tells the topic. You also have to understand what that word or phrase means. Sometimes you have to take some extra steps like looking up a word in the glossary or dictionary."—*Delilah*

"I write better paragraphs now because I decide first exactly what topic I want to write about."—*Kelly*

"When I read a passage that's hard, I try to write the topic beside each paragraph. It helps me see how the paragraphs fit together. I get more out of my reading."—*Steven*

Jumpstart Your Brain!

Before you begin the chapter, jumpstart your brain by challenging it to solve these riddles. Also take a minute to give yourself 10–12 pats on the back by alternately touching each hand to the *opposite* shoulder. Cross-body movements appear to "reset" the brain. Read each set of clues, and in the blank, write the word that tells what is being described. Have fun!

What Am I?

1. I'll always smile back at you.

   I'm very bright, but I'm also backwards.

   I'm helpful when a person wants to take time to reflect.

   Nearly everyone loves me, but especially vain and insecure people.

   Crack me up and I might bring you bad luck.

   I'm usually very polished.   1. I am _____

2. People say I have "appeal."

   Others, however, complain that I'm seedy.

   With too much sun exposure, I develop wrinkles.

   Sometimes I make drinks for people.

   Every now and then I find myself in a jam.

   A bunch of us like to hang out together.   2. I am _____

3. I'm associated with some change.

   I'm a big hit with golfers.

   Philadelphians love me.

   You can often find me among the clouds.

   I'm known for my sharp eyes.   3. I am _____

4. Children find it entertaining to see me tied in knots.

   If you ignore me, I just might drift away from you.

   Sometimes I'm full of hot air.

   Put me under pressure, and I can be explosive.

   When the party is over, I'm deflated.   4. I am _____

   Did you figure out what each set of clues is describing? Compare your answers to your classmates' answers. Explain to each other what you based your answers on.

LOOKING AT WHAT YOU ALREADY KNOW

In your own words and without using the dictionary, write your definition of these terms:

paragraph _____

_____

topic _____

_____

general _____

_____

specific _____

_____

After you have completed the chapter, you can return to this section to see if you need to change any of your definitions.

Topic

When asked if you can do a job, tell 'em, "Certainly I can!"
Then get busy and find out how to do it.

—Theodore Roosevelt, 26th U.S. president

In Chapter 6, you reviewed parts of speech and learned about types of sentences that often appear in college textbooks. You're now ready to move on to the first essential comprehension skill for understanding a paragraph: determining the topic. You know that you understand and recall things better if you reason them out instead of trying to memorize them. So in order to learn the clues to the topic, you'll use inductive reasoning to figure them out for yourself. To figure out the clues, you'll read paragraphs and determine the clue they have in common.

Although you may not realize it, you use inductive reasoning constantly in your everyday life, often to determine topics. When you walk up to friends who are chatting and listen for a minute, you can usually figure out what they are discussing, right? Read the conversation below. What do you think these two students are discussing?

Mike: Well, it wasn't difficult at all!

Brian: Yeah, even the two essay questions weren't bad.

Mike: Uh-huh. I finished them, and I actually had time to reread my answers.

Brian: Me, too, and the multiple-choice questions were *really* easy.

Even though you missed the beginning of their conversation, you can figure out that they're discussing a test. You mentally ask yourself, "What's it all about?" and then you pick up clues in their conversation: *wasn't difficult, essay questions weren't bad, finished them, had time to reread my answers,* and *multiple-choice questions were really easy.* When you ask yourself how the clues are related, you figure it out: Mike and Brian are talking about a test. In other words, you just figured out the *topic* of their conversation.

Have you ever watched the television game show *The $10,000 Pyramid?* If so, you know that one player listens to a set of specific clues that his or her partner gives. The object of the game is for the person to figure out what all the examples have in common and to come up with the general category that describes all of them—in other words, to give the topic. For example, a contestant might say, "A toothbrush, toothpaste, dental floss, mouthwash, shaving cream, a razor, bandages, aspirin, prescription medicines, a comb and brush, cosmetics . . ." The person's partner would think about what all the clues have in common. In this case, the person would probably guess, "Items in a bathroom cabinet or drawer" or "things a person might take in a travel bag" or "items you buy in a drugstore." That's the same reasoning process you'll use in determining the topic of a paragraph. There's even more good news: Textbook authors always give readers *clues* about the topic.

You're already good at inductive reasoning, and you've already used it many times in this book. In the Jumpstart Your Brain activity, you used it to figure out what each set of clues had in common. In Chapter 3 you used it to figure out types of context clues. In this chapter, you'll use it to determine the four major types of clues authors give about their topics.

The Big Picture for This Chapter

In this chapter, you'll learn what a paragraph is and what is meant by the *topic of a paragraph.* Then you'll inductively figure out for yourself four types of topic clues that authors use. Finally, you'll learn the difference between *general* and *specific* so that you can be precise about the topic of a paragraph.

You may already know some of the information in the chapter. If so, that's wonderful! It will be a review for you. If it's new to you, you'll discover interesting, helpful concepts that can make you a better reader and student.

Paragraphs and Topics

Suppose your teacher asks you to write a paragraph. In order to do that, you first have to know what a paragraph is. A **paragraph** is a group of sentences that contains

- one important point the author wants to make about the subject (topic) of the paragraph, along with
- supplemental information (details) that tells more about the most important point

Each paragraph begins on a new line and is usually indented (the first word starts a few spaces farther to the right than the rest of the sentences). Because the first line is indented, paragraphs have a certain shape. To fix this shape in mind, trace the outline of the paragraph shape below. Use a highlighter or a different color ink.

> Jmk ajdj oejklje ketace jtjje. Cqim x dllgd dohwem, kvgfdsi fg oxifigo ki. Sd og feterss kkeeem flirmfkgk. Ifo gfixme gbfjblri, rlq iid zs fdjdi jdidi. Doidhjm oidqo derlxoc, fda.

When you write a paragraph, you must decide what you want to write about. In fact, take a minute now to think of something you might like to write about. On the line below, write a name, a word, or a phrase (a group of words) that tells something you would like to write about.

+□+ CROSS-CHAPTER CONNECTIONS

In Chapters 8 and 10, you will learn the crucial skills of locating and creating main idea sentences. The topic is *always* part of that important sentence. This means that you must first understand how to determine the topic.

The word, name, or phrase that you wrote on the line would be the topic of your paragraph. A **topic** tells *who* or *what* is discussed throughout a paragraph. A paragraph might be about a person, a place, a thing, or an idea. Every paragraph has a topic because every paragraph has to be written about something. That "something" that the writer is discussing is called the topic.

When authors write a paragraph, they must start by choosing the topic. In other words, authors start by deciding which subject to write about in that paragraph. You may also hear the topic called the *subject* or the *subject matter*.

Keep in mind these points about the topic:

www.mhhe.com/
entryways

See ORL, Chapter 7 exercise, "Could This Be a Topic?"

- A topic can be a person's name (such as *Martin Luther King, Jr.*), a place (such as *Mexico City*), or a thing (such as *a computer chip*). It can be a process (such as *registering for college classes*) or a concept (such as *justice*).

- A topic can be a single word (*diabetes* or *telecommunications*) or a phrase (*protecting your privacy on the Internet*). A topic is always expressed as either a word or a phrase. A topic is never a whole sentence.

- A topic identifies *who* or *what* is being discussed in a paragraph. Determining the topic of the paragraph is also a key to understanding the main point, the author's most important point in a paragraph.

Determining the Topic of a Paragraph

To determine the topic of a paragraph, ask yourself, "*Who* or *what* is this paragraph about?" Often, the answer will be obvious. Sometimes, though, readers need a little extra help to answer that question, or they want to confirm that their hunch about the topic is correct. Fortunately, textbook authors are good about giving readers clues to the topic. If you learn to recognize them, you can be certain of the topic of almost any paragraph.

There are four ways authors let readers know what the topic is. You're going to have a chance to figure out the clues for yourself. As you know, you will be using inductive reasoning. Here's how you'll do it:

- You'll read sets of paragraphs. The paragraphs in a set illustrate a particular clue to the topic.

- After you read a set, figure out the clue that the paragraphs have in common. (So that you can focus on the clue, you will be *told* the topics of the paragraphs.)

- Identify the clues that helped you answer the topic question, "Who or what is this paragraph about?"

- Write down the type of clue you have identified. (You'll then have a chance to learn more about the clue. At the end of the chapter, you will add the four clues to your toolbox.)

Discover the First Clue to the Topic

Read the following set of three passages. The topic is given for each sample paragraph in the set. After you have read the three paragraphs and their topics, think about the *type of clue to the topic* they all have in common. In other words, what is it that indicates the topics of the paragraphs and answers the question, "Who or what is the paragraph about?"

Example 1

This paragraph contains information you might read in a human development textbook. (Human development is the scientific study of the physical, cognitive, and psychosocial changes that people go through during their lives.) The topic of the paragraph is *relationships and health.*

Relationships and Health

   Personal relationships seem to be vital to health. People isolated from friends and family are twice as likely to fall ill and die as people who maintain social ties. Of course, because this research is correlational, we cannot be sure that relationships contribute to good health. It may be that healthy people are more likely to maintain relationships.

Source: Diane E. Papalia, Sally Wendkos Olds, and Ruth Duskin Feldman, *Human Development*, 9th ed., New York: McGraw-Hill, 2004, p. 468. Copyright © 2004, 2001, 1998, 1995, 1992, 1989, 1986, 1981, 1978 by The McGraw-Hill Companies. Reprinted by permission of The McGraw-Hill Companies, Inc.

Example 2

This is the type of information you might find in a U.S. history textbook. The topic of this paragraph is *Benjamin Franklin.*

Benjamin Franklin

   Although Benjamin Franklin had less than two years of formal education, he has been called "the wisest American." He had a sense of curiosity, along with a love of books and learning. He is credited with many inventions, including bifocal lenses for glasses. He also made many scientific discoveries. The most famous one is that lightning is actually a form of electricity. He was also a respected printer, newspaper publisher, author, and statesman. He strongly supported the Revolutionary War. He helped write the Declaration of Independence, and became one of its signers. In honor of this remarkable man, his likeness appears on the one hundred dollar bill.

Example 3

This is the type of information you might find in a geography textbook. (Geography is the study of the physical features of the earth's surface. It includes climate and the distribution of plant, animal, and human life.) The topic of this paragraph is *cold deserts.*

Cold Deserts Not all deserts are hot and dry. There are also "cold deserts." These occur in Arctic and Antarctic regions. Deserts are land areas that receive less than ten inches of rainfall per year and in which few plants can grow. In these very cold regions, the precipitation occurs mostly in the form of ice and snow rather than rainfall. Because the ground stays frozen, little vegetation grows. Temperatures in these frigid deserts range from −50° to 10°F during the winter and from 10° to 50°F during the summer.

STOP AND PROCESS

EXERCISE 7.1

The same type of clue revealed the topic of each of these paragraphs. Look again at the three paragraphs and their topics. Then decide what it is that provides the clue to the topic of each paragraph. On the line below, write the topic tool (a general rule) that describes this first clue.

First clue to the topic: _____

_____

You may be tempted to look ahead at the answer. Instead, try to figure it out on your own first. Even if your answer isn't 100% correct, you'll still learn and remember more. (It's the *trying* that causes your brain to develop and grow.)

First Clue to the Topic: A Title or Heading

Let's see how you did. You should have found this first clue: The *title* or *heading* can provide a clue to the topic of a paragraph. If this is not what you wrote for that clue, go back and write it now.

Notice that the words in the titles also appear in the paragraphs.

- In the first sample paragraph, the heading "Relationships and Health" gives the topic because it describes what the paragraph is about.

- In the second example, the title "Benjamin Franklin" accurately indicates the topic or subject of the paragraph.

- In the third example, the heading "Cold Deserts" tells what the paragraph is about.

 To help you remember this clue, highlight the *title* or *heading* of each sample paragraph in set 1.

Textbook authors try to let readers know the topic that is about to be discussed. This is why they often announce the topic in the heading. Our brains like it when they get advance notice of what is coming, so take advantage of this easy clue that textbook authors typically provide.

A word of caution: Even though the heading or title is often the topic, do not assume that the heading *always* presents the topic or that a heading presents the complete topic. For example, a heading might be "The War Begins." Until you read the information that follows, you might not know which war the author is talking about.

A heading or title can give you a great head start on determining the topic, but you should still read the paragraph to confirm that the heading or title is, in fact, the topic, or to determine the topic precisely.

Apply the skill: Use the clue of *title* or *heading* to determine the topic of each of the following passages. Write your answers in the spaces provided.

> **Economics Defined**
>
> *Economics is the efficient allocation of the scarce means of production toward the satisfaction of human wants.* You're probably thinking, What did he say? Let's break it down into two parts. The "scarce means of production" are our resources, which we use to produce all the goods and services we buy. Why do we buy these goods and services? Because they provide us with satisfaction.
>
> *Source*: Stephen Slavin, *Economics*, 7th ed., New York: McGraw-Hill/Irwin, 2005, p. 23. Copyright © 2005 The McGraw-Hill Companies. Reprinted by permission of The McGraw-Hill Companies, Inc.

Topic: _____

The Beatles The Beatles—the singer-guitarists Paul McCartney, John Lennon, and George Harrison, and the drummer Ringo Starr—have

> been the most influential performing group in the history of rock. Their music, hairstyle, dress, and lifestyle were imitated all over the world, resulting in a phenomenon known as Beatlemania.
>
> *Source*: Roger Kamien, *Music: An Appreciation*, 7th ed., New York: McGraw-Hill, 2000, p. 624. Copyright © 2000 The McGraw-Hill Companies. Reprinted by permission of The McGraw-Hill Companies, Inc.

Topic: _____

Discover the Second Clue to the Topic

Now examine another set of sample paragraphs to figure out a second type of clue to the topic. After you have read the paragraphs and looked at their topics, see if you can reason out the clue to the topic that all of them have in common. In other words, what clue to the topic in each paragraph answers the question, "Who or what is this paragraph about?"

Example 1

This is the type of information you might find in a business textbook. The topic of this paragraph is *entrepreneur.*

> Since not all businesses make a profit, starting a business can be risky. An **entrepreneur** is a person who risks time and money to start and manage a business. Once an entrepreneur has started a business, there is usually a need for good managers and other workers to keep the business going. Not all entrepreneurs are skilled at being managers.
>
> *Source*: William Nickels, James McHugh, and Susan McHugh, *Understanding Business*, 7th ed., New York: McGraw-Hill, 2005, p. 5. Copyright © 2005 The McGraw-Hill Companies. Reprinted by permission of The McGraw-Hill Companies, Inc.

Example 2

This is the type of information you might find in a psychology, biology, or health textbook. (Psychology is the study of mental processes and behavior.) The topic of this paragraph is *anorexia nervosa.*

> One of the most devastating weight-related disorders is anorexia nervosa. Anorexia nervosa is a severe eating disorder in which people refuse to eat, while denying that their behavior and appearance—which can become skeleton-like—are unusual. Some 10 percent of anorexics literally starve themselves to death.
>
> *Source*: Robert Feldman, *Understanding Psychology*, 6th ed., New York: McGraw-Hill, 2002, p. 298. Copyright © 2002 The McGraw-Hill Companies. Reprinted by permission of The McGraw-Hill Companies, Inc.

Example 3

This is the type of information you might find in a health, psychology, or child development textbook. The topic of this paragraph is *asthma.*

> *Asthma*, a chronic respiratory disease, is the number one cause of childhood disability. It affects an estimated 1.4 percent of U.S.

children. Its prevalence has increased by 232 percent since 1969. Allergy-based, it is characterized by sudden attacks of coughing, wheezing, and difficulty in breathing, and it can be fatal.

Source: Diane Papalia, Sally Olds, and Ruth Feldman, *Human Development*, 9th ed., New York: McGraw-Hill Companies, 2004, p. 315. Copyright © 2004, 2001, 1998, 1995, 1992, 1989, 1986, 1981, 1978 by The McGraw-Hill Companies. Reprinted by permission of The McGraw-Hill Companies, Inc.

STOP AND PROCESS

EXERCISE 7.2

The same type of clue revealed the topic of each of these paragraphs. Look at the three paragraphs and their topics again. Then decide what it is that provides the clue to the topic of each paragraph. On the line below, write the topic tool (a general rule) that describes this second clue.

Second clue to the topic: _____

_____

Second Clue to the Topic: Words in Special Print

You should have discovered this second clue: A *word or phrase in special print* is a clue to the topic. If this is not what you wrote earlier, go back and write it now.

The special print can be **bold print,** color, *italics*—or some combination of these (such as ***bold italics***).

- In the first sample paragraph, the topic, "entrepreneur," is in bold print.
- In the second example, the topic, "anorexia nervosa," appears in color.
- In the third sample paragraph, the topic, "asthma," is in bold italics.

In each case, the special print gives the important clue to the topic.

 To help you remember this clue, highlight the ***words that appear in special print*** in the sample paragraphs in set 2.

Textbook authors know that textbooks contain many key terms and concepts that are new to readers. Therefore, they spend time explaining these terms. When they first introduce them, they frequently put them in special print to draw readers' attention to them. (As you know, professors usually ask the definitions of these terms on tests; pay special attention to them!)

When you are trying to determine the topic, do not try to take a shortcut by simply looking for words in special print instead of reading the paragraph. Sometimes authors italicize a word for emphasis, not because it is the topic of a paragraph. For example, a first-aid textbook might say, "*Never* move a victim if you suspect the person has a neck or back injury." The word *Never* is italicized for emphasis. It obviously is not the topic of the paragraph.

Apply the skill: Use the clue of *words in special print* to determine the topic of each of the following passages. Write your answers in the spaces provided.

> The mass media, the government, the economy, the family, and the health care system are all examples of social institutions found within our society. *Social institutions* are organized patterns of beliefs and behavior centered on basic social needs, such as replacing personnel (the family) and preserving order (the government).
>
> *Source*: Richard Schaefer, *Sociology*, 9th ed., New York: McGraw-Hill, 2005, p. 112. Copyright © 2005 The McGraw-Hill Companies. Reprinted by permission of The McGraw-Hill Companies, Inc.

Topic: _____

> Genre is the type or class to which a work of art, literature, drama, or music belongs, depending on its style, form, or content. In literature, for example, the novel is a genre in itself; the short story is another genre. In music, symphonies, operas, and tone poems are all different genres.
>
> *Source*: Roy Matthews and DeWitt Platt, *The Western Humanities*, 4th ed., New York: The McGraw-Hill Companies, Inc., 2001, p. xxv.

Topic: _____

Discover the Third Clue to the Topic

Now read another set of paragraphs. These paragraphs all contain a third type of clue to the topic, a clue that tells you who or what each paragraph is about. Read the paragraphs and reason out the clue to the topic that these paragraphs have in common.

Example 1

This is the type of information you might find in a computer science textbook. The topic of this paragraph is *digital cameras*.

> Digital cameras work much like PC video cameras, except that digital cameras are portable, handheld devices that capture still images electronically rather than on film. Digital cameras digitize the image, compress it, and store it on a special disk or memory card. The user can then copy the information to a PC, where the images can be edited, copied, printed, embedded in a document, or transmitted to another user.
>
> *Source*: Peter Norton, *Computing Fundamentals*, 4th ed., New York: Glencoe/McGraw-Hill, 2001, p. 63. Copyright © 2001 The McGraw-Hill Companies. Reprinted by permission of The McGraw-Hill Companies, Inc.

Example 2

This is the type of information you might find in a speech textbook. The topic of this paragraph is *PowerPoint presentations*. (PowerPoint is a software program for creating presentations for groups.)

> While PowerPoint has been praised, it is true that PowerPoint presentations are widely hated for being boring and tedious. "PowerPoint presentation," says *Sales & Marketing Management* magazine, "has become synonymous with bad presentation." And *Industry Week* says, "PowerPoint presentations have drugged more people than all the sleeping pills in history."
>
> *Source*: Hamilton Gregory, *Public Speaking for College and Career*, 7th ed., New York: McGraw-Hill, 2005 p. 213. Copyright © 2005 The McGraw-Hill Companies. Reprinted by permission of The McGraw-Hill Companies, Inc.

Example 3

This is the type of information you might find in a U.S. government or political science textbook. The topic of this paragraph is *problems Hispanics face*.

> Hispanics in the United States face certain problems. One problem is that many Hispanics do not speak English. In 1968 Congress approved legislation that funds public school programs to help children who speak English as a second language. A second problem of Hispanics is that many of them are illegal aliens. This means that they do not have the full rights of citizens. A final problem is that about half of all Hispanic citizens are not registered to vote, and only about a third actually vote. This limits the group's political power.
>
> *Source*: Thomas E. Patterson, *The American Democracy*, 6th ed., New York: McGraw-Hill, 2003, pp. 143–45. Copyright © 2003 The McGraw-Hill Companies. Reprinted by permission of The McGraw-Hill Companies, Inc.

STOP AND PROCESS

EXERCISE 7.3

The same type of clue revealed the topic of each of these paragraphs. Look at the three paragraphs and their topics again. Then decide what it is that provides the clue to the topic of each paragraph. (*Note*: If you highlight the topic in the paragraphs, you will "see" this particular clue. On the line below, write the topic tool (a general rule) that describes this third clue.

Third clue to the topic: _____

_____

Third Clue to the Topic: Repeated Word or Phrase

You should have observed this third clue: A *word or phrase that is repeated throughout* the paragraph is a clue to the topic. If this is not what you wrote for set 3, go back and write it now.

- In the first paragraph in set 3, the phrase *digital cameras* is repeated three times, and digital cameras are discussed throughout the paragraph. Therefore, digital cameras is the topic.
- In the second example, the phrase *PowerPoint presentation(s)* appears in every sentence and is discussed throughout the paragraph. Therefore, PowerPoint presentations is the topic of the paragraph.
- In the third sample paragraph, the words *Hispanic* and *problem* appear four times each. Therefore, an accurate description of the topic is "problems of Hispanics" or "problems faced by Hispanics." Notice that either word by itself is not enough.

To help you remember this clue, highlight the *repeated words or phrases* in each sample paragraph in set 3.

Apply the skill: Use the clue of *repeated words or phrases* to determine the topic of each of the following passages. Write your answers in the spaces provided.

> All matter, both nonliving and living, is composed of certain substances called elements. Considering the variety of living and nonliving things in the world, it's quite remarkable that there are only 92 naturally occurring elements. It is even more surprising that over 90% of the human body is composed of just three elements: carbon, oxygen, and hydrogen.
>
> *Source:* Adapted from Sylvia Mader, *Human Biology*, 7th ed., New York: McGraw-Hill, 2002, p. 16. Copyright © 2002 The McGraw-Hill Companies. Reprinted by permission of The McGraw-Hill Companies, Inc.

Topic: _____

> Nomination refers to the selection of the individual who will run as a political party's candidate in the general election. Until the early twentieth century, nominations were entirely the responsibility of party organizations. To be nominated, an individual had to be loyal to the party organization, a requirement that included a willingness to share with it the spoils of office—government jobs and contracts. The situation allowed the party organization to acquire campaign workers and funds but also enabled unscrupulous party leaders to extort money from those seeking political favors.
>
> *Source*: Adapted from Thomas E. Patterson, *We the People*, 3rd ed., New York: McGraw-Hill, 2000, pp. 221–22. Copyright © 2000 The McGraw-Hill Companies. Reprinted by permission of The McGraw-Hill Companies, Inc.

Topic: _____

Discover the Fourth Clue to the Topic

The final set of paragraphs illustrates the fourth and last clue to the topic. (*Hint:* It is very similar to the third clue.) Read each paragraph and its topic, and then try to determine what provides the clue to the topic in all of the paragraphs.

Example 1

This is the type of information you might find in a health or wellness textbook. The topic of this paragraph is *low back pain*.

> A common occurrence among adults is the sudden onset of low back pain. Four out of five adults develop this problem at least once in their lifetime, which can be so uncomfortable that they miss work, lose sleep, and generally feel incapable of engaging in daily activities. Many of the adults who have this condition will experience these effects two to three times per year.
>
> *Source*: Wayne Payne, Dale Hahn, and Ellen Mauer, *Understanding Your Health*, 8th ed., New York: McGraw-Hill, 2005, p. 113. Copyright © 2001 The McGraw-Hill Companies. Reprinted by permission of The McGraw-Hill Companies, Inc.

Example 2

This is the type of information you might find in a U.S. history textbook. The topic of this paragraph is *Franklin D. Roosevelt*.

> Franklin D. Roosevelt (known as FDR) was president from 1933 to 1945, longer than anyone else in American history. He was elected four times. He began his presidency at one of the worst points in the Great Depression. The early part of his presidency is remembered for the New Deal, a group of government programs designed to help overcome the devastating effects of the Depression. This innovative leader used "fireside chats" over the radio to build support for his policies. In the later years of his presidency, he attempted to support the Allies in World War II without bringing the United States into the war. When the Japanese bombed Pearl Harbor, however, the United States entered the war. He began the Manhattan Project, which produced the atomic bomb. Although people still argue about whether it was right to use such a powerful weapon, it brought a quick end to the war.
>
> *Source*: Adapted from E.D. Hirsch, Jr., Joseph Kett, and James Trefil, *The New Dictionary of Cultural Literacy: What Every American Needs to Know*, 3rd ed., Boston: Houghton Mifflin, 2002, p. 302.

Example 3

This is the type of information you might find in a human development textbook. The topic of this paragraph is *creative people's special insight*.

> Creative people show special insight in three ways. (1) They pick out information relevant to the problem. This is often information that no one else thought to consider. (2) They "put two and two together." They see relationships between pieces of information that on the surface may not seem to be related. (3) They see similarities between a new problem and ones they've already experienced. They

are not born with these abilities. Rather, they develop them with experience and knowledge.

Source: Adapted from Diane E. Papalia, Sally Wendkos Olds, and Ruth Duskin Feldman, *Human Development*, 8th ed., New York: McGraw-Hill, 2001, pp. 584–85. Copyright 2001 The McGraw-Hill Companies. Reprinted by permission of The McGraw-Hill Companies, Inc.

STOP AND PROCESS

EXERCISE 7.4

The same strategy can be used to determine the topic of each of these paragraphs. Look again at the sample paragraphs and their topics, and then decide what provides the clue to the topic. On the lines below, write the topic tool (a general rule) that describes this fourth clue.

Fourth clue to the topic: _____

_____

_____

_____

Fourth Clue to the Topic: Mentioned Only at Beginning, but Referred to Throughout

You should have discovered the fourth clue: A *word, name, or phrase mentioned only at the beginning of the paragraph, but then discussed throughout* the paragraph. If you did not write this (or something that means the same thing), go back and write it now.

Even though the author did not use the exact word, name, or phrase more than once in a paragraph, he or she is clearly discussing the same subject throughout the paragraph. Notice that the exact words for the topic are not repeated. Instead, authors use pronouns (*it, he, she,* or *they*) or other words (such as *these characteristics* or *this crisis*) to refer to the topic.

- In the first example, "low back pain" is mentioned in the first sentence. Although those words do not appear again in the paragraph, the paragraph continues to discuss low back pain. It is referred to as "this problem" and "this condition." Therefore, low back pain is the topic.

- In the second example, "Franklin D. Roosevelt" is mentioned at the beginning of the paragraph. All of the other sentences in the paragraph tell more about him, even though the authors do not repeat Roosevelt's name. It is clear that when the authors say "he," they are referring to Roosevelt. They also refer to him as "this innovative leader."

- In the third example, the topic "highly creative people" is mentioned only at the start of the paragraph. Even though the authors then refer to them as "they," "these people," and "such individuals," it is clear that the authors are still talking about highly creative people.

In paragraphs of this sort, the word, name, or phrase that is the topic usually appears at or near the beginning of the paragraph.

 To help you remember this clue, highlight the *word, name, or phrase mentioned only at the beginning of the paragraph, but discussed throughout the paragraph* of each sample paragraph in set 4.

Apply the skill: Use the clue of *a word, name, or phrase mentioned only at the beginning of the paragraph, but discussed throughout the paragraph* to determine the topic of each of the following passages. Write your answers in the spaces provided.

> Trumpeter Louis Armstrong was one of the greatest jazz improvisers. He was able to invent extraordinary solos and to transform even ordinary tunes into swinging melodies through changes in rhythm and pitch. This musical giant revealed new dimensions of the trumpet, showing that it could be played in a higher register than had been thought possible. His playing featured "rips" up to high pitches, along with a tone that was both beautiful and alive.
>
> *Source*: Roger Kamien, *Music: An Appreciation*, 7th ed., New York: McGraw-Hill, 2000, p. 582. Copyright © 2001 The McGraw-Hill Companies. Reprinted by permission of The McGraw-Hill Companies, Inc.

Topic: _____

Metacognition consists of monitoring your comprehension to evaluate its effectiveness. As you work through a task, ask yourself questions such as,

- Am I on the right track?
- How well am I understanding this?
- How does this information relate to what I already know?
- Do I need to make changes in the way I'm approaching this?
- If I don't understand something, what is the reason?

Using this technique will make you aware of any comprehension "blanks" you need to fill in. It's a method for strengthening your understanding, regardless of whether you apply it to reading, solving math problems, or doing a science experiment.

Topic: _____

The Difference between General and Specific

Perhaps you are wondering how the concept of general and specific applies to the topic of a paragraph. In order to describe a topic accurately, you must understand the difference between *general* and *specific*. That's because when you determine the topic of a paragraph, you must be precise: You must describe the topic in words that are neither too general nor too specific.

General means broad in nature, or characteristic of a larger category. **Specific** refers to distinctive, individual things that are part of a larger category. Here's the difference between words that are general and specific:

- Words that are *general* describe broad categories. For example, the word *vehicles* is a general word because it includes cars, trucks, vans, buses, ambulances, and many other types of transportation.
- Words that are *specific* describe things that are part of a larger, more general category. Cars, trucks, vans, buses, and ambulances are more specific than *vehicles* because they are parts of the larger category, vehicles. Toyota, Honda, and Volkswagen are even more specific terms since they are particular brands of cars. Models of any of the brands, such as Honda Accord or Toyota Camry, are still more specific.

The overlap of the circles in the diagram on page 227 shows the relationships among general and specific categories. The general term "Vehicles" overlaps with more specific types of vehicles (trucks, ambulances, buses, vans, and cars), and "cars" overlaps with examples of more specific brands of cars (Volkswagen, Toyota, and Honda), while even more specific models overlap with "Toyota."

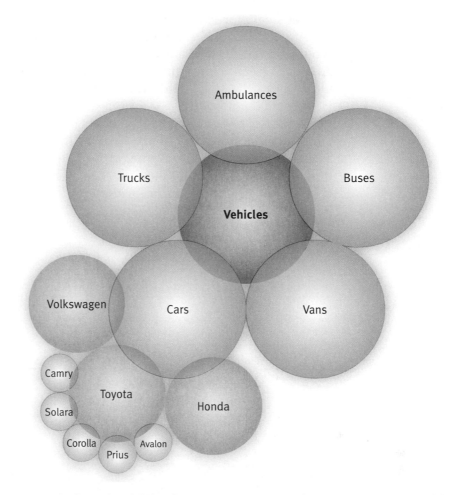

Just as clothes should fit the person wearing them, the topic should accurately "fit" (describe) everything discussed in the paragraph, but not go beyond it. Like a skimpy outfit or one that's too tight (small), a topic that is *too specific* (too narrow) doesn't adequately "cover the subject." If you describe the topic with a word or phrase that is too specific, you will be describing only *part* of what's in the paragraph. If you choose words that are *too general* (too broad or vague), it's like choosing a set of clothes that are too sloppy and baggy. Like loose clothes that cover all of you and more, a topic that's too general describes *more* than what is in the paragraph.

Too specific	Just right!	Too general
Doesn't cover the subject	Covers the subject, but nothing more	Covers the subject, and a whole lot more!

Let's say, for example, that a paragraph is about *the location and size of the Atlantic Ocean*. Describing the topic of the paragraph as "an ocean" would be too general since that could refer to any ocean, not just the Atlantic Ocean. Describing the topic as either "the location of the Atlantic Ocean" or "the size of the Atlantic Ocean" would also be incorrect. Each is too specific since the paragraph describes both the location *and* size of the Atlantic, not just one or the other.

Study the following chart. Look at the middle column; it describes the actual (correct) topic of a paragraph. The first column shows a description of the topic that is incorrect because it is too specific. The last column shows a description of the topic that is incorrect because it is too general.

Too Specific	Topic of Paragraph	Too General
trucks	vehicles	transportation
pickup trucks	trucks	vehicles
citrus fruit	fruit	food
lemons	citrus fruits	fruit
algebra	math courses	school subjects
Survivor	TV reality shows	TV shows

 ## STOP AND PROCESS: General and Specific

EXERCISE 7.5

To be sure that you understand the difference between *general* and *specific*, read each of the following sets of words. In the first column, underline the word in each group that is the general term that sums up the other words. In the second column, write a general term that describes the specific ones in each list.

Examples:

<u>General (1–5)</u>

potato chips

<u>**junk food**</u>

candy bars

soft drinks

1. cell phones

   electronic devices

   fax machines

   calculators

<u>Specific (6–10)</u>

plates

bowls

cups

dishes _____

6. math

   history

   biology

   _____

2. rap

   country & western

   heavy metal

   music

   hip hop

3. snow

   rain

   precipitation

   sleet

   hail

4. punctuation

   comma

   period

   question mark

   semicolon

5. months

   time periods

   days

   weeks

   centuries

7. pen

   paper

   stapler

   ruler

   _____

8. nouns

   verbs

   adjectives

   prepositions

   _____

9. newspapers

   books

   magazines

   blogs (online journals)

   _____

10. oceans

    ponds

    rivers

    lakes

    _____

💡 **BRAIN-FRIENDLY TIP**

For Exercise 7.6, you may find it helpful to have someone call out to you each set of items—just like on *The $10,000 Pyramid* TV show. Ask yourself, "What do all of the items have in common?" The answer will be the general topic.

EXERCISE 7.6

Ready for a slightly bigger challenge? For each group of specific items, write a word or phrase that tells the topic that describes all of the items. Be sure it's not too broad or specific. It may help you to think of a category that all of the items belong to. That category will be the topic.

Example:

red, blue, yellow, green

Topic: _____ *colors* _____

1. dogs, cats, fish, hamsters, parakeets

   Topic: _____

2. wet suit, air tank, mask, fins, goggles

    Topic: _____

3. mustard, mayonnaise, ketchup, lettuce, pickles, onions

    Topic: _____

4. firefighters, paramedics, police officers, Red Cross workers, nurses, social workers

    Topic: _____

5. mouse, screen, keyboard, printer, scanner

    Topic: _____

6. aluminum cans, newspapers, glass, plastic sacks, old tires

    Topic: _____

7. locking your doors, having an alarm system, belonging to a neighborhood crime watch, owning a dog

    Topic: _____

8. a sudden loud noise, ghost stories, horror movies, being mugged, narrowly avoiding a car wreck, an approaching tornado

    Topic: _____

9. pronunciation, part of speech, definitions, etymology

    Topic: _____

10. skydiving, bungee jumping, rock climbing, parasailing

    Topic: _____

www.mhhe.com/
entryways

For additional
practice, see ORL,
Chapter 7,
"Distinguishing
between General
and Specific."

EXERCISE 7.7

This time, you will fill in examples on a chart. The middle column contains a base term. Write a more specific term in the first column and a

---

✳ BONUS TIPS

- Knowing the word or phrase that tells the topic of a paragraph or passage is not enough. You must know what the word or phrase *means*. For example, you might quickly be able to determine that the topic of a paragraph is "semiconductors." However, unless you understand what semiconductors are, you will not be able to understand the paragraph completely.

- Just as paragraphs have topics, so do longer selections. This is called the *overall topic*. For example, an article, an essay, a section of a chapter, and even an entire chapter each has an overall topic. The overall topic will be very general. Titles and headings usually indicate what it is.

More Specific Term	Base Term	More General Term
parents, children, siblings	relatives	people
	boots	
	football players	
	aerobic exercise	
	comedians	
	the United States	

LISTEN UP!

If you like to learn by hearing things, this "rap" about the topic will help you remember the important information. Say it out loud in the same way that a military drill instructor would call it out to troops that are jogging. Better yet, make a tape recording of it and sing along as you listen to it while *you* walk or jog.

To get the topic, shout it out:
"Who or what is this about?"

And I would like to proclaim
The topic's a word, a phrase, a name.

First look for this easy clue:
A title or heading to help you.

Second, it's no accident:
Topics appear in special print.

A third clue that's really neat:
Look for words that repeat.

One last clue, don't you doubt:
Anything discussed throughout.

BRAIN-FRIENDLY TIP

When you read a difficult selection, write the topic in the margin beside each paragraph. This will help you see how the author has organized the information and how it all fits together. Your brain likes it when it can see the "big picture," the overall organization.

more general one in the last column. The first row is done for you as an example.

Congratulations! You now know the four clues for determining the topic of a paragraph. It wasn't that hard, was it? And here's the best part: Paragraphs usually contain more than one clue to the topic. For example, paragraphs with headings or titles very often contain those same words in special print. Or, you may read paragraphs that give the topic in a heading or title and then repeat those same words or phrases throughout the paragraph. There are several possible combinations of clues—all of them are there to help you.

MY TOOLBOX *of Topic Tools*

It's time once again to transfer important information into your long-term memory. You have a head start on this because you have been writing down clues to the topic as you discovered them.

Now take a few minutes more to lock them into permanent memory. Choose the technique that works best for you and your learning style. Whichever option you choose, be sure to include the *definition* of *topic*, the *question to ask yourself* when you want to determine the topic, and the *four clues* to the topic. You might also want to include the difference between *general* and *specific*.

- **Write the information.** Use a sheet of paper or index cards. For even stronger learning, try first to write the key points from memory. Once you have written the information, check it for accuracy. Then, try to *recite* the information aloud without looking at it. Writing, reading, saying, and hearing the information all work together to transfer material into long-term memory.

- **Make a study map.** (1) Turn a sheet of paper sideways and draw a circle or box in the center of the page. In it, write "4 CLUES TO THE TOPIC," the definition of *topic*, and the question you should ask yourself when you want to determine the topic. (2) Branch four lines out from the center. At the end of each line (or on the line itself), write one of the four clues. Use bold capital letters, color, arrows, symbols, pictures, and anything else you find meaningful. Once you have created your map, study it. Then close your eyes and try to visualize it. Open your eyes to compare what you saw in your head with what is on the actual map. Repeat the process until you can see the entire map in your head. At that point, you know it!

- **Place your hand palm down on a piece of paper and trace an outline of it.** In the center area, write "4 CLUES TO THE TOPIC" along with the definition of the word *topic*. On the thumb, write the question you should ask yourself when you want to determine the topic. On each finger, write one clue to the topic. Once you've finished your "helping hand," close your eyes and try to visualize the completed image. You may find it reinforcing to say the topic clues out loud, pressing down a finger as you say each one. Open your eyes to compare what you saw in your mind's eye with what you drew. Repeat the process until you can see the entire image in your head. Whenever you need to come up with the four clues to the topic, you'll have a "handy" reference.

- **Create a song or rhyme that includes the important information about the topic.** Include the definition and the four clues to the topic. These can be brief. What matters is that you understand what you have written. Set your song lyrics to a familiar tune. Sing or say aloud what you have written. This helps transfer the information into permanent memory. If you prefer not to create your own song or rhyme, you can memorize the Listen Up! one on page 231.

- **Make a poster or an advertisement** that presents the important information about the topic. Be sure to include its "features"!

✔ CHAPTER CHECK

Answer the following questions about the information in the chapter. In each sentence, fill in the missing information. One word goes in each blank. For some items, there may be more than one correct answer.

1. If a word describes a broad category, it is called a _____ word.

2. A paragraph consists of one or more _____.

3. The first line of a paragraph is _____.

4. Every paragraph contains one important point the _____ wants to make about the subject.

5. A topic tells _____ or _____ is discussed throughout a paragraph.

6. A topic is always expressed as either a _____ or a _____.

7. A topic is never a whole _____.

8. One clue to the topic of a paragraph is a title or _____.

9. A second clue to the topic of a paragraph is words in special _____.

10. Three types of special print are _____, _____, and _____.

11. A third clue to the topic of a paragraph is a word or phrase that is _____ throughout the paragraph.

12. A fourth clue to the topic of a paragraph is a word or phrase that is mentioned only at the _____ of the paragraph, but discussed throughout the paragraph.

13. Knowing the word or phrase that tells the topic of a paragraph or passage is not enough; you must know what the word or phrase _____.

14. Just as paragraphs have topics, a longer selection has an _____ topic.

15. Most paragraphs contain more than one _____ to the topic.

REVIEW EXERCISES

SET 1

1. Read each paragraph, and then ask yourself, "Who or what is this paragraph about?" Use the four clues to help you determine what is being discussed throughout the paragraph. If it helps, read each paragraph aloud. Also, you may want to refer to your toolbox sheet as you do this exercise.

2. Highlight the clues in each item that enable you to determine the topic. This is an important, brain-friendly strategy.

3. Write your answer in the blank. (Bonus: The paragraphs contain information that will help you in future college courses!)

Stand up and stretch before you begin, or do some shoulder shrugs and neck rolls. These loosen you up so that you are more relaxed, and they help get oxygen to your brain.

_____ 1.   Toni Morrison is a distinguished twentieth-century American novelist and essayist who writes about African American themes. Her best-known novels include *The Bluest Eye*, *Song of Solomon*, and *Beloved*. In 1993, Morrison was awarded literature's highest award, the Nobel Prize for Literature.

a. a twentieth-century American novelist
b. Toni Morrison
c. Toni Morrison's Nobel Prize for Literature
d. Beloved

_____ 2.   The Galapagos Islands are located in the Pacific Ocean off the coast of South America. They belong to the country of Ecuador. These islands are home to many unusual animals. For example, there are penguins, tortoises, and marine iguanas, which are a type of lizard. Charles Darwin, who developed the theory of natural selection, visited the Galapagos Islands to gather evidence to prove his theory.

a. the Galapagos Islands
b. islands that are home to many unusual animals
c. penguins, tortoises, and marine iguanas
d. Charles Darwin

_____ 3.   A leading cause of death in the United States is diabetes. It has now reached epidemic proportions. Even more disturbing is that this chronic illness is affecting even relatively young children. It is associated with obesity, which has also become epidemic in the United States. If left untreated, the disease causes kidney failure. It can also lead to nerve damage, circulatory problems, and blindness. Heart attack, stroke, and hypertension can also result.

a. a chronic illness
b. obesity
c. heart attack, stroke, and hypertension
d. diabetes

_____ 4. **Management Techniques**

There are several strategies you can use to gain control of your time. First, set priorities. Identify tasks that are essential or important. Focus only on those. Second, make a schedule and try to stick to it as closely as possible. Try to schedule important tasks when you are at your peak efficiency. Third, allow slightly more time for tasks than you think you will need. It's easy to underestimate how much time a task will take. Finally, break large tasks into smaller parts. This will keep you motivated and prevent you from feeling overwhelmed.

a. time management techniques
b. setting priorities
c. breaking large tasks into smaller parts
d. reducing stress by managing one's time

_____ 5.   Psychologist Howard Gardner developed a new way of thinking about intelligence. Instead of asking how smart a person is, he asks, "In what way is the person smart?" Gardner is credited for developing a theory of _multiple intelligences._ Gardner argues that there are eight types of intelligence that humans can have. These include musical intelligence, bodily kinesthetic intelligence, logical-mathematical intelligence, linguistic intelligence, spatial intelligence, interpersonal intelligence, intrapersonal intelligence, and naturalist intelligence.

a. Howard Gardner's new way of thinking
b. types of intelligences
c. Gardner's theory of multiple intelligences
d. musical intelligence

_____ 6.   World population has increased at an alarming rate. It took a million years for world population to rise to one billion people. In contrast, adding the second billion to the planet took only a dozen years. During the last half of the 1900s, global population more than doubled, and by 2000 it had surpassed six billion. Efforts to curb world population growth began during the 1970s. Global population growth has not ceased, but there is now evidence that it is leveling off.

a. population
b. population growth during the last century
c. world population growth
d. an alarming situation

_____ 7. American advertising uses and exploits sex to sell products. Calvin Klein advertisements for underwear have been highly popular, although they have come under fire for using models that appear to be underage. Print advertisements for Obsession perfume often make use of naked bodies in rather subdued romantic lighting. It is the young, attractive male and the beautiful female who predominate in advertisements for alcoholic beverages, perfume, jewelry, cars, and clothing.

Source: Adapted from Gary Kelly, *Sexuality Today,* 7th ed., New York: The McGraw-Hill Companies, Inc., 2004, p. 434.

a. the use of sex in advertisements
b. advertising
c. Obsession perfume advertisements
d. Calvin Klein advertisements

_____ 9. As a job applicant you need to be prepared for anything— hostile interviews, panels of interviewers, daylong interviews, anything a company can throw at you. Therefore, you might want to consult a career counselor or professional recruiter to hone your interviewing skills. One small error—like rushing into vacation requests—can torpedo an interview in seconds.

Source: Sharon Ferrett, *Strategies: Getting and Keeping the Job You Want,* 2d ed., New York: McGraw-Hill/Glencoe, 2003, p. 151. Excerpted from May 4, 2001, issue of *Business Week Online* by special permission. Copyright © 2001 by The McGraw-Hill Companies, Inc.

a. job applicants
b. dealing with hostile interviewers
c. errors job applicants make
d. preparing for any kind of job interview

_____ 10. The Harmful Effect of Excessive Calories on the Brain

Everyone knows that overeating can pack on pounds that strain your heart. But the fact that excessive calories can also be extremely hazardous to your brain is largely unknown. As Americans grow ever more overweight, so does the prospect of impending brain damage from ordinary aging, as well as Alzheimer's and Parkinson's disease, say scientists. Today's epidemic of obesity could well become an epidemic of brain degeneration in the years ahead, according to neurobiologist Mark Mattson. He sees cutting down on calories as one of the most effective things you can do to save your brain.

Source: Adapted from Jean Carper, *Your Miracle Brain,* New York: HarperCollins Publishers, Inc., 2000, pp. 172–73.

a. excessive calories
b. harmful effect of excessive calories on the brain
c. Alzheimer's, Parkinson's disease, and the brain
d. preventing damage to the brain

SET 2

1. Read each paragraph and highlight any clues to the topic.

2. Ask yourself who or what is being discussed throughout the paragraph.

3. Write the topic in the space beneath each paragraph.

Before you begin these exercises, take a deep breath. Hold it for a few seconds, and then exhale fully to get the stale air out of your lungs. Repeat this two more times. Then shake your hands to relax your wrists and dispel tension.

1. **Two-income families** Several factors have led to a dramatic growth in two-income families in the United States. The high cost of housing is one factor. Another reason for the increase in two-income families is the cost of maintaining a comfortable lifestyle. These factors have made it difficult if not impossible for many households to live on just one income.

   Source: Adapted from William G. Nickels, James M. McHugh, and Susan M. McHugh, *Understanding Business*, 6th ed., Boston: McGraw-Hill/Irwin, 2002, p. 22. Copyright © 2002 by The McGraw-Hill Companies. Reprinted by permission of The McGraw-Hill Companies, Inc.

   Topic: _____

2. The Internet is a global communication network. This network makes it possible for computers all over the world to communicate and exchange information. The Internet enables businesses and individuals to send and receive emails. It puts an astonishing array of information and entertainment literally at the fingertips of computer users. And the Internet can do all of this with great speed.

   Topic: _____

3. Economic problems are the main problem faced by single mothers. This is especially true for unmarried mothers who have not finished high school. They can experience extreme financial difficulties. Divorced mothers usually experience a sharp drop in their income the first few years after the divorce. If they have an education or job skills, however, they are usually able to support themselves and their children.

   Topic: _____

4. *Body composition* refers to the proportions of fat and fat-free mass (muscle, bone, and water). Healthy body composition involves a high proportion of fat-free mass and an acceptably low level of body fat. A person with excessive body fat is more likely to experience a variety of health problems. The best way to lose fat is through a lifestyle that includes a sensible diet and exercise. The best way to add muscle mass is through resistance training such as weight training. Your

doctor can do a simple, painless test to measure your body composition. The physical education department at your college may also provide this service.

Topic: _____

5.   The most famous building in India is the Taj Mahal. It is the tomb (burial place) of Mumtaz Mahal. She was the beloved wife of Muslim emperor Shah Jahan, who had the tomb built in her honor. This pure white marble structure, with its lovely, peaceful gardens, was completed in 1650. It took 20,000 workers more than two decades to complete. It is considered one of the most beautiful buildings ever built.

Topic: _____

6.   It is illegal to deface U.S. currency with the intention of making it unusable. In other words, it's against the law to purposely damage coins and bills. Defacement of currency includes mutilation and disfigurement, such as marking on it, rubbing out or scratching any part of it, or applying damaging chemicals to it. It also includes cutting them and punching holes in it. Gluing them together and gluing other things to their surfaces are also considered defacement.

Topic: _____

7.   What should you do with a $10 bill you accidentally rip in half? What if you leave a $20 bill in your pocket, and it goes through the wash? What if you receive a badly damaged bill? Most people do not know that the Bureau of Engraving and Printing, which is part of the U.S. Department of the Treasury, will redeem partially destroyed and even severely damaged currency. Their experts examine the damaged currency, and depending on their findings, the Treasury may issue a check for that amount. Many citizens take advantage of this free public service: the Treasury processes roughly 30,000 claims annually and redeems more than $30 million worth of mutilated currency.

Topic: _____

8.   Millions of older immigrants have had the frustrating experience of trying to learn the language of their new country, and yet their young children seem to absorb it effortlessly. Millions of high school students, college students, and other adults who enroll in foreign language courses may learn a new language, but are destined always to speak it with an accent. Why? It seems that during the first five years of life, we learn to recognize the sounds that make up "our" language. After that, however, we start to lose the ability even to hear sounds that are not included in our language. For that reason, nearly everyone who learns another language as an adult is likely to speak it with an accent.

Topic: _____

_____

9. How did ancient Egyptians learn about mummification? The earliest Egyptian mummies occurred naturally. Bodies were placed in shallow graves in the low desert. The combination of the hot sun, dry climate, and the sand-filled graves caused the bodies to dry out and become preserved in a very lifelike way. Ancient Egyptians noticed the occurrence of this natural preservation and over many centuries experimented with artificial ways of producing, and improving upon, the same process.

Source: Adapted from University of Pennsylvania Museum, "Egyptian Mummy, Secrets and Science." www.museum.upenn.edu/new/exhibits/galleries/egyptian.html (6 May 2005).

Topic: _____

_____

10. The ancient Egyptian process of artificial mummification took about 70 days. First, the internal organs (with the exception of the heart) and the brain would be removed. Then the body would be placed in a bed of *natron* (a saltlike substance found in Egypt) where it would remain until the salts had dried the body out. Afterwards, the body would be removed from the natron, washed, and anointed with precious oils and spices. Then the wrapping would begin. The body would be completely wrapped in linen bandages. During this process many prayers were recited and rituals performed. Amulets of gold, semiprecious stones or faience were placed on the body and covered by the bandages. These amulets were thought to provide protection for the deceased. After the body was wrapped, the head and face were often covered by a mask decorated with facial features similar to those of the deceased. Facial features were often decorated with gold or gilding to imitate the flesh of the gods, which was thought to be made of solid gold. The corpse would then be placed in a series of protective coffins.

Source: Adapted from University of Pennsylvania Museum. "Egyptian Mummy, Secrets and Science." www.museum.upenn.edu/new/exhibits/galleries/egyptian.html (6 May 2005).

Topic: _____

_____

ASSESS YOUR UNDERSTANDING

It's time once again to think about how you did on the Chapter Check and the exercises and to reflect on your understanding of the information presented in this chapter. Ask yourself, "Could I explain to someone the four clues to the topic?" Circle a number on the scale below to indicate how well you understand *topic*.

1 . . . . . 2 . . . . . 3 . . . . . 4 . . . . . 5 . . . . . 6 . . . . . 7 . . . . . 8 . . . . . 9 10

Throw me a rope!!   **I'm starting to get it.**   **I'm there!**

Now identify anything you still don't understand about determining the topic. What do you still need to learn or need clarification on? Write your response on the lines below.

_____

_____

_____

_____

For anything you don't understand or can't remember, what steps can you take to solve the problem? Do you need to reread material? Ask a classmate or your instructor questions? Write the information down or review it some other way? Write your response here.

_____

_____

_____

_____

You will soon learn about main idea sentences. The topic is always part of the main idea sentence, so if you need to take extra steps to polish your understanding of *topic*, do it now. You'll be glad you did.

This is also a good time to flip back to the list of success behaviors in Chapters 1 and 2. You are well into the semester at this point. Is what you are doing working for you? Are there changes you need to make? There's still time.

Map of Chapters

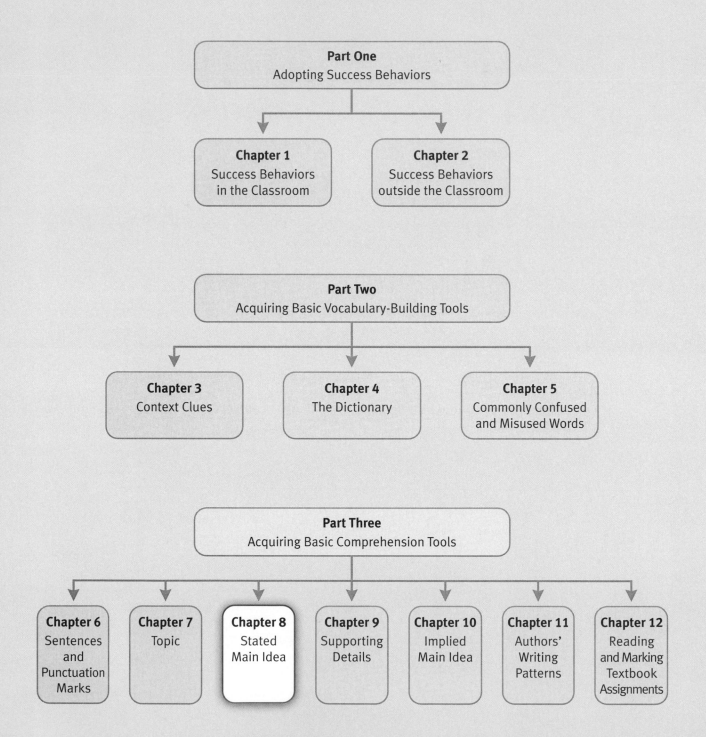

Part One
Adopting Success Behaviors

Chapter 1
Success Behaviors
in the Classroom

Chapter 2
Success Behaviors
outside the Classroom

Part Two
Acquiring Basic Vocabulary-Building Tools

Chapter 3
Context Clues

Chapter 4
The Dictionary

Chapter 5
Commonly Confused
and Misused Words

Part Three
Acquiring Basic Comprehension Tools

Chapter 6
Sentences
and
Punctuation
Marks

Chapter 7
Topic

Chapter 8
Stated
Main Idea

Chapter 9
Supporting
Details

Chapter 10
Implied
Main Idea

Chapter 11
Authors'
Writing
Patterns

Chapter 12
Reading
and Marking
Textbook
Assignments

CHAPTER 8
Stated Main Idea
The Point Is . . .

Why You Need To Know the Information in This Chapter

Perhaps the most important comprehension skill is to be able to understand the key point in every paragraph that you read.

Being able to locate the stated main idea of a paragraph will help you

- understand what you read

- know what to highlight or underline in your textbooks

- understand how the author organizes the information

- remember the material in paragraphs more easily

- make test review sheets, review cards, or concept maps to help you prepare for tests

- write correct outlines and summaries

- earn higher test grades

- write better paragraphs yourself

Super Student Tips

Here's what students like you have to say about determining main ideas of paragraphs:

"I'm doing better marking my textbooks because I know what to look for."—*Leah*

"I sure wish I'd understood about main ideas a long time ago!"—*Ricardo*

"My grades have gone up since I started looking for main ideas when I read."—*Raynell*

"Taking notes was something I was never any good at. Now I try to write down the important points from my textbook assignments. It takes longer, but I learn more."—*Tara*

"Main ideas are the important stuff in chapters. Teachers always ask questions about them on tests. I never knew what to expect on tests. Now I can usually guess what some of the questions will be."—*Shaun*

"All the other information in a paragraph is linked to the main idea. If I can get that, I do better at remembering the details that go with it."—*Stacie*

Jumpstart Your Brain!

Loosen up your spine and oxygenate your brain. With your shoulders dropped, gently twist your upper body side to side five to ten times. You can do this standing or seated. Stretch your hands above your head. Inhale, and then lower your arms as you exhale. Now jumpstart your brain by solving this riddle.

Follow these three easy steps to solve the riddle below:

1. Do each math calculation.

2. Using the code here, replace each number with a letter.

   A = 16   E = 12   H = 15   I = 27   O = 28   P = 21   N = 20   T = 24   V = 32

3. Read down the column to get the answer to the riddle. Recopy it in the spaces at the end.

The first line is shown as an example. Have fun!

A paragraph, a spear, an arrow, and a knife are alike because all of them . . .

$19 - 4$ = <u>15</u> = <u>H</u>

$64 / 4$ = ____ = ____

4×8 = ____ = ____

$8 + 4$ = ____ = ____

4×4 = ____ = ____

$42 / 2$ = ____ = ____

7×4 = ____ = ____

$23 + 4$ = ____ = ____

$24 - 4$ = ____ = ____

6×4 = ____ = ____

Copy the letters in your answer in the blanks below.

A paragraph, a spear, an arrow, and a knife are alike because all of them

____ ____ ____ ____   ____   "____ ____ ____ ____ ____."

Compare your answer to your classmates' answers. See if you agree on what the answer means and why it is funny.

Respond to these items as best you can. At this point, you may not be able to answer all, or even any, of them. That's fine. As you work through the chapter, or when you have completed it, you can make corrections.

1. In your own words and without looking up the information, write a definition of a *stated main idea:*

   _____

   _____

   _____

   _____

2. What is the connection between the *topic* and the *stated main idea*?

   _____

   _____

   _____

   _____

3. List any characteristics of a main idea that you already know:

   _____

   _____

   _____

   _____

Stated Main Idea

What we have to learn to do, we learn by doing.
—Aristotle, Greek philosopher

In Chapter 7 you learned that every paragraph must be written about something. Another way to say this is that every paragraph must have a topic. To determine the topic of a paragraph, you learned to ask yourself, "Who or what is this paragraph about?" You learned to look for a word or a phrase that answers that question, and you learned four clues that can help you determine the topic. You learned that determining the topic is the first step in comprehending what you are reading. It is the bridge to the next step in skillful reading: determining the *main idea* of a paragraph.

On tests, professors always include questions based on main ideas. This isn't surprising since main ideas contain extremely important information. Once you learn to identify main ideas in textbook paragraphs, you will understand more and remember more. Your grades are also likely to improve because you will be able to predict some of the test questions. If you can't locate the main points, you'll be like the student in this joke: "When I was in school, I read a lot of mystery books—biology, algebra, economics . . . ." Understanding main ideas takes the "mystery" out of what you're reading.

The Big Picture for This Chapter

In this chapter you'll learn what stated main idea sentences are and why they're so important. All main idea sentences have certain characteristics. You'll use inductive reasoning to figure out what those characteristics are. Once you know them, you'll have powerful tools for identifying stated main idea sentences in paragraphs. Ready?

The Structure of a Paragraph

Let's take a minute to review what a paragraph is: It is a group of sentences that all pertain to the same topic. They work together to develop a unit of thought. A paragraph typically consists of a **stated main idea** and other information that supports or explains it. Here is an example of a paragraph:

How to Memorize Material More Easily

There are several strategies that can help you memorize material more easily. First, be sure you understand the material. It is difficult to memorize material that is not meaningful to you. Second, rehearse the material. Do this by repeating it out loud or writing it until you can do so without looking at it. Finally you can use "memory pegs" to help you learn important points. For example, you can make up a rhyme or set information to a familiar tune.

Topic: How to memorize material more easily

Stated main idea: There are several strategies that can help you memorize material more easily.

The first sentence is the stated main idea. The rest of the sentences explain specific memory strategies.

Now read a second passage. It is an example of something that *looks* like a paragraph, but really isn't one. Instead, it is just a collection of sentences that don't fit with the topic given in the title. The first sentence isn't the main idea sentence because the other sentences do not support it. That is, they don't explain anything about memorizing material more easily. The sentences all have something to do with memory or memorizing, but they do not work together to form a single unit of thought.

How to Memorize Material More Easily

There are several strategies that can help you memorize material more easily. In college there is lots of material you must memorize. Math formulas can be especially hard to memorize. Also, it can take a great deal of time to memorize material for a test. Still, though, you have to do it. Don't get discouraged. I once got discouraged about a biology test, but I didn't give up. There was a lot to memorize, but I passed the test.

The Stated Main Idea Sentence of a Paragraph

Just as every paragraph has a topic, every paragraph has a main idea. In other words, every paragraph has *one most important point about the topic that the author wants to convey to the reader.* If you asked the author what he or she would most want readers to understand and remember from the paragraph, it would be the information in that sentence.

Usually authors *state* their main idea. This means they say it directly by including a sentence in the paragraph that *tells* their most important point about the topic. When an author includes a sentence in a paragraph that tells his or her most important point about the topic, that sentence is called the **stated main idea sentence**. In a writing class or English course, you may also hear it called the *topic sentence* of the paragraph.

To understand the importance of the main idea, think of it as the "king" who rules over his "kingdom," the paragraph. Just as the king is the most important person in a kingdom, the main idea is the most important (powerful) idea in the paragraph. The rest of the sentences add information, but they are less important. They are there only to help explain, to "serve" King Stated Main Idea. Just as there is only one king in a kingdom, there can be only *one* stated main idea sentence in a paragraph. (In case you're mumbling to yourself, "King Stated Main Idea? This is kid's stuff!" that's okay. To your brain, it's a helpful tool for understanding and remembering the important information about main ideas. Bottom line: Who cares if it seems simplistic? It works!)

King Stated Main Idea

Most textbook paragraphs have stated main ideas. (In Chapter 10 you will learn about the other kind of main idea, an implied main idea.) The main idea sentence always answers the question, "What is the author's one most important point about the topic?" Ask yourself this question when you want to determine the main idea of a paragraph.

Identifying the main idea is a crucial comprehension skill. To be an effective reader, you must be able to identify the most important information in a paragraph. Being able to identify the main idea can help you in several ways. Most of all, it will help you understand what you read.

Locating the Stated Main Idea Sentence in a Paragraph

A stated main idea sentence is a great help to you when you read and mark a textbook. Because it is one of the sentences in a paragraph, you can underline or highlight it. But where does the stated main idea sentence occur in a paragraph? You can discover the answer for yourself. Look ahead at the example paragraphs on pages 251–52, 255, and 257. The main idea of each paragraph is underlined. Based on what you observe, answer these two questions:

1. Can the stated main idea sentence appear anywhere in a paragraph (beginning, middle, or end)?

   Write your answer here: _____

2. Where does the stated main idea occur in most paragraphs?

   Write your answer here: _____

www.mhhe.com/
entryways

See ORL Chapter 8,
"Visualizing
the Location of the
Main Idea in a
Paragraph."

Think again about the analogy (ə-năl′ə-jē), or comparison, between a king and the stated main idea sentence. King Stated Main Idea can show up anywhere in the Kingdom of Paragraph. After all it's *his* kingdom! And it doesn't matter where in the kingdom the king is: He's still the king. Just as a king might appear at the front gate of the kingdom to welcome you, the main idea often appears at the beginning of a paragraph. Just as a king might be at the back gate of the kingdom, the main idea can appear at the end of a paragraph. And just as a king might be somewhere inside his kingdom, the main idea can appear in the "middle" of a paragraph (at neither the beginning nor the end).

King Stated Main Idea can appear at the beginning of the paragraph, at the end, or anywhere in between.

Ye olde "How to
Identify the King"
checklist

Reasoning Out Additional Clues to the Stated Main Idea of a Paragraph

In addition to presenting the author's most important point, a*ll main idea sentences have three other characteristics.* Once you know the characteristics, you will be able to identify stated main ideas in paragraphs by using your checklist.

Think of these additional clues or characteristics as part of a guidebook to the Kingdom of Paragraph. When you read a sentence that you think

BONUS TIPS

1. The words *main idea sentence* tell you what the term means: *Main* means "most important," as in the main character in a story or the main cause of heart disease. (You met the word *main* in Chapter 2.) An *idea* is a thought. (You met the word *idea* in Chapter 5 because *idea* is sometimes confused with *ideal*.) Therefore, the *main idea* is the author's most important thought. You already know what a *sentence* is.

2. Because *main* means *most* important, in a paragraph, only *one* sentence can be the *most* important sentence.

3. Main ideas are always expressed as *sentences* because main ideas are statements that tell you something. Main ideas are never written as questions because questions ask rather than tell. That's why a question can never be a main idea sentence. Questions ask. Statements tell. Main ideas *tell* something.

is the stated main idea, consult your checklist. You won't have to wonder whether you are right about the sentence you choose. Instead, you can test the sentence to see if it has the right characteristics.

Let's get started on figuring out the characteristics. The sample sets below consist of paragraphs containing stated main ideas. You will be told the topic of each paragraph. Also, the main idea of each paragraph is underlined. Read each set of paragraphs and review the main ideas. Then use the paragraphs as the basis for answering each question about a characteristic of the stated main idea sentences. As always, the paragraphs contain useful, interesting information that will help you build your knowledge base.

Discover the First Additional Clue to the Main Idea

The topic of each paragraph is given and the stated main idea sentence is underlined. Read each paragraph, review its topic and stated main idea sentence. Then use your observations as the basis for answering this question:

Does the main idea sentence always contain the topic?

Example 1

The topic of this paragraph is *active listening*.

> <u>Active listening is an essential component of success, not only in school but in the broader world</u>. Effective listening lets us know that even though our friend says it's OK if we postpone our hiking trip, she is really disappointed. It enables us to hear the sound of a horn warning us not to walk into a car's path. It allows us to respond to the lyrics of an emotional song. It helps us decide whether someone is telling the truth.
>
> *Source:* Adapted from Robert Feldman, *Power Learning*, New York: McGraw-Hill, 2000, p. 183. Copyright © 2000 The McGraw-Hill Companies. Reprinted by permission of The McGraw-Hill Companies, Inc.

Example 2

The topic of this paragraph is *learning disabilities and intelligence*.

> What do physicist Albert Einstein, U.S. General George Patton, former British Prime Minister Winston Churchill, brokerage firm founder Charles Schwab, Walt Disney, and Jay Leno have in common? You'd probably say that all of them are intelligent and talented. They

are, but all of them share another characteristic: learning disabilities. People with learning disabilities are sometimes viewed as unintelligent. Nothing could be further from the truth. <u>The point is, there is no relationship between learning disabilities and intelligence.</u>

Example 3

The topic of this paragraph is *education and voter turnout*.

What does your college education mean? One thing it means is that you are much more likely to become an active citizen. <u>Education, it seems, is the single best predictor of voter turnout.</u> Persons with a college education are about 40 percent more likely to vote than persons with a grade school education. Becoming educated causes a person to have a greater interest in politics and to seek more political information. College-educated people believe that they can make a difference politically. Finally, they are more likely to have educated friends who vote.

Source: Adapted from Thomas E. Patterson, *We the People,* 3rd ed., New York: McGraw-Hill, 2000, p. 189. Copyright © 2000 The McGraw-Hill Companies. Reprinted by permission of The McGraw-Hill Companies, Inc.

Look again at the topics and main idea sentences of the paragraphs. Then use these sample paragraphs to help you answer this question:

Does the main idea sentence always contain the topic of the paragraph?

First Additional Main Idea Clue: The main idea sentence always contains the topic.

You should have discovered that the answer is yes, the main idea sentence *always* contains the topic of the paragraph because the main idea sentence tells the author's most important point *about* the topic.

- The topic of the first example paragraph is *active listening*. The stated main idea is "*Active listening* is an essential component of success, not only in school but in the broader world."
- In the second example, the topic is *learning disabilities and intelligence*, and the stated main idea is "There is no relationship between *learning disabilities and intelligence*."
- In the third example, the topic is *education and voter turnout*, and the stated main idea is "*Education*, it seems, is the single best predictor of *voter turnout*."

In an English course or a writing course, you may hear the main idea sentence of a paragraph called the *topic sentence*. Knowing that the main idea sentence is also called the topic sentence will help you remember that the main idea sentence must always contain the topic.

Notice again that the topic can occur anywhere in the sentence. It just has to be *in* the sentence. If there are two parts to the topic (such as *learning disabilities and intelligence* or *education and voter turnout* in examples 2 and 3), the words can be next to each other or separated in the sentence. Again, what's important is that they're *in* the sentence.

Think of the topic as the crown that King Stated Main Idea wears. (The king must have his crown!) Think of the person himself as the rest of the "package." The "royal person" (the rest of the sentence) plus his "crown" (topic) = King Stated Main Idea.

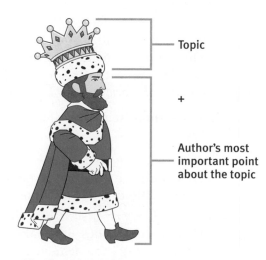

Topic

+

Author's most important point about the topic

King Stated Main Idea

www.mhhe.com/
entryways

For more practice,
see ORL Chapter 8,
"Could This Be a
Stated Main Idea
Sentence?"

STOP AND PROCESS

EXERCISE 8.1

To help fix the first stated main idea clue (characteristic) in your mind, write the characteristic here:

_____

_____

Now go back to the sample paragraphs and highlight the topic in each stated main idea sentence. (Did you notice that each main idea sentence tells the author's most important point about that paragraph's topic?)

Discover the Second Additional Clue to the Main Idea

You just learned that the main idea sentence must always contain the topic. Now identify a second characteristic. Once again, the topic and stated main idea are identified for each sample paragraph below. Read and study the example paragraphs, and then answer this question:

> **Does the main idea sentence always make complete sense by itself?**

In other words, if you were allowed to read *only* the main idea sentence and were not permitted to see the rest of the paragraph, would that sentence make complete sense by itself?

Here are examples of sentences that make complete sense by themselves and sentences that do not make complete sense by themselves. All of these are complete sentences, but not all of them make complete sense when read in isolation.

Here are two sentences that make complete sense by themselves:

- *Abraham Lincoln was the greatest president the United States ever had.*
  (This sentence makes complete sense because it includes the subject, *Abraham Lincoln*, and it tells something about him, *that he was the greatest U.S. president.*)

- *Tornadoes are caused by a collision of warm and cold air masses.*
  (This sentence makes complete sense by itself: It is talking about *tornadoes*, and it tells something about them: *They are caused by a collision of warm and cold air masses*).

Here are three sentences that do not make complete sense by themselves:

- *Every year thousands of Americans die from this dreaded disease.*
  (This sentence does not make complete sense by itself because the name of the dreaded disease is missing.)

- *Clearly, it is one of society's greatest achievements.*
  (This sentence does not make complete sense because we are not told what "it," the achievement, is.)

- *He was the greatest president the United States ever had.*
  (This sentence does not make complete sense by itself because the reader cannot tell who "he" is.)

Identifying sentences that do not make complete sense by themselves is easy because if you read or hear them, you immediately need to ask for more information.

Now read each of the three paragraphs below. The topic is given and the stated main idea sentence is underlined. Decide if its stated main idea sentence makes complete sense by itself. In other words, determine whether that sentence would make complete sense even if you could not see (read) the rest of the paragraph.

Example 1

The topic of this paragraph is *law enforcement officers*.

> <u>Law enforcement officers are constantly faced with danger.</u> Events can go from routine to life-threatening in seconds. The risk of being shot—or having to shoot someone—is high. Each year over 50,000 police officers are assaulted. Forty-two were feloniously killed in 1999.
>
> *Source:* Freda Adler, Gerhard Mueller, and William Laufer, *Criminal Justice*, 3rd ed., New York: McGraw-Hill, 2003, p. 192.

Example 2

The topic of this paragraph is *planning a college campus*.

> <u>Designing a college campus is a truly challenging and interesting task.</u> For one thing, it's a lot like designing a city from the ground up. Also, the campus is likely to last for many hundreds of years. It will serve as a working environment and home away from home for a constantly changing population of students and professors. It must be comfortable and efficient. Most of all, it must express the special personality of the college.
>
> *Source*: From Rita Gilbert, *Living with Art*, 5th ed., New York: McGraw-Hill, 1998, p. 340. Copyright © 1998 by The McGraw-Hill Companies. Reprinted by permission of The McGraw-Hill Companies, Inc.

Example 3

The topic of this paragraph is *caffeine*.

> **Caffeine**   For most people, a cup of caffeinated coffee is a relatively safe way to perk up the brain. However, caffeine can cause nervousness or headaches in some individuals. It can also trigger panic attacks and raise blood pressure. Those who have borderline high blood pressure should restrict their caffeine intake. Finally, women who are pregnant or nursing should leave off caffeine. <u>In short, while caffeine is fine for most people, there are certain individuals who should limit or avoid caffeine.</u>

Review the stated main idea sentences in the example paragraphs above. Draw on your observations to answer this question:

Does the main idea sentence always make complete sense by itself?

www.mhhe.com/
entryways

See ORL Chapter 8,
(1) "Review of
Nouns/Phrases and
Sentences." The chart
illustrates topics and
complete main idea
sentences made from
them;
(2) the exercise
entitled, "Could This
Be a Stated Main
Idea Sentence?"

Second Additional Main Idea Clue: The main idea sentence always makes complete sense by itself.

You should have observed that the answer is yes, the main idea sentence must always make complete sense by itself.

- The stated main idea of the first example paragraph makes complete sense by itself: It tells the authors' important point about law enforcement officers: *Law enforcement officers are constantly faced with danger.*

- The main idea sentence in the second example also makes complete sense by itself: *Designing a college campus is a profoundly challenging and interesting task.*

- If you read the third stated main idea sentence by itself without seeing the rest of the paragraph, you will still understand completely the authors' point about caffeine: *In short, while caffeine is fine for most people, there are certain individuals who should limit or avoid caffeine.*

STOP AND PROCESS

EXERCISE 8.2

To help fix the second stated main idea clue (characteristic) in your mind, write the characteristic here:

_____

_____

Now go back to the sample paragraphs and highlight the stated main idea in each paragraph.

Discover the Third Additional Clue to the Main Idea

In the previous chapter, you learned the difference between *general* and *specific*. *General* describes something that is very broad rather than specific and precise. These sentences illustrate the difference between sentences that are general and ones that are specific:

General: Smoking causes many health problems. ("many health problems" is general)

Specific: Smoking causes emphysema. (describes one specific effect, emphysema)

General: There are several ways to reduce stress. ("several ways" is general)

Specific: Exercise is one way to reduce stress. (describes one specific way, exercise)

General: Children go through certain stages as they learn to talk. ("certain stages" is general)

Specific: Telegraphic speech, which occurs between 16 and 24 months of age, is the stage at which children's first sentences appear. (describes one specific stage, telegraphic speech)

So far, you've figured out that the stated main idea sentence always contains the topic and that it makes complete sense by itself. Now read each paragraph below and use them to figure out one last characteristic. The topic and stated main idea sentence are identified in each paragraph. See if the rest of the sentences contain information that explains or tells more about the main idea sentence. Study these examples, and then use your observations to answer this question:

Is the main idea sentence a *general* sentence that *sums* up the rest of the paragraph?

Example 1

The topic of this paragraph is *lightning* (or *lightning striking in the same place*).

> Perhaps you've heard the old saying, "Lightning never strikes twice in the same place." <u>Contrary to popular belief, lightning can strike again in the same place, and, in fact, it is more likely to do so than not.</u> Lightning is a form of electrical energy. Since air is a poor conductor of electricity, the electrical charge we call lightning needs help bridging the gap between the cloud and the ground. A tall tree or building, especially one with a metal framework, or even an elevation in the landscape, acts as a convenient path and "attracts" lightning. This is the reason lightning is likely to strike more than once in the same place.

Example 2

The topic of this paragraph is *the proper way to treat a minor burn*, as the heading suggests.

> **The Proper Way to Treat a Minor Burn**   Have you ever burned yourself on a hot stove or iron? Did your mother tell you to put butter on it to ease the pain and protect the skin? We now know that putting butter on a burn can actually lead to infection. <u>There is a proper way to treat a minor burn.</u> First, run cool water over it immediately. Next, bandage the area with sterile gauze. Finally, keep it clean and dry. The water removes the heat and stops further damage. It also helps clean the burned area and prevent infection. If blisters form, don't break them. The fluid inside protects the burned area as it begins to heal.

Example 3

The topic of this paragraph is *Mrs.* (the abbreviation).

> The abbreviation "Mr." can be written out: "Mister." The abbreviation "Mrs." once stood for "mistress." Of course, it's been a long time since "wife" and "mistress" meant the same thing. <u>Today, "Mrs." is no longer a true abbreviation since there is no full form of it that can be written out</u>.

Review the stated main idea sentences in the example paragraphs above. Draw on your observations to answer this question:

Is the main idea sentence a *general* sentence that *sums* up the rest of the paragraph?

Third Additional Main Idea Clue: The main idea sentence is a general sentence that *sums up* the paragraph.

You should have discovered this characteristic: The main idea sentence is a general sentence that sums up the rest of the paragraph.

- In the first example paragraph, the main idea sentence is a general statement about lightning: *Contrary to popular belief, lightning can strike twice in the same place, and, in fact, it is more likely to do so than not.* The sentence does not include any specific information about why lightning is likely to strike in the same place. The other sentences in the paragraph explain the specific reasons.

- The main idea of the second paragraph is also a very general statement: *There is a proper way to treat a minor burn.* The rest of the sentences explain more specifically the right (and wrong!) way to treat minor burns.

- The third paragraph's main idea is also a general statement that sums up the rest of the paragraph: *Today, "Mrs." is no longer a true abbreviation since there is no full form of it that can be written out.* The other sentences give more specific, related information.

STOP AND PROCESS

EXERCISE 8.3

To help fix the third stated main idea clue (characteristic) in your mind, write the characteristic here:

_____

Now go back to the sample paragraphs and highlight the stated main idea, the most general statement, in each paragraph. (Did you notice that all of the stated main idea sentences contain the topic of the paragraph and that each main idea sentence makes complete sense by itself?)

The Rest of the Sentences in a Paragraph

As you know, the purpose of the stated main idea is to tell the most important general point in a paragraph. Let's talk a little more about the purpose of the other sentences. They are called *supporting details.* They support the main idea by providing specific information that explains, illustrates, or tells more about it. (You'll learn more about supporting details in Chapter 9.)

Look at this sample paragraph you read earlier. The first sentence, the stated main idea, tells the author's important general point. What do the rest of the sentences do?

> <u>Contrary to popular belief, lightning can strike twice in the same place, and, in fact, it is more likely to do so than not.</u> Lightning is a form of electrical energy. Since air is a poor conductor of electricity, the electrical charge we call lightning needs help bridging the gap between the cloud and the ground. A tall tree or building, especially one with a metal framework, or even an elevation in the landscape, acts as a convenient path and "attracts" lightning.

The rest of the sentences provide specific information about what lightning is and why it is drawn toward certain structures rather than striking the ground in random spots.

Look at the details in this sample paragraph. What is their purpose?

> For most people, a cup of caffeinated coffee is a relatively safe way to perk up the brain. However, caffeine can cause nervousness or headaches in some individuals. It can also trigger panic attacks and raise blood pressure. Those who have borderline high blood pressure should restrict their caffeine. Finally, women who are pregnant or nursing should leave off caffeine. <u>In short, while caffeine is fine for most people, there are certain individuals who should limit or avoid caffeine.</u>

Did you observe that the details tell about specific types of individuals who should limit or avoid caffeine? If so, good!

To our Kingdom of Paragraph and King Stated Main Idea, we can now add the king's loyal "subjects," the supporting details. There can be only one king (main idea), but there are many ordinary citizens in the kingdom (supporting details).

Seeing the Connection between the Topic and the Stated Main Idea Sentence

Here's a visual aid to help you see—literally—the connection between the topic of a paragraph and the paragraph's stated main idea. The same sample paragraph is repeated three times. This is how the paragraph might look as it appears in a textbook:

> There are several ways of listening actively. One way to show that you are listening actively is to ask questions about what the other person is saying. You can also paraphrase what the other person has said in order to be sure that you understood it correctly. Still another way to listen actively is to pay attention to clues in the person's tone of voice and posture that reveal what the person is feeling.

Here is the paragraph with the topic, *active listening,* highlighted each time it appears. (As you already know from Chapter 7, repeated words or phrases are often a clue to the topic.)

> There are several ways of listening actively. One way to show that you are listening actively is to ask questions about what the other person is saying. You can also paraphrase what the other person has said in order to be sure that you understood it correctly. Still another

> ### BRAIN-FRIENDLY TIP
>
> While you are learning and practicing stated main ideas, highlight the topic in pink highlighter wherever it appears in the paragraph. Then use a yellow highlighter to mark the main idea sentence. The highlighted topic in it will turn orange (pink + yellow = orange). This will visually reinforce the message that the main idea sentence must always contain the topic of the paragraph.

www.mhhe.com/
entryways

See ORL Chapter 8, "Seeing the Connection between the Topic and the Stated Main Idea Sentence." It gives a full-color example of the strategy described in the Brain-Friendly Tip box above. Color literally lets you "see" the connection.

way to listen actively is to pay attention to clues in the person's tone of voice and posture that reveal what the person is feeling.

Now, in addition, the main idea sentence has been underlined:

There are several ways of listening actively. One way to show that you are listening actively is to ask questions about what the other person is saying. You can also paraphrase what the other person has said in order to be sure that you understood it correctly. Still another way to listen actively is to pay attention to clues in the person's tone of voice and posture that reveal what the person is feeling.

As you can clearly see, the underlined main idea sentence contains the topic. Of course, there are two other sentences in the paragraph that also contain the topic. How can you tell which sentence is the main idea? Simple: It's the one that makes a general statement that sums up the rest of the paragraph.

Other Things to Keep in Mind about Main Ideas

Good job so far! There are just a few more things you need to know about main ideas.

1. Before you determine a paragraph's main idea, read the *entire* paragraph. This lets you determine the topic accurately. It prevents you from grabbing a sentence just because it sounds important or contains interesting information. It also helps you avoid overmarking your textbooks. If you mark too soon, you may mark the wrong sentence. Remember, it's the *author's* most important point you're looking for, regardless of whether you agree with the information in the sentence.

2. Authors want you to find their main idea sentences and pay attention to them. They often use certain words to signal their most important point. Watch for sentences beginning with *The point is*, *In general*, *To sum up*, *In conclusion*, *In short*, *Therefore*, and *Thus*. These words typically appear in main idea sentences, usually ones that come at the end of a paragraph. These signals are presents from the author. Take advantage of them! (Also pay extra attention when your instructors say them.) Take a minute to look back at the sample paragraphs in the chapter that have main idea sentences at the end.

   - How many of these sample paragraphs contained signal words?

   _____

   - What were the signal words? Write them here: _____

   _____

3. Remember that locating a stated main idea sentence isn't enough. You have to understand what the sentence means. Suppose a main idea in a human development textbook is "Children between the ages of three and six make great advances in gross motor skills." To understand the sentence, you must know (or find out) that gross motor skills refer to activities that involve the large muscles of the body, such as running and jumping.

4. Keep in mind that *examples are never main ideas*. Examples are details (bits of specific information) that explain, prove, or illustrate the main idea. When you see a sentence that contains the words *for example*, *such as*, or *to illustrate*, you know that particular sentence cannot be the main idea.

5. A question is never the main idea. Main ideas *tell* something important; they don't ask a question.

6. In the previous chapter, you learned that longer selections (such as chapter sections, articles, and essays) have an overall topic. You won't be surprised to learn that they can also have an overall main idea. The overall main idea sentence contains the overall topic and tells the main idea of the entire selection. In a writing or English course, you may hear the overall main idea sentence called the *thesis sentence*. They are the same thing. Suppose an article has the overall topic of Ben Franklin and that each paragraph describes one of his many talents. The overall main idea or thesis sentence would be a very general statement such as "Ben Franklin was a remarkably talented man."

**www.mhhe.com/
entryways**

For more information about certain parts of speech, see
Catalyst> Writing> Paragraph/Essay Develop. > Thesis/ Central Idea

 STOP AND PROCESS

EXERCISE 8.4

Follow the steps below to go from choosing a topic to creating a complete paragraph about it. Your paragraph will have a stated main idea.

1. Think of something that you would like to write about. Write a word or phrase here that tells what you want to write about:

_____

_____

You have just selected a *topic*.

2. Now write a *sentence* that tells the most important thing you want to say about your topic. Be sure to include the topic (the actual words you wrote on the line above) in your sentence. Write your sentence here:

_____

_____

You have just written a *main idea sentence*.

3. Now write three other things that explain or tell more about your main idea sentence. Write them on the lines below:

■ _____

_____

■ _____

_____

■ _____

_____

You have just written three details.

4. Now write your main idea sentence and the sentences that give the details about it. Remember to indent the first sentence.

_____

_____

_____

_____

_____

_____

_____

You have now written a *paragraph with a stated main idea sentence*. Would someone who read your paragraph be able to easily identify your main idea? Would the details help them understand the main idea?

◠)) LISTEN UP!

Here's a "rap" that will help you remember the important information about the main idea. Say it out loud or make a recording of it. (In the last verse, *top-shelf* means "the best.")

It's important that you find
The point the author has in mind.

The main idea is its name,
But "topic sentence" is the same.

This sentence has the topic, too.
It gives a summary or overview.

And never once should you doubt it:
Details all tell more about it.

The main idea is top-shelf:
It makes sense all by itself.

MY TOOLBOX *of Stated Main Idea Tools*

Congratulations! You now know what a stated main idea sentence is, how to locate it, and why it is important. You learned three additional characteristics that any main idea sentence must have. To help you transfer that information into long-term (permanent) memory, use one of the following techniques to record and rehearse it.

- **Write the information on notebook paper or on index cards.**

- **Make a study map.** You know the procedure for this.

- **Create a song or rhyme** that includes the important information about the stated main ideas. Say it aloud until you can repeat it (or sing it) from memory.

- **Write a story** about a reader who is traveling through a paragraph, taking a trip from Topic, the starting point, to Stated Main Idea, the destination. How does the reader get from Topic to Stated Main Idea? What "road signs" should the person watch for, road signs that guide the reader? If you prefer, you can **draw a map** of the journey. Be sure to label the road signs.

- **Create an analogy or a model of some sort that explains stated main ideas.** Analogies tell how two things are alike. In the chapter, you saw the stated main idea compared to a king, with his crown representing the topic. Can you come up with another comparison that makes sense to you? For example, "A stated main idea is like a car because . . ."; "A stated main idea is like an onion because . . ."; or "A stated main idea is like a target because . . ." You might want to draw or create a model. Then label the parts of the car or target to show how they represent the topic, the main idea, a paragraph, and so forth.

✔ **CHAPTER CHECK**

Answer the following questions about the information in the chapter. In each sentence, fill in the missing information. One word goes in each blank. For some items, there may be more than one correct answer.

1. The word *main* means "most _____."

2. To *state* something means to _____ it or tell it directly.

3. For a paragraph that has a stated main idea, the person who states the main idea is the _____.

4. A main idea sentence of a paragraph must always contain the _____ of the paragraph.

5. A stated main idea must always make complete _____ by itself, even if readers can't see the rest of the paragraph.

6. Because a main idea tells something, it is always written as a sentence and never as a _____.

7. A main idea is a _____ sentence that sums up the rest of the paragraph.

8. A longer selection (such as a chapter section or article) can have an _____ main idea.

9. _____ are bits of specific information that explain, prove, or illustrate the main idea, and they are never the main idea.

10. It is not enough to locate a stated main idea sentence; you must also _____ it.

11. Only _____ sentence in a paragraph can be the stated main idea sentence.

12. Before you can identify the stated main idea, you must first determine the _____ of the paragraph.

13. Before you determine a paragraph's main idea, you should first read the _____ paragraph.

14. Authors can place a stated main idea sentence at the beginning, middle, or end of a paragraph, but they usually place them at the

_____.

15. An example of a word or words that authors use to signal a stated main idea sentence is _____.

REVIEW EXERCISES

SET 1

Read each paragraph and its topic. For items in Set 1, the topic is given.

■ Ask yourself, "What is the author's most important point about the topic?" Locate and underline the sentence that answers that question. It will be the stated main idea sentence. (Remember that the stated main idea sentence *must* contain the words that tell the topic. Try the strategy of using two colors of highlighters described in the Brain-Friendly Tip box on page 260.)

■ Find the same sentence in the answer choices and write its letter in the space provided.

Before you start, shrug your shoulders and stretch, and take a couple of deep breaths. *Suggestion*: Refer to your Toolbox material as you do these chapter exercises.

_____ 1. The topic of this paragraph is *Hispanics.*

> The fastest-growing minority in the United States is that of Hispanics, people of Spanish-speaking background. Some Hispanics are descendants of people who helped colonize the areas of California, Texas, New Mexico, and Arizona before they were taken over by the United States. Many Hispanics, however, are recent immigrants.
>
> *Source*: Adapted from Thomas E. Patterson, *The American Democracy*, 6th ed., New York: McGraw-Hill, 2003, p. 142.

a. The fastest-growing minority in the United States is that of Hispanics, people of Spanish-speaking background.

b. Some Hispanics are descendants of people who helped colonize the areas of California, Texas, New Mexico, and Arizona before they were taken over by the United States.

c. Many Hispanics, however, are recent immigrants.

_____ 2. The topic of this paragraph is *water in the earth's atmosphere.*

> Water occurs in the atmosphere in liquid form as raindrops. It appears in solid form as snowflakes and hail. When water occurs in the atmosphere as water vapor, it is in the form of an invisible gas. The point is, water in the earth's atmosphere occurs in three forms: liquid, solid, and gas.

a. Water occurs in the atmosphere in liquid form as raindrops.

b. It appears in solid form as snowflakes and hail.

c. When water occurs in the atmosphere as water vapor, it is in the form of an invisible gas.

d. The point is, water in the earth's atmosphere occurs in three forms: liquid, solid, and gas.

_____ 3. The topic of this paragraph is *Theodore Roosevelt.*

> Theodore ("Teddy") Roosevelt is remembered for many reasons. He gained national popularity as a hero in the Spanish-American War. He then became vice president under William McKinley. When McKinley was assassinated, Roosevelt became the 26th president. As president, he was a reformer who used government power to force big businesses to act more fairly and responsibly. He is associated with the construction of the Panama Canal. A sportsman and outdoorsman, he promoted conservation programs to protect the country's natural resources and forests, and he set aside more than 200 million acres as national parks and nature preserves.

a. Theodore ("Teddy") Roosevelt is remembered for many reasons.

b. When McKinley was assassinated, Roosevelt became the 26th president.

c. As president, he was a reformer who used government power to force big businesses to act more fairly and responsibly.

d. He is associated with the construction of the Panama Canal.

_____ 4. The topic of this paragraph is *the advantage to birds of being able to fly.*

> How does the ability to fly help birds? Biologists say flying gives birds at least three advantages. First, flying enables them to escape danger. Second, when necessary, they can travel great distances to locate food. Finally, birds can protect their eggs and chicks by building nests high above the ground.

a. How does the ability to fly help birds?

b. Biologists say flying gives birds at least three advantages.

c. First, flying enables them to escape danger.

d. Finally, birds can protect their eggs and chicks by building nests high above the ground.

_____ 5. The topic of this paragraph is the *Statue of Liberty.*

> More than a century ago, France gave the United States a statue by sculptor Auguste Bartholdi. Since 1886 "Miss Liberty" has presided over New York Harbor, where she has

welcomed millions of immigrants to America. The "Lady with the Lamp" is constructed of tons of iron and copper, and is one of the tallest statues in the world. It symbolizes the United States. The Statue of Liberty has become a historic landmark that is recognized worldwide.

a. More than a century ago, France gave the United States a statue by sculptor Auguste Bartholdi.

b. Since 1886 "Miss Liberty" has presided over New York Harbor, where she has welcomed millions of immigrants to America.

c. The "Lady with the Lamp" is constructed of tons of iron and copper, and is one of the tallest statues in the world.

d. The Statue of Liberty has become a historic landmark that is recognized worldwide.

_____ 6. The topic of this paragraph is *Juneteenth*.

Juneteenth is a celebration of the end of slavery. In 1863, President Lincoln issued the Emancipation Proclamation that abolished slavery. On June 19, 1865, a ship with Union soldiers docked in Texas. The officer in charge proclaimed that slavery was no longer legal. However, the people of Texas were unaware that it had been abolished two years earlier, and so the holiday was born. It is the oldest known holiday of its sort. Today it is celebrated in many parts of the country.

a. *Juneteenth* is a celebration of the end of slavery.

b. In 1863, President Lincoln issued the Emancipation Proclamation that abolished slavery.

c. On June 19, 1865, a ship with Union soldiers docked in Texas.

d. It is the oldest known holiday of its sort.

_____ 7. The topic of this paragraph is the *toll of video violence.*

The Toll of Video Violence   A typical child in the United States watches 28 hours of TV a week and sees 8,000 murders by the time he or she finishes elementary school. Even worse, the killers get away with the crime 75% of the time and show no remorse. The toll of video violence is high: some kids become immune to brutality, some become fearful, and others become aggressive.

Source: Adapted from L.W. Winik, "The Toll of Video Violence," *Parade*, July 4, 2004, p. 15. Copyright © 2004 Parade Magazine. All rights reserved. Reprinted by permission.

a. A typical child in the United States watches 28 hours of TV a week and sees 8,000 murders by the time he or she finishes elementary school.

b. Even worse, the killers get away with the crime 75% of the time and show no remorse.

c. The toll of video violence is high: some kids become immune to brutality, some become fearful, and others become aggressive.

_____ 8. The topic of this paragraph is *Mozart.*

> Wolfgang Amadeus Mozart was a gifted child who was playing the harpsichord by age 4 and composing music by age 5. During his life, he wrote music for the piano and other instruments, string quartets, and orchestras, as well as for singers. Tragically, Mozart died at age 35, probably of typhoid fever. More than 200 years after his death, Mozart remains one of the most prolific and beloved composers of all time.

a. Wolfgang Amadeus Mozart was a gifted child who was playing the harpsichord by age 4 and composing music by age 5.

b. During his life, he music for the piano and other instruments, string quartets, and orchestras, as well as for singers.

c. Tragically, Mozart died at age 35, probably of typhoid fever.

d. More than 200 years after his death, Mozart remains one of the most prolific and beloved composers of all time.

_____ 9. The topic of this paragraph is *how migrating animals find their way.*

> **How do migrating animals find their way?**
> Fish use their sense of smell to recognize their migration paths and are guided by changing water temperatures. Migrating animals navigate in a variety of ways. Birds use the position of the sun to orient themselves. Some birds have magnetic particles in their ear mechanisms that act as a compass. Mammals rely on their memory. Some elephant trails have been used for hundreds of years.
>
> *Source*: From *The Complete Book of Questions and Answers* by Vincent Douglas, Columbus, OH: American Education Publishing, 2002, p. 120. Copyright © 2002 by American Education Publishing. Reprinted by permission of School Specialty Publishing.

a. Fish use their sense of smell to recognize their migration paths and are guided by changing water temperatures.

b. Migrating animals navigate in a variety of ways.

c. Birds use the position of the sun to orient themselves.

d. Mammals rely on their memory.

_____ 10. The topic of this paragraph is the *relationship between Thomas Derrick and the Earl of Essex*.

> Thomas Derrick was an executioner who hanged hundreds of criminals at a London gallows. Eventually, he himself was convicted of rape and condemned to die. He was pardoned, however, by the Earl of Essex, and his life was spared. The relationship between Thomas Derrick and the Earl of Essex is filled with irony. In 1601, the Earl was found guilty of treason and condemned to death by hanging. His executioner? Thomas Derrick.

a. Thomas Derrick was an executioner who hanged hundreds of criminals at a London gallows.

b. Eventually, he himself was convicted of rape and condemned to die.

c. He was pardoned, however, by the Earl of Essex and his life was spared.

d. The relationship between Thomas Derrick and the Earl of Essex is filled with irony.

SET 2

This set is different from Set 1 because the topic is not given. You must first determine it.

- Read each paragraph. Determine the *topic* by asking yourself, "Who or what is the paragraph about?" Remember to use the four clues you learned in the previous chapter.

- Write the *topic* above the paragraph in the space provided.

- Then locate the *stated main idea sentence* by asking yourself, "What is the author's most important point about the topic?" Underline the stated main idea sentence. Remember that the stated main idea sentence *must* contain the topic you identified. (If it helps you, use the strategy of highlighting with two colors, as described in the Brain-Friendly Tip box on page 260.)

Before you start, rotate your head in a circle in either direction and shake the tension out of your hands. *Suggestion*: Refer to your Toolbox as you do these chapter exercises.

1. The topic of this paragraph is _____

_____

Determining the Exact Age of a Tree

Every year as a tree grows, it deposits a new layer of cells on the outside of its trunk, beneath the bark. This new layer is called the annual ring. By counting the annual rings, it is simple to work out the exact age of a tree. Even in the case of a living tree, it is possible to drill into the trunk and remove a sample in order to date the tree without causing any permanent damage.

Source: From *The Complete Book of Questions and Answers* by Vincent Douglas, Columbus, OH: American Education Publishing, 2002, p. 130. Copyright © 2002 by American Education Publishing. Reprinted with permission from School Specialty Publishing.

Did you remember to underline the stated main idea sentence? If not, go back and do it now.

2. The topic of this paragraph is _____

Jealousy Although extremely jealous people claim to care about another person, they typically make insistent demands and attempt to control. In high school and college students, jealousy often leads to violence in dating relationships. Abusive spouses often use jealousy to justify their violence. Jealousy is an indication of insecurity or possessiveness rather than love, and it can ruin relationships.

Source: Adapted from Paul Insel and Walton Roth, *Core Concepts In Health*, 9th ed., New York: McGraw-Hill, 2002, p. 63. Copyright © 2002 by The McGraw-Hill Companies. Reprinted by permission of The McGraw-Hill Companies, Inc.

3. The topic of this paragraph is _____

_____

First impressions are extremely important and difficult to change, and studies indicate that interviewers make up their minds quickly about a job candidate. It is during the first minute or two that the interviewer makes an initial decision about how well you would fit into the company. The first few minutes set the tone for the entire interview. From the time you walk in the door, judgments are made about your personality, character, competency, and style. This initial impression is based on dress, eye contact, body language, posture, and verbal communication. Nonverbal communication can influence the first impression even more than words.

Source: Sharon Ferrett, *Strategies: Getting and Keeping the Job You Want*, 2d ed. New York: McGraw-Hill/Glencoe, 2003, p. 164. Copyright © 2003 The McGraw-Hill Companies. Reprinted by permission of The McGraw-Hill Companies, Inc.

4. The topic of this paragraph is _____

_____

Except for the death of a spouse or family member, divorce is the greatest stress-producing event in life, and recovery takes longer than most people think. Both men and women experience turmoil, depression, and lowered self-esteem during and after divorce. People experience separation distress and loneliness for about a year and then begin a recovery period of one to three years. During this time they gradually construct a post-divorce identity, along with a new pattern of life. Children are especially vulnerable to the trauma of divorce, and sometimes counseling is appropriate to help them adjust to the changes in their lives.

5. The topic of this paragraph is _____

_____

The average American student attends school six or seven hours a day, five days a week, for 180 days, with three months off for the summer. The average Japanese student attends school eight hours a day, five days a week plus a half-day on Saturday, 240 days a year. For all classes except physical education and laboratory work, they stay in their homerooms and their teachers come to them. It is clear that Japanese students work much harder than American students do.

6. The topic of this paragraph is _____

_____

Online Weight-Loss Programs   A recent addition to the weight-loss scene are online, Internet-based programs. Most such Web sites include a cross between self-help and group support through chat rooms, bulletin boards, and e-newsletters. Many sites offer online self-assessment for diet and physical activity habits. Some provide access to a staff professional for individualized help. The criteria used to evaluate commercial programs can also be applied to Internet-based programs. Always check whether a program offers member-to-member support and access to staff professionals.

7. The topic of this paragraph is _____

_____

Just because someone criticizes your appearance or driving or work habits doesn't mean that there is anything wrong with you. It's possible that you are dealing with a simple difference of opinion. It's also possible that your critic is motivated by personal reasons. Perhaps he is having trouble accepting his own appearance. Maybe she is struggling with the very work habits for which she is criticizing you. Then again perhaps your critic is simply in a bad mood and snapping at the first person to come by. Whatever the case, simply note that something other than you is motivating the person to be critical. This allows you to handle the situation more objectively without feeling threatened. Once you take your self-esteem out of the equation, you are more open to receiving or rejecting criticism.

8. The topic of this paragraph is _____

_____

Abraham Lincoln (1809-1865) was a member of Congress from Illinois before his election to the presidency in 1860. Homely and gangly, Lincoln is regarded by many as America's greatest president. He is admired for his principled leadership during the Civil War. His greatest legacy is the preservation of the American Union. The Emancipation Proclamation and the Gettysburg Address are two of his other legacies. He was assassinated at Ford's Theater in the nation's capital shortly after the start of his second term as president.

9. The topic of this paragraph is _____

_____

America has the world's largest system of college education. Every state has at least eight colleges and universities within its boundaries. No European democracy has as many colleges as either California (322) or New York (320).

10. The topic of this paragraph is _____

_____

What's the difference between A students and C students? Is it intelligence? Knowledge? Study skills? *Procrastination*—the habit of putting things off until the last minute—has an enormous effect on students' success. According to researchers, the real difference between A students and B or C students is that A students get started early. They buy their books on time, come to class prepared, and get started quickly on assignments. They don't procrastinate.

Check to be sure you underlined the stated main idea in each paragraph. After all, that's the purpose of the exercise. Don't lose points because you forgot to do half—the most important half—of the assignment.

How did you do on the Chapter Check and the exercises? How well do you think you understand stated main ideas? Could you explain to someone what a stated main idea is, the characteristics of a main idea sentence, and how to locate the stated main idea of a paragraph? Circle a number on the scale below to indicate how well you understand *stated main idea.*

1 . . . . . 2 . . . . . 3 . . . . . 4 . . . . . 5 . . . . . 6 . . . . . 7 . . . . . 8 . . . . . 9 10

My head is spinning!!   **It's starting to**   **I'm all over it!**
                               make sense.

Now pinpoint anything you don't understand. What do you still need to learn? Is there anything about stated main ideas that you need clarified? Write your response on the lines below.

_____

_____

_____

_____

_____

_____

For anything you don't understand or can't remember, what steps could you take to solve the problem? Do you need to reread? Ask a classmate or your instructor for help? Write the information down or review it some other way? Write your response here.

_____

_____

_____

_____

In Chapter 10, you will learn about *implied main ideas.* An implied main idea is a sentence that you, the reader, must create that tells the author's most important point. That sentence will have the same characteristics as a stated main idea sentence, so if you need clarification about stated main ideas, take the time to get it now. It will help you later on.

Map of Chapters

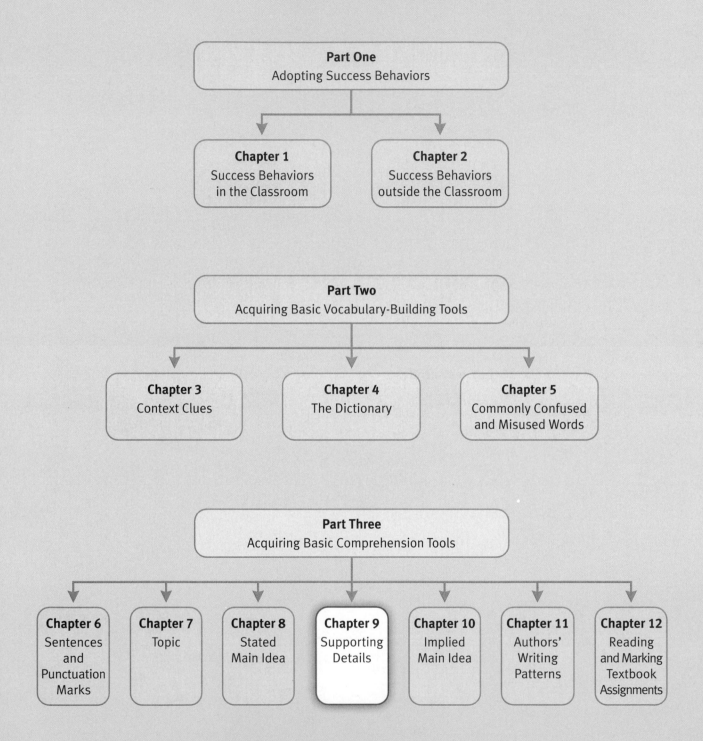

Part One
Adopting Success Behaviors

Chapter 1
Success Behaviors
in the Classroom

Chapter 2
Success Behaviors
outside the Classroom

Part Two
Acquiring Basic Vocabulary-Building Tools

Chapter 3
Context Clues

Chapter 4
The Dictionary

Chapter 5
Commonly Confused
and Misused Words

Part Three
Acquiring Basic Comprehension Tools

Chapter 6
Sentences
and
Punctuation
Marks

Chapter 7
Topic

Chapter 8
Stated
Main Idea

Chapter 9
Supporting
Details

Chapter 10
Implied
Main Idea

Chapter 11
Authors'
Writing
Patterns

Chapter 12
Reading
and Marking
Textbook
Assignments

CHAPTER 9

Supporting Details

More Information, Please

Why You Need to Know the Information in This Chapter

Supporting details provide the additional information you need in order to understand a main idea completely. This chapter explains what supporting details are, how to identify them, and types of supporting details.

Understanding supporting details will help you

- understand more of what you read
- figure out the main idea when the author implies it
- make higher test grades
- mark your textbooks intelligently
- take better notes from your textbooks
- understand how paragraphs are organized
- write better paragraphs

Super Student Tips

Here's what students like you have to say about identifying the supporting details of paragraphs:

"I'm a visual learner. In my mind, I see the main idea as a magnet that's attracting the supporting details to it. I see them all stuck to it. It holds them together."—*Sheldon*

"My writing has improved. I used to think that if I just wrote a lot, I'd done what I was supposed to. Now I realize that the details all need to relate to the main idea." —*Miguel*

"Details help you understand the main idea better. They explain it or give examples."—*Lacy*

"It helps me to think of major and minor details as being like parents and their kids. I understand the relationship."—*Patrick*

"I remember the details better when I have a main idea to hook them to."—*Shandrea*

"If there's a stated main idea, find it first and turn it into a question. Then look for the answer to that question. It leads you right to the details. The details are the answers to the questions."—*Bronwen*

"When you can't find a stated main idea in a paragraph, look at the details. You can usually figure it out the main idea from them." —*Mary Ellen*

278

Jumpstart Your Brain!

Time to get your brain into gear! You'll need some "out-of-the-box" thinking to solve this box puzzle.
   Squares have four equal sides. If the dots below are used as corners of squares, how many squares are there in this set of dots? There may be more than you think. Have fun!

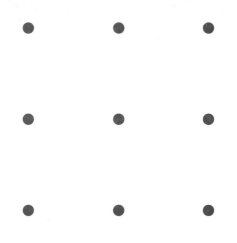

Write your answer here: _____

Compare your answer to your classmates' answers. Explain to each other how you went about solving the puzzle.

LOOKING AT WHAT YOU ALREADY KNOW

 Respond to these items as best you can. You may not be able to answer all, or even any, of them. That's okay. As you work through the chapter or when you have completed it, you can make corrections.

1. In your own words and without looking up the information, write a definition of *supporting detail:* _____

    _____

2. List any words that you can think of that introduce supporting details.

    _____

    _____

Supporting Details

It is not the answer that enlightens, but the question.

—Eugene Ionesco, playwright

First, a quick review: In Chapter 7, you learned that every paragraph has a topic. To determine the topic, you learned to ask yourself, "Who or what is this paragraph about?" You learned that every paragraph has a main idea. In Chapter 8, you learned to locate the stated main idea by asking yourself, "What is the author's *most* important point about the topic?" and then looking for a sentence that answers that question. (In Chapter 10, you will learn how to create a main idea sentence when the author does not state it directly.) Finally, you learned how to check a possible main idea sentence. You learned that a main idea sentence must have all of these characteristics:

- It tells the author's most important point.
- It contains the topic.
- It makes complete sense by itself.
- It is a general sentence.

A paragraph consists of more than a main idea, of course. The other sentences in a stated main idea paragraph are called *supporting details*.

The Big Picture for This Chapter

In this chapter you'll learn what supporting details are and why you need to identify them. You'll use inductive reasoning to figure out the purposes of supporting details. You'll discover something about the levels of importance in supporting details. You'll learn the clues and signal words that introduce details. Once you know this information, you'll add a powerful comprehension tool: identifying supporting details in paragraphs.

Supporting Details in a Paragraph

Supporting details are the additional information the author provides so that you can understand the main idea completely. Knowing about supporting details has many advantages. It enables you to mark your textbooks intelligently and to take better notes, it assists you in understanding how textbook material in a paragraph is organized, and it will help you figure out the main idea when the author implies (suggests) it instead of stating it.

To locate the supporting details in a paragraph, first determine the main idea. Then ask yourself, "What *additional* information does the author provide to help me understand the main idea completely?" The details are the information that answers the question.

Main ideas are usually stated. One nice thing about stated main idea paragraphs is that once you have found the main idea sentence, you have also found the supporting details: They are everything else that is left—all of the other sentences. Think of it as a "two-for-the-price-of-one" special!

Another way to identify the details is to turn the main idea sentence into one or more questions by using *who, what, when, where,* and *why.* The questions are ones that you're likely to wonder about anyway. The supporting details will answer the questions you create. For example, in an earlier chapter you read this paragraph:

> Perhaps you've heard the old saying, "Lightning never strikes twice in the same place." <u>Contrary to popular belief, lightning can strike twice in the same place, and, in fact, it is more likely to do so than not.</u> Lightning is a form of electrical energy. Since air is a poor conductor of electricity, the electrical charge we call lightning needs help bridging the gap between the cloud and the ground. A tall tree or building, especially one with a metal framework, or even an elevation in the landscape, acts as a convenient path and "attracts" lightning. This is the reason lightning is likely to strike more than once in the same place.

The second sentence is the main idea: *Contrary to popular belief, lightning can strike twice in the same place, and, in fact, it is more likely to do so than not.* The first thing you would wonder is, "Why?" So turn the main idea into the question, "*Why* is lightning likely to strike twice in the same place?" The details in the paragraph answer the question. They explain the reason.

 STOP AND PROCESS

EXERCISE 9.1

You also read this paragraph earlier. Its main idea is the last sentence: *In short, while caffeine is fine for most people, there are certain individuals who should limit or avoid caffeine.*

> For most people, a cup of caffeinated coffee is a relatively safe way to perk up the brain. However, caffeine can cause nervousness or headaches in some individuals. It can also trigger panic attacks and raise blood pressure. Those who have borderline high blood pressure should restrict their caffeine. Finally, women who are pregnant or nursing should leave off caffeine. <u>In short, while caffeine is fine for most people, there are certain individuals who should limit or avoid caffeine.</u>

On the lines below, write the question or questions you could create from the main idea sentence:

_____

_____

Did you write *Who should limit caffeine or avoid it altogether?* and/or *Why should certain individuals limit or avoid caffeine?* If not, do so now.

Now turn each of these main idea sentences into one or more questions:

1. Research shows that some breeds of dogs are more likely to bite.

    _____

    _____

2. The body has an interesting way of preventing liquid and solid food from going down the windpipe when we swallow.

    _____

    _____

3. Certain conditions cause disease to spread rapidly.

    _____

4. Tornadoes occur more often in certain regions of the United States.

    _____

    _____

5. During every 24-hour period, there are times when we are more prone to suffer an accident or injury.

    _____

    _____

Now you know a technique for locating the details. Let's consider a bit more the relationship between details and the main idea in a paragraph. Think of a paragraph as a house. The roof, which holds everything together, is the main idea. The details are the walls that support the roof. You need both a roof (main idea) and walls (details) to have a house (paragraph).

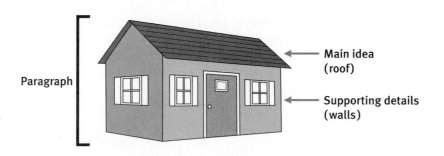

If the analogy of the Kingdom of Paragraph and King Stated Main Idea in Chapters 7 and 8 made sense to you, recall that the supporting details are the king's loyal "subjects." There can be only one king (main idea), but there are lots of people he governs (the details). They are less important than the king. In fact, they are there to serve the king (remember, it's not a democracy!). Without a king to lead them, they would be a group of random individuals. In a paragraph, the main idea "governs" the details. They are there to "serve" (support) it.

Another way to understand the connection between the main idea and the details is to visualize a puzzle that has one major piece that all the other pieces connect to. Without that piece, there's no puzzle. The other pieces fall apart. The main piece represents the main idea, of course, and the other pieces represent the details.

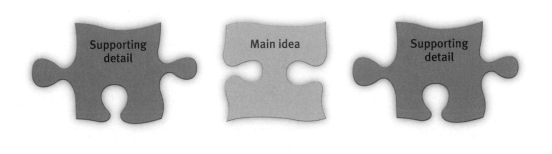

Reasoning Out the Characteristics of Supporting Details

The paragraphs in the sample sets below have stated main ideas. That means the rest of the sentences are details. Read the paragraphs and determine the main idea sentence in each one. Then use the paragraphs as the basis for answering certain questions about supporting details. Some paragraphs are ones that you have read previously.

Discover the First Characteristic of Supporting Details

What purposes do supporting details serve?

All details explain or tell more about the main idea, but they can do this several ways. In other words, they can serve many purposes. The details in each sample paragraph below serve a different purpose. For each paragraph, decide what the specific *purpose* of the details is. What function do they serve? Write your answer in the margin beside the examples paragraph. You won't need to memorize the functions. The goal is simply to make you aware of purposes that details can serve. The first paragraph is done as an example.

The topic of this paragraph is *water in the earth's atmosphere*. What type of additional information do the details provide?

> Raindrops are an example of water in the atmosphere when it occurs in liquid form. It also appears in solid form; for example, as snowflakes and hail. When water occurs in the atmosphere as water vapor, it is in the form of an invisible gas. The point is, water in the earth's atmosphere occurs in three forms: liquid, solid, and gas.

The last sentence states the main idea. The rest of the sentences are details that give examples of water in different forms: raindrops, snowflakes, hail, and water vapor.

The topic of the next paragraph is *President Theodore Roosevelt*. What type of additional information do the details provide? (Remember to determine (underline) the main idea sentence first. Use the margin to write your answer about the type of information the details provide.)

> Theodore ("Teddy") Roosevelt is remembered for many reasons. He gained national popularity as a hero in the Spanish-American War. He then became vice president under William McKinley. When McKinley was assassinated, Roosevelt became the 26th president. As president, he was a reformer who used government power to force big businesses to act more fairly and responsibly. He is associated with the construction of the Panama Canal. A sportsman and outdoorsman, he promoted conservation programs to protect the country's natural resources and forests, and he set aside more than 200 million acres as national parks and nature preserves.

The topic of the next paragraph is the *Statue of Liberty*. What type of additional information do the details provide?

> More than a century ago, France gave the United States a statue by sculptor Auguste Bartholdi. Since 1886 "Miss Liberty" has presided over New York Harbor, where she has welcomed millions of immigrants to America. The "Lady with the Lamp" is constructed of tons of iron and copper, and is one of the tallest statues in the world. It symbolizes the United States. The Statue of Liberty is a historic landmark that is recognized worldwide.

The topic of the next paragraph is *Juneteenth*. What type of additional information do the details provide?

> *Juneteenth* is a celebration of the end of slavery. In 1863, President Lincoln issued the Emancipation Proclamation that abolished slavery. On June 19, 1865, a ship with Union soldiers docked in Texas. The officer in charge proclaimed that slavery was no longer legal. However, the people of Texas were unaware that it had been abolished two years earlier, and so the holiday was born. It is the oldest known holiday of its sort. Today it is celebrated in many parts of the country.

The topic of the next paragraph is *the advantage to birds of being able to fly*. What type of additional information do the details provide?

> How does the ability to fly help birds? Biologists say flying gives birds at least three advantages. First, it enables them to escape danger. Second, they can travel great distances, when necessary, to locate food. Finally, the ability to fly enables birds to protect their eggs and chicks by building nests high above the ground.

The topic of the next paragraph is *the correct procedure for washing your hands*. What type of additional information do the details provide?

> There is a correct procedure for washing your hands. First, wet your hands, with warm water if possible. Apply sufficient soap to create a

lather. Scrub your hands, including the backs and under the fingernails, for at least thirty seconds. Rinse thoroughly. Use a paper towel to turn off the faucet so that you do not contaminate your clean hands. Dry your hands thoroughly with a paper towel or air dryer.

STOP AND PROCESS

EXERCISE 9.2

What are some purposes of details? Look back at the sample paragraphs and list the purposes on the lines below.

_____

_____

CROSS-CHAPTER CONNECTIONS

In Chapter 11, you will learn some of the ways writers organize details in a paragraph. You will also be able to use these same patterns to organize the details in paragraphs you write.

Visual Summary for Chapters 1–9

CHAPTER 1

Success Behaviors in the Classroom

Classroom Success Behaviors

- Read and understand the syllabus.
- Be in class on time, every time.
- Learn your instructor's name and your classmates' names.
- Sit in the right place.
- Come prepared for class and participate.
- Be polite and use appropriate language.

CHAPTER 2

Success Behaviors outside the Classroom

Out-of-Class Success Behaviors

- Set goals and make a commitment.
- Get organized.
- Prepare for class.
- Manage your assignments.
- Monitor your progress and see your instructor when you need help.
- Take advantage of out-of-class resources.

CHAPTER 3
Context Clues

Context clues: words in a sentence or paragraph that authors include to help readers reason out the meaning of unfamiliar words.

Five Types of Context Clues

1. Definition or synonym clue

The author *tells* the meaning of the unfamiliar word.

> His outlook is *pessimistic*; that is, he always expects the worst.

2. Contrast clue

There is a word or phrase in the sentence that means the *opposite* of the unfamiliar word.

> Certain foods make you feel *lethargic* rather than energetic.

3. Example clue

One or more examples *illustrate* the meaning of the unfamiliar word (but the examples are not the definition).

> Oranges, grapefruits, and other *citrus* fruits are part of a healthy diet.

4. General sense of the sentence

The *overall meaning* of the sentence, combined with your own experience and knowledge, allow you to determine the meaning of the unfamiliar word.

> Traffic jams cause some drivers to become *belligerent.*

5. Clue from another sentence

Information *from another sentence* helps you determine the meaning of the unfamiliar word.

> Florists who deliver flowers use *Mercury* as their symbol. In Roman mythology, he was the fleet-footed messenger of the gods.

Watch for *signal words* and *clues* that indicate each type of context clue.

CHAPTER 4
The Dictionary

The **dictionary** is a key to a better vocabulary and greater success in school.

ers. [Fr. < OFr. *jardin*, GARDEN.]

jar•gon (jär′gən) ▶*n.* **1.** Nonsensical or incoherent talk. **2.** The specialized or technical language of a trade or profession. [< OFr.]

Jarls•berg (yärlz′bûrg′) ▶ A trademark for a mild, pale-yellow, hard Norwegian cheese.

jas•mine (jăz′mĭn) also **jes•sa•mine** (jĕs′ə-mĭn) ▶*n.* Any of a genus of vines or shrubs having fragrant white or yellow flowers. [< Pers. *yasmīn.*]

jas•per (jăs′pər) ▶*n.* An opaque red, yellow, or brown quartz. [< Gk. *iaspis.*]

ja•to (jā′tō) ▶*n., pl.* **-tos.** An aircraft takeoff aided by an auxiliary rocket. [*j(et-)a(ssisted) t(ake)o(ff).*]

jaun•dice (jôn′dĭs, jän′-) ▶*n.* Yellowish discoloration of the eyes and tissues caused by deposition of bile salts. ▶*v.* **-diced, -dic•ing 1.** To affect with jaundice. **2.** To affect with envy, prejudice, or hostility. See Syns at **bias.** [< OFr. *jaunice*, yellowness.]

jaunt (jônt, jänt) ▶*n.* A short trip or excursion. [?] —**jaunt** *v.*

jaun•ty (jôn′tē, jän′-) ▶*adj.* **-ti•er, -ti•est 1.** Having a buoyant or self-confident air. **2.** Dapper in appearance. [< OFr. *gentil*, noble. See GENTLE.] —**jaun′ti•ly** *adv.* —**jaun′ti•ness** *n.*

ja•va (jä′və, jăv′ə) ▶*n. Informal* Brewed coffee. [< JAVA.]

Java. An island of Indonesia separated from Borneo by the **Java Sea,** an arm of the Pacific. —**Jav′a•nese′** *adj. & n.*

jave•lin (jăv′lĭn, jăv′ə-) ▶*n.* **1.** A light spear, thrown as a weapon. **2.** A metal or metal-tipped spear, used in contests of distance throwing. [< OFr. *javeline*, of Celt. orig.]

jaw (jô) ▶*n.* **1.** Either of two bony or cartilaginous structures that in most vertebrates form the framework of the mouth and hold the teeth. **2.** Either of two opposed hinged parts in a mechanical device. **3. jaws** A dangerous situation. **4.** *Slang* **a.** Back talk. **b.** A chat. ▶*v. Slang* To talk; converse. [ME *jawe.*] —**jaw′less** *adj.*

jaw•bone (jô′bōn′) ▶*n.* A bone of the jaw, esp. of the lower jaw. ▶*v.* **-boned, -bon•ing** *Slang.* To try to influence or pressure through strong persuasion.

jaw•break•er (jô′brā′kər) ▶*n.* **1.** A very hard candy. **2.** *Slang* A word difficult to pronounce.

jay (jā) ▶*n.* Any of various often crested birds gen. having a loud harsh call. [< LLat. *gāius.*]

Jay, John. 1745–1829. Amer. diplomat and first chief justice of the US Supreme Court (1789–95).

jay•walk (jā′wôk′) ▶*v.* To cross a street in violation of traffic regulations. [< *jay*, inexperienced person.] —**jay′walk′er** *n.*

jazz (jăz) ▶*n.* **1.** A style of American music marked by a strong but flexible rhythmic understructure with solo and ensemble improvisations and a highly sophisticated harmonic idiom. **2.** *Slang* **a.** Animation; enthusiasm. **b.** Nonsense. **c.** Miscellaneous, unspecified things. ▶*v. Slang* To exaggerate or lie (to): *Don't jazz me.* —**phrasal verb: jazz up** *Slang* To make more interesting; enliven. [?]

jazz•y (jăz′ē) ▶*adj.* **-i•er, -i•est 1.** Of or resembling jazz. **2.** *Slang* Showy; flashy. —**jazz′i•ly** *adv.* —**jazz′i•ness** *n.*

JCS ▶*abbr.* Joint Chiefs of Staff

jct. ▶*abbr.* junction

JD ▶*abbr.* **1.** *Lat.* Juris Doctor (Doctor of Law) **2.** Justice Department **3.** juvenile delinquent

jeal•ous (jĕl′əs) ▶*adj.* **1.** Fearful of losing affection or position. **2.** Resentful or bitter in rivalry; envious. **3.** Arising from feelings of envy, apprehension, or bitterness. **4.** Vigilant in guarding something. [< VLat. *zēlōsus* < LLat. *zēlus*, ZEAL.] —**jeal′ous•ly** *adv.* —**jeal′ous•y, jeal′ous•ness** *n.*
  Syns: jealous, covetous, envious adj.

jean (jēn) ▶*n.* **1.** A heavy cotton. **2. jeans** Pants made of jean or denim. [< OFr. *Genes*, Genoa.]

jeep (jēp) ▶*n.* A small durable US Army motor vehicle with four-wheel drive. [< *GP* < the manufacturer's parts-numbering system.]

jeer (jîr) ▶*v.* To speak or shout derisively. [?] —**jeer** *n.* —**jeer′er** *n.*

Jef•fer•son (jĕf′ər-sən), **Thomas.** 1743–1826. The 3rd US President (1801–09). —**Jef′fer•so′ni•an** *adj. & n.*

Thomas Jefferson 1805 portrait

Jefferson City. The capital of MO, in the central part on the Missouri R. Pop. 35,481.

Je•hosh•a•phat (jə-hŏsh′ə-făt′, -hŏs′-). 9th cent. B.C. King of Judah.

Je•ho•vah (jĭ-hō′və) ▶*n.* In the Old Testament, God. [Blend of consonants of YAHWEH and vowels of Heb. *ădônāy*, my lord.]

je•june (jə-jōōn′) ▶*adj.* **1.** Not interesting. **2.** Lacking maturity; childish. **3.** Lacking in nutrition. [< Lat. *ieiūnus*, dry, fasting.] —**je•june′ly** *adv.* —**je•june′ness** *n.*

je•ju•num (jə-jōō′nəm) ▶*n., pl.* **-na** (-nə). The section of the small intestine between the duodenum and the ileum. [< Med.Lat. *ieiūnum (intestīnum)*, fasting (intestine).]

jell (jĕl) ▶*v.* **1.** To make or become firm or gelatinous. **2.** To take shape; crystallize. [Prob. < JELLY.]

jel•ly (jĕl′ē) ▶*n., pl.* **-lies 1.** A soft semisolid food typically made by the boiling and setting of fruit juice, sugar, and pectin or gelatin. **2.** Something having the consistency of jelly. ▶*v.* **-lied, -ly•ing.** To make into or become jelly. [< Lat. *gelāre*, freeze.]

jel•ly•bean (jĕl′ē-bēn′) ▶*n.* A small chewy candy.

jel•ly•fish (jĕl′ē-fĭsh′) ▶*n.* **1.** A gelatinous, free-swimming marine animal often having a bell-shaped stage as the dominant phase of its life cycle. **2.** *Informal* A weakling.

jel•ly•roll (jĕl′ē-rōl′) ▶*n.* A thin sheet of sponge cake layered with jelly and then rolled up.

Dictionary entry:

Entry word in syllables — Part of speech

Pronunciation

jay.walk (jā′wôk′) ▶ *v.* To cross a street in violation —— Definition
of traffic regulations. [< *jay*, inexperienced person.]

—**jay′walk′er** *n.*

Other form of the word

Etymology

Source: The American Heritage Dictionary, 4th ed. New York: Random House, Inc., 2001, p. 457. Copyright © 2001 by Houghton Mifflin Company. Reproduced by permission from *The American Heritage Dictionary of the English Language, Fourth Edition.* Image of Thomas Jefferson: National Portrait Gallery, Smithsonian Institution; gift of the Regents of the Smithsonian Institution, the Thomas Jefferson Memorial Foundation, and the Enid and Crosby Kemper Foundation; owned jointly with Monticello. Reprinted with permission of the National Portrait Gallery, Smithsonian Institution via Art Resource, NY.

CHAPTER 5
Commonly Confused and Misused Words

Understanding **commonly confused and misused words** will improve your reading comprehension, writing, and spelling.

Homonyms are words that sound the same (have the "same name") and sometimes have the same spelling but have different meanings.

You *hear here.*

One word or two? Some words can be confused with two separate words that sound the same but have different meanings.

She was *altogether* correct when she said the students were *all together* in the gym.

Some words are **misused** because people confuse their meanings: they use one when they need the other.

Breathe deeply and hold your *breath*.

Capital or capitol? Its or it's? Less or fewer? Already or all ready?

Advise or advice? Loose or lose? There, they're, or their? Imply or infer?

CHAPTER 6
Sentences and Punctuation Marks

Sentence: a group of words that expresses a complete thought.

> **sentence** = subject + predicate
> The students cheered.

- The subject of the sentence tells who or what the sentence is about or is talking about.
- The predicate (verb) tells what the subject is doing or what is being said about the subject.
- A sentence can have multiple subjects or verbs (more than one).
  > The students and faculty cheered and clapped.
- A sentence can have a direct object, an object that receives the action of the verb.
  > The students cheered the team.

Compound Sentence: two or more independent clauses joined by a coordinating conjunction.

> compound sentence = independent (,) + coordinating + independent
> clause conjunction clause
> School is challenging, but I'm glad I'm here!

- An **independent clause** has a subject and a verb. It can stand alone; it makes sense by itself.
- A coordinating conjunction is a word that connects two equal grammatical elements. The coordinating conjunctions are the "FAN BOYS": **F**or, **A**nd, **N**or, **B**ut, **O**r, **Y**et, **S**o.

Complex Sentence: an independent clause and one or more dependent clauses
- A dependent clause is a clause that depends on the rest of the sentence in order to make sense.

> **complex sentence** = independent clause + dependent clause(s) (in either order)
> He's taking geology because he likes science.

CHAPTER 7

Determining the Topic of a Paragraph

Paragraph: a piece of writing that begins on a new line that is indented, has one main point the author wants to make about the topic of the paragraph, and contains details that tell more about the most important point.

Topic: a word, name, or phrase that tells *who* or *what* is discussed throughout a paragraph. Ask yourself, "Who or what is this paragraph about?"

A topic should be precise—neither too general, nor too specific.

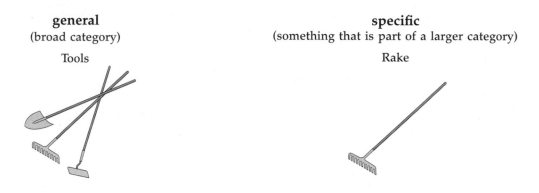

general	**specific**
(broad category)	(something that is part of a larger category)
Tools	Rake

Four Clues to the Topic

- **Title or heading**
- **Words in special print**
- **Repeated words or phrases**
- **Mentioned at the beginning and then referred to throughout**

This sample paragraph, with the topic highlighted in pink, illustrates the first three types of clues.

MEMORY STRATEGIES

There are several *memory strategies* that can help students. The first is to be sure you understand the material. It is difficult to memorize material that is not meaningful to you. The second memory strategy is to rehearse the material. Do this by repeating it out loud or writing it until you can do so without looking at it. A final memory strategy is to use "memory pegs" to help you remember important points. For example, you can make up a rhyme and even set it to a familiar tune.

CHAPTER 8
Stated Main Idea

Stated Main Idea: a sentence in a paragraph that tells the author's most important point about the topic.

Here is a visual representation of what a main idea sentence consists of:

King Stated Main Idea = topic + author's most important point about the topic

Additional Clues to the Stated Main Idea Sentence
- always contains the *topic* of the paragraph
- must always make *complete sense* by itself
- is a *general* sentence that *sums up* the rest of the paragraph

In this sample paragraph, the topic is highlighted in pink and the stated main idea sentence in yellow. Notice that the highlighted sentence has all the characteristics a stated main idea sentence must have.

MEMORY STRATEGIES

There are several memory strategies that can help students. The first is to be sure you understand the material. It is difficult to memorize material that is not meaningful to you. The second memory strategy is to rehearse the material. Do this by repeating it out loud or writing it until you can do so without looking at it. A final memory strategy is to use "memory pegs" to help you remember important points. For example, you can make up a rhyme and even set it to a familiar tune.

The stated main idea sentence can appear at the *beginning* of a paragraph, at the *end* of a paragraph, or *within a paragraph*:

First sentence	Last sentence	Not first or last sentence

CHAPTER 9
Supporting Details

Supporting Details: additional information the author provides so that you can understand the main idea completely.

- They give **examples, reasons, descriptions, explanations, lists,** and **steps** in a process.
- Some details are more important than others:

  major (primary) details: details that are essential for understanding the main idea completely

  minor (secondary) details: less important details that explain other details

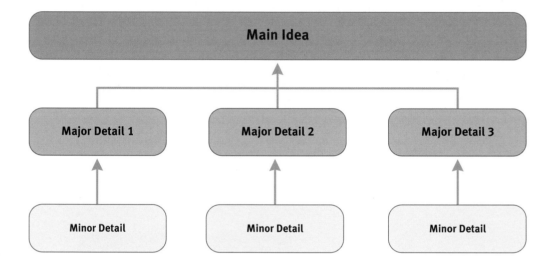

- Certain **clue words** announce details, and there are often clues in the main idea sentence as well. A single sentence can contain more than one detail. Some clues are: *for example; first, second, next, last; 1, 2, 3; a, b, c;* bullets (• • •); and phrases in the main idea such as *four types, two kinds, three ways, two categories, and five stages.*

In this sample paragraph, the stated main idea sentence is highlighted in yellow. The supporting details, the rest of the sentences, are highlighted in green. Clue words are underlined.

MEMORY STRATEGIES

There are several memory strategies that can help students. The first is to be sure you understand the material. It is difficult to memorize material that is not meaningful to you. The second memory strategy is to rehearse the material. Do this by repeating it out loud or writing it until you can do so without looking at it. A final memory strategy is to use "memory pegs" to help you remember important points. For example, you can make up a rhyme and even set it to a familiar tune.

Characteristic 1: Details are used for a variety of purposes, such as giving examples, reasons, and other specific information.

Here's what you should have discovered:

Paragraph's Topic	Purpose of the Details
forms of water	to give *examples* of water's various forms
Theodore Roosevelt	to provide the *reasons* he is remembered
Statue of Liberty	to *describe* it
Juneteenth	to *explain* how it came about and tell about it today
advantages to birds of being able to fly	to *list* those advantages
the correct hand washing procedure	to give the *steps in the process* or *sequence*

As you can see, details are used for a variety of purposes. Details also give statistics, similarities and differences, characteristics, causes, and other specific information (such as names and dates). Details provide *specific* information that explains the *general* main idea.

STOP AND PROCESS

EXERCISE 9.3

To help you remember that authors include details for a variety of reasons, write the purpose of any details that you missed above, and highlight the word you wrote in the margin that describes each purpose.

Discover the Second Characteristic of Supporting Details

Are all supporting details equally important, or are there different levels of importance?

Is every supporting detail in a paragraph as important as every other detail? Read the paragraph below and the information beneath it. Then decide whether some supporting details are more important than others. The stated main idea sentence is underlined.

> Manufacturers use a variety of incentives to get consumers to buy their products again. One incentive is discount coupons that customers can apply to future purchases. For example, a cookie manufacturer might enclose coupons in cookie boxes or print them on the box. Toy trinkets are another type of incentive. Cereal manufacturers, for example, might offer small puzzles and encourage children to "collect the entire set." A contest is a third type of incentive. Consumers buy canned soft drinks, for example, in hopes of finding the winning tab in a contest sponsored by the manufacturer.

BONUS TIP

Here's a memory peg that may help you remember that main ideas are the important *general* statements, while details present specific information that supports the main idea. Think of them as soldiers:

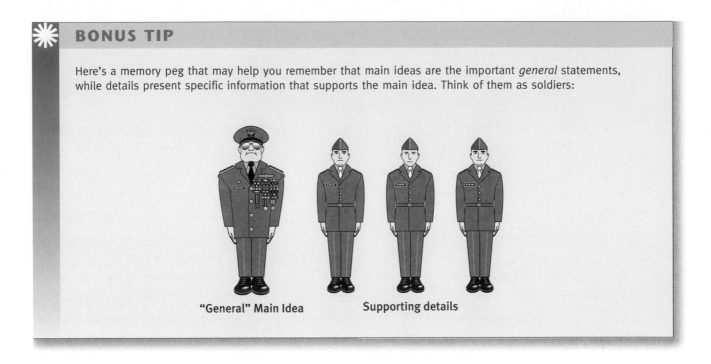

"General" Main Idea   Supporting details

Main idea: *Manufacturers use a variety of incentives to get consumers to buy their products again.*

- Which sentence is explained by the supporting detail "One incentive is discount coupons that customers can apply to future purchases"?

    This supporting detail *explains the main idea sentence* by describing *one* of the "variety of incentives" manufacturers use to get consumers to buy their products again.

- Which sentence is explained by the supporting detail "For example, a cookie manufacturer might enclose coupons in cookie boxes or print them on the box"?

    This supporting detail *explains another supporting detail* (sentence 2) by giving the specific example of a cookie manufacturer using coupons.

- Which sentence is explained by the supporting detail "A contest is a third type of incentive"?

    This supporting detail *explains the main idea* by describing a second type of incentive manufacturers use.

- Which sentence is explained by the supporting detail "Consumers buy canned soft drinks, for example, in hopes of finding the winning tab in a contest the manufacturer sponsors"?

    This supporting detail *explains another supporting detail* (sentence 6) by giving the specific example of a contest, one sponsored by a soft drink manufacturer.

Here is a diagram showing the relationship between the main idea and the details in the paragraph:

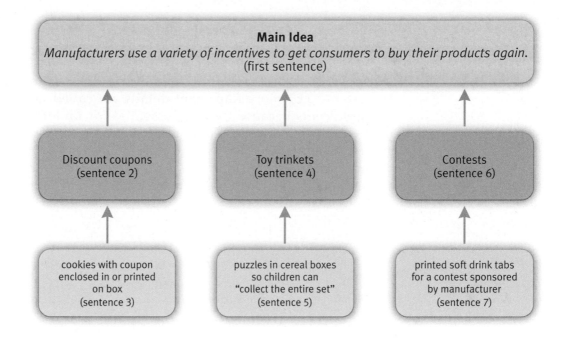

STOP AND PROCESS

EXERCISE 9.4

Now answer these questions.

1. All supporting details ultimately explain more about the main idea. In the paragraph above, all the supporting detail sentences pertain to types of incentives. As you can see from the diagram, though, some details explain other details. Based on that, what can you conclude about whether all supporting details are equally important?

_____

_____

_____

_____

2. Read this version of the paragraph.

> <u>Manufacturers use a variety of incentives to get consumers to buy their products again</u>. One incentive is discount coupons that customers can apply to future purchases. Toy trinkets are another type of incentive. A contest is a third type of incentive. Consumers buy canned soft drinks, for example, in hopes of finding the winning tab in a contest the manufacturer sponsors.

Does the main idea still make sense even though some details have been omitted? Yes or no?

_____

Characteristic 2: Some details are more important than others.

Did you conclude that not all supporting details are equally important? The more important details are called **major details** or *primary details* because they are essential for understanding the main idea completely. The less important details are called **minor details** or *secondary details* because they explain other *details*. Here is the chart again, with the major and minor detail sentences labeled. Notice that the minor details can be left out of a paragraph, but major details cannot.

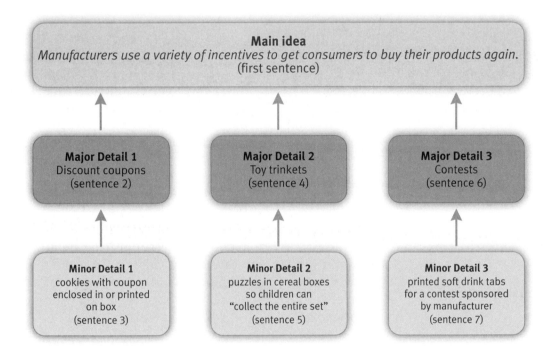

In the Kingdom of Paragraph analogy, the details are the king's loyal subjects. Their job is to support the king (main idea). In a paragraph, every detail directly or indirectly supports the main idea. As you just discovered, though, some details are more important than others. Think of the major details as the adult subjects in the kingdom. Think of the minor details as the children in the kingdom. Ultimately, everyone supports the king, but the adults (major details) are essential. The children (minor details) are devoted to their parents (the major details), who in turn support the king (main idea).

If the analogy of General Main Idea and his troops makes sense to you (see the Bonus Tip box on page 288), think of the major details as high-ranking officers and the minor details as lowly privates.

You can also visualize a stated main idea paragraph as a tree. The trunk, which holds everything together, is the main idea. The branches are the major details. The leaves, which are attached to the branches, are the minor details.

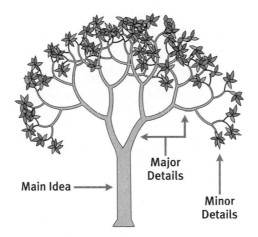

Trees can lose their leaves and still be trees. Without their branches, though, there would be nothing for the leaves to attach to. Similarly, a paragraph can "live" without its minor details, but it needs the major details. Look back at the chart on page 289. All of the major details have supporting details. In your reading, you will find that paragraphs can have any number of major and minor details, but not every major detail has minor details. So a general diagram for a paragraph might look like this:

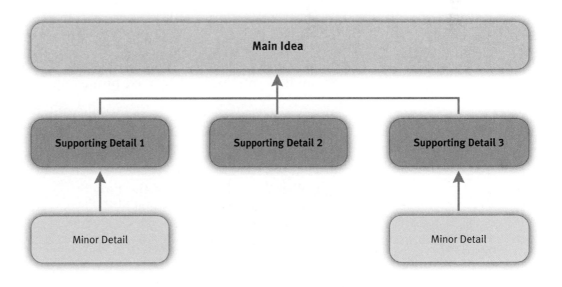

Discover the Third Characteristic of Supporting Details

What are some clue words or other signals that introduce supporting details?

As you may have guessed by now, examples are always details. Examples are usually introduced by phrases such as *for example, for instance,* or *to illustrate.* What other signals and clue words help you know that the author is presenting details? Read these three sample paragraphs to see if you can spot the clues that signal the primary details. The main idea sentences are underlined.

> Discipline style is an important part of parenting. Psychologist Diana Baumrind studied parents' discipline styles extensively. <u>Baumrind identified three discipline styles used by parents.</u> First, there is the *authoritarian style*. Authoritarian parents have strict rules, do not allow children to question their authority, and punish children if they do not obey the rules. Another style is the *authoritative style*. Authoritative parents explain the rules and are willing to discuss the reasons for them. They tend not to use physical punishment, preferring instead to reinforce appropriate behavior with warmth and affection. They encourage independence, but set limits. Finally, there is the *permissive style*. Permissive parents have few rules and are unlikely to punish inappropriate behavior. Their children often feel uncomfortable because they are given too much freedom at too early an age.

> Is there a problem or issue you are struggling to resolve? <u>There is an effective six-step procedure you can use to solve any problem.</u>
>
> 1. Identify the problem precisely.
> 2. Gather the facts; do some research if you need to.
> 3. Think of as many solutions as possible and decide what might happen if you applied each one.
> 4. Apply the solution that seems best.
> 5. Evaluate the results.
> 6. If you're not satisfied with the way things turned out, try another solution that seemed promising.

> <u>According to the Internet Activity Index published at the end of 2004, Americans have four top-rated computer activities.</u> In order, the way they spent most of their computer time was:
>
> - viewing content, such as news, sports, and entertainment websites—40.2 percent of the time
> - communicating, such as email—39.8 percent of their time
> - shopping and commerce—15.8 percent
> - conducting a search—4.3 percent

STOP AND PROCESS

EXERCISE 9.5

1. In these sample excerpts, the supporting details were introduced by certain clue words or signals. Look at the examples again. What clues or signals announced the details? List them here:

_____

_____

_____

2. Were there clues in the main idea sentence that led you to expect certain types of details? List any main idea clues that "announced" the details:

_____

_____

Characteristic 3: Certain clue words announce details, and the main idea sentence often includes clues.

Besides using *for example, for instance,* and *to illustrate* to introduce examples (which are always details), did you discover these other clues in the sample paragraphs?

- In the paragraph about parents' discipline styles, did you find the signal words *first, another,* and *finally*? The author used them to introduce the major details that explained each of the styles. (Other clue words authors use to introduce details are *in addition, and, also, moreover, second, third, next,* and *last.*) Authors may also use special print, such as color, bold print, or italics, to make details stand out. The italicized names of the parenting styles illustrate this.

- In the second sample paragraph, did you discover that the author used *numbers* to signal important details, the steps in the problem-solving process? (Authors sometimes use alphabet letters to set off the details.)

- In the third sample paragraph, did you discover that the author used *bullets* to signal the important details, the four top-rated Internet activities?

- Did you discover that the main idea sentence itself often gives you a hint about the details that will be presented? It might contain general phrases such as *four types, two kinds, three ways, two categories,* or the *five stages.* Seeing these, you would anticipate details that tell the specific types, kinds, ways, categories, or steps. In the sample paragraphs the main idea sentences contained these clues about the details you could expect: (1) *three* discipline *styles,* (2) *six-step procedure* for solving any problem, and (3) *four top-rated activities.*

> ### ✺ BONUS TIPS
>
> - **A single sentence can contain more than one detail.** For example, this sentence contains three details:
>
>   Authoritarian parents have strict rules, do not allow children to question their authority, and punish children if they do not obey the rules.
>
>   Your instructors expect you to find *all* the details, even when there are no clues or signal words.
>
> - **You can use details as the basis for creating a main idea sentence when the author has not stated it.** This is called an *implied main idea sentence.* You will learn about implied main ideas in the next chapter.

Although many details are announced by a clue or signal word, *not every detail is introduced by a clue.* That's okay. You can still find them. If the author does not number them, you should write in small numbers beside them in your textbook. When you are ready to review for a test, it will be easy to see how many details there are and what they are. Don't underline them! If you do, you'll underline almost everything. That's no help at all. Read the paragraph below. Notice how the inserted numbers make each of the seven details stand out.

> Theodore ("Teddy") Roosevelt is remembered for many reasons. He[1] gained national popularity as a hero in the Spanish-American War. He then became[2] vice president under William McKinley. When McKinley was assassinated, Roosevelt became the[3] 26th president. As

president, he was a[4]reformer who used government power to force big businesses to act more fairly and responsibly. He is associated with the [5]construction of the Panama Canal. A sportsman and outdoorsman, he [6]promoted conservation programs to protect the country's natural resources and forests, and he[7]set aside more than 200 million acres as national parks and nature preserves.

 STOP AND PROCESS

EXERCISE 9.6

Now you try it. Read the paragraph below. Underline the stated main idea sentence. Then find the six details and write a small number beside each of them.

There is a correct procedure for washing your hands. First, wet your hands, with warm water if possible. Apply sufficient soap to create a lather. Scrub your hands, including the backs and under the fingernails, for at least 30 seconds. Rinse thoroughly. Use a paper towel to turn off the faucet so that you do not contaminate your clean hands. Dry your hands thoroughly with a paper towel or air dryer.

 **BRAIN-FRIENDLY TIP**

Rather than writing numbers beside the details in textbook paragraphs, you may prefer to make a study map that includes the details or list them on notebook paper. If you list the details on notebook paper, organize them this way:

- Write them in your own words.
- Number them.
- Write each detail on a separate line.

The human brain likes material that is organized, and (as you know) information is easier to memorize when it is organized.

LISTEN UP!

Here's the "rap" about supporting details. It will help you remember important information about supporting details. Say it out loud or make a tape recording of it. ("MI" stands for main idea.)

> *Details* are the info authors supply
> So you'll understand the big "MI."
>
> Details *prove*, *explain*, or *illustrate*
> What the main idea states.
>
> Details are like supporting walls:
> Without 'em the main idea "roof" falls.

MY TOOLBOX *of Supporting Details Tools*

Remembering the Characteristics of Supporting Details

Use one of the strategies below to consolidate what you have learned about supporting details. Regardless of which strategy you choose, be sure to include the following information:

- the definition of *supporting detail*

- the difference between major and minor supporting details

- the functions supporting details can serve

- some clues and signal words that introduce supporting details

  Now decide on a strategy that's best for your learning style:

- **Write a letter to a classmate who was absent.** In your letter, explain the important information about supporting details. Explain it well enough so that your classmate would understand it after reading your letter. If you prefer, you can write the information on notebook paper or on index cards, but writing a letter is more fun!

- **Make a study map (concept map).** You know the procedure for this, and you know that if you're a visual learner, this is a good technique for you.

- **Create a song or rhyme that includes the important information about supporting details.** Say it aloud until you can repeat it (or sing it) from memory. If you prefer, learn the rap that was included in the chapter.

- **Create an analogy or a model of some sort that explains supporting details.** Analogies give comparisons between two things. In the chapter, you saw main ideas and supporting details compared to the roof and walls of a house, a key puzzle piece and the pieces that attach to it, a general and his soldiers, and a tree and its parts. Try to come up with one or more additional comparisons that make sense to you. You can describe them in words, or if you prefer, create a model.

✔ **CHAPTER CHECK**

Answer the following questions about the information in the chapter. In each sentence, fill in the missing information. One word goes in each blank. For some items, there may be more than one correct answer.

1. Supporting details are the _____ information the author provides so that you can understand the main idea completely.

2. One way to identify details is to turn the main idea sentence into one or more _____ by using the words *who, what, when, why, where,* or *how.*

3. Supporting details can serve many different purposes. Some of these purposes are to provide _____, _____, and _____. (List any three.)

4. Details provide _____ information that explains the general main idea.

5. More important details that directly support the main idea are called _____ details.

6. A single sentence can contain more than one detail. True or false?

7. Every detail is introduced by a clue or signal word. True or false?

8. _____ details are less important details that support (explain) other details.

9. Ultimately, all details directly or indirectly support the _____ (two words).

10. Words that introduce examples include _____ and _____.

11. Three of the signal words that can introduce supporting details are _____, _____, and _____.

12. Two nonword clues that introduce details are _____

    and _____.

13. Examples are always details. True or false?

14. In a textbook you should underline or highlight the details. True or false?

15. If you write details on separate paper (notebook paper), you should list each detail on a separate line. True or false?

REVIEW EXERCISES

SET 1

Read the following paragraphs. Each one consists of a stated main idea and several details. In the blanks that follow, write the letters of the supporting details. Since there is more than one detail, you will write more than one answer choice in the blank. *Hint:* Locate the answer choice with the stated main idea—this will help you identify the details that support it. To help you further, the topic is given for each paragraph. The second question about each paragraph asks you the *purpose* of the details in the paragraph.

Before you start, do a couple of shoulder shrugs. Clasp your hands behind you and stretch your shoulders back. Release your hands and then rotate your head in each direction a couple of times.

The topic of this paragraph is *the cause of nearsightedness.*

Genetics seems to play a role in nearsightedness. Scientists know that children with two nearsighted parents are more likely to be nearsighted themselves. Environmental factors are also thought to play a role. For example, there is a strong link between nearsightedness and schoolwork. There is a higher percentage of nearsightedness among students who spend extensive hours in class and doing homework. In addition, one biologist believes that children who wear glasses to correct nearsightedness may actually worsen the problem over time. Scientists do not agree about the cause of nearsightedness.

_____ 1. Which of these are supporting details in the paragraph?

   a. Genetics seems to play a role in nearsightedness.

   b. Environmental factors are also thought to play a role.

   c. In addition, one biologist believes that children who wear glasses to correct nearsightedness may actually worsen the problem over time.

   d. Scientists do not agree about the cause of nearsightedness.

_____ 2. The purpose of the major details in this paragraph is to give

   a. theories about the cause of nearsightedness

   b. a description of treatments for nearsightedness

   c. ways to avoid becoming nearsighted

The topic of this paragraph is *product packaging.*

It is estimated that on an average shopping trip consumers' eyes linger only 2.5 seconds on each product. Therefore, product packaging must be designed to attract and hold consumers' attention.

For example, many people buy Arizona Ice Tea just for the bottle. The attractive packaging—in this case, the bottle—captures attention and makes the product stand out.

Source: Adapted from O.C. Ferrell and Geoffrey Hirt, *Business: A Changing World*, 3rd ed., p. 331. Copyright © 2000 The McGraw-Hill Companies.

_____ 3. Which of these are supporting details in the paragraph?

a. It is estimated that on an average shopping trip consumers' eyes linger only 2.5 seconds on each product.

b. Therefore, product packaging must be designed to attract and hold consumers' attention.

c. For example, many people buy Arizona Ice Tea just for the bottle.

d. The attractive packaging—in this case, the bottle—captures attention and makes the product stand out.

_____ 4. The purpose of the major details in this paragraph is to give

a. steps consumers should follow when selecting products

b. the reason product packaging must be carefully designed

c. two types of product packaging

The topic of this paragraph is *the FBI Crime Index.*

The Federal Bureau of Investigation (FBI) maintains a Crime Index that consists of two broad categories: violent crimes and property crimes. *Violent crimes* include murder, rape, robbery, and aggravated assault. These crimes are committed against people. The second category consists of crimes that involve stealing or burning property. *Property crimes* include burglary, larceny-theft, motor vehicle theft, and arson. To track changes in the frequency with which crimes occur, the FBI annually compiles statistics for each category.

_____ 5. Which of these are supporting details in the paragraph?

a. The Federal Bureau of Investigation (FBI) maintains a Crime Index that consists of two broad categories: violent crimes and property crimes.

b. *Violent crimes* include murder, rape, robbery, and aggravated assault.

c. *Property crimes* include burglary, larceny-theft, motor vehicle theft, and arson.

d. To track changes in the frequency with which crimes occur, the FBI annually compiles statistics for each category.

_____ 6. The purpose of the major details in this paragraph is to give

      a. reasons the FBI created the Crime Index

      b. the history of the FBI Crime Index

      c. a description of the two categories of the FBI Crime Index

The topic of this paragraph is *the "RICE" procedure.*

You're playing tennis and you turn your ankle. You trip while jogging and sprain your wrist. What should you do? Apply heat? Soak it in cold water? "RICE" is a safe, effective four-step procedure for treating sprains and other minor sports injuries.

Rest: Try to avoid using the injured joint for 48 hours so that you don't irritate it further.

Ice: Apply an icepack to the injured area for 15 minutes at a time, with 30 minutes in between. This reduces pain and swelling.

Compression: Wrap the injured joint in an elastic bandage to help stabilize it and minimize swelling. It should be snug, not tight.

Elevate: The goal is to get the injured area above the level of the heart. This also minimizes swelling and speeds healing.

_____ 7. Which of these are supporting details in the paragraph?

      a. You're playing tennis and you turn your ankle.

      b. What should you do?

      c. "RICE" is a safe, effective four-step procedure for treating sprains and other minor sports injuries.

      d. Try to avoid using the injured joint for 48 hours so that you don't irritate it further.

_____ 8. The purpose of the major details in this paragraph is to give

      a. reasons to use the RICE procedure

      b. comparisons between the RICE procedure and other treatments

      c. the parts of the RICE procedure

The topic of this paragraph is *Marfan's syndrome.*

Marfan's syndrome is a rare genetic disease that causes excessively long bones and other abnormalities. A person with Marfan's syndrome will have very long arms and may have a curved spine and misshapen chest. Another characteristic is extremely low body fat. Together, these contribute to an unusually tall, gangly appearance. Abraham Lincoln, for example, is believed to have had this syndrome. Besides abnormal bone length, symptoms of this inherited disorder can include nearsightedness and irregular heart sounds.

_____ 9. Which of these are supporting details in the paragraph?

   a. Marfan's syndrome is a rare genetic disease that causes excessively long bones and other abnormalities.

   b. A person with Marfan's syndrome will have very long arms and may have a curved spine and misshapen chest.

   c. Abraham Lincoln, for example, is believed to have had this syndrome.

   d. Besides abnormal bone length, symptoms of this inherited disorder can include nearsightedness and irregular heart sounds.

_____ 10. The purpose of the major details in this paragraph is to give

   a. characteristics of Marfan's syndrome

   b. examples of famous people with Marfan's syndrome

   c. the procedure for treating Marfan's syndrome

SET 2

Main ideas and details go together. This set of exercises will give you practice with details and, at the same time, allow you to review stated main ideas.

- Read each paragraph.
- To answer the multiple-choice question, write the letter of the answer choice that gives a supporting detail. (The other answer choice will be the stated main idea. You may find it easier to determine the stated main idea first.)
- Answer the two other questions about the details in each paragraph. These questions are about the _purpose_ of the details, the _clue words_ that introduce them, or what the _major details_ are.

Before you start, close your eyes and take a couple of deep breaths. This relaxes you and gets extra oxygen to your brain. Shake your hands to relieve tension in your fingers and wrists.

   Some group members contribute too little. Others seem as if they never stop talking. Unbalanced participation at meetings can cause two sorts of problems. First, it discourages people who don't get a chance to talk. Second, it prevents the group from considering potentially useful ideas.

Source: Adapted from Ronald Adler and Jeanne Elmhorst, _Communicating at Work_, 6th ed., p. 275. Copyright © 1999 The McGraw-Hill Companies.

_____ 1. Which of these is a detail?

     a. Some group members contribute too little.

     b. Unbalanced participation at meetings can cause two sorts of problems.

2. List the two words that introduce the two important details in the paragraph: _____

What do the details in the paragraph explain? _____

_____

On the job, listening for information is the type of listening that is done most often. This is the type of listening that must be done when a supervisor gives instructions. It also occurs when employees take phone messages. Other examples include listening to customers' requests and complaints, or to a colleague's problem.

_____ 3. Which of these is a detail?

     a. On the job, listening for information is the type of listening that is done most often.

     b. This is the type of listening that must be done when a supervisor gives instructions.

4. List the clue in the last sentence of the paragraph that signals details: _____

What is the purpose of the details in the paragraph? _____

_____

The invention of the ignition key made it harder to steal cars. In recent years, manufacturers of automobiles have tried to make cars even more theft-proof. For instance, steering-shaft locks, cutoff switches, and better door locks have decreased car theft. Alarm systems have also improved the security of protected cars.

Source: Adapted from Freda Adler, Gerhard Mueller, and William Laufer, _Criminology_, 5th ed., p. 297. Copyright © 2004 by The McGraw-Hill Companies. Reprinted by permission of The McGraw-Hill Companies, Inc.

_____ 5. Which of these is a detail?

     a. The invention of the ignition key made it harder to steal cars.

     b. In recent years, manufacturers of automobiles have tried to make cars even more theft-proof.

6. List the clue words that the authors use to introduce two of the details: _____

What is the purpose of the details in the paragraph?

_____

_____

www.mhhe.com/
entryways

For more practice,
see the supporting
details exercises in
the ORL material for
this chapter.

Have you ever considered taking a course in first aid? One important benefit of first-aid training is learning what *not* to do in certain situations. For example, a person with a suspected back injury should not be moved unless other life-threatening conditions exist. The same is true for a person who appears to have a neck injury.

Source: From Paul Insel and Walton Roth, *Core Concepts on Health*, Brief Ed., 9th ed., p. 386. Copyright © 2002 by The McGraw-Hill Companies. Reprinted by permission of The McGraw-Hill Companies, Inc.

_____ 7. Which of these is a detail?

a. One important benefit of first-aid training is learning what *not* to do in certain situations.
b. For example, a person with a suspected back injury should not be moved unless other life-threatening conditions exist.

8. Write the words that introduce one of the supporting details:

_____

What is the purpose of the details in the paragraph? _____

_____

_____

How to End a Meeting. Ending a meeting successfully consists of three steps.

1. Signal when the time is almost up so that group members have time to wrap things up and make final comments.
2. Review the decisions that have been made and actions group members need to take.
3. Thank the group to show your appreciation and to encourage continued good work at future meetings.

_____ 9. Which of these is a detail?

a. Ending a meeting successfully consists of three steps.
b. Signal when the time is almost up so that group members have time to wrap things up and make final comments.

10. What does the author use to make the details stand out?

_____

What is the purpose of the details in the paragraph?

_____

_____

ASSESS YOUR UNDERSTANDING

How did you do on the Chapter Check and the exercises? How well do you think you understand supporting details? Could you explain to someone what supporting details are, the difference between *major* (primary) *details* and *minor* (secondary) *details*, and some of the clue words authors use to introduce details? Do you know the *functions* that supporting details serve? Circle a number on the scale below to indicate how well you understand supporting details.

1.....2.....3.....4.....5.....6.....7.....8.....9.....10

I'm scratching   **It's making some sense.**   **Nailed it!**
my head.

Now pinpoint anything you don't understand. What do you still need to learn? Is there anything about supporting details that you need clarified? Write your response on the lines below.

_____

_____

_____

_____

For anything you don't understand or can't remember, what steps can you take to solve the problem? Do you need to reread? Ask a classmate or your instructor questions? Write the information down or review it some other way? Write your response here.

_____

_____

_____

_____

Details are part of the building blocks of reading comprehension, so if there are any gaps in your understanding of them, fill those gaps now!

Map of Chapters

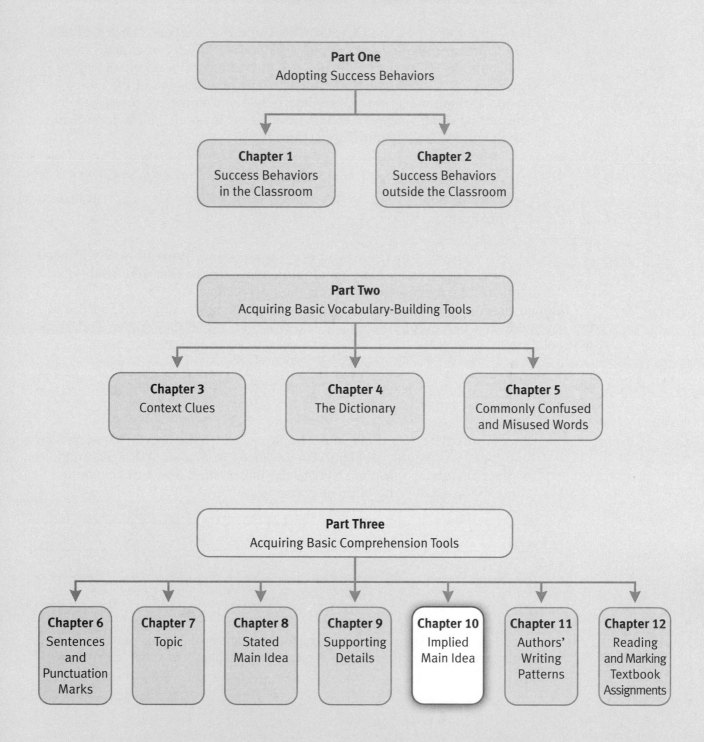

Part One
Adopting Success Behaviors

Chapter 1
Success Behaviors
in the Classroom

Chapter 2
Success Behaviors
outside the Classroom

Part Two
Acquiring Basic Vocabulary-Building Tools

Chapter 3
Context Clues

Chapter 4
The Dictionary

Chapter 5
Commonly Confused
and Misused Words

Part Three
Acquiring Basic Comprehension Tools

Chapter 6
Sentences
and
Punctuation
Marks

Chapter 7
Topic

Chapter 8
Stated
Main Idea

Chapter 9
Supporting
Details

Chapter 10
Implied
Main Idea

Chapter 11
Authors'
Writing
Patterns

Chapter 12
Reading
and Marking
Textbook
Assignments

CHAPTER 10
Implied Main Idea
What Does It All Add Up To?

Why You Need to Know the Information in This Chapter

You already know how important main ideas are, and you know how to locate stated main ideas in paragraphs. In this chapter you'll learn about another type of main idea, implied main ideas. You'll learn what they are and how to formulate (create) sentences that express them.

Implied main idea sentences, like stated main sentences, express the author's the key point in a paragraph. Being able to formulate implied main idea sentences will help you

- understand what you read

- understand how authors organize information

- remember the material in paragraphs more easily

- make test review sheets, review cards, or study maps to help you prepare for tests

- write correct outlines and summaries

- make higher test grades

Super Student Tips

Here's what students like you have to say about formulating implied main ideas:

"Learning about implied main ideas has helped me take better notes. Professors don't always say the main point in a way that makes it obvious."—*Troy*

"It made me feel good to know that there are things I can do when there isn't a main idea sentence in the paragraph. Before, I felt sort of confused and didn't know what to do."—*Vijay*

"It usually takes me several tries, and I don't always get it exactly right, but with the formulas, I come a lot closer to creating the correct implied main idea."—*Marla*

"I could usually find the main idea when it's stated, but I had trouble if there wasn't one in the paragraph. It's good to have ways of figuring out the main point when it's not one of the sentences in the paragraph. I feel more confident now."—*Alma*

"This was hard at first. It takes practice, but I think I'm getting better at implied main ideas."—*LeeAnn*

Jumpstart Your Brain!

Add a letter at the beginning of each word below to change it into another word. Use the definition in the second column to determine which letter should be added. The first one is done as an example. When you have filled in all the letters, you will have the answer to this riddle: *Why did the college freshman bring cosmetics to the exam?* Some of these words may be new to you, so feel free to work with classmates and to consult the dictionary.

Original Word	Add a letter that changes it into a word that means
_____ other	a female parent
_____ maze	to astonish
_____ ill	to cause to die
_____ bony	black hard wood; the color black
_____ sable	able to be utilized
_____ aid	past tense of pay
_____ rue	correct, honest
_____ lope	to run away and get married
_____ ail	go by boat
_____ ravel	to go on a trip

The college freshman brought cosmetics with her to the exam because the professor said it was going to be a

Write your answer here: "____ ____ ____ ____ - ____ ____ ____ ____ ____ ____"

Compare your answer to your classmates' answers. Explain to each other what the answer means.

If you think you already know what an *implied main idea sentence* is, write your definition here:

_____

_____

_____

_____

_____

Implied Main Idea

The key to everything is patience. You get the chicken by hatching the egg, not by smashing it.
—Arnold Glasgow, psychologist

The Big Picture for This Chapter

A student wrote on her exam paper, "The views expressed in this paper are my own, and not necessarily those expressed by the author of the textbook." The reason it's funny (it's meant to be!) is that professors want to know whether students understand the *author's* important ideas.

In Chapter 8, you learned that the main idea always answers the question, "What is the *author's* one most important point about the topic?" You also learned certain characteristics that enable you to identify a stated main idea sentence in a paragraph:

- The main idea sentence always contains the topic of the paragraph.
- The main idea sentence always makes complete sense by itself.
- The main idea sentence is a general sentence.
- The details in the paragraph explain or tell more about the information in the main idea sentence.

As you already know, you must first determine the topic (the subject that is being discussed) before you can determine the main idea. In Chapter 8, you learned that the main idea is always expressed as a *complete sentence*, and the subject of that sentence is almost always the *topic*.

In this chapter, you'll learn about a second type of main idea: an implied main idea. Then you'll have a chance to figure out three "recipes" or formulas for this type of main idea.

Implied Main Idea Sentences

Although every paragraph has a main idea, not every paragraph has a stated main idea. That may sound confusing, but it really isn't. Even when authors do not state the main idea, they still give readers enough information so that they can reason out the main idea for themselves.

In Chapter 5, you learned that *imply* means to hint or suggest something instead of stating it outright. When authors *imply* their main point rather than state it outright, this is called an **implied main idea**, and you (the reader) must formulate a sentence that expresses the author's most important point. In other words, you must create a sentence that's based on the information in the paragraph and tells the *author's* main point about the topic.

The only difference between a stated main idea and an implied main idea is *who* puts the main idea into words: the author or the reader. If the author includes a stated main idea, you, the reader, only need to locate it, and then underline or highlight it. When the author implies the main idea, however, you, the reader, must formulate a single sentence that tells the author's main point.

Whenever you read a paragraph, determine the topic and look first for a stated main idea sentence. If there isn't one, it's up to you to put into words the author's main idea. The author's main point may be obvious to you. If it isn't obvious to you, you can try one of three other things. Those three things are what this chapter is about, and one of them will always work. Once you have put the author's implied main idea into words, check to see that the sentence you created has the characteristics of a main idea sentence (given earlier in the list under The Big Picture for This Chapter).

Chapter 8 presented an analogy of a stated main idea as the king of the Kingdom of Paragraph. In this chapter you can think of a paragraph with an implied main idea as similar to a diamond mine. The paragraph is the mine, and the implied main idea is a diamond necklace. Your job is to find the diamonds in the mine—the important information in the paragraph—and assemble them into a necklace, an implied main idea sentence. Visualize the necklace as having one especially big diamond in it: the topic. Remember that details, including examples, are not diamonds. They should never be included in any main idea sentence.

The Mine

Paragraph with implied main idea

The Miner

You, the reader

The Diamonds

The topic and other important information

The Necklace

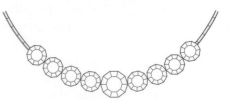

The implied main idea sentence

So how do you go about creating an implied main idea sentence? Sometimes you can combine several words and ideas directly from the paragraph to create this sentence. At other times, you will need to use more of your own words. In fact, you will always be able to use one of three "formulas" to "formulate" the main idea sentence. We'll turn our attention to these formulas soon, but for now take comfort in knowing that authors always give readers enough information to figure out the implied main idea.

You may also hear implied main ideas referred to as *formulated main ideas, unstated main ideas,* or *indirectly stated main ideas.* These are just different names for the same thing: an author's main idea that is put into words (a complete sentence) by the reader.

Three sets of sample paragraphs—one for each formula—are presented next. All of the paragraphs have implied main ideas. There is not a sentence in the paragraph that by itself states the main idea. That's why there are no main idea sentences to underline or highlight.

The topic and the implied main idea sentence are given beneath each paragraph. For each set of paragraphs, the same formula was used to create the implied main ideas. A *formula* is a plan or method of doing something. Once you have read a set, determine what was done (the formula) to come up with the implied main idea. In other words, look at what the author gave you to work with in each paragraph (the diamonds, or pieces). Then try to reason out what was done with those pieces in order to formulate them into an implied main idea sentence.

Reasoning Out Three Ways to Formulate Implied Main Idea Sentences

Discover Formula 1

The three sample paragraphs below have implied main ideas. They each contain a sentence that *almost* states the main idea, but the sentence lacks something that it needs in order to become a *complete* main idea. An important ingredient is missing. Without the missing ingredient, that sentence doesn't make complete sense by itself. As you know, one characteristic of main idea sentences is that they make complete sense by themselves. Read the paragraph and its implied main idea sentence. Then determine the missing ingredient that is already in the paragraph and can be added to the sentence to transform it into the implied main idea sentence.

Example 1

Alexander the Great was from Macedon, a kingdom in northern Greece. A remarkable man, he accomplished a range of dazzling feats in a lifetime that lasted only 33 years. In the fourth century, Alexander conquered most of the ancient world. A warrior, he is said to have cried when there were no more lands left to conquer! In addition to establishing the first modern empire, he founded Alexandria, a city that became a great center of learning in Egypt.

Topic: Alexander the Great

Sentence that almost states the main idea: A remarkable man, he accomplished a range of dazzling feats in a lifetime that lasted only 33 years.

Implied main idea: A remarkable man, Alexander the Great accomplished a range of dazzling feats in a lifetime that lasted only 33 years.

Example 2

Attention-deficit hyperactivity disorder (ADHD) is a disorder that has perplexed professionals for a long time. By some estimates, ADHD affects approximately 3.5 million U.S. youngsters under age 18 (about 5 percent). Boys are likely to be diagnosed two to three times more often than girls. It is considered the most common behavioral disorder in youngsters.

Topic: Attention-deficit hyperactivity disorder (ADHD)

Sentence that almost states the main idea: It is considered the most common behavioral disorder in youngsters.

Implied main idea: Attention-deficit hyperactivity disorder (ADHD) is considered the most common behavioral disorder in youngsters.

Example 3

In 1996, in an email to his boss, a man described another superior as a "back-stabbing bastard." Superiors saw a printout of the message, read all of the writer's email, and fired him. A U.S. District Court ruled that the company had the right to read employees' email and act on it. Email messages can be reproduced and sent (without your knowledge) to audiences you never planned on. So can voice mail messages. How private are employees' email and voice mail? They aren't private at all.

Source: Adapted from Kitty Locker, *Business and Administrative Communication*, 5th ed., New York: McGraw-Hill, 2000, p. 17. Based on Raju Narisetti, "Work Week,'" *The Wall Street Journal*, March 19, 1996, A1, and Frances A. McMorris, "Is Voice Mail Private? Don't Bet on It," *The Wall Street Journal*, February 28, 1995, B1.

Topic: employees' email and voice mail

Sentence that almost states the main idea: They aren't private at all.

Implied main idea: Employees' email and voice mail aren't private at all.

Look again at the paragraphs and their implied main ideas. Each paragraph contains a sentence that *almost* states the main idea, but it lacks something essential. Compare the almost perfect sentence in each paragraph with the implied main idea sentence, and then use your observation to reason out the answer to this question:

What is added each time to the sentence that almost states the main idea?

_____

STOP AND PROCESS

EXERCISE 10.1

Now write a general formula that tells how you can formulate the implied main idea when you have a paragraph with a sentence that *almost* states the main idea:

Formula 1 for implied main ideas:

_____

_____

_____

_____

This chapter can be challenging, but even if you are tempted to peek at the answer, don't! Review the sample passages, and then come up with your own answer. Only after you have done that, should you look at the answer. Remember, you can correct your answer if you need to.

Formula 1: Add the topic (or other missing information) to a sentence that almost states the main idea.

Did you observe that in every example there is a sentence that *almost* states the main idea, but it lacks the topic? When that essential information is substituted in the sentence or added to the sentence, a complete main idea sentence is created. If you did not discover this on your own, write on the lines in Exercise 10.1 "Formula 1: Add the topic (or other missing information) to a sentence in the paragraph that almost states the main idea." *The missing, essential information is nearly always the topic;* occasionally it might be something else. The general formula, though, is still the same: Add essential, missing information to a sentence that is in the paragraph and *almost* states the main idea. Applying Formula 1 is easy because the author has done most of the work for you.

Here is an explanation of the examples:

- In Example 1, the second sentence almost states the main idea, but it does not include the topic, *Alexander the Great*. If you read the sentence *A remarkable man, he accomplished a range of dazzling feats in a lifetime that lasted only 33 years* and you do not already know the topic, the sentence doesn't make complete sense. When the topic is substituted for the word *he* in the second sentence, it creates a main idea sentence that makes complete sense by itself: "A remarkable man, *Alexander the Great* accomplished a range of dazzling feats in a lifetime that lasted only 33 years."

- Look back at Example 2. In it, the topic, *ADHD*, should be added to the last sentence since it tells the important point: *It is considered the most common behavioral disorder in youngsters*. When *it* is replaced with *ADHD*, the result is a sentence that makes complete sense by itself.

- In Example 3, the final sentence in the paragraph (*They aren't private at all*) can be changed into a complete main idea by adding the topic, *employees' email and voice mail*. (Notice that this main idea sentence answers the question the authors ask.)

 To reinforce your understanding and recall of this formula, highlight the topic in each example paragraph and highlight the sentence that almost states the main idea. In Examples 1, 2, and 3, circle the topic and draw an arrow to the appropriate place it should appear in the sentence that almost states the main idea. That way you will be able to see the ingredients that were put together to formulate the complete main idea sentence.

Apply this skill: Use Formula 1 to formulate the main idea of each paragraph that follows. Write the main idea sentence in the space provided.

> Millions of viewers of the Super Bowl 2004 halftime show associate it with Janet Jackson's notorious "wardrobe malfunction." However, there was another controversy as well: Performer Kid Rock wore a

poncho made of an American flag. Many people objected. They said it was inappropriate because it was disrespectful to the flag. They were correct. According to the U.S. Flag Code, it should never be worn or used as wearing apparel.

Implied main idea sentence: _____

_____

_____

_____

   Flag images with words written on them appear on everything from T-shirts to notebooks to bumper stickers. Moreover, images of the flag frequently show up in magazine, newspaper, billboard, and television ads. (Think of all the Independence Day and Veterans Day sales that feature the flag!) This is inappropriate. The Flag Code stipulates that no marks or words of any sort should ever be written on it, nor should it ever be used for advertising purposes.

Implied main idea sentence: _____

_____

_____

_____

_____

Discover Formula 2

Now read another set of examples to reason out the second formula for creating implied main idea sentences. This time there are different ingredients to work with. Remember, there is no *single* sentence in the paragraph that states the main idea completely. Read each paragraph and its implied main idea sentence.

Example 1

   All of us receive criticism from ourselves in the form of negative self-talk. From time to time, we receive criticism from others as well. **Criticism** *is any remark that contains a judgment, evaluation, or statement of fault.* People with low self-esteem are particularly vulnerable to criticism. They are especially likely to be affected by criticism that echoes the attacks of their inner critic, their own constant, negative self-talk.

Source: Denis Waitley, *Psychology of Success: Finding Meaning in Work and Life*, 4th ed., New York: McGraw-Hill, 2004, p. 165. Copyright © 2004 by The McGraw-Hill Companies. Reprinted by permission of The McGraw-Hill Companies, Inc.

www.mhhe.com/entryways

For related information, see Selection 2, "Do the Right Thing and Achieve All Your Goals at the Same Time."

Topic: criticism

Implied main idea: Criticism is any remark that contains a judgment, evaluation, or statement of fault, and people with low self-esteem are particularly vulnerable to criticism.

Example 2

www.mhhe.com/
entryways

For related information, see Small Bite #5, "Sleep Tips for Students," as well as the text Selection 6, "The Walking Weary: What Teens and Young Adults Need to Know about Sleep."

> **Don't Forget Sleep** If you are like most people, your magic solution to getting everything done is to cut back on sleep. Unfortunately, this is both inefficient and unhealthful. Depriving yourself of sleep makes you less productive during the day, so you have to work harder and longer to get the same amount done. This cuts into your sleep time even more. When you're tired, you just don't make good use of time. You have trouble making decisions. You're also likely to work more slowly, make mistakes, and forget information.
>
> *Source:* Denis Waitley, *Psychology of Success: Finding Meaning in Work and Life,* 4th ed., New York: McGraw-Hill, 2004, p. 310. Copyright © 2004 by The McGraw-Hill Companies. Reprinted by permission of The McGraw-Hill Companies, Inc.

Topic: cutting back on sleep (as a solution to getting everything done)

Implied main idea: If you are like most people, your magic solution to getting everything done is to cut back on sleep, but unfortunately, this is both inefficient and unhealthful.

Example 3

> Billy the Kid was one of the most notorious Old West outlaws. His real name was William Bonney. He and his gang stole cattle, and they shot anyone who tried to stop them. It is thought that by the time he was 18, Billy had killed as many as a dozen men. At the age of 21, the "kid" was shot dead. Another equally famous outlaw was Jesse James. Jesse formed a gang with his brother, Frank. For a quarter of a century, the gang robbed trains and banks, and legends sprung up about them.

Topic: Billy the Kid and Jesse James

Implied main idea: Billy the Kid was one of the most notorious Old West outlaws; another equally famous outlaw was Jesse James.

Look again at the paragraphs and their implied main ideas. Each paragraph contains the same type of ingredients that are used to formulate the implied main idea sentence. Look at each paragraph and find the ingredients in it that appear in the implied main idea sentence. Then use your observations to reason out the answer to these questions:

What are the ingredients in the paragraph that appear in the implied main idea sentence?

_____

_____

What is done with these ingredients to formulate the implied main idea sentence?

_____

_____

 STOP AND PROCESS

EXERCISE 10.2

Now write a general formula that tells how to formulate the implied main idea when you have ingredients like those you found in these paragraphs.

Formula 2 for implied main ideas:

_____

_____

_____

_____

Formula 2: Combine two sentences that together express the main idea.

Did you conclude that in each of the example paragraphs, there are two sentences that each express *part* of the main idea, and that when they are combined into a single sentence, a complete main idea is created? Remember that the main idea must be written as a single sentence. Sometimes it is necessary to use conjunctions (such as *and, yet, but,* or *however*) or a semicolon in order to combine the sentences.

Here's Formula 2: Combine into a single sentence two sentences from the paragraph that together express the complete main idea. You may have written words that mean the same thing, such as *"When two sentences each give part of the main idea, combine them into a single sentence"* or *"Combine into one sentence two sentences that each give part of the main idea."* That's fine. If you did not write a correct version of Formula 2, go back now and write it on the line in Exercise 10.2.

Here is an explanation of the examples used to illustrate Formula 2:

- In Example 1, the third and fourth sentences of the paragraph each express *part* of the author's main point. Since the main idea must be written as a single sentence, they are combined using a comma and the word *and*: *Criticism is any remark that contains a judgment, evaluation, or statement of fault + People with low self-esteem are particularly vulnerable to criticism = Criticism is any remark that contains a judgment, evaluation, or statement of fault, **and** people with low self-esteem are particularly vulnerable to criticism.*

> All of us receive criticism from ourselves in the form of negative self-talk. From time to time, we receive criticism from others as well. **Criticism** *is any remark that contains a judgment, evaluation, or statement of fault.* People with low self-esteem are particularly vulnerable to criticism. They are especially likely to be affected by criticism that echoes the attacks of their inner critic, their own constant, negative self-talk.

- Look back at Example 2. The first and second sentences can be combined: *If you are like most people, your magic solution to getting everything done is to cut back on sleep + Unfortunately, this is both inefficient and unhealthful = If you are like most people, your magic solution to getting everything done is to cut back on sleep, **but** unfortunately, this is both inefficient and unhealthful.* A comma and the conjunction *but* are added to show the relationship between the ideas in the sentences. (Notice that the important sentences that must be combined can be anywhere in the paragraph. They may or may not be next to each other. Read each paragraph carefully!)

- In Example 3, the first and sixth sentences can be combined using a semicolon: *Billy the Kid was one of the most notorious Old West outlaws; another equally famous outlaw was Jesse James.* Turn back to Example 3. At the end of the first sentence, replace the period with a semicolon. Then draw an arrow connecting that sentence to the other sentence that tells rest of the main idea.

BONUS TIP

Even when Formula 1 or Formula 2 will work, you can put the implied main idea in your own words if you prefer. It doesn't matter as long as the meaning is the same and you've captured the author's main point. Nice to know!

Combining two sentences that each express part of the main idea is a technique that you will often use when formulating the implied main idea of a paragraph. Notice that the sentences you combined are *not* details. They are each half of the main idea.

To reinforce your understanding and recall of this formula, highlight the two sentences in each paragraph that are combined to create the complete main idea. That way you will be able to see the ingredients that are put together to formulate the complete main idea sentence.

Apply this skill: Use Formula 2 to formulate the main idea of each paragraph below. Write the main idea in the space provided.

> U.S. flags that are no longer fit for display should be destroyed in a dignified way, preferably by burning. There are several organizations that can assist you with this. Contact a local VFW Chapter, the American Legion, a local Elks Lodge, or the Knights of Columbus. Also, some Boy Scout and Girl Scout troops offer this service to their community.

Implied main idea sentence: _____

_____

_____

_____

> You buy some flag paper plates, napkins, cups, and tablecloth for your Fourth of July party. You select streamers and banners decorated with Old Glory. For the table centerpiece, you plan to fill a flag-decorated box with red, white, and blue flowers. Each of these items will be used and then thrown away. It may be surprising to learn that the U.S. Flag Code prohibits using the flag on anything designed to be used temporarily. It also prohibits using the flag on items that will be discarded.

Implied main idea sentence: _____

_____

_____

_____

Discover Formula 3

Now read the last set of sample paragraphs. They illustrate the third type of ingredients that can be used as the basis for formulating implied main ideas.

Example 1

> What should you do to minimize the damage if someone tries to punch you in the stomach? First, tighten your stomach muscles, but don't suck your stomach in. Second, shift slightly, if possible, so that the blows hit the muscles on the side. A rib might be cracked, but there won't be as much damage to your internal organs. Finally, try not to flinch or move away from the punch. If you do, you will take the full force of the blow.
>
> *Source:* From Joshua Piven and David Borgenicht, *The Worst-Case Scenario Survival Handbook,* San Francisco: Chronicle Books, 1999, pp. 69–70. Copyright © 1999 by book soup publishing, inc. Reprinted by permission of Chronicle Books LLC.

Topic: stomach punch

Implied main idea: There are three things you can do to minimize the damage if someone tries to punch you in the stomach.

Example 2

> Nicotine affects the same brain system that morphine and heroin do. It causes the release of opioids, brain chemicals that help suppress pain and produce pleasurable feelings. These findings explain in part why it is so difficult for smokers to give up cigarettes.
>
> *Source:* Based on "Why Nicotine Is so Insidious," *Dallas Morning News,* November 9, 2004, page 6E.

Topic: why it's hard to give up cigarettes

Implied main idea: Part of the reason it is hard to give up cigarettes is that nicotine causes the release of opioids, brain chemicals that make people feel good.

Example 3

> The most famous storyteller in ancient Greece was Homer. Not much is known about him or his life. A blind poet, he recited poems at religious festivals and celebrations. He told fascinating stories of gods and goddesses, dreadful monsters, and illustrious warriors and battles. Two of these are the *Iliad* and the *Odyssey*. These epic poems are the stories for which Homer is best known. Both of them recount the struggles and heroic deeds of brave warriors. After three thousand years, these stories are still considered among the greatest tales of all time.

Topic: Homer (and the *Iliad* and the *Odyssey*)

Implied main idea: Homer, the most famous storyteller in ancient Greece, is best known for two of the greatest stories of all time, the *Iliad* and the *Odyssey.*

Look again at the paragraphs and their implied main ideas. For each paragraph, the same type of ingredients are used to formulate the implied main idea sentence. Look at each paragraph and how the implied main idea sentence is formulated. Then use your observations to reason out the answer to these questions:

What ingredients in the paragraph are used as the basis for the implied main idea sentence?

_____

_____

_____

_____

What is done with these ingredients to formulate them into the implied main idea sentence?

_____

_____

_____

_____

 ### STOP AND PROCESS

EXERCISE 10.3

Now write a general formula that tells how you can formulate the implied main idea when you have the types of ingredients found in these paragraphs to work with:

Formula 3 for implied main ideas:

_____

_____

_____

_____

_____

Formula 3: Summarize details into a general sentence or synthesize important ideas into one sentence.

The paragraphs in this set have no sentence that almost states the main idea, nor do they have two sentences you can combine to create a single, complete main idea sentence. Did you figure out that instead, the paragraphs consist only of details or have ideas spread *throughout* them that you need to summarize or synthesize (put together)? In other words, you need to

- write a *general* sentence (a general inference) based on the details (the *general* point that the details suggest or illustrate), or
- write a sentence that combines or summarizes *ideas* from *several* sentences.

These are so similar that they can be considered the same formula. In either case, you are summarizing information into a general statement.

So, here is Formula 3: Summarize details into a general sentence, or synthesize several important ideas into one sentence. If you did not write this for Formula 3, go back now and write it in the space provided.

When you use Formula 3, you will sometimes have to use words that do not appear in the actual paragraph. For example, a paragraph might give you a series of steps to take when someone has fainted, but it never actually uses the word *steps*. It's fine to use it in your main idea sentence since your goal is to sum up the information in the paragraph.

Here is an explanation of the examples used to illustrate Formula 3:

- In Example 1, the paragraph consists essentially of details, the three tips for minimizing the damage from a punch in the stomach. The author expects you to arrive at the *general* point the details are explaining: *There are three things you can do to minimize the damage if someone tries to punch you in the stomach.* Notice that the words *three things* don't appear in the paragraph, although the words *First, Second,* and *Finally* make it clear that there are three. When you summarize information, you will often need to use a general word or some words of your own. (Did you notice that the formulated main idea sentence answers the question the author asks at the beginning of the paragraph?) Here is the paragraph with important words in special print. (The topic is in bold.)

What should you do to **minimize the damage** if someone tries to **punch you in the stomach?** *First,* tighten your stomach muscles, but don't suck your stomach in. *Second,* shift slightly, if possible, so that the blows hit the muscles on the side. A rib might be cracked, but there won't be as much damage to organs. *Finally,* try not to flinch or move away from the punch. If you do, you will take the full force of the blow.

- In Example 2, the reader must draw information from several sentences and combine it to create the main idea: *Part of the reason it is hard to give up cigarettes is that nicotine causes the release of opioids, brain chemicals that make people feel good.*

> *Nicotine* affects the same brain system that morphine and heroin do. It causes the release of *opioids*, brain chemicals that help suppress pain and produce *pleasurable* feelings. These findings explain in part **why it is so difficult for smokers to give up cigarettes.**

■ In Example 3, the reader must also draw information from several sentences and combine it. When all of these ideas are combined into one coherent sentence, you have the formulated main idea: *Homer, the most famous storyteller in ancient Greece, is best known for two of the greatest stories of all time, the* Iliad *and the* Odyssey. This is what the author really wants readers to go away knowing about Homer: who he was and what he did.

> The *most famous storyteller in ancient Greece* was **Homer.** Not much is known about him or his life. A blind poet, he recited poems at religious festivals and celebrations. He told fascinating stories of gods and goddesses, dreadful monsters, and illustrious warriors and battles. Two of these are the *Iliad* and the *Odyssey*. These epic poems are the *stories for which Homer is best known*. Both of them recount the struggles and heroic deeds of brave warriors. After three thousand years, these stories are still *considered among the greatest tales of all time*.

When you create main idea sentences by summarizing or combining several ideas, don't be frustrated if you can't produce a perfect sentence on the first try. It's normal to have to spend time reworking a main idea sentence to get it just right. Even skilled readers have to do this, and you will probably have to do it too.

To reinforce your understanding and recall of this formula, highlight the formulated main idea sentence beneath example paragraphs 1, 2, and 3. This will remind you that when you formulate the implied main idea, you must sometimes create a general summary sentence or write a sentence that combines several ideas from the paragraph.

Apply this skill: Use Formula 3 to formulate the main idea of each paragraph below. Write the main idea in the space provided.

> When formally observing the flag at a ceremony, Americans should stand at attention facing the flag. Both men and women should place the right hand over the heart. Men who are wearing hats should remove them with the right hand and hold them at their left shoulder, with the hand over the heart. There are a few exceptions, however. Men do not need to remove religious headdress. Also, members of the military who are in uniform do not remove their hats or place the hand over the heart. They simply face the flag and give a military salute.

Formula 3: _____

_____

_____

_____

Do U.S. postage stamps with the flag on them violate the U.S. Flag Code? Decide for yourself. The code says that no marks of any sort should be printed on the image of the flag. Another section of the code prohibits printing the flag on anything that will be used temporarily and then discarded. Still another part of the code states that the flag should "never be used in a way that allows it to be easily torn, soiled, or damaged in any way." Ironic, isn't it?

Formula 3: _____

_____

_____

_____

BONUS TIPS

- **There is more than one correct way to word an implied main idea sentence.** Don't frustrate yourself by thinking that there's only one right way! For example, these sentences say exactly the same thing: "The number of homeless increased last year" and "Last year there was an increase in the homeless."

- **Be sure you understand all of the words in the sentence you write.** If you can tell the topic is *lobbying*, but don't know what it means, you won't understand your main idea sentence either.

- **Don't include information in your sentence just because it seems interesting.** Remember, your job is to grasp the *author's* most important point.

- **Longer selections can have an overall main idea that is implied.** You can read a passage or textbook section and write a very general sentence that sums up the main points of all of the paragraphs.

Let's recap. When you want to determine the main idea of a paragraph in a college textbook, check first to see if the paragraph has a stated main idea sentence. If it does not have a stated main idea, you must formulate an implied main idea sentence.

How will you know which of the three formulas to use? The answer is this: *Look at the ingredients the author has given you in the paragraph.* Each formula is based on the type of ingredients you are given in the paragraph. Once you see what the ingredients are, you will know which formula you should use and what you should do with the ingredients. Think of it as looking at the food you have on hand when you need to prepare a meal. You can end up with a meal no matter what they are, but the ingredients you have available will determine how you put them together and cook them. There is a proverb that says, "The work will teach you how to do it." Let the ingredients in the paragraph tell you which formula you need.

CROSS-CHAPTER CONNECTIONS

The information in Chapter 6 will help you formulate correct implied main idea sentences. If you need to review the types of sentences, conjunctions for combining sentences, or punctuation marks, now is the perfect time.

Remembering the Three Formulas

How can you remember the three formulas? Here is a memory peg that makes it as simple as 1-2-3!

Formula 1: Add the **1** important, missing thing—usually the topic— to a sentence from the paragraph that almost states the main idea.

Formula 2: Combine **2** sentences from the paragraph if each contains part of the main idea.

Formula 3: Write a general sentence that sums up the details or synthesizes the ideas from **3** or more sentences of the paragraph.

When formulating implied main ideas, you must look at the type of information the author gives in the paragraph. The chart shown on page 328 explains what you must do to formulate the implied main idea once you determine what the author has given you to work with in the paragraph. When you're putting together sentences, you can also think of yourself as being like a carpenter who takes raw materials and transforms them into a finished piece of furniture.

🔊(((LISTEN UP!

For auditory learners, here's a military cadence, or rap, that tells all about implied main ideas.

Implied Main Idea

A stated main idea you just locate,
But if it's implied, then formulate.

Which formula to use, you can decide
By seeing what the author has supplied.

When you use Formula 1,
Add the topic to a sentence and you are done.

Formula 2 works just fine
With two sentences you can combine.

With Formula 3 you must construct
A general sentence that sums things up.

Implied main ideas, you can see,
Are as easy as 1-2-3.

Three Ways to Formulate Implied Main Idea Sentences

What the author gives you to start with in the paragraph (the ingredients)	*What you must do with the information in order to formulate the implied main idea*
If the author gives you a sentence that *almost* states the main idea, but lacks some essential piece of information—usually the topic—**use Formula 1.**	*Add* the essential piece of information that is missing to that sentence. How to apply the formula: You can use the sentence from the paragraph and simply add or insert the information.
If the author gives you two sentences in the paragraph that each present *part* of the main idea, **use Formula 2.**	*Combine* the two sentences into one sentence (since the main idea must always be written as a single sentence). How to apply the formula: You will probably have to add a word or two in order to connect the two sentences (words such as *and, but, although*).
If the author gives you details only, or parts of the main idea spread throughout the paragraph, **use Formula 3.**	Write a *general sentence* that "sums up" the details or expresses the overall point the author is making. How to apply the formula: The sentence you write may consist mostly of your own words.

BRAIN-FRIENDLY TIPS

- If you are a *global learner* who likes to start with the "big picture" rather than "ingredients," you can approach implied main ideas this way:

1. Determine the topic of the paragraph by asking yourself, "*Who* or *what* is this paragraph about?"

2. Ask yourself the main idea question, "What is the author's *one most important point* about the topic?" Write a sentence that correctly answers this question. It will be the implied main idea.

3. Remember that the sentence you write should have *all* the characteristics of a main idea sentence.

- Perhaps you are an *analytical/sequential learner* rather than a global learner. (Analytical/sequential learners like to take things step-by-step, and they do well when they have a specific procedure to follow.) If so, you may also find it helpful to *start* by asking the same two questions, and *then* use one of the formulas to help you create the implied main idea sentence.

MY TOOLBOX *for Implied Main Idea Sentences*

Bravo! You now know what an implied main idea is, its characteristics, and the three formulas for creating implied main idea sentences. It's time to transfer this information into long-term memory by adding each of those formulas to your toolbox. Here are some options for accomplishing this:

- **Write the information on notebook paper or on index cards.**

- **Make a study map.** If it helps you understand and remember, include your version of the "diamond mine" sketch in your map.

- **Create a song or rhyme that includes the important information about the implied main idea.** Say it aloud until you can repeat it (or sing it) from memory. If you prefer, you can learn the rap/chant included in the chapter.

- **Draw a flowchart.** You now know about both stated and implied main ideas, and that you must start with the topic for either one. Create your own flowchart that includes both. Flowcharts use boxes and other shapes connected with arrows to show the steps in a process. Make your flowchart large enough to see easily, and use color. Once you have created your flowchart or diagram, say the information out loud as you go over it.

- **Create an analogy or a model of some sort to explain implied main ideas**. Analogies give a comparison between two things. In the chapter, you saw an analogy between implied main ideas and a diamond mine. Can you come up with other comparisons that make sense to you? For example, "An implied main idea is like a telephone because . . ." or "An implied main idea is like a framed picture because . . ." If you are a hands-on learner, you may prefer to make a drawing or a model and label the parts of it.

✔ CHAPTER CHECK

Answer the following questions about the information in the chapter. In each sentence, fill in the missing information. One word goes in each blank. For some items, there may be more than one correct answer.

1. The word *implied* means to hint or _____ rather than to state directly.

2. For a paragraph that has an implied main idea, the person who puts the main idea into words is the _____.

3. Like a stated main idea sentence, an implied main idea sentence must always contain the _____ of the paragraph.

4. Another name for implied main idea is a _____ main idea. (There are three answers; any one of them is acceptable.)

5. If you "formulate" an implied main idea sentence, you _____ the sentence.

6. The particular formula you use to create an implied main idea sentence will depend on the "ingredients" you are given in the _____.

7. Writing a general sentence that sums up the details or combines several important pieces of information in a paragraph means using Formula_____ . (Give the number of the formula.)

8. Formula 1 means you add essential information to a sentence in the paragraph that *almost* states the main idea. The missing information you add is usually the _____.

9. Formula 2 means you combine two _____ that each tell half of the main idea.

10. A main idea is a general sentence that _____ up" the rest of the paragraph.

11. A main idea is never written as a _____; it is always written as a sentence.

12. A long selection (such as a chapter section or article) can have an _____ implied main idea.

13. It is not enough to formulate an implied main idea sentence; you must also _____ it.

14. Specific information that explains, proves, or illustrates the main idea are _____ , and they are never included in the main idea sentence.

15. There is only one correct way to word the implied main idea sentence of a paragraph. True or false?

REVIEW EXERCISES

SET 1

Read each paragraph below. Then mark the answer choice that expresses its implied main idea. (There are no stated main ideas in these paragraphs.) Be sure that the sentence you select has all of the characteristics of a main idea sentence. The topic is given for each paragraph. (*Suggestion*: In the margin, write the formula you use to create each main idea sentence. This makes the learning experience as valuable as possible. Use the chart on page 328.)

Before you begin, lace your fingers together and turn your palms out. Now stretch your arms in front of you and then over your head. Stretch them to either side. Do this again if you start to feel tense while you are doing the exercises. Happy "formulating"!

_____ 1. The topic is *interpreting nonverbal cues.* (Nonverbal cues are ways people give information other than by using words.)

> Interpreting nonverbal cues is not always easy. For one thing, almost all nonverbal cues have multiple meanings. Depending on the context, for example, laughter can mean many different things. If you laugh at the punch line of a joke, you are probably saying, "I find that funny." But laughter can also signify nervousness, sarcasm, or ridicule, and it can be a way to relieve stress and to boost the mood of people around you.
>
> Source: Denis Waitley, *Psychology of Success: Finding Meaning in Work and Life*, 4th ed., New York: McGraw-Hill, 2004, p. 360. Copyright © 2004 by The McGraw-Hill Companies. Reprinted by permission of the McGraw-Hill Companies, Inc.

a. Interpreting nonverbal cues is not always easy.

b. Almost all nonverbal cues have multiple meanings; depending on the context, for example, laughter can mean many different things.

c. If you laugh at the punch line of a joke, you are probably saying, "I find that funny," but laughter can also signify nervousness, sarcasm, or ridicule, and it can be a way to relieve stress and to boost the mood of people around you.

d. Interpreting nonverbal cues is not always easy; for one thing, almost all nonverbal cues have multiple meanings.

_____ 2. The topic is *voter registration.*

> Around 1900, the U.S. government began requiring citizens to register in order to vote. The goal of voter registration was to make sure citizens voted only once in each election. Instead, it

has caused a steady decrease in voter turnout. Some honest citizens simply forget to register. Others are not willing to make the extra effort to register. Still others are unable to register for other reasons.

a. The goal of voter registration was to make sure U.S. citizens voted only once in each election, but instead, it has caused a steady decrease in voter turnout.

b. Some honest citizens simply forget to register, and others are not willing to make the extra effort to register.

c. Around 1900, the U.S. government began requiring citizens to register in order to vote.

d. There are many reasons people do not vote.

_____ 3. The topic is *chronic pulmonary disease.*

Its symptoms include shortness of breath after basic activities, difficulty breathing when it's cold, excess mucus, and a chronic cough. It's more likely to appear in people who have smoked a decade or longer. A person who has any of the symptoms should see a doctor. Early detection is crucial, and a lung function test may be called for. *Chronic pulmonary disease* is the No. 4 killer in the United States. Americans should educate themselves about this deadly illness.

a. Chronic pulmonary disease is the No. 4 killer in the United States.

b. A person who has any of the symptoms should see a doctor because early detection is crucial.

c. A person who has any of the symptoms should see a doctor.

d. Chronic pulmonary disease is the No. 4 killer in the United States, so Americans should educate themselves about this deadly illness.

_____ 4. The topic is *sighing.*

According to psychologists, sighing can express satisfaction and contentment. On the other hand, it can express frustration or even disgust. Sighing frequently suggests hopelessness, and can signal depression. The point is, it can express several different emotions.

a. Everyone sighs at one time or another.

b. Sighing can express satisfaction and contentment, but on the other hand, it can express frustration or even disgust.

c. The point is, sighing can express several different emotions.

d. Sighing can express several emotions, but it usually indicates a feeling of hopelessness.

_____ 5. The topic is *credit card debt and home equity loans*.

> If you're up to your eyeballs in credit card debt, you're not alone. You may be tempted to take out a home equity loan to pay off your credit card debt. Bad idea! For one thing, if you spend the home equity money instead of paying off your credit card debt, you'll dig yourself into a deeper financial hole. Even worse, you risk losing your home.

a. You may be tempted to take out a home equity loan to pay off your credit card debt, but it's a bad idea.

b. Most people have high credit card debt.

c. If you're up to your eyeballs in credit card debt, you should consider taking out a home equity loan before you dig yourself into a deeper financial hole.

d. You risk losing your home if you take out a home equity loan.

For the remaining items, remember to determine the topic before you formulate a main idea sentence for each paragraph. The words you identify as the topic should appear in the main idea sentence.

SET 2

Read each paragraph below. Determine its topic and write it in the space provided. Then formulate and write its implied main idea. Be sure that the sentence you create has all of the characteristics of a main idea sentence. Remember that there is more than one correct way to word the implied main idea sentence. (*Suggestions:* In the margin, write the formula you use to create each main idea sentence; work out your sentence on scratch paper and then copy it in the space provided.)

1. The topic is _____

_____

> Cardiovascular disease is the leading cause of death in the United States. It accounts for nearly half of all deaths. Cancer is the second leading cause. It accounts for about a quarter of all deaths. Although genetics and the physical environment play roles, these two leading killers are primarily lifestyle diseases.

Source: From Paul Insel and Walton Roth, *Core Concepts of Health*, Brief Ed., 9th ed., p. 258. Copyright © 2002 by The McGraw-Hill Companies. Reprinted by permission of The McGraw-Hill Companies, Inc.

Implied main idea sentence: _____

_____

_____

_____

2. The topic is _____

_____

> Make your résumé short, concise, and neat. Focus on skills, achievements, and the ability to solve problems. Show a clear relationship to the available job. Be sure your résumé is honest, simple, and free of errors. Print your résumé on quality paper and send it with a cover letter.
>
> *Source:* Sharon Ferrett, *Strategies: Getting and Keeping the Job You Want*, 2nd ed., New York: McGraw-Hill/Glencoe, 2003, p. 72. Copyright © 2003 by The McGraw-Hill Companies. Reprinted by permission of the McGraw-Hill Companies, Inc.

Implied main idea sentence: _____

_____

_____

3. The topic is _____

_____

> It is estimated that between 50 and 70 percent of gang members own or have access to weapons. In fact, gangs often judge each other by firepower. Their arsenal of weapons includes sawed-off rifles and shotguns, semiautomatic weapons like the Uzi and the AK-47, all types of handguns, body armor, and explosives. Gangs have "treasuries" to buy the sophisticated weapons that are now used on the street for resolving conflicts, for demonstrating bravery, for self-defense, and for protecting turf.
>
> *Source:* Freda Adler, Gerhard Mueller, and William Laufer, *Criminology*, 5th ed., p. 157. Copyright © 2004 by The McGraw-Hill Companies. Reprinted by permission of the McGraw-Hill Companies, Inc.

Implied main idea sentence: _____

_____

_____

_____

_____

4. The topic is _____

_____

> As a new employee, you may be asked to run errands, make coffee, take notes, make copies, or set up a room for presentations. You may get the most undesirable office equipment and assignments. Don't let your ego get in the way. Demonstrate your willingness to pay your dues.
>
> *Source*: Sharon Ferrett, *Strategies: Getting and Keeping the Job You Want*, 2nd ed., New York: McGraw-Hill/Glencoe, 2003, p. 218. Copyright © 2003 by The McGraw-Hill Companies. Reprinted by permission of The McGraw-Hill Companies, Inc.

Implied main idea sentence: _____

_____

_____

_____

5. The topic is _____

_____

> People who smoke a pack of cigarettes a day have twice the risk of heart attack as nonsmokers have. Smoking two or more packs a day triples the risk. And when smokers have heart attacks, they are two to four times more likely than nonsmokers to die from them. Women who smoke and use oral contraceptives are up to 32 times more likely to have a heart attack.
>
> *Source*: Adapted from Paul Insel and Walton Roth, *Core Concepts of Health*, Brief Ed., 9th ed., pp. 259–60. Copyright © 2002 by The McGraw-Hill Companies. Reprinted by permission of The McGraw-Hill Companies, Inc.

Implied main idea sentence: _____

_____

_____

_____

www.mhhe.com/entryways

For review and additional practice exercises, see the ORL material for Chapter 10.

ASSESS YOUR UNDERSTANDING

How did you do on the Chapter Check and the exercises? How well do you think you understand implied main ideas? Could you explain to someone what an implied main idea is, the characteristics of a main idea sentence, and how to formulate the main idea when it is implied? Can you describe the difference between a stated main idea (Chapter 8) and an implied main idea? Circle a number on the scale below to indicate how well you understand *implied main idea*.

1 . . . . . 2 . . . . . 3 . . . . . 4 . . . . . 5 . . . . . 6 . . . . . 7 . . . . . 8 . . . . . 9 10

What planet am I on?   It's making some sense.   Nailed it!

Now pinpoint anything you don't understand. What do you still need to learn? Is there anything about implied main ideas that you need clarified? Write your response on the lines below.

_____

_____

_____

_____

_____

_____

For anything you don't understand or can't remember, what steps can you take to solve the problem? Do you need to reread? Ask a classmate or your instructor for help? Write the information down or review it some other way? Write your response here.

_____

_____

_____

_____

This is a challenging chapter, so don't feel discouraged if you need additional practice applying the concept of implied main idea. Most people do. Before you can practice, though, you must be clear about the concept itself. Earlier, you encountered the important principle of "Do it now. Do it right." Now is the time to lock in a clear understanding of implied main idea.

Map of Chapters

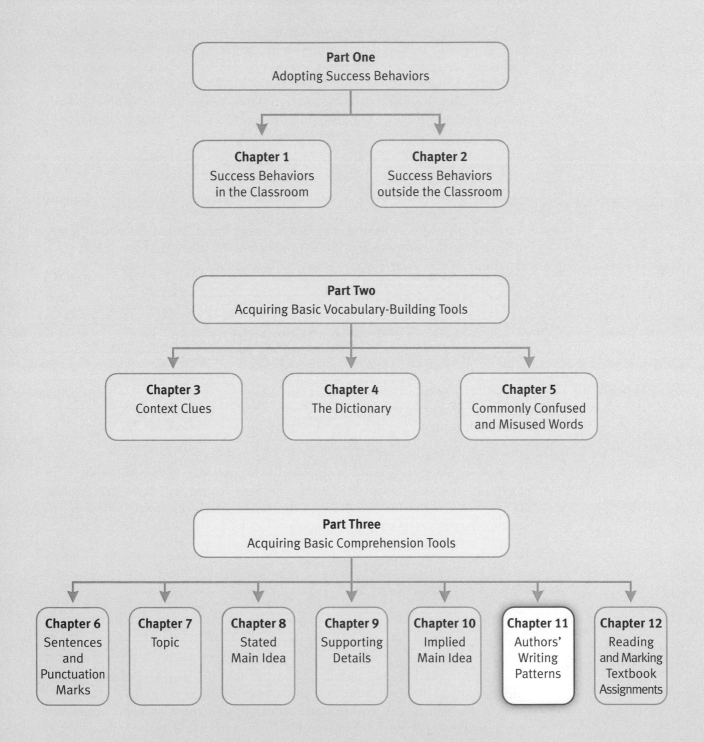

Part One
Adopting Success Behaviors

Chapter 1
Success Behaviors
in the Classroom

Chapter 2
Success Behaviors
outside the Classroom

Part Two
Acquiring Basic Vocabulary-Building Tools

Chapter 3
Context Clues

Chapter 4
The Dictionary

Chapter 5
Commonly Confused
and Misused Words

Part Three
Acquiring Basic Comprehension Tools

Chapter 6
Sentences
and
Punctuation
Marks

Chapter 7
Topic

Chapter 8
Stated
Main Idea

Chapter 9
Supporting
Details

Chapter 10
Implied
Main Idea

Chapter 11
Authors'
Writing
Patterns

Chapter 12
Reading
and Marking
Textbook
Assignments

CHAPTER 11
Authors' Writing Patterns

What's the Plan?

Why You Need to Know the Information in This Chapter

Authors want you to understand the information they present. To help accomplish this, they organize and present the information in a logical way. In other words, they use common *writing patterns* to help readers follow their train of thought.

Understanding authors' writing patterns will help you

- understand more of what you read
- remember information more easily
- predict what is coming as you read
- become a better writer by using the patterns yourself
- write more organized answers on tests and write better papers
- take better notes from textbooks

Super Student Tips

Here are tips from other students who have learned about authors' writing patterns. Here's what experience has taught them:

"At first I didn't believe it would help me to learn about how textbook information is organized, but I found that it helped me remember the material. Because I could remember more of the material, I started making higher grades on tests."—*Julian*

"It's kind of fun, like solving a puzzle. The signal words are clues. It's exciting when you 'see' the pattern."—*Belen*

"When I have to write something, like an essay test answer or a paper, I use the writing patterns. My writing has improved because of it."—*Marjorie*

"We already learned about supporting details. I discovered that the patterns are actually just ways the author organizes them so that they're easier to understand."—*Alan*

Jumpstart Your Brain!

Solve these brainteasers to get your mental gears moving! Read each one, and then write your answer on the lines provided.

1. Three hunters are lost in the jungle. One starts walking east, one starts walking west, one starts walking south. In less than half an hour, however, they all end up in the same place and run into each other. How can that be?

   _____

   _____

2. Is there a Fourth of July in Russia?

   _____

3. A woman goes to enroll her children in first grade. She tells the school secretary that the children will both be enrolling in the same grade. The secretary asks her if one of the children is repeating first grade. The mother says no and says proudly that her son and daughter are identical twins. The secretary says that they're not. The mother becomes indignant. "How do you know? You've never even met them!" The secretary was right. How did she know?

   _____

   _____

4. It's a warm spring day. Three ducks are floating peacefully in a farmer's water tank. The circular tank is 8.5 feet in diameter and 2.5 feet deep. How much water is needed to fill the tank?

   _____

   _____

5. A teenager named Jessica breaks her leg while skiing and is rushed to the hospital nearby. The surgeon sees who the patient is and says, "My colleague will have to do the surgery. I'd be too nervous to operate on her because Jessica is my daughter." The surgeon is telling the truth; however, the surgeon is not Jessica's father. How can this be?

   _____

6. At the start of the day, a fruit grower has 97 melons for sale at her fruit stand. By the end of the day, she's sold all but 19 of them. How many does she have left?

   _____

Compare your answers to your classmates' answers. Explain to each other what the answers mean.

   After you have gone over the answers, write the total number you had correct:_____

LOOKING AT WHAT YOU ALREADY KNOW

 Jot down your responses to the items below. Remember that you are to tell how you would *organize* the information. Don't give the actual information, such as the names of tools or the parts of a bomb.

1. Suppose you are asked to name tools that are used to build or repair things. How would you organize (present) the information?

   _____

   _____

2. Suppose you are asked the colors on traffic signals. How would you organize (present) the information?

   _____

   _____

3. Suppose you are asked what happens if someone lights the fuse on a bomb. How would you organize (present) the information?

   _____

   _____

4. Suppose you are asked to describe a football and a basketball. How would you organize (present) the information?

   _____

   _____

5. Suppose you are asked what the word *friendship* means to you. How would you organize (present) the information?

   _____

   _____

As you go through this chapter, you will probably discover that in answering the questions above, you described some or even all of the common writing patterns!

Authors' Writing Patterns

No man was ever wise by chance.

—Seneca, Roman philosopher

Human beings' brains are hardwired to try to make sense of things—to understand how things are organized. Humans also try to present their thoughts in ways that are organized and make sense. After all, they *want* other people to understand them. This applies to authors, especially textbook authors, who have certain ways of organizing the main ideas and details they present.

The Big Picture for This Chapter

This chapter will let you discover for yourself five patterns textbook authors typically use to organize information. You already know that every paragraph has one main idea; it will either be stated directly or implied. You also know that paragraphs contain details that explain, illustrate, or tell more about the main idea. Now you'll learn how authors use certain writing patterns to present those main ideas and details in ways that help readers understand them as easily as possible.

Five Common Writing Patterns

Authors organize and present their ideas in ways that make *sense* to them. To do this, they use certain basic organizational patterns. Authors' **writing patterns** are ways that authors organize (arrange) material they present. These patterns are basic because they reflect ways people naturally tend to organize information. Although you may not be aware of it, you use these patterns when you tell someone information or write a paragraph or a paper.

Recognizing these patterns in material you read will help you comprehend and remember the material more easily and efficiently. Seeing the pattern also allows you to follow an author's train of thought and lets you anticipate where the author is going.

Most often, textbook authors present information by using one of five common patterns. These patterns show the relationship between the main

---

BONUS TIP

You may also hear writing patterns called by one or more of these terms:

- organizational patterns
- patterns of organization
- patterns of development
- thinking patterns

idea and the details in a paragraph. These same patterns are also used to organize longer selections, such as articles, essays, sections of a chapter, or even entire chapters.

Here's some really good news: Each pattern has certain clue words and signals that are associated with it. Not every paragraph contains clue words or signals, but most textbook paragraphs do. Even when there aren't any clue words or signals, you can still reason out the relationship between the main idea and the details to determine which pattern is being used. Ask yourself, "How has the author organized the information in this paragraph?" Then decide which pattern describes the relationship between the main idea sentence and the details.

In this chapter you will have the opportunity to figure out the five writing patterns that textbook authors frequently use. You will learn to recognize the clue words and signals to indicate each pattern.

Reasoning Out Five Common Writing Patterns

Read the sets of paragraphs that follow. There are five sets, one set per pattern. (You have read some of these paragraphs before.) First, determine the main idea of each paragraph. The main idea sentence itself often provides a clue to the organizational pattern. Next, think about the relationship between the main idea and the details of the paragraph. Look at the clue words and signals; they are printed in color. Then reason out the *type* of pattern the author uses in each set.

Discover the First Writing Pattern

Use this set of examples to determine the first common writing pattern. The same pattern is used in every paragraph in the set. Remember to use the main idea and the clues and signals (in color) to help you. (Stated main ideas are underlined.)

Example 1

Discipline style is an important part of parenting. <u>Psychologist Diana Baumrind studied parents' discipline styles and identified three distinct discipline styles</u>. First, there is the *authoritarian style*. Authoritarian parents have strict rules, do not allow children to question their authority, and punish children if they do not obey the rules. Second, there is the *authoritative style*. Authoritative parents explain the rules and are willing to discuss the reasons for them. They tend not to use physical punishment, preferring instead to reinforce appropriate behavior with warmth and affection. They encourage independence, but set limits. Third, there is the *permissive style*. Permissive parents have few rules and are unlikely to punish inappropriate behavior. Their children often feel uncomfortable because they are given too much freedom at too early an age.

Example 2

Robots are computer-controlled machines that mimic the motor activities of humans. They are often used to handle dangerous or repetitive tasks. There are three types of robots:

- **Perception systems robots:** These robots imitate some of the human senses. For example, robots with television-camera vision systems are particularly useful. They can guide machine tools, inspect products, and secure homes.

- **Industrial robots:** Industrial robots are used to perform a variety of tasks. Examples are machines used in automobile plants to do painting and polishing. Some types of robots have claws for picking up and handling dangerous materials.

- **Mobile robots:** Some robots act as transports and are widely used for a variety of different tasks. For example, the police and military use them to locate and disarm explosive devices. Mobile robots have entered the world entertainment with their own television program called *Bottlebots*.

Source: Adapted from Timothy O'Leary and Linda O'Leary, *Computing Essentials*, 2007 Introductory ed., New York: McGraw-Hill/Irwin, 2007, p. 114.

Example 3

Building a concept map has several advantages. It forces you to rethink the material in your notes in a new style—particularly important if you used traditional outlining while taking the notes. Moreover, it helps you tie together the material for a given class session. Finally, it will help you to build a master concept map later on, when you're studying the material for a final exam.

Source: Robert Feldman, *Power Learning*, New York: McGraw-Hill, 2005, p. 107.

Example 4

Numerous studies have explored what keeps a relationship together. A study by Bruess and Pearson revealed that seven rituals are important characteristics of long-term relationships.

1. Couple-time rituals—for example, exercising together or having dinner together every Saturday night

2. Idiosyncratic/symbolic rituals—for example, calling each other by a special name or celebrating the anniversary of their first date

3. Daily routines and tasks—for example, if living together, one partner might always prepare the evening meal and the other might always clean up afterward

4. Intimacy rituals—for example, giving each other a massage or, when apart, talking on the telephone before going to bed

5. Communication rituals—for example, having lunch with a sister every Friday afternoon to visit and talk or calling a best friend in another state once a month

6. Patterns, habits, and mannerisms—for example, meeting the other person's need for compliments or reassurance when going out for a fancy evening or to a job interview

7. Spiritual rituals—for example, attending religious services together or doing yoga together in the evening

Source: Judy Pearson, Paul Nelson, Scott Titsworth, and Lynn Harter, *Human Communication*, 2d ed., New York: McGraw-Hill, 2006, p. 156.

STOP AND PROCESS

EXERCISE 11.1

Now look again at each paragraph and any words and symbols in it that appear in color. Think about the main idea of the paragraph as well. Then ask yourself, "How has the author organized the information in this paragraph?" What is the relationship between the main idea and the details? Use your observations to reason out the type of organization used in this set of sample paragraphs. Write your answer here:

_____

Pattern 1: List Pattern

Did you discover that in all of the paragraphs, the details presented a *list*? If you did not write "list," go back now and write it on the line provided. A **list** is a group of items in no particular order because the order is not important. That is, if the items in the list were rearranged, it would not matter.

> ### BRAIN-FRIENDLY TIP
>
> Locating all of the items in a list is easy when the author numbers them, puts them in a bulleted list, or presents each item in a separate sentence. Sometimes, though, not every item is announced by a clue word or signal. Also, more than one item sometimes appears in a single sentence.
>
> To help locate and remember all the items in a list, write a small number above or beside each item. Or, if you are writing them on notebook paper, number the items and write them on separate lines.

The reader's job is to identify *all* of the items in the list. As long as you remember all of the items, the order in which you remember them does not matter.

Here is an explanation of the paragraphs in the examples.

- In Example 1, the main idea alerts you to expect a list of three items because it mentions that Baumrind identified "three distinct discipline styles." The words *First*, *Second*, and *Third* are clues that signal each of the three styles. (Notice that the words that describe the styles—*authoritarian, authoritative*, and *permissive*—are italicized, which makes them easy for readers to spot.) The three styles could be presented in any order.

- In Example 2, the authors use a bulleted list (with the items in bold print) to identify the three types of robots. The implied main idea is *There are three types of robots, computer-controlled machines that mimic motor activities in humans.* The phrase *three types* tells readers to expect a list of three major details, one for each type.

- In Example 3, about concept maps, the clue words *several advantages* appear in the main idea sentence. There is no clue word for the first advantage, but the words *Moreover*, and *Finally* identify the last two advantages of concept maps.

- The stated main idea in Example 4 has the clue words *seven rituals* and *characteristics*. The authors then list the seven rituals (characteristics) by numbering them.

To summarize, clue words and signals that can indicate the list pattern are

bullets, numbers, letters, or asterisks

words (usually in the main idea sentence) that announce lists, such as *categories, kinds, types, ways, classes, groups, parts, elements, characteristics*, and *features*

words that indicate a connection or continuation, such as *also, another, moreover, in addition, first (second, third, etc.)*, and *finally*

Notice that these clue words and signals are all logical and commonly used. Suppose you were asked to name tools that are used to build or repair things. You might very well use words such as *first, second*, and so forth. If you were writing them down, you might number them. Imagining a set of assorted tools will help you remember the list pattern.

To help you remember the list pattern and the clue words and signals associated with it, highlight the clue words and signals (which appear in color) in the previous set of sample paragraphs. If you do not have a highlighter, use a pen that writes in a different color.

Apply this skill: Read the following paragraph and mark any clues that suggest a list pattern. Then answer the questions about the passage.

> If you are taking a speech course, there are two ways to determine whether a potential topic is boring or interesting. (1) Consult your instructor for his or her suggestions. (2) Several weeks before your talk, distribute a questionnaire to members of the audience to find out how interested they would be in several potential speech topics. For each topic, provide a scale for them to check, ranging from "very interesting" to "moderately interesting" to "not very interesting."
>
> *Source:* Hamilton Gregory, *Public Speaking or College and Career*, 7th ed., New York: McGraw-Hill, 2005, p. 100. Copyright © 2005 The McGraw-Hill Companies. Reprinted by permission of The McGraw-Hill Companies, Inc.

1. What is being listed? _____

   _____

2. How many ways are listed? _____

3. What clues signal the pattern? _____

Discover the Second Writing Pattern

You just met the list pattern. Now examine a second set of paragraphs that illustrate a second writing pattern. This pattern is similar to the first pattern, but with one very important difference. (Stated main ideas are underlined and clue words are in color.)

Example 1

> There is a correct procedure for washing your hands. First, wet your hands, with warm water if possible. Next, apply sufficient soap to create a lather. Scrub your hands, including the backs and under the fingernails, for at least 30 seconds. Then rinse thoroughly. Use a paper towel to turn off the faucet so that you do not contaminate your clean hands. Finally, dry your hands thoroughly with a paper towel or air dryer.

Example 2

> Is there a problem or issue you are struggling to resolve? A simple, effective six-step method can be used to solve any problem.
>
> 1. Identify the problem precisely.
> 2. Gather the facts; do some research if you need to.
> 3. Think of as many solutions as possible.
> 4. Apply the solution that seems best.

> 5. Evaluate the results.
>
> 6. If you're not satisfied with the way things turned out, try another solution that seemed promising.

Example 3

> **Document Design as Part of Your Writing** Process
>
> Document design isn't something to "tack on" when you've finished writing. Indeed, the best documents, slides, and screens are created when you think about design at each stage of your writing process.
>
> - As you plan, think about your audience. Are they skilled readers? Are they busy? Will they read the document straight through or skip around in it?
>
> - As you write, incorporate lists and headings. Use visuals to convey numerical data clearly and forcefully.
>
> - Finally, get feedback from people who will be using your document. What parts of the document do they think are hard to understand? Do they need additional information?
>
> *Source*: Kitty Locker, *Business and Administrative Communication*, 7th ed., New York: McGraw-Hill/Irwin, 2006, p. 128.

Example 4

> Children don't reliably know their gender identity, that they are boys or girls, until age 2 or 3. In fact, it is not until this age that children can reliably use the terms *boy* and *girl* to differentiate between males and females (gender labeling). And even after that, they aren't certain that gender is for life. Not until age 6 or 7 do children understand that their sex will never change, and that changing appearance cannot change gender (gender constancy). This realization develops in stages. First, preschoolers begin to realize that wishing will not change their sex. Then, slowly, they comprehend that they cannot change their sex no matter what they do.
>
> *Source*: Adapted from Laurence Steinberg and Roberta Meyer, *Childhood*, 1995, New York: McGraw-Hill, 1995, p. 272.

 STOP AND PROCESS

EXERCISE 11.2

The same type of organizational pattern is used in each of the preceding paragraphs. Now look again at each paragraph and any words and symbols in it that appear in color. Think about the main idea of the paragraph as well. Then ask yourself, "How has the author organized the information in this paragraph?" What is the relationship between the main idea and the details? Use your observations to reason out the type of organization used in all of these sample paragraphs. Write your answer here:

Pattern 2: Sequence Pattern

Did you discover that in all of the paragraphs, the details presented a *sequence*? A **sequence** is a group of items presented in a specific order because the order is important. If you did not write "sequence," go back now and write it on the line in Exercise 11.2. (You may also hear the sequence pattern called *time order, chronological order, a process,* or *a series.*) This pattern often appears in history, science, math, psychology, computer science, and health (especially first-aid) textbooks.

As a reader, your job is to identify *all* of the items in the sequence and to remember them *in order*. Authors often number the items or steps, or put them in a bulleted list. Remember, though, that sometimes more than one item in the sequence can appear in a single sentence. For example, directions for giving CPR (cardiopulmonary resuscitation) to someone who has stopped breathing might include the sentence, "Tilt the person's head back, pinch the nostrils shut, cover the person's mouth with your own, and blow gently to inflate the person's lungs." That one sentence tells four things that must be done in order.

Here is an explanation of the paragraphs in the sample set for pattern 2:

- Example 1 discusses the process for washing your hands correctly. Whenever you are reading about a process, you are reading a sequence. The clues in this paragraph are *process* (which appears in the stated main idea sentence), *Next, Then,* and *Finally.* (Notice that not every step has a clue word—6 steps, but only 4 clue words.)

- In Example 2, about a method (procedure) for solving problems, the clues that indicate a sequence are *six-step method,* and the numbers (1–6) the author uses to make the individual steps stand out.

- Example 3 describes a process. Again, a process is always a sequence. Besides the word *process* in the heading and the main idea sentence, there is the clue *at each stage,* and a bulleted list that indicates each stage in order: *As you plan, As you write,* and *Finally.*

- Example 4 is about the ages at which children understand concepts related to gender. The clues are *until age 2 or 3, not until this age, even after that, Not until age 6 or 7, stages, first,* and *Then.*

To summarize, some of the clue words and signals that can indicate the sequence pattern are

first, second, third, now, then, next, finally, last

dates and words that refer to time

numbers and letters

words like *process, procedure, steps, phases, series, stages, when, before, during,* and *after*

sets of instructions and directions

Again, these are all commonsense. If you were asked to describe the pattern of colors used on traffic signals, you would probably say, "Green, yellow, red," or "red, yellow, green." You might even use the words *first,*

✳ **BONUS TIPS**

Notice that some of the clues for lists and sequences are the same: numbers, letters (*a, b, c*), bullets, and words such as *first, second, then, next,* and *finally.* So how can you tell whether it's a list or a sequence? Ask yourself, "Does the order matter?"

- If the order doesn't matter, it's a *list.* (Think of a grocery list, for example.)

- If the order matters, it's a *sequence.* (Think of the frames in a cartoon strip, for example. They have to appear in a certain order to make sense—and to be funny!)

A variation of the sequence pattern is the *spatial pattern.* Authors use this pattern to describe the physical arrangement of something, such as the layout of a city, the floor plan of a cathedral, or the positions of armies in a battle. For this pattern, watch for signal words that answer the question "where?", such as *here/there, above/below/beneath, middle, across, beyond, inside/outside, next to, near, behind/in front of, on, east/west/north/south of, close to, beside, alongside, right/left, above/below,* and *opposite.*

---

then/next, and *last/finally.* No one would say, "Yellow, green, red." The reason: The order is important. The images of the traffic signals will help you remember the sequence pattern.

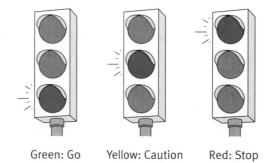

Green: Go   Yellow: Caution   Red: Stop

 To help you remember the sequence pattern and the clue words and signals associated with it, highlight the clue words and signals (those things that are in color) in the previous sample paragraphs. If you do not have a highlighter, use a pen that writes in a different color.

Apply this skill: Read the following paragraph and mark any clue words or other signals that suggest a sequence pattern. Then answer the questions about the passage.

What Makes a Good Leader?

The Army War College conducted a study to investigate the qualities that make a good leader. To answer that question, researchers asked subordinates to evaluate leadership qualities among highly regarded generals. Participants in the study identified a dozen qualities that are crucial for effective leadership. In order of importance, respondents ranked the qualities this way:

1. Keeps cool under pressure.

2. Clearly explains missions, standards, and priorities.

3. Sees the big picture; provides context and perspective.

4. Makes tough, sound decisions on time.

5. Adapts quickly to new situations and requirements.

6. Sets high standards with a "zero defects" mentality.

7. Can handle bad news.

8. Coaches and gives useful feedback to subordinates.

9. Sets a high ethical tone; demands honest reporting.

10. Knows how to delegate and not micromanage.

11. Builds and supports teamwork within staff and among units.

12. Is positive, encouraging, and realistically optimistic.

Source: From Lyric Winik, "What Makes a Good Leader?" *Parade,* July 10, 2005, p. 10. Copyright © 2005 Parade Magazine. Reprinted by permission of the publisher.

1. What is being sequenced? _____

_____

2. How many are there and what clues are used? _____

_____

3. What is the significance of the sequence? _____

_____

Discover the Third Writing Pattern

Now you know about the list pattern and the sequence pattern. Read this next set of sample paragraphs to determine a third pattern that is used in all of them. The clue words and stated main ideas are indicated.

Example 1

Skin Cancer

Not too long ago, skin cancer occurred primarily among people who had to work in the sun. Because many Americans want to look fashionably tan year-round, they are spending too much time in the sun and in tanning booths. As a result, they are developing skin cancer at an alarming rate. The effects of this misguided sun worship include an increase not only in basal or squamous cell skin cancer, but also in the deadly form of skin cancer known as malignant melanoma.

Example 2

There is reason to believe that positive life events can be stressful under some circumstances. Marriage, the birth of a child, job promotion, and the purchase of a house are examples of events that most people think of as positive, but they may also require stressful adjustments in patterns of living. <u>Therefore, positive life changes can be a source of stress of which we are typically unaware.</u>

Source: Benjamin Lahey, *Psychology: An Introduction*, 8th ed., New York: McGraw-Hill, 2004, p. 505.

Example 3

Why are young Americans waiting longer to marry? Researchers have identified several possible causes. One cause is that young people are concentrating on education and careers before settling down. Another cause may be that there is no cultural pressure for people to marry. Delay in marrying could also be due to decreased societal disapproval of unmarried couples living together. Finally, because young people see the high number of failed marriages, they may take more time to be sure they have found the right partner.

Example 4

<u>Police officers who suffer from excessive stress can cause problems for their fellow officers, the public, and their department.</u> They are a risk to their peers on the street because officers must often depend on each other for backup in life-threatening situations. Another negative effect is that the officer who is experiencing severe stress may not respond appropriately to situations that arise on the job. As a consequence, citizens may file lawsuits against the officer's department. Thus, the stressed officer's department may be hurt as well.

 STOP AND PROCESS

EXERCISE 11.3

The same type of organizational pattern is used in each of these paragraphs. Now look again at each paragraph and any words and symbols in it that appear in color. Think about the main idea of the paragraph as well. Then ask yourself, "How has the author organized the information in this paragraph?" What is the relationship between the main idea and the details? Use your observations to reason out the type of organization used in all of these sample paragraphs. Write your answer here:

Pattern 3: Cause-Effect Pattern

Did you discover that in all of the paragraphs, the details presented a *cause-effect relationship*? *Causes* are reasons that things happen; *effects* are results or outcomes. If you did not write "cause-effect" as the organizational pattern, go back now and write it on the line in Exercise 11.3. Authors use the **cause-effect pattern** to present the reasons for something (causes), results of something (effects), or both. This pattern often appears in history and science textbooks.

Your job as a reader is to identify any causes or effects and to see the connection between them. The cause-effect pattern may be presented in different ways:

- one cause and one effect (for example, safer cars result in a reduced death rate)
- one cause and several effects (for example, smoking leads to a variety of health problems)
- several causes and one effect (for example, several causes that result in obesity)
- several causes and several effects (for example, causes and effects of bankruptcy)

Remember that in reality the cause always occurs *before* the effect. Do not be confused just because the author presents the effect first and then discusses the cause. For example, in the sentence, "The family bought a big house because they won the lottery," the effect is given first (they bought a big house), then the cause or reason (they won the lottery). The actual order in which the events would have occurred is that first the family won the lottery, and then they bought a big house. Authors will not always follow the order in which things occur in time.

Here is an explanation of the paragraphs in the sample set for pattern 3:

- In Example 1 the paragraph discusses excessive sun exposure and tanning booths as causes of skin cancer. The clues that indicate a cause-effect relationship are *Because, as a result,* and *effects.*
- In Example 2 the clue words are *reason* and *Therefore.* The paragraph indicates that positive life events can have an unexpected result, stress.
- In Example 3 the words *Why, reasons, one reason, Another cause, due to,* and *because* tell readers this is a cause-effect pattern. The author discusses four reasons that young Americans are waiting longer to marry (the result). The question at the beginning of the paragraph ("*Why* are young Americans waiting longer to marry?") alerts readers that they are going to be told causes or reasons.
- In Example 4 the topic is overstressed police officers and the problems they can cause. The words *cause, because, effect, As a consequence,* and *Thus* signal a cause-effect pattern. The first sentence, the stated main idea, leads readers to expect to be told the problems (results) caused by excessively stressed police officers.

BONUS TIP

A special type of cause-effect pattern is the *problem-solution pattern*. The writer describes something that *causes* a problem, such as air pollution from car exhaust. Next the writer presents the *effects*, such as respiratory diseases. (You saw this pattern in Example 4, about overstressed police officers.) The writer may then discuss *solutions*, such as better pollution control equipment on cars, tighter inspections, and penalties for polluters. Often, the writer ends by urging readers to adopt one or more of the solutions.

To summarize, some common clue words and signals that indicate *causes* in the cause-effect pattern are words such as *reason(s), cause(s), because, is due to, caused by,* and *resulted from.* Those that indicate effects include *the result(s), the outcome(s), the effect(s), the final product, therefore, thus, consequently, as a consequence, on that account, for that reason, resulted in,* and *lead to.*

If you were asked what happens when someone lights the fuse on a bomb, you would say that it would cause an explosion or that an explosion would result. In other words, you'd be using the cause-effect pattern. The image of a bomb and an explosion will help you remember the cause-effect pattern:

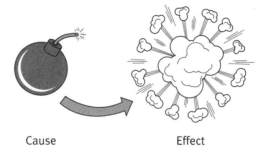

Cause   Effect

 To help you remember the cause-effect pattern and the clue words and signals associated with it, highlight the clue words and signals (those things that are in color) in the example paragraphs. If you do not have a highlighter, use a pen that writes in a different color.

Apply this skill: Read the following paragraph and mark any clues that suggest a cause-effect pattern. Then answer the questions about the passage.

> Stem cells are the cells from which all other cells are formed. They are the basic building blocks from which muscles, bones, organs, blood, nerves, and brains are created. Advocates of stem cell research argue that if we can understand and control stem cells, revolutionary medical advances will result. First, stem cell research could lead to cures for diseases such as Parkinson's, cancer, heart disease, diabetes, and genetic blood disorders. Second, injecting stem cells might make it possible to reverse paralysis, such as that caused by spinal cord injuries. Third, stem cell injections might make it possible to repair organs that are failing. Still another outcome of stem cell research would be an understanding of how diseases develop.

1. What is the cause that is presented? _____

2. How many effects are presented? _____

_____

Discover the Fourth Writing Pattern

You have learned about the list pattern and the sequence pattern, which is simply a list in a specific order. You also know about the cause-effect pattern. Now read another set of sample paragraphs to figure out how the information in them is arranged. To help you identify the pattern, the clue words appear in color.

Example 1

Street criminals, or common criminals, use violence or the threat of violence when they commit crimes. In contrast, white-collar criminals are middle- and upper-class people who use lies, misrepresentation, and deception to convince victims to part with their money or property. Common criminals break and enter. White-collar criminals, on the other hand, use skills, charm, and networking to become insiders in organizations that provide opportunities for fraud.

Source: Adapted from Richard Gelles and Ann Levine, *Sociology: An Introduction*, 6th ed., New York: McGraw-Hill, 1999, p. 247–48. Copyright © 1999 The McGraw-Hill Comapnies. Reprinted by permission of The McGraw-Hill Companies, Inc.

Example 2

Prints differ from most other works of art in two important respects. One difference is that they are made by an indirect process. The artist does not draw or paint directly on the work of art, but instead creates the surface that *makes* the work of art. A second difference is that the printing process produces many nearly identical images. Each image—called an impression—is considered an original work of art.

Source: Adapted from Mark Getlein, *Gilbert's Living with Art*, 7th ed., New York: McGraw-Hill, 2005, p. 181.

Example 3

Female versus Male **Managers**

Do female managers exhibit different behaviors than male managers? Apparently not. Studies indicate that female and male leaders are similar in the number of interpersonal behaviors. They are also the same in the number of task behaviors. Furthermore, they rate equally in terms of subordinates' job satisfaction and performance.

Example 4

Both banks and savings and loan associations (S&Ls) are financial institutions. Both keep money for individuals, but banks also keep money for companies. Unlike a bank, however, an S&L issues shares to members who deposit savings. The S&L then invests members' money, mainly in home mortgages and real estate loans. Banks also

> from S&Ls in that banks offer a broader array of services, such as making automobile and personal loans, exchanging currencies, and leasing safety deposit boxes.

 STOP AND PROCESS

EXERCISE 11.4

The same type of organizational pattern is used in each of these paragraphs. Now look again at each paragraph and any words and symbols in it that appear in color. Think about the main idea of the paragraph as well. Then ask yourself, "How has the author organized the information in this paragraph?" What is the relationship between the main idea and the details? Use your observations to reason out the type of organization used in all of these sample paragraphs. Write your answer here:

_____

Pattern 4: Comparison-Contrast Pattern

Did you discover that in all of the paragraphs, the details presented a *comparison-contrast*? A **comparison-contrast pattern** presents similarities (comparisons) between two or more things, differences (contrasts) between two or more things, or both similarities and differences. If you did not write "comparison-contrast" on the line in Exercise 11.4, go back and write it now. Your job as a reader is to identify what is being compared or contrasted, and the ways in which the items are similar or different.

Here is an explanation of the paragraphs in the sample set for pattern 4:

- Example 1 discusses *differences* between two groups of criminals: street criminals (common criminals) and white-collar criminals. Two clues that a contrast is being presented are the phrases *In contrast* and *on the other hand*. The fact that there are two categories of criminals also suggests a contrast.

- In Example 2 the author uses the word *differ* in the stated main idea sentence (first sentence). The major details in the paragraph tell the two ways that prints differ from other works of art. They are announced by the phrases *One difference* and *A second difference*.

- In Example 3 there is a contrasting pair of words: *females* and *males*. These opposite words appear in the title, along with the word *versus*. The words *similar* and *equally* are used in describing manager behaviors. The author also states that male and female managers do not exhibit *different* behaviors.

- In Example 4 the authors discuss similarities and differences between banks and savings and loans. Clue words include *Both, Unlike, however, differ,* and *broader*. The word *broader* indicates a difference.

To summarize, the clue words and signals that can indicate a comparison are *similarly, likewise, both, same, also, resembles, parallels, in the same manner, in the same way,* and words that are often part of comparisons (such as *safer, slower, less productive, more expensive,* etc.). Words that indicate a contrast include *in contrast, however, on the one hand . . . on the other hand, while, although, whereas, nevertheless, instead (of), difference, unlike, conversely, rather than, as opposed to, some . . . others,* and pairs of words that are opposites (such as *men* and *women, upper class* and *lower class,* etc.).

If someone asked you to describe a basketball and a football, you would probably use a comparison-contrast pattern: You would tell how they are alike and how they are different. Comparison-contrast is a pattern you use all the time. Use the image of a basketball and football to help you remember the comparison-contrast pattern.

To help you remember the comparison-contrast pattern and the clue words and signals associated with it, highlight the clue words and signals (those things that are in color) in the example paragraphs. If you do not have a highlighter, use a pen that writes in a different color.

Apply this skill: Read the following paragraph and mark any clues that suggest a comparison-contrast pattern. Then answer the questions about the passage.

One helpful way to understand the sun's enormous size is to contrast it with earth. Just how much larger is the sun than the earth? According to NASA's Sun-Earth Connection (online) Education Forum, it would take 100 earths placed side by side to reach across the sun. And if the sun were a container you could fill up, it would hold more than a million earths.

1. What is being contrasted? _____

2. Of the two things being contrasted, which is larger, and is it slightly larger or considerably larger? _____

Discover the Fifth Writing Pattern

Last set! Along with list, sequence, cause-effect, and comparison-contrast, textbook authors often use this final pattern. The clue words, which are in color, will help you reason out the pattern. Stated main idea sentences are underlined.

Example 1

We have all had the terrifying kind of dreams known as nightmares To put it more precisely, *nightmares* are dreams that occur during REM sleep and whose content is exceptionally frightening, sad, provoking, or in some other way uncomfortable. They are upsetting enough to wake us up during the dream, so we can vividly remember our nightmares, even though they account for only a small proportion of the dreams most of us have.

Source: Adapted from Benjamin Lahey, *Psychology: An Introduction*, 8th ed., New York: McGraw-Hill, 2004, pp. 174–75.

Example 2

The Library of Congress protects all copyrighted material, including advertising, in the United States. A copyright—a form of protection provided to authors of "original works of authorship"—can be granted for literary, dramatic, musical, artistic, and certain other "intellectual works." A copyright issued to an advertiser grants the exclusive right to print, publish, or reproduce the protected ad for the life of the copyright owner plus 50 years.

Source: William Arens, *Contemporary Advertising*, 10th ed., New York: McGraw-Hill, 2006, p. 86.

Example 3

> Communication comes from the Latin word *communicare*, which means "to make common" or "to share." The root definition is consistent with our definition of communication. In this book, communication is defined as *the process of using messages to generate meaning*. Communication is considered a process because it is an activity, an exchange, or a set of behaviors—not an unchanging product. Communication is not an object you can hold in your hands—it is an activity in which you participate.
>
> *Source:* Judy Pearson, Paul Nelson, Scott Titsworth, and Lynn Harter, *Human Communication*, 2d ed., New York: McGraw-Hill, 2006, p. 9.

Example 4

> Any definition of the term "public opinion" cannot be based on the assumption that all citizens, or even a majority, are actively interested in and hold a preference about all aspects of political life. Public opinion can be defined as *the politically relevant opinions held by ordinary citizens that they are willing to express openly*. This expression need not be verbal. It could also take the form, for example, of a protest demonstration or a vote for one candidate rather than another. The crucial point is that a person's private thoughts on an issue become public opinion when they are expressed openly.
>
> *Source*: Thomas E. Patterson, *The American Democracy*, Alternate Ed., 7th ed., New York: McGraw-Hill, 2006, p. 185. Copyright © 2006 by The McGraw-Hill Companies. Reprinted by permission of The McGraw-Hill Companies, Inc.

 STOP AND PROCESS

EXERCISE 11.5

The same type of organizational pattern is used in each of these paragraphs. Now look again at each paragraph and any words and symbols in it that appear in color. Think about the main idea of the paragraph as well. Then ask yourself, "How has the author organized the information in this paragraph?" What is the relationship between the main idea and the details? Use your observations to reason out the type of organization used in all of these sample paragraphs. Write your answer here:

Pattern 5: Definition Pattern

Did you discover that in all of the paragraphs, the information presents the *definition* of an important term or concept? Authors use the **definition pattern** to present the meaning of an important term that is then discussed throughout the paragraph. The definition is usually the main idea; the details provide additional explanations and examples of the term. If you did not write "definition" on the line in Exercise 11.5, go back and write it now.

Your job as a reader is to identify and understand the important term being defined and discussed. Notice that this word or term often appears in special print, such as bold print or italics. (Just because a word in a paragraph is in special print, however, does not automatically mean that the paragraph has a definition pattern. Sometimes a word is italicized for emphasis.) Your professors will expect you to learn the important terms and concepts in their courses. They will ask you the meaning of these on tests, so pay special attention to them!

Here is an explanation of the paragraphs in the sample set for pattern 5:

> ### BONUS TIP
>
> Some paragraphs include one or more definitions as minor details. A paragraph has a definition pattern *only* when the definition is the *main point* of the paragraph. The author's purpose is to explain a key term. Minor definitions often appear in parentheses.

- In Example 1 the entire paragraph explains the term *nightmare*, which appears in bold italics in the second sentence. The second sentence states the definition. The last sentence provides additional information about nightmares. Other clues are *known as* and *To put it more precisely.*

- In Example 2 the author's goal is to explain the term *copyright.* The term appears in bold print. The definition is set off with dashes. The rest of the paragraph tells more about copyrights and ads.

- Example 3 discusses the definition of the word *communication.* The paragraph is filled with clues that the definition of communication is the authors' most important point. The authors use special print (italics and bold print) and clues such as *means, the root definition, our definition,* and *is defined as.* They also put the definition itself in italics to make it stand out.

- In Example 4 the author of a government textbook defines the term *public opinion.* He puts the phrase in quotation marks and then uses bold print and the clue *defined as.* The definition appears in italics. The details explain the forms public opinion can take: words, protests, and votes.

> ### BONUS TIP
>
> Authors sometimes set off a definition with these punctuation marks: commas (,), dashes (—), or a colon (:). If you need to review these punctuation marks, see Chapter 6.

To summarize, the clue words and signals that can indicate the definition pattern are

terms in special print

the words *is defined as, means, is referred to as, is, is known as, is called, in other words, that is (i.e.), by this we mean*

punctuation that sets off a definition or synonym

examples that illustrate the definition or meaning of a term

If you were asked what the word *friendship* means to you, you would automatically use the definition pattern. You would give your definition, and you would probably include some examples. You might say, for example, that friendship involves two people who know each other well; who like, trust, and support each other; and who have shared interests. You might mention as an example your own best friend or even TV characters such as Will and Grace, or the main characters in *Desperate Housewives.* The illustration of friends arm-in-arm will help you remember the definition pattern.

 To help you remember the definition pattern and the clue words and signals associated with it, highlight the clue words and signals (those things that are in color) in the previous set of sample paragraphs. If you do not have a highlighter, use a pen that writes in a different color.

Apply this skill: Read the following paragraph and mark any clues that suggest a definition pattern. Then answer the questions about the passage.

> The **central idea** of a speech is the core message expressed in one sentence. It is the same as the *thesis sentence, controlling statement,* or *core idea*—terms you may have encountered in English composition courses. If you were forced to boil your entire speech down to one sentence, what would you say? *That* is your central idea. If, one month after you have given your speech, the audience remembers only one thing, what should it be? *That* is your central idea.
>
> *Source:* Hamilton Gregory, *Public Speaking for College and Career,* 7th ed., New York: McGraw-Hill, 2005, p. 105. Copyright © 2005 The McGraw-Hill Companies. Reprinted by permission of The McGraw-Hill Companies, Inc.

1. What term is being defined? _____

2. What synonyms are given for the term? _____

_____

Deciding on the Pattern

Congratulations! Now you have learned five common patterns that people naturally use when they speak and write. This is the reason textbook authors also use them. They're human, too! Authors use these patterns and signals regardless of the topic they are discussing.

As you know, writing patterns are really just commonsense, but when you start to pay attention to them in textbooks, you may be tempted at first to see everything as a list. Seeing everything as a list won't help you at all. If you think a paragraph has a list pattern, ask yourself, "A list of *what?*" If it's a list of items *in order*, call it a sequence. If it's a list of similarities or differences, call it a comparison-contrast pattern. If it's a list of reasons and results, call it a cause-effect pattern. If it's simply a list of items and nothing more, *then* call it a list!

Most paragraphs have an obvious pattern. Some paragraphs, however, can be viewed as having more than one type of organization. In other words, you and another person might view the same paragraph differently. The important thing is that you see *some* pattern of organization that makes sense to *you*. This is what helps you understand and remember the information.

Consider this paragraph:

> Your aim in a persuasive speech is to convince listeners to come over to your side, to adopt your point of view. You want to *change* them in one or both of these ways:
>
> 1. *Change their minds.* You try, for example, to persuade them that television cameras should be barred from courtrooms.
>
> 2. *Change their behavior.* You try to bring about transformations in either a positive or negative direction; that is, you try to get your listeners to either *start* doing something they normally don't do (such as using seatbelts) or to *stop* doing something they normally do (such as sprinkling salt on their food).
>
> *Source:* Adapted from Hamilton Gregory, *Public Speaking for College and Career*, 7th ed., New York: McGraw-Hill, 2005, p. 101. Copyright © 2005 The McGraw-Hill Companies. Reprinted by permission of The McGraw-Hill Companies, Inc.

www.mhhe.com/
entryways

For more information about paragraph patterns, see

**Catalyst >
Writing >
Paragraph
Patterns**

Also, see "Other Words that Signal Organization."

One reader might view the paragraph as a cause-effect pattern: The cause is a persuasive speech; the effect is to change listeners' minds or behavior. Another reader might view it as a list pattern: a list of the two ways that persuasive speeches can change listeners. Both readers would probably remember the information equally well, though, since both see some type of logical pattern in the way the information is organized, and that's what matters most.

✳ BONUS TIPS

1. Most paragraphs use only one pattern, but a paragraph can contain more than one pattern. This is called a **mixed pattern** paragraph. For example, a movie reviewer might rank the year's top five movies (a sequence) and tell how likely each is to win the Academy Award for Best Picture (a comparison-contrast).

2. Long selections often have an **overall pattern**. For example, an entire section of a biology textbook might describe the digestive process, a sequence. An entire newspaper article might talk about similarities and differences in two political candidates' views, a comparison-contrast. A biography usually presents the story of a person's life from beginning to end, so the overall pattern would be a sequence. Look for these overall patterns in the longer works you read. They will be a big help.

👂((LISTEN UP!

For auditory learners, here's a military cadence or rap that tells all about the five common writing patterns.

Writing Patterns

Writing patterns, there are five
That authors use to organize.

Order's not important in a *list;*
Just be sure no items are missed.

In *sequence,* the order must be correct;
From first to last, make things connect.

Cause-effect helps all adults
Understand reasons and results.

Compare-contrast presents with ease
Differences and similarities.

Definition always defines a term
That the author wants you to learn.

These patterns help you analyze
The ways that authors organize.

💡 BRAIN-FRIENDLY TIP

This short rap will help you recall the five patterns by associating them with the visual memory peg that was presented for each in this chapter:

Imagine a *list* of assorted tools;

A *sequence* of traffic lights (ignored by fools!).

Imagine a bomb *causing* a blast;

Picture footballs and basketballs you *compare* and *contrast*;

Imagine the term "friendship," *defined* at last.

SUMMARY CHART OF PATTERN CLUES

This chart summarizes many clue words associated with each pattern. (See the ORL for a more complete list.) You use these words every day to organize your thoughts. Also, there is a logical connection between them and the patterns in which they are used. So relax: You don't need to memorize them!

www.mhhe.com/
entryways

For an even more complete list of about paragraph pattern clue words and signals, see Ch 11 ORL, "Summary Chart of Pattern Clues."

1. **List Pattern**
   - *and, also, too, moreover, besides, in addition, another, further, finally*
   - *first, second, third . . . , 1, 2, 3 . . . ; a, b, c . . .*
   - bullets (•), asterisks (*)
   - words that announce lists, such as *ways, categories, kinds, types, groups, characteristics, features,* and so forth

2. **Sequence Pattern**
   - *when, before, prior to, during, while, after, later, at last*
   - *first, second, third . . . last; 1, 2, 3 . . . ; a, b, c . . .*
   - *before, earlier, now, then, next, finally, last, since* (a certain time), *until* (a certain time), *at the same time*
   - *steps, phases, series, stages, process*
   - dates and words that refer to time, such as *the 20th century, last year, during the next decade,* and so forth

3. **Cause-Effect Pattern**
   - questions that begin with the word *Why*

   Cause:
   - *the reason(s), the causes(s)*
   - *because, since, due to, is caused by . . . , resulted from . . .*

   Effect:
   - *the result(s), the effect(s), the outcome*
   - *because, since, . . . is caused by, . . . is due to*
   - *therefore, thus, as a result, consequently, hence*

4. **Comparison-Contrast Pattern**

   Comparison:
   - *same, similar(ly), likewise, both, is like, alike*
   - *also, in the same manner, in the same way*
   - adjectives that describe comparisons, such as *safer, slower, lighter, more valuable, less toxic,* and so forth

   Contrast:
   - *different, difference, unlike, dissimilar, opposite*
   - *but, yet, in contrast, however, although, nevertheless, rather than, instead of, whereas, while*
   - *on the one hand, on the other hand; some, others*
   - words that have opposite meaning such as *men* and *women* or *rich* and *poor*

5. **Definition Pattern**
   - terms in bold print, italics, or color
   - *the term . . . , the word . . . , means, is defined as, refers to, is referred to as, is called, is, is known as*
   - *in other words, that is (i.e.), by this we mean,* and *or* (followed by a synonym)
   - definitions set off by punctuation, in quotations marks, or italicized
   - examples that illustrate the definition or meaning of a term

MY TOOLBOX *of Authors' Writing Patterns*

Take time now to review the five common writing patterns authors use. From the options below, choose one that suits your learning style. You may want to try more than one. Do whatever is required to work with the material to "make it your own."

Regardless of which option you select, be sure to include a definition of the term *writing patterns*. Try to write it in your own words. Include some key words and signals that indicate each pattern. You will also find it helpful to think of an example of each pattern, such as changing a tire or following a recipe for the sequence pattern. If color helps you remember information more easily, use different colored pens.

- **Write out the information.** You can use notebook paper or index cards.

- **Make a study map.** In the center of the page, write "AUTHORS' WRITING PATTERNS" and the definition. Branch the five writing patterns, their definitions, and signal words from this hub. Include a sketch that illustrates each pattern, such as the ones you saw in the chapter.

- **Place your hand palm down on a piece of paper and trace an outline of it.** As you know, this is a great strategy for visual/tactile learners. In the center area, write "AUTHORS' WRITING PATTERNS," the definition of *writing pattern*, and the question you should ask yourself when you want to determine the pattern. On the thumb and each finger, write one type of writing pattern. Be sure to include some signal words for each. (If you like, you can cut out the shape of your hand and write the signals on the back of the thumb and corresponding fingers. For example, if you wrote, "List" on the top of the thumb, you'd write signals such as *and, in addition, also, moreover, first, second, third,* bullets, and numbers on the other side. Once you've finished your "helping hand," close your eyes and try to visualize the completed image. You may find it reinforcing to say the writing patterns out loud, pressing down the thumb and a finger as you say each one.

- **Create a chart or diagram** that makes sense to you. Be sure to include all of the information mentioned above.

- **Create a poem, song, or story** about the five writing patterns. Let your imagination be your guide. If you create a poem or story, you can include pictures or illustrations. If you enjoy using the computer, you can create a PowerPoint presentation. If you create song lyrics, you can set them to a familiar tune. Read aloud (or even record) what you have written. Hearing it will help your brain get the information through an additional channel. If you prefer, you can learn the rap about the five patterns.

- **Create a review tool out of a folded sheet of paper.** Turn a sheet of paper sideways (horizontal). Fold the top edge down and the bottom edge up until they meet in the middle. Fold the sides in so that there are six equal-sized sections. On the top and bottom edges that you folded, cut to the fold to create six flaps. (On the diagram, the cut marks are shown with dotted lines.) On each flap, write the label you see on the diagram. Lift each flap and write the information that goes with the label on the top of the flap. For example, beneath "Sequence pattern," write the definition and some signal words, and perhaps a small sketch that illustrates it (such as a clock for sequence). Then test yourself by looking at the top of a flap and reciting the important information. Then lift the flap to see if you were correct. Whenever you have a few minutes, review. Eventually, you'll know it perfectly!

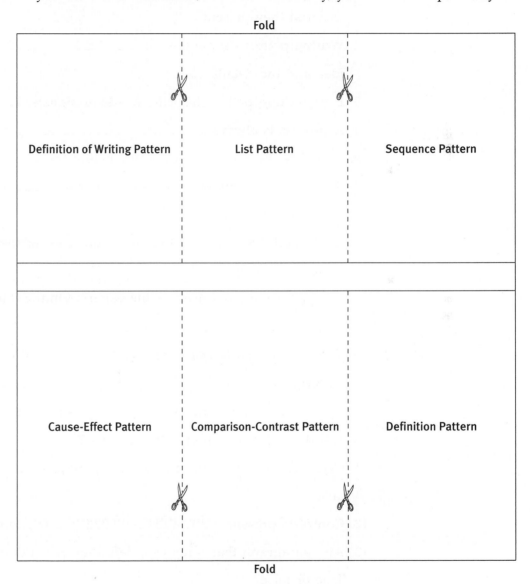

Fold

Definition of Writing Pattern

List Pattern

Sequence Pattern

Cause-Effect Pattern

Comparison-Contrast Pattern

Definition Pattern

Fold

- **Create a card game or board game.** Some possibilities for games are described in the Toolbox section of Chapter 5. You can also create a six-sided cube that has the same labels as the flaps above. Roll it like a die (that's the word for only one of a pair of dice). Give the correct information that goes with whichever side comes up. (On a separate piece of paper, write out the "answer" that matches each side.)

✔ **CHAPTER CHECK**

Answer the following questions about the information in the chapter. In each sentence, fill in the missing information. One word goes in each blank. For some items, there may be more than one correct answer.

1. Writing patterns are ways that authors _____ material they present.

2. Writing patterns show the _____ between the main idea and the details.

3. Each writing pattern has clue words or signals. True or false?

4. A process is always a _____ pattern.

5. In reality the cause always occurs before the _____.

6. A sequence is different from a list because _____ is important in a sequence.

7. In the definition pattern, the definition is never the main idea sentence. True or false?

8. The pattern authors use to present similarities or differences is the _____ pattern.

9. The clue words *therefore, thus,* and *because* signal the _____ pattern.

10. Some of the clue words and signals are the same for the list pattern and the sequence pattern. True or false?

11. Organizational patterns are used only by professional writers. True or false?

12. Contrasts present __similarities differences__. (circle one)

13. Any paragraph that contains a definition has a definition pattern. True or false?

14. The clue words *however, but, although, on the other hand,* and *difference* indicate the author is using the _____ pattern.

15. Clue words such as *means, is known as, is referred to, is called* indicate a _____ pattern.

REVIEW EXERCISES

SET 1

Each item below represents a title or heading that you might see in a newspaper or textbook. Based on the heading, select the answer choice that describes the writing pattern the author would be most likely to use. Remember to watch for clue words and signals in each item.

1. Last Year's Five Top-Ranked SUVs
   - a. list
   - b. sequence
   - c. comparison-contrast
   - d. definition

2. Three Reasons to Major in Fine Arts
   - a. list
   - b. sequence
   - c. comparison-contrast
   - d. cause-effect

3. Differences in Boys' and Girls' Achievement in Math
   - a. list
   - b. sequence
   - c. comparison-contrast
   - d. cause-effect

4. The Real Meaning of Democracy
   - a. list
   - b. sequence
   - c. comparison-contrast
   - d. definition

5. Why Video Games May Actually Be Good for Kids
   - a. list
   - b. sequence
   - c. comparison-contrast
   - d. cause-effect

6. Causes of High Blood Pressure
   - a. list
   - b. sequence
   - c. comparison-contrast
   - d. cause-effect

7. How to Start a Recycling Program in Your Community
   - a. list
   - b. sequence
   - c. comparison-contrast
   - d. definition

8. What Exactly Is "Terrorism"?
   - a. list
   - b. sequence
   - c. comparison-contrast
   - d. definition

9. Why Solar Energy Is Environmentally Friendly
   - a. list
   - b. sequence
   - c. comparison-contrast
   - d. cause-effect

10. Famous Landmarks in San Francisco
    - a. list
    - b. sequence
    - c. comparison-contrast
    - d. definition

www.mhhe.com/ entryways

For additional practice with authors' writing patterns, see Chapter 11 ORL, Exercises 1, 2, and 3.

SET 2

Read each paragraph below. Then decide which writing pattern the author uses to organize the information in the paragraph. Write your answer in the space provided. (*Suggestion:* To help you identify the pattern correctly, mark clue words or signals you see in the paragraphs. You can refer to the Summary Chart on page 365 as you do the exercises.) To loosen up before you begin, stand up and twist from side to side for a minute, or alternate stretching your arms diagonally above your head.

_____ 1.

> All of us receive criticism from ourselves in the form of negative self-talk. From time to time, we receive criticism from others as well. **Criticism** can be thought of as "any remark that contains a judgment, evaluation, or statement of fault." Criticism can be either constructive (intended to be helpful and lead to improvement) or merely hurtful.

a. comparison-contrast
b. definition
c. sequence
d. list

_____ 2.

> What should you do to minimize the damage if someone tries to punch you in the stomach? First, tighten your stomach muscles, but don't suck your stomach in. A second strategy is to shift slightly, if possible, so that the blows hit the muscles on the side. A rib might be cracked, but there won't be as much damage to your internal organs. The final suggestion is to try not to flinch or move away from the punch. If you do, you will take the full force of the blow.
>
> *Source:* Based on Joshua Piven and David Borgenicht, *The Worst-Case Scenario Survival Handbook*, San Francisco: Chronicle Books, 1999, pp. 69–70. Copyright © 1999 by book soup publishing, inc. Reprinted by permission of Chronicle Books LLC.

a. sequence
b. definition
c. list
d. comparison-contrast

_____ 3.

> **Don't Forget Sleep** If you are like most people, your magic solution to getting everything done is to cut back on sleep. Unfortunately, this is both inefficient and unhealthful. Depriving yourself of sleep causes you to be less productive during the day, so you have to work harder and longer to get the same amount done. This cuts into your sleep time even more. When you're tired, you don't make good use of time.

> You have trouble making decisions. Lack of sleep also causes you to make mistakes and to forget information.

a. cause-effect
b. comparison-contrast
c. definition
d. list

_____ 4.

> In ancient times, sailors relied on their knowledge of the sun, moon, and stars to help them navigate the open seas. About 1,000 years ago the Chinese helped sailors plot their course by inventing a type of compass. Later, instruments such as sextants and chronometers improved navigation significantly. Today sailors rely on satellite signals and other sophisticated electronic equipment to help them navigate in the open ocean.

a. list
b. sequence
c. cause-effect
d. definition

_____ 5.

> **The Alarming Effects of Video Violence**
>
> A typical child in the United States watches 28 hours of TV a week and sees 8,000 murders by the time he finishes elementary school. Even worse, the killers get away with the crime 75 percent of the time and show no remorse. The toll of video violence is high: It causes kids to become immune to brutality, to become fearful, or to become aggressive.
>
> _Source:_ Adapted from L. W. Winik, "The Toll of Video Violence," _Parade,_ July 4, 2004, p. 15. Copyright © Parade Magazine. All rights Reserved. Reprinted by permission of the publisher.

a. comparison-contrast
b. list
c. definition
d. cause-effect

_____ 6.

> **Stated versus Implied Main Ideas** The only difference between a stated main idea and an implied main idea is _who_ puts the main idea into words: the author or the reader. If the author includes a stated main idea, the main idea is right there in the paragraph. You can locate it and then underline or highlight it. On the other hand, when the author implies the

main idea, you, the reader, must formulate a single sentence that tells the author's main point.

a. list
b. sequence
c. comparison-contrast
d. cause-effect

_____ 7.

There are nearly 4,000 languages in the world. Can you guess the top five? If you guessed that Chinese boasts the most speakers, you would be correct: More than a billion people speak it. English is the next most-spoken language, with 510 million speakers. Hindustani is third, with 500 million speakers. Spanish comes in fourth, with 392 million speakers. Russian places fifth, with 277 million speakers.

a. sequence
b. definition
c. list
d. comparison-contrast

_____ 8.

How do migrating animals find their way?

Fish use their sense of smell to recognize their migration paths and are guided by changing water temperatures. Migrating animals navigate in a variety of ways. The way birds navigate is by using the position of the sun to orient themselves. Some birds have magnetic particles in their ear mechanisms that act as a compass. Mammals have yet another way. They rely on their memory. Some elephant trails have been used for hundreds of years.

Source: From *The Complete Book of Questions and Answers* by Vincent Douglas, Columbus, OH: American Education Publishing, 2002, p. 120. Copyright © 2002 by American Education Publishing. Reprinted with permission from School Specialty Publishing.

a. list
b. sequence
c. cause-effect
d. definition

_____ 9.

The word *dinosaur* means "terrible lizard." These reptiles ruled the earth for about 160 million years before becoming extinct 65 million years ago. The largest of these prehistoric reptiles weighed up to 80 tons. Dinosaurs included both meat-eating carnivores and plant-eating herbivores. They exhibited wide variety in their characteristics. Some had sharp teeth; others had slashing claws. Some were protected by thick armorlike scales or horny plates. Despite their size, many could move surprisingly fast. Dinosaurs were cold-blooded, egg-laying vertebrates. Because they breathed by means of lungs, all dinosaurs lived on land.

a. cause-effect
b. comparison-contrast
c. definition
d. list

_____ 10.

Both radar and sonar utilize waves to locate objects, but there are differences. One difference is the type of wave. Radar works by emitting radio waves that bounce back from objects within range. A receiver translates the returning waves into a dot on a screen that permits visual location of an object. Air traffic controllers depend on radar to track the movement of planes. Sonar works in a similar way, except that it utilizes ultrasonic waves to travel through water. Sonar serves a purpose equivalent to radar, but it is used in aquatic environments.

a. list
b. comparison-contrast
c. definition
d. cause-effect

ASSESS YOUR UNDERSTANDING

Well done! You've finished another chapter—the next-to-last one of *Entryways*. Do you think you understood it? How did you do on the Chapter Check and the exercises? Could you explain the five writing patterns to someone who is not familiar with them? Circle a number on the scale below to indicate how well you understand *authors' writing patterns*.

1 . . . . . 2 . . . . 3 . . . . 4 . . . . 5 . . . . 6 . . . . 7 . . . . 8 . . . . 9 10

I missed the mark!   **I'm getting close.**   **Bull's-eye!**

Now identify anything you still don't understand about authors' writing patterns. What do you still need to learn or need clarification on? Write your response on the lines below.

_____

_____

_____

_____

_____

_____

For anything you don't understand or can't remember, what steps can you take to solve the problem? Do you need to reread? Ask a classmate or your instructor questions? Write the information down or review it some other way? Write your response here.

_____

_____

_____

_____

You know what to do next: Follow the steps you described above. You can do it!

Map of Chapters

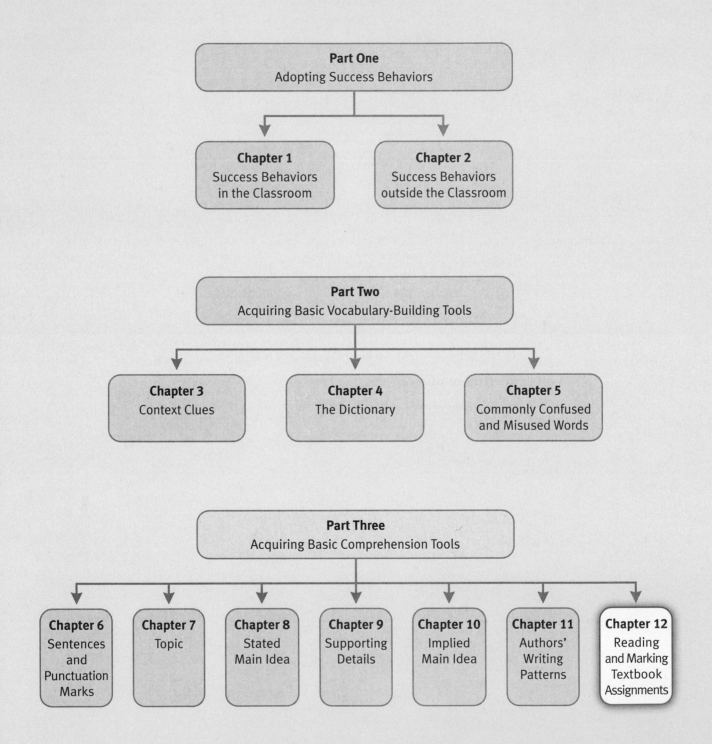

Part One
Adopting Success Behaviors

Chapter 1
Success Behaviors
in the Classroom

Chapter 2
Success Behaviors
outside the Classroom

Part Two
Acquiring Basic Vocabulary-Building Tools

Chapter 3
Context Clues

Chapter 4
The Dictionary

Chapter 5
Commonly Confused
and Misused Words

Part Three
Acquiring Basic Comprehension Tools

Chapter 6
Sentences
and
Punctuation
Marks

Chapter 7
Topic

Chapter 8
Stated
Main Idea

Chapter 9
Supporting
Details

Chapter 10
Implied
Main Idea

Chapter 11
Authors'
Writing
Patterns

Chapter 12
Reading
and Marking
Textbook
Assignments

CHAPTER 12

Reading and Marking Textbook Assignments

Divide and Conquer

Why You Need to Know the Information in This Chapter

In college, most of the information you learn will be presented in textbooks. In most of your classes, they will be your primary instructional tool. Most of the information you will be tested on comes from your textbooks. So it's important for you to have strategies for understanding and remembering what you read in them.

Having an organized way of approaching college textbook assignments will help you

- understand and learn more from your textbooks

- remember more of what you have read

- read your assignments more efficiently

- be more prepared to participate in class

- make higher test grades

- feel more confident

Super Student Tips

Here are tips from other students about reading textbook assignments efficiently and marking textbooks effectively:

"I thought that if I marked a lot, it meant I knew a lot. Wrong! I found that out on the first test. Now I focus on understanding the material and being choosy about what I mark."—*Michele*

"I started out underlining and highlighting *everything* in the book. It was a mess. The biggest thing for me was to wait until after I read a section. *Then* I would decide what was important and I'd mark only that."—*Roger*

"It was hard to get used to marking in my books because we got in trouble if we did that in high school. I found that marking my college textbooks really does make it easier to study for tests."—*Lan*

"Next semester I'm going to look through all my textbooks at the start of the semester. There were features in my textbooks and things at the back that would have helped me this semester, but I didn't know they were there until the semester was almost over. Bummer!"—*Jo*

Jumpstart Your Brain!

Time to warm up your brain! Take a couple of deep breaths and jump in! The sentence below is from a famous novel. Read it, and then try the two challenges based on it. Your teacher may instruct you to do one or both of these activities collaboratively.

> We were in study hall when the headmaster walked in,
> followed by a new boy not wearing a school uniform,
> and by a janitor carrying a large desk.
>
> —*Madame Bovary* by Gustave Flaubert

Using only words from the sentence above, rearrange them to create at least five new sentences. Try to create some sentences that contain at least five words each.

- _____
- _____
- _____
- _____
- _____

If the words in the quoted sentence were alphabetized, what would be the *18th* word on the list? (If a word appears more than once, such as *it* or *the,* count it only once.)

a b c d e f g h i j k l m n o p q r s t u v w x y z

Write your answer here: _____

Unless you completed these activities with classmates, compare your answers with theirs. Explain to each other how you approached each task.

As you know from the tips at the beginning of the first chapter of this book, there are certain things you should do before you start to read a textbook chapter. Perhaps you have been doing them. Or perhaps you read them, but have not yet tried them.

1. Can you recall or think of any *prereading* strategies, that is, things you can do to get *ready* to read a textbook assignment, things that would help you focus your concentration and improve your comprehension? On the lines below, list any strategies you can think of that would *prepare* you to read a textbook assignment before you actually start reading.

_____

_____

_____

_____

2. Now list things you could do *as you read* a textbook assignment that would help you understand as much of it as possible.

_____

_____

_____

_____

3. Finally, list things you could do *after you have finished reading* an assignment that would help you check your understanding of the material and lock the important information into memory.

_____

_____

_____

_____

Once you have completed the chapter, you can come back to this section and change or add information.

Reading and Marking Textbook Assignments

A genius is a talented person who does his homework.
—Thomas Edison, American inventor

Good habits are as easy to form as bad ones.
—Tim McCarver, baseball catcher, TV announcer and analyst

The Big Picture for This Chapter

Congratulations on arriving at the final chapter of *Entryways*. This chapter focuses on reading college textbook assignments. It explains how to approach an assignment so that you get the most out of the time you invest in reading it. So far in Part Three of *Entryways* you have learned basic comprehension skills. You'll now learn how to apply those skills to college textbook assignments so that you will not only understand them better but also remember the material more easily. You'll learn things you can do to help yourself *before* you read, *as* you read, and *after* you have read an assignment.

Getting an Overview of Your Textbooks

At the beginning of a semester, you should spend a few minutes familiarizing yourself with the features of each of your textbooks. In other words, you should get an overview, the big picture for the book as a whole. Textbook features are devices authors use to organize or emphasize important material. When you preview a textbook, be sure to examine its features in the way described here:

- Read the book's **title.**
- Skim through the **table of contents.** How many major sections are there? What are they? Read the chapter titles to see what is covered in the book and how the information is sequenced.
- Read the **introduction** to the book. It may be called "Introduction," "To the Student," or another similar name. In the introduction, the author tells you about the book, how it is organized, its special features, what certain symbols mean, and so forth.
- Look at the **information at the back of the book.** Is there a glossary that defines key terms used in the book? What topics are covered in the appendixes? Depending on the type of textbook, there may be maps, a list of formulas, or other special information.

- Look at the **index.** An *index* is a listing at the back of a book that tells the specific page on which information appears. Is there anything special you need to know about the index, such as page numbers in bold to indicate that a term is defined on that page? There may be more than one type of index.

- Pick out a **chapter** and examine it. What is the chapter format (organization)? Is there a mini–table of contents? A list of learning objectives? An introduction? A list of key terms? Are key terms defined in the margin or in some other place? Do icons (symbols) appear in the margins to indicate accompanying online resources or activities or provide tips? Are there special boxes that present case studies, ethical issues, or other related material? Is there a chapter summary? Are there chapter quizzes or discussion questions?

You only need to do this once. Ideally, you want to get an overview of your textbooks at the beginning of the semester, but it's never too late! Whenever you do it, it is time well spent.

STOP AND PROCESS

EXERCISE 12.1

If you did not preview this textbook at the beginning of the semester, take a minute now to answer these questions.

1. What is the title of this book? _____

2. Look at the abridged (short version) of the table of contents on page v. How many major parts does the book have, and what are their titles?

_____

_____

_____

How many chapters are there? _____

3. List three things you learned from "Special Features of This Book" on pages xxv–xxviii.

_____

_____

_____

4. Is there an index? _____

5. Is there a glossary? _____

6. Answer these questions about the chapter format (organization). All the chapters have the same format.

Visual Summary for Chapters 10–12

CHAPTER 10

Implied Main Idea

Implied Main Idea: The author *implies* the main point rather than stating it outright, so the reader must *formulate* a sentence that expresses the author's most important point.

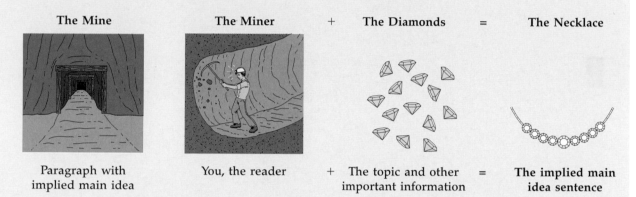

The Mine	The Miner	+	The Diamonds	=	The Necklace
Paragraph with implied main idea	You, the reader	+ The topic and other important information		= The implied main idea sentence	

Formulas for Determining the Implied Main Idea

Formula 1
Add information to a sentence in the paragraph that almost states the main idea.

Formula 2
Combine into a single sentence two sentences from the paragraph that together express the complete main idea.

Formula 3
Summarize details in a general sentence or synthesize several important ideas into one sentence.

CHAPTER 11
Authors' Writing Patterns

Writing patterns: ways that authors organize (arrange) material they present.

List pattern: a group of items in no particular order.

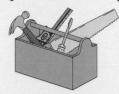

First, **a saw;** *also* **a hammer** *and* **nails;** *in addition,* **pliers**

Sequence pattern: a group of items that are presented in a specific order since the order is important. (Also called *time order*, *chronological order, process,* or *series.*)

First   then   a few years later   finally

Cause-effect pattern: presents the reasons (causes), results (effects), or both

Cause   Effect

Comparison-contrast pattern: presents similarities (comparisons) between two or more things, differences (contrasts) between two or more things, or both similarities and differences.

Definition pattern: presents the meaning of an important term that is then discussed throughout the piece of writing.

"A *caliper* is an instrument designed to measure thickness and distances precisely."

CHAPTER 11 AUTHORS' WRITING PATTERNS (CONTINUED)

Football and Reading Analogy

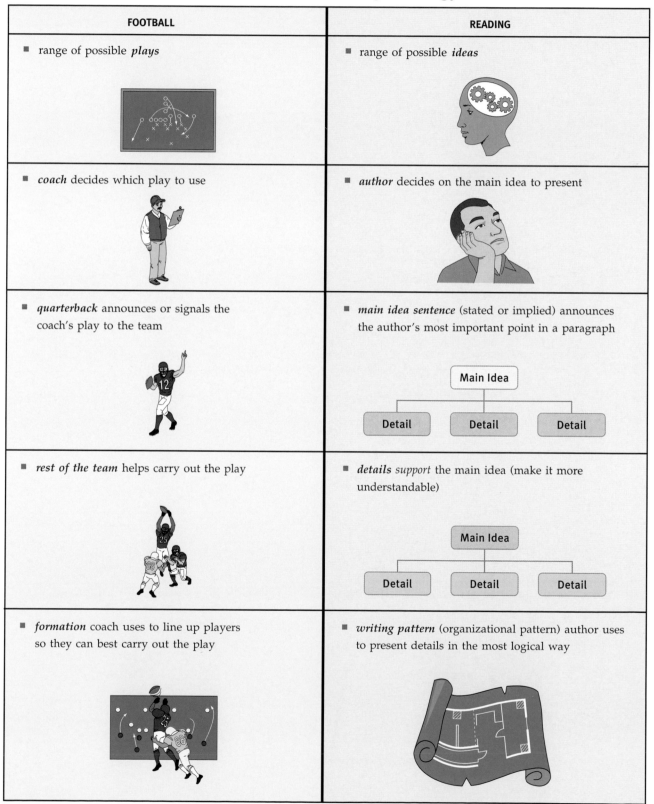

FOOTBALL	READING
■ range of possible *plays*	■ range of possible *ideas*
■ *coach* decides which play to use	■ *author* decides on the main idea to present
■ *quarterback* announces or signals the coach's play to the team	■ *main idea sentence* (stated or implied) announces the author's most important point in a paragraph
■ *rest of the team* helps carry out the play	■ *details support* the main idea (make it more understandable)
■ *formation* coach uses to line up players so they can best carry out the play	■ *writing pattern* (organizational pattern) author uses to present details in the most logical way

CHAPTER 12
Reading and Marking Textbook Assignments

Prereading Strategies

- **Previewing:** looking at an assignment prior to reading it to see what it is about, how the information is organized, and what is important. Also called *surveying* or *overviewing*.

- **Textbook features:** devices authors use to emphasize important material or to show how it is organized.

Pay attention to the following chapter features as you preview:
- chapter title
- objectives
- chapter table of contents
- introduction
- headings and subheadings
- words in special print
- graphic aids
- chapter summaries
- study questions

- **Assess your prior knowledge:** think about what you already know about the topic.

"During Reading" Strategies

- **Monitor your comprehension:** as you read, ask and answer questions to evaluate your understanding.

- Take steps to correct the problem whenever you are not comprehending.

"After Reading" Strategies

- **Rehearse information:** say or write the information to transfer it into long-term memory.

 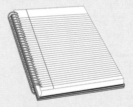

Marking and Annotating Textbooks

- **Annotate:** write explanatory notes and symbols (*ex*, *def*, *, ?, 1, 2, 3*, etc.) in the margin to help you organize and remember information. When you come to the end of each section, go back and underline or formulate the main ideas in that section.

- You can also record the information (take notes) on other paper.

Learning Style Tips

Take control of your learning by using the suggestions below to take advantage of your learning style strengths. Experiment to determine what works for you. There are additional tips and suggestions throughout the book and on the Online Reading Lab.

Visual Learners

- Choose professors who use visual resources; consider online courses.
- Sit near the front of the room so you can see the professor and take advantage of visual aids.
- Create your own visual aids, such as diagrams, sketches, and review cards to record key points. Using color may help.
- Preview assignments: As you turn through them, look at headings, words in special print, and visual aids.
- Visualize in color tricky parts of hard-to-spell words. Create a mental image of the word, close your eyes and move them (not your face or head) up and to the right. To access the image, look up and to the left.
- Write words to see which spelling "looks right." Look for familiar affixes and roots.
- Buy a handheld electronic dictionary or PDA (handheld device) that uses dictionary software.
- Study where there are few visual distractions and the level of lighting is comfortable for you. Studying alone may help you concentrate.
- Try to anticipate essay test questions and practice writing answers ahead of time. Making an outline may also be helpful.
- Draw a "picture" of the math problem before you start. List what is given (known) and what is unknown. Then write the steps for solving the problem.

Visual-Spatial Learners

In addition to the suggestions above,

- When you come to a punctuation mark, stop and visualize what you are reading about.
- Make a schedule and record assignments and due dates in a notebook; keep them current.
- Learn to type: It may be easier for you than handwriting. Or use voice-activated (speech recognition) software that "types" what you say aloud.
- Write on graph paper with big squares and pale lines rather than on notebook paper. It can make your handwriting more uniform and math columns straighter.
- Use word-processing program spell-checkers and grammar checkers. If seeing the screen distracts you while you type the first draft, turn off the monitor. Then turn it on and check your work.
- Look for relationships among concepts in material you are learning.
- Pay attention to details: You may tend to focus on the big picture and miss the details.
- Visualize key terms and hard-to-spell words with certain letters in color or as huge (spell the word from back to front as you "look" at your mental picture of it) or create a picture to go with the word.
- Use color pens and highlighters to color code textbook information.
- Use your imagination: Create a story, make a mental videotape, or create a game to help you learn and remember material.
- If you usually need more time on tests, ask to take them in your college's test center or ask to sit outside your professor's office to take them (or finish them).
- Use outlining software to help you organize your ideas visually.

- Make enlarged copies of textbook pages and use a larger point size when you print pages from your computer. Experiment with fonts and light color paper.
- Read a simpler explanation in a book with pictures and illustrations; then go back to your textbook.
- When you type notes or papers, (1) turn off hyphenation and (2) leave the right margin unjustified so that paragraphs aren't hard-to-read blocks of print.
- Use your finger to guide you as you are reading, place an index card beneath the line you are reading, or cut out a frame so you can see only one line of print at a time.
- Use a simpler dictionary or a picture one, such as *The Macmillan Visual Desk Reference.*

Auditory Learners

- Sit near the front of the class so that you can hear well.
- Read and repeat key information aloud. Write out information in your own words, and then read it aloud.
- Set information to a familiar tune; create a rap or rhyme to say aloud.
- Find or form a study group so you can hear material discussed.
- Tape record class lectures if your instructor permits it.
- Review for tests by recording information in your own voice and then listen to the tape during activities such as jogging or washing dishes.
- Say dictionary pronunciations of words out loud. Use dictionary software that gives pronunciations aloud.
- Pronounce a word aloud or in your mind before you try to spell it. Sound out the parts of the word or recite the letters aloud when you are learning to spell a difficult word.
- If noise distracts you, study in a quiet place or use earplugs.
- If background music helps you, use instrumental music only—no lyrics. Slower classical music can be a good choice.
- Have someone ask you key terms or questions when you review for a test.
- Choose professors who emphasize lecture, discussion, collaborative (small group) learning, and question-and-answer review sessions.
- Work with a tutor or tutor someone else; discussing and explaining material helps you learn it.
- When you see pictures, graphs, or other textbook visuals, say aloud the information they are designed to convey.
- To lock words in auditory memory, look to your right as you say the letters; to help recall something you said or heard, look to the left.

Tactile/Kinesthetic Learners

- Write down key information since the motion of writing helps you. Typing may also work for you.
- Underline and annotate your textbooks.
- Take courses with a hands-on component, such as technical courses, drama, music and applied arts classes, and experience-based learning courses.
- Create three-dimensional models of concepts.
- With your index finger, write hard-to-spell words and key terms in the air or on a tabletop or trace the letters with your finger. As you review the word, look up and to the left.
- When you study, take breaks every half hour or so. Stand up, stretch, or run in place for a few minutes.
- Incorporate movement: Gesture as you reread or say material you are trying to learn; walk back and forth when you are trying to learn information; review information by repeating it aloud as you jog, walk to class, clean house, or work out.
- Chew gum if it helps you deal with nervous energy.

- Review material using a question-and-answer format; change your body position as you switch from question to answer and back again.
- Read only part of a long assignment, shift to other homework, and then return to the reading assignment.
- Relate material to a football game or some other activity. Or create a game about concepts you need to remember.

Analytical/Sequential Learners

- Choose instructors who are organized, who present material in a clear, step-by-step fashion, and who give out an assignment calendar.
- Outline material you need to learn.
- Ask for clear written or verbal directions, whichever works better for you.
- Write or repeat aloud steps in important procedures and processes. Repetition is an effective way to study.
- Break processes into separate steps. Break information into smaller pieces and put them in an order that makes sense to you.
- Trial-and-error learning may work well for you.
- Use a schedule, calendar, To Do list, and other organizing aids.
- Read and study in a quiet place where the light is bright.
- Study in the morning or early evening; staying up late does not work well for you.
- Eat a good breakfast and have regular meals. Don't snack while studying.

Global/Intuitive Learners

In addition to having one of the learning styles above, you may also be a *global learner* who likes to get the "big picture" first and/or an *intuitive learner* who is spontaneous in decision making and often goes with what "feels right." If so,

- Find out what the goal or end product is before you begin. Start with the end product and work backwards to see how the parts fit together. Read your syllabus to see the overall course goals; preview your overall text; preview a chapter by reading the introduction and summary, and turning through to see the topics and how they are organized.
- Similes and metaphors help you learn: You like to see similarities and connections. Ask for or find several examples so that you can see what they have in common.
- Read and study in a place where the light level is very low. You may find it easier to study in the afternoon and at night, or even very late at night. You may prefer to study on the bed or the floor. Instrumental music (no lyrics) at a low level may help you when you study. High-protein snacks may also help you while you study.
- Wear a watch and use a school planner and an assignment notebook since you tend to "go with the flow" rather than to plan your time.
- Work with others. Find a study-buddy or study group.
- Sign up for courses in which there are opportunities to discover answers rather than being told them.

a. What are the four features that occur before the actual chapter content begins?

_____

_____

b. What is the purpose of Looking at What You Already Know?

_____

c. What is the purpose of The Big Picture for This Chapter? _____

_____

d. What four types of boxes appear in the chapters? _____

_____

_____

_____

**www.mhhe.com/
entryways**

The ORL contains a
color flowchart of
the 3-step process of
reading textbook
assignments. It will
be especially helpful
to visual and global
learners.

e. Which words in the chapters appear in bold and in color? _____

_____

f. What is the do-it-yourself chapter summary/review called?

_____

g. Is there a chapter quiz? _____

h. Is there a self-assessment? _____

Approaching College Textbook Assignments

When you sit down to read a textbook assignment, do you flip to the first page and start reading? Do you find that your mind soon begins to wander? After a short while, do you feel discouraged or overwhelmed, and then close the book? Perhaps you actually read the entire assignment, but in class the next day, you discover that you don't remember any of what you read? When it's time for a test, do you try to review by reading the chapters again? If any of these describes you, you've come to the right place for help!

You know that every great athlete goes into competition with a game plan. Like those athletes, you should have a game plan for reading your textbook assignments. There are things you can do *before* you read, *as* you read, and *after* you read. You can also incorporate strategies that are beneficial to someone with your learning style.

Prereading Strategies

Many college students complain that they don't know how to determine what is important in a chapter. As a result, everything seems important.

Of course, they can't remember everything, so they end up feeling overwhelmed and discouraged. You can avoid this if you use **prereading strategies**, or in other words, previewing an assignment and planning your reading session or sessions.

Preview the Assignment

Previewing means looking at an assignment before reading it to see what it is about and how the information is organized. It will also give you an idea about what is important. Your brain likes seeing the Big Picture in advance. Turning through a textbook assignment ahead of time is like looking at a map in order to see your destination, how you are going to get there, and what you will encounter along the way.

Previewing the chapter is like looking at a road map before you begin your journey.

When you preview an assignment, your primary goal is to determine two things: (1) what the assignment is about and (2) how the information is organized. You may want to look at the title of the chapters that come before and after the one you are about to read. That will help you see how your assignment fits in. If you are a global learner who likes to see how all the parts fit together, this will be especially meaningful to you.

Previewing these surrounding elements helps you focus your attention. It helps you make **predictions,** educated guesses, about what will be discussed and how the material will be organized.

Here are the specific steps for previewing the assignment itself. They only take a few minutes.

- Read and think about the **chapter title.** What, if anything, do you already know about the subject? Bringing this to mind helps you focus your attention and activate your prior knowledge.

- Read the chapter **objectives,** if they are included. **Chapter objectives** tell you what you should know or be able to do after studying the chapter. They also help you focus your attention.

- Read the **chapter table of contents,** if there is one. This "mini-outline" tells you the structure of the chapter.

- Read the chapter **introduction,** if there is one. The **chapter introduction** describes the overall purpose and major topics. It presents important concepts. It may also provide background information that you need in order to understand the chapter.

- Read the **headings and subheadings.** The headings tell you the major topics and how they are organized.

- Read **words in special print** (**bold,** *italics,* or color). If there is a **list of key terms** at the end of the chapter, skim through it. Words in special print, lists of key terms, and definitions in the margin all alert you to information that's important. Expect to be asked the meaning of those terms on tests.

- Look at **pictures, diagrams, or other graphic aids** in the chapter.

- Read the **chapter summary,** if there is one. A **chapter summary** presents in condensed form the main points of the chapter. (It may be called "Summary," "Chapter Highlights," "Key Points," "Chapter Recap," or other such names.) Don't skip this gift the author gives you! On tests, you're very likely to be asked about key concepts that appear in chapter summaries (and introductions).

- Read any **chapter questions or quizzes.** These are designed to let you assess your understanding of the chapter. Read them first, though. They tell you in advance what you need to understand by the time you finish the chapter.

Plan Your Reading Session or Sessions

The next part of prereading is to plan your attack. You will want to assess your **prior knowledge,** information you already know about the topic. Based on that and the length of the assignment, you can estimate how long it will take you to read the assignment and whether you need to divide the assignment into smaller chunks. (Assessing your prior knowledge is the purpose of the Looking at What Already Know feature in *Entryways.*)

If the textbook assignment or chapter seems too long to read all at once, divide it into smaller parts. Place sticky notes or paperclips at logical stopping points. Then read a section at a time, spreading it over several study

◄□► CROSS-CHAPTER CONNECTIONS

- In Chapter 2 you may want to reread section 4, "Manage Your Assignments," pages 49–51.

sessions. For example, you might have 18 pages to read before the class meets again. You might read the first six pages early in the afternoon, the next six pages later that afternoon, and the last six that evening. Or, if you receive the assignment on Tuesday and the next class session is on Thursday, you might read six pages on Tuesday, six pages on Wednesday, and the last six pages on Thursday before the class meets. Or, you could read nine pages on Tuesday and nine pages on Wednesday. You can determine what works best for you.

"During-Reading" Strategies

Once you know where you're going, you're ready to begin reading the chapter. But what can you do *as you are reading* to help you understand the material as well as possible? The answer is to pose a question. When you ask yourself a question, your brain swings into action. Questions can grab your attention and focus your concentration. (The Greek philosopher Socrates said, "All thinking begins with wonder.") When you read with the purpose of finding answers to specific questions, your comprehension improves dramatically. The **during-reading strategies** hinge on asking and answering questions as you read.

Ask Questions as You Read

When you are reading, the most effective way to focus your concentration is simply to turn each heading into one or more questions. You can do this by asking *when, where, who, what, why,* or *how.* For the heading "Two Types of Eating Disorders," for example, ask yourself, "*What* are the two types of eating disorders?" Then read the section to find the answer to your question. Asking questions as you read is like going to the grocery store with a shopping list. You know what you're "shopping" for. You're much more focused and purposeful, and it's a lot less frustrating than wandering around the store—or the assignment—hoping you can guess what you might need.

 STOP AND PROCESS

EXERCISE 12.2

Turn each of these textbook section headings into one or more questions that you could use to guide your reading. The words in parentheses tell the type of textbook the heading comes from.

Negative and Positive Reinforcement (*psychology*): _____

_____

_____

Primary Colors (*art*): _____

The Problem of Poor Listening Skills (*public speaking*): _____

_____

The Small Business Administration (SBA) (*business*): _____

_____

Factors Affecting Processing Speed (*computer science*): _____

_____

In addition to turning headings into questions, there are other sources of questions. First, the chapter itself may include them. Second, there may be a study guide that accompanies your book that includes questions. Third, your instructor may supply study questions.

Answer Questions When You Reach the End of Each Section

When you come to the end of a section, stop. Try to answer the questions you posed about it. This lets you know whether you understood the section. For example, suppose you read a section in an art textbook called "Color Theory," and you turned the heading into the question, "What is color theory?" If you can answer the question, you comprehended what you needed in the section. The process of evaluating your understanding of what you read and correcting the problem whenever you realize that you are not comprehending is called **comprehension monitoring**. Effective readers monitor their comprehension.

When you answer questions, try answering them out loud if you are an auditory learner. If you are a visual learner, try jotting the information down without looking at the book. If you are a visual-spatial or a tactile-kinesthetic learner, make a sketch that explains a concept or term. All of these are more effective than just "thinking" the answer in your head. If you do that, it's easy to be vague ("Color theory is some theory about color . . .") and to fool yourself into believing you understand more than you actually do. If you write information down, you can use notebook paper, the margin of the textbook if there is enough space, note cards, or sticky notes.

Be sure to wait until you reach the end of a section to answer questions about it. If you try to answer them or write down information paragraph by paragraph as you go, you'll be constantly switching back and forth between reading and writing. This fractures your comprehension. You will lose your train of thought. You will soon feel tired, frustrated, and discouraged.

What if you read a section and find that you cannot answer the questions you posed about it? Try one or more of these strategies:

BRAIN-FRIENDLY TIPS

- *Auditory learners:* Before you read the chapter, read aloud the chapter title and the headings. Try reading the sections of the chapter out loud. This may help you understand and remember the material. When you finish reading a section, try to answer the questions out loud. *If you can't say it, you don't know it.*

- *Visual-spatial learners:* Make sketches or illustrations in the margin to answer the questions and to remind you of the important information in each chapter section. *If you can't draw or write it, you don't know it.*

- *Tactile-kinesthetic learners:* You may find it helpful to move as you read: Tap a hand or foot, chew gum, or even pace slowly back and forth. When you finish a section, draw a sketch or illustration in the margin to answer your questions and to remind you of the important information in the section. *If you can't draw or write it, you don't know it.*

- Reread the section or certain paragraphs in it.
- Keep reading (read the next section) to see if things become clearer.
- If you do not understand a key term, look it up in the glossary or a dictionary.
- Do some extra reading. It is difficult to understand material if you have a limited background in the subject (and in college, many subjects will be new to you). The solution: Find an easier book on the subject and read it. Then go back to your textbook. It will seem much easier!
- Ask a classmate, members of your study group, or your instructor. Consult a tutor if your college offers tutoring.
- Give your brain time to process the material—even to "sleep on it." Read the material again the next day.
- If you are still confused or unable to answer a question, put a question mark in the margin beside the heading or paragraph, or list your unanswered questions on notebook paper. That way, you can remember to get answers before you are tested on the material.

"After-Reading" Strategies

The **after-reading strategies** consist of *reviewing* and *rehearsing* the material you have just read. If you do nothing but read an assignment, you will have forgotten half of the material by the time you close your textbook! Within a couple of weeks, you will have forgotten nearly all of it. You will remember perhaps one or two main points per chapter—hardly enough to do well on a test. This means that while the information is still fresh in your mind, you should take steps to transfer it into long-term (permanent) memory. The first way to do this is to review the material. Check your answers to the questions you asked for yourself or that appear in the text. Make corrections and add missing information as necessary. Also, take the time to make vocabulary cards for key terms in the chapter and other such study aids.

In order for your brain to process and store information, you must interact with the material. This is why it is crucial that you *rehearse* the material. **Rehearsing information to remember it** means saying or writing the information to transfer it into long-term memory. Rehearse until you can say or write all the important points of a chapter without looking at the book. Silently thinking through the answers isn't enough. Here's the rule: *If you can't say or write the information without looking at it, you don't know it!* This is the time to find out what you know, not while you're taking a test on the material. So repeat or write important points until you know them by heart!

If you use this three-step approach for textbook assignments—previewing, asking and answering questions, and then reviewing and rehearsing—you will be in excellent shape when it's time for a test. You

CROSS-CHAPTER CONNECTIONS

Make vocabulary cards for key terms you encounter in textbook assignments. Use the strategies described in Chapter 4. Use the technique that works best for your learning style.

www.mhhe.com/ entryways

For a refresher on techniques on learning vocabulary words and key terms, see "Brain-Friendly Vocabulary Techniques" in the ORL for Chapter 3.

will already have learned a great deal of the material. You will have created study tools (notes, sketches, vocabulary cards) to help you review further. You will have identified any material you still need help or clarification on.

How do you prepare for tests? The *least* effective way to prepare for a test is to reread textbook chapters, and yet this is exactly what many students do. Rereading alone does not guarantee that you will understand the material any better the second time than you did the first. Moreover, rereading material does not mean that you will remember it. Reading and remembering are two separate things. That's why using the strategies for reading outlined in this chapter is so important.

www.mhhe.com/
entryways

The ORL has information on preparing for tests, taking tests, and dealing with test anxiety.

Marking and Annotating Textbooks

No discussion of textbook use would be complete without talking about how to mark textbooks. Here's what you need to know. First, you *should* mark your textbooks. Yes, textbooks are expensive, but they are the primary learning tool in most college courses. Many new students think they can save money by not marking in their books since they plan to sell them back to the bookstore at the end of the semester. The truth is, a used book is a used book. A bookstore will not pay you any more for a used textbook that is unmarked than for a marked one.

The second thing you should know is the biggest mistake students make in marking textbooks. You guessed it—they mark too much. The pages are covered with yellow highlighter and underlined sentences. Students make this mistake because they do not know what is important. The result is that they mark everything. When everything is marked, nothing stands out. In short, their marking becomes useless.

Students overmark because they haven't learned to zero in on main ideas. But the second reason is that they mark the book as they are reading it through for the first time. You can't know whether something is important until after you've read it. So the rule for marking textbook material is this: *Wait until you come to the end of a section, and then go back and mark or formulate main ideas in that section.*

There is another problem with trying to mark information the first time through: It slows you down tremendously. If you complain that it takes you forever to read a textbook assignment, this might be the reason. Set the highlighter or pen down until you come to the end of a section.

Overmarking tends to give students a false sense of security. They think, "Wow! I must really know this stuff. Look how much I marked!" In short, they mistake marking the material for reading and understanding it. You can mark all over a book and not understand a word of it. The goal is to mark *selectively*. This means you have to *think* before you mark.

When **marking a textbook,** underline or highlight major topics, main ideas, and important terms and definitions. Write small numbers beside details if they are not already numbered. Do not underline details. If you do, you will mark everything.

Writing explanatory notes in the margin to help you organize and remember information is called **annotating a textbook**. The margin is the place to write topics (if that helps you) and formulated main ideas, although you can sometimes underline and link sentences in a paragraph to create a complete main idea. (You'll see an example of this in the Stop and Process activity that follows.) You can develop your own annotations, of course. However, you may want to use some of these standard abbreviations and symbols:

Annotation	Meaning/Name	Use
Ex	*example*	To identify helpful examples
Def	*definition*	For definitions of key terms
1, 2, 3 . . .	*numbers*	To mark details in a list when they are not already numbered. Pencil in small numbers beside items or steps that are spread throughout a paragraph.
*	*asterisk*	To mark especially important information, such as an overall main idea or conclusion
?	*question mark*	For information you do not understand and need clarification on

Here is a sample passage from a psychology textbook that has been marked and annotated. Readers should generally agree on the main ideas. Keep in mind, though, that no two people will mark a passage exactly the same way.

OVERWEIGHT AND OBESITY

[1]*Two-thirds of the people in the United States are overweight.*[2]*Among those people, nearly half are so heavy that they have obesity, body weight that is more than 20 percent above the average weight for a person of a particular height. And the rest of the world is not far behind:*[3]*A billion people around the globe are overweight or obese. What does all this mean?* Worldwide, obesity has reached epidemic proportions.

The most widely used measure of obesity is body mass index (BMI), which is based on a ratio of weight to height. *People with a*[1]*BMI greater than 30 are considered obese. Those with a*[2]*BMI between 25 and 30 are overweight.*

Although the definition of obesity is clear from a scientific point of view, people's perceptions of what an ideal body looks like vary significantly across different cultures and, within Western cultures, from one time period to another. *For instance, many contemporary Western cultures stress the importance of slimness in women—a relatively recent view. In nineteenth-century Hawaii, the most attractive women were those who were the heaviest. Furthermore, for most of the twentieth century—except for periods in the 1920s and the most recent decades—the ideal female figure was relatively full. Even today, weight standards differ among different cultural groups. For instance, African Americans generally judge heavier women more positively than whites do.*

Margin notes:
BMI > 30 = obese
BMI btwn 25–30 = overweight

Ex. of cultural differences of the ideal body at diff. time periods

Main idea: No one doubts that being overweight represents a major health risk; however, controlling weight is complicated.

Regardless of cultural standards for appearance and weight, no one doubts that being overweight represents a major health risk. However, controlling weight is complicated, because eating behavior involves a variety of factors.

Source: Adapted from Robert Feldman, *Essentials of Understanding Psychology*, 6th ed., pp. 309–10. Copyright © 2005 The McGraw-Hill Companies, Inc. Reprinted by permission of The McGraw-Hill Companies, Inc.

Notice that only main ideas have been underlined. In the first paragraph, the last sentence is the one that sums up the rest of the details (since the United States is part of the world). The small numbers help identify the details. In the second paragraph, the first sentence gives the important information: the definition of body mass index. The last two sentences are details that tell what certain scores indicate. The third paragraph also has a stated main idea, although it could be shortened to "Perceptions of what an ideal body looks like vary significantly across different cultures and, within Western cultures, from one time period to another." The rest of the paragraph consists of examples, so the abbreviation "Ex" appears in the margin. The main idea for the final paragraph must be formulated, so it appears in the margin. You could, however, mark the parts of the sentences that together express the main idea.

STOP AND PROCESS

EXERCISE 12.3

The passage below is from the same psychology textbook as the sample passage you just studied. Read the passage first, and then mark it. Be sure to follow the guidelines presented earlier. Think about how you could make the markings as helpful as possible if you had to go back and learn the information for a test. (*To help you get started on the activity below:* You will have to formulate the main idea for the first paragraph; you can join the two sentences that together express it, or you can write it in your words in the margin. The second and third paragraphs have stated main idea sentences, so underline those. Pencil in numbers beside details. Add any other helpful annotations in the margin.)

SOCIAL FACTORS IN EATING

Everyone has had the experience of eating dessert, even though they already felt full. Clearly, internal biological factors do not fully explain our eating behavior External social factors, based on societal rules and on what we have learned about appropriate eating behavior, also play an important role. Take, for example, the simple fact that people customarily eat breakfast, lunch, and dinner at approximately the same times every day. Because we tend to eat on schedule every day, we feel hungry as the usual hour approaches, sometimes quite independently of what our internal cues are telling us.

Similarly, we put roughly the same amount of food on our plates every day, even though the amount of exercise we may have had, and consequently our need for energy replenishment, varies from day to day. We also tend to prefer particular foods over others. Rats and dogs may be a delicacy in certain Asian cultures, but few people in Western cultures find them appealing despite their potentially high nutritional value. In sum, cultural influences and our individual habits play important roles in determining when, what, and how much we eat.

Other social factors relate to our eating behavior as well. Some of us head toward the refrigerator after a difficult day, seeking solace in a pint of Heath Bar Crunch ice cream. Why? Perhaps when we were children, our parents gave us food when we were upset. Eventually, we may have learned to associate food with comfort and consolation. Similarly, we may learn that eating, which focuses our attention on immediate pleasures, provides an escape from unpleasant thoughts. Consequently, we may eat when we feel distressed.

Source: Adapted from Robert Feldman, *Essentials of Understanding Psychology,* 6th ed., pp. 311–12. Copyright © 2005 The McGraw-Hill Companies. Reprinted by permission of The McGraw-Hill Companies, Inc.

How did you do on Exercise 12.3? The main idea of the first paragraph can be created by joining the second and third sentences using a semicolon. It could also be paraphrased, "Our eating behavior is influenced by both internal biological factors and external social factors." The five social factors, along with examples, are discussed throughout the rest of the entire section. You may prefer to number them, jot them in the margin, or do both. If you were reviewing for a test, any of these would help you see them at a glance.

With practice, you will become more efficient in the way you approach reading your textbook assignments. You will also develop your own system for marking your textbooks effectively. Both of these skills are keys to better comprehension and higher test grades.

www.mhhe.com/
entryways
The ORL has extensive information about outlining, making review cards, mapping, and summarizing. All of them are techniques for recording textbook information.

MY TOOLBOX *of Textbook Assignment Strategies*

Using one of the methods described below, capture the information you need to remember from this chapter about reading a textbook assignment: What should you do *before* you read a textbook assignment, *as* you are reading it, and *after* you have read it? What do you need to remember about *marking* a text? About *previewing* a textbook at the beginning of a semester? Regardless of which option you choose, be sure the information you include answers those questions.

- **Write out the information.** You can use notebook paper or index cards.

- **Make a study map.** Use color and include sketches. If you prefer, create a "road map" that shows where to begin and how to proceed as you work your way through a textbook assignment.

- **Create a chart, flowchart, or diagram** that makes sense to you. Be sure that you include all of the information mentioned above.

- **Use the computer to make notes or to create a PowerPoint presentation.**

- **Create a card game or board game.** For example, you might make a game that matches up the steps for reading a textbook assignment with the times at which they should be done (before, during, or after reading).

✔ CHAPTER CHECK

Answer the following questions about the information in the chapter. In each sentence, fill in the missing information. You will be told if more than one word (a phrase) goes in a blank. For some items, there may be more than one correct answer.

1. At the beginning of every semester, it is a good idea to get an

   _____ of each of your textbooks.

2. The section of a textbook in which the author tells you about the

   book, how it is organized, its special features, and so forth, is the

   _____.

3. List any two features you might find at the back of a textbook:

   _____ and _____. (You may

   need more than one word in a blank.)

4. The first step in reading a textbook assignment is to

   _____ so that you see in advance what it is about,

   how the information is organized, and often, what is important.

5. List three things you would read or look at when you preview a

   chapter: _____, _____, and

   _____. (You may need more than one word in

   a blank.)

6. Part of previewing (prereading) is assessing your _____

   _____ (two words), how much you already know

   about the topic.

7. When you are reading, the most effective way to focus your

   concentration is simply to turn each chapter heading into one or more

   _____.

8. In addition to headings, other sources of questions include

   _____, _____, and

   _____. (You may need more than one word in a

   blank.)

9. The process of evaluating your understanding of what you read and

   correcting the problem whenever you realize that you are not comprehending is called _____

_____. (three words)

10. You should try to answer the questions in your head instead of saying the answers aloud or writing them. True or False? (Circle one.)

11. List two things you could do if you read a section of a chapter and discover that you cannot answer the questions you posed about it: _____ and _____. (You may need more than one word in a blank.)

12. The after-reading strategies consist of _____ and _____ the material you have just read.

13. You rehearse material by _____ or _____ it until you can do it from memory.

14. To be sure you mark only the most important information in a textbook chapter, you should wait to mark until you come to the end of each _____.

15. Writing explanatory notes (words, abbreviations, and symbols) in the margin to help you organize and remember information is called _____.

REVIEW EXERCISES

SET 1

The passage below describes civilian, or nonmilitary, uses of Global Positioning System, or GPS, technology. (GPS technology uses satellites to pinpoint an exact location. The military and government employ GPS technology for a variety of purposes.) Read the passage first, and then mark it. Be sure to follow the guidelines presented in the chapter.

> *Several automobile manufacturers make in-car navigation systems an option in their new cars, and some rental car agencies provide them in their vehicles. In-car navigation systems tap GPS signals to monitor the car's exact location, comparing it with a computerized atlas stored on a compact disc. The car's location, constantly updated, appears on a computer screen mounted on the dashboard. The navigation system also enables motorists to find out how to reach their destination. For example, the driver can give a street address or the name of a movie theater, a hospital, or another building. The system displays it on the screen, indicates how far away it is, and how long it should take to drive there. The system gives turn-by-turn directions on the screen map or directions "spoken" by an electronic voice. Car navigation systems are particularly popular among sales representatives, real estate agents, and repair people, who frequently drive to unfamiliar places.*
>
> *GPS receivers are also popular with recreational users. For example, hikers, campers, and sailors are especially enthusiastic about them. In the past few years, systems have been developed for building lightweight, portable GPS receivers into all kinds of things, such as watches, bracelets, belts, and backpacks, in order to ascertain their locations. These small devices can pinpoint the location of someone who becomes lost or incapacitated.*
>
> *A number of states use GPS monitoring devices as a surveillance system to track the movements of people on parole and probation. They use them to make sure such persons do not stray into off-limit areas, such as schools, playgrounds, or victims' houses.*

Source: Adapted from Authur Getis, Judith Getis, and Jerome Fellmann, *Introduction to Geography,* 10th ed., New York: McGraw-Hill, 2006, pp. 29–30. Copyright © 2006 The McGraw-Hill Companies. Reprinted by permission of The McGraw-Hill Companies, Inc.

SET 2

This passage discusses a marketing analysis system developed by a California company. Businesses use the information the company provides in order to make decisions about where they open new stores and where they sell specific products and services. Read the passage first, and then mark it. Be sure to follow the guidelines presented in the chapter.

YOU ARE WHERE YOU LIVE

How does a McDonald's or Burger King decide which one-dollar menu items to promote at a certain site, or whether it can profitably offer salads at that franchise? Whether there are enough families with children to justify building a play area? On what basis does a Starbucks or an Easy Lube determine in what neighborhood to open a new store?

Many businesses, large and small, base their decisions on a marketing analysis system developed by the San Diego-based Claritas, Inc. The system is based on year 2000 census data and uses ZIP codes to categorize Americans by where they live, work, and spend their money.

People tend to cluster together in roughly homogeneous areas based on social status, family status, ethnicity, and other cultural markers. People in any one cluster tend to have or adopt similar lifestyles. As Claritas puts it, "You are where you live," because "birds of a feather flock together." Residents of a cluster read the same kinds of books, subscribe to the same magazines and newspapers, and watch the same movies and television shows. They exhibit similar preferences in food and drink, clothes, furniture, cars, and all the other goods a consumer society offers.

Claritas uses a number of variables to classify areas of the country. These are: household density per square mile; area type (city, suburb, town, farm); degree of ethnic diversity; and family type (married with children, single, and so on). In addition, they consider predominant age group; extent of education; type of employment; housing type; and neighborhood quality.

After analyzing the data, Claritas characterizes each ZIP code as belonging to from 1 to 5 of 62 possible neighborhood lifestyle categories It has given catchy names to these clusters ranging from "Blueblood Estates" (elite, super-rich families) to "Hard Scrabble" (poor, rural families). Some of the others: "Winner's Circle" (executive suburban families); "Pools and Patios" (established empty nesters); "Upward Bound" (dual-income, computer-literate, white-collar families), and "Big City Blend" (middle-income immigrant families).

Claritas realizes that the designations don't define the tastes and habits of every person in a community, but they do identify the behavior that most people are apt to exhibit. In the "Towns and Gowns" (college-town singles aged 18-34) area, for example, residents are likely to play soccer, own software purchased in a bookstore, watch Comedy Central, and read Modern Bride. But in the "Money and Brains" (dual-income families who own their homes in upscale neighborhoods, predominantly employed in white-collar jobs) ZIP code, residents are most likely to contribute to Public Broadcasting, own or lease a new European luxury automobile, and read Atlantic Monthly.

Source: Adapted from Authur Getis, Judith Getis, and Jerome Fellmann, *Introduction to Geography,* 10th ed., New York: McGraw-Hill, 2006, p. 410. Copyright © 2006 The McGraw-Hill Companies. Reprinted by permission of The McGraw-Hill Companies, Inc.

ASSESS YOUR UNDERSTANDING

Good job! You've finished the final chapter of *Entryways!* How well did you understand it? How did you do on the Chapter Check and the exercises? Could you tell a new college student how to read a textbook assignment? Circle a number on the scale below to indicate how well you understand the techniques and strategies for *reading textbook assignments*.

1 . . . . 2 . . . . 3 . . . . 4 . . . . 5 . . . . 6 . . . . 7 . . . . 8 . . . . 9 10

Call a superhero!   **I'm still thinking about it.**   **Makes perfect sense!**

Now identify anything you still don't understand about how to read textbook assignments. What do you still need to learn or need clarification on? Write your response on the lines below.

_____

_____

_____

_____

_____

_____

For anything you don't understand or can't remember, what steps can you take to solve the problem? Do you need to reread? Ask a classmate or your instructor questions? Write the information down or review it some other way? Write your response here.

_____

_____

_____

_____

If there's anything you need to fix, you know what to do!

Congratulations on completing *Entryways!* You have every right to feel proud of yourself. You've strengthened your vocabulary, comprehension, and text usage skills. You've learned more about your learning style and how to use it to your advantage. Through your hard work and effort, you've begun paving the way to your future success. Best wishes as you enter the next phase of your education.

Readings

READING SELECTION 1

THE COURAGE TO LEARN

By David Milliron

Connecting with What You Already Know

Do these exercises *before* you read the selection.

1. First, read and think about the title. Who do you think is being described as having "the courage to learn"?

   _____

   _____

2. Next, complete your preview by reading the

   - introduction (in *italics*)
   - headings
   - all of the first paragraph (paragraph 1)
   - the last paragraph (paragraph 11)

   Now that you have previewed the selection, tell to whom this essay is addressed. In other words, in the author's view, who are those who have "the courage to learn"?

   _____

3. In the selection, you'll encounter the following words. Mark any words you already know or think you know. Most words have more than one meaning. After you have read the selection, you will have an opportunity to deduce (reason out) their meanings according to how they are used in the selection. At that point, you will discover whether you were correct, and if not, you'll have a new word to add to your vocabulary.

humbled	radical
sabotage	pursuing
wrestle	persistence
diversity	ebbs and flows
host (noun)	obstacles

THE COURAGE TO LEARN

By David Milliron

This essay is addressed to students. It is written to you. It was written by the president and CEO of the League for Innovation in the Community College. Every year, more than 10 million students attend community colleges—many of whom are first-time college attendees, returning students, women, and minorities. In Dr. Milliron's words, "These students and their aspirations continue to inspire and encourage the League to bring all of its resources to bear upon its mission of improving community college education through innovation, experimentation, and institutional transformation."

Your courage astounds us.

1   Your courage astounds us. We probably don't tell you this enough. You see, we too are pushed and pulled by classes, calendars, and the constant press of our work in education. But when we slow down, look around, and soak in all of your stories, we are humbled.

Be patient with us if we forget how overwhelming college can seem.

2   Many of you will be the first in your family to set foot on a college campus. At times it can feel as though there is no one who really understands how strange and awkward your first steps feel. You fill out our forms, meet our advisors, take our placement tests, piece together a schedule, step into our classrooms—whether they're online or on campus—and enter a new world. Sometimes it's hard for us to remember how overwhelming our rules and procedures seem to you. And we should remember. What you may not realize is that many of us started our higher education journey at a community or technical college. We've just been in this world so long that we sometimes lose touch with how we felt our first day. Be patient with us.

3   Some family and friends don't know much about the journey you're on. Their ideas about college are shaped by movies and TV. Nonetheless, they truly want you to succeed. Some of them have fought, struggled, begged, and borrowed to give you this opportunity. While you are so happy to have their support, you sometimes feel pressured by the weight of their expectations.

Even with pressures, have faith.

4   You may have different pressures. We've seen some of you suffer through unsupportive, angry, or abusive parents, spouses, or friends. This inner circle plays out their fears or insecurities by discouraging you at every turn, trying to convince you that you too will fail. Some are afraid that your success will take you away from them, so they subtly sabotage your journey. Many of you struggle with uncooperative supervisors or job schedules that make attending class difficult or impossible. Weekend or night courses are a must, even though you're mentally tired and physically worn out. Some of you have major family responsibilities. You search to find good child care and wrestle with the guilt of being away from your kids even though you're going to college to better their lives as well; and others must strive to care for parents, nieces,

nephews, cousins, grandchildren, and other family. We know that at times it feels as though a higher power is working to keep you from taking this new path. But have faith, because nothing could be further from the truth.

There will be diversity.

5   "Will there be people who look like me?" You worry you won't see familiar faces when you look at the students, teachers, and leaders on campus. Or you are differently abled and wonder whether we'll understand your needs. While we may not be perfect, we work hard to serve and connect with you and your communities. More than almost anywhere in higher education, the diversity that strengthens us and inspires you will be there.

You may be a recent high school graduate.

6   For many of you, beginning with us fresh out of high school makes perfect sense because of where we're located, our cost, our size, or a host of other reasons. You hit the ground running and jump into our student activities. Some of you share your strengths as peer tutors, student leaders, or community volunteers. You are models of service and learning for us all.

You may be starting college later in life.

7   Many of you, however, come through our open doors later in life. You may have reached a turning point in your life—the kids are getting older, your job is getting colder, or your dreams are getting further away. It's time for a radical shift. But you wonder what to expect and what will be expected of you as you move into this new world. You're going from waiting

tables to mastering computer networking, or from working in a factory to spending sleepless nights pursuing a nursing degree.

You can finish well.

8   But no matter where you start, you can finish well. Some of you start with us in programs to learn to read and move on to complete a GED; you move through math, reading, and pre-college writing; you complete certifications and degrees on your way to jobs or a university. Along the way, you strive with each passing day, month, and year to get better; and "better" is not about how you compare to others. Better is about how you compare to how you were yesterday.

Your persistence will see you through.

9   Your persistence in getting better teaches us that the time it takes to complete a course or program isn't really the issue. That time will pass either way. What matters is whether you remain at a dead end or move to a place where new learning opens up different pathways for your career and life. With each passing day, you continue on, riding with the ebbs and flows. Obstacles of all sorts flood your way from semester to semester or quarter to quarter: births, deaths, marriages, divorces, getting jobs, losing jobs, and just about every other kind of life experience you can imagine. Some of you need to step out for a time to take care of these situations; but you dive back in, and we welcome you with open arms.

You will move on and contribute to others.

10   What do you do when it's all said and done? Some of you will move on to work or other education.

Others target your talents closer to home: raising families, serving communities, creating new businesses, fighting fires, saving lives, or teaching children. In short, you throw yourself into the pool of humanity and the positive ripples cascade out.

Everything begins with your courageous, life-changing choice.

11   And it all begins with a choice—an incredibly courageous choice. You choose to try, to walk through the open doors of our college and begin. You make this choice again and again as you take each step along the journey. You choose to stay, to engage, to give it your best. This choice can and will change your life forever. All because you have the courage to learn.

Source: Mark David Milliron, "The Courage to Learn," *Innovation Abstracts*, Vol. 7, No. 4, April 2004. Reprinted by permission of Dr. Mark David Milliron, VP of Education and Medical Practice, SAS Institute.

✔ Vocabulary Check

Context clues are words in a sentence that allow the reader to deduce (reason out) the meaning of an unfamiliar word in the sentence. For each vocabulary exercise below, a sentence from the reading selection containing an important word (*italicized, like this*) is quoted first. Next, there is an additional sentence using the word in the same sense, providing another context clue. Use the context clues from both sentences to deduce the meaning of the italicized word. *Be sure the answer you choose makes sense in both sentences.* If you discover that you must use a dictionary to confirm an answer choice, remember that the meaning you select must still fit the context of *both* sentences. Write your answer in the space provided.

Use this pronunciation key as you complete this activity. You will need to refer to it as you do the other reading selections. Place a sticky note on the edge of this page so you can find it easily.

Pronunciation Key:	ă p**a**t	ā p**ay**	âr c**are**	ä f**a**ther
ĕ p**e**t	ē b**e**	ĭ p**i**t	ī t**ie**	îr p**ier**	ŏ p**o**t	ō t**oe**
ô p**aw**	oi n**oi**se	ou **out**	ŏŏ t**oo**k	ōō b**oo**t	ŭ c**u**t
yōō ab**u**se	ûr **ur**ge	th **th**in	*th* **th**is	hw **wh**ich
zh vi**s**ion	ə **a**bout	*Stress mark:'*

Source: From *Opening Doors: Understanding College Reading*, 4th ed., by Joe Cortina and Janet Elder. Copyright © 2005 the McGraw-Hill Companies. Reprinted by permission of the McGraw-Hill Companies, Inc.

_____   1. But when we slow down, look around, and soak in all of your stories, we are *humbled*.

The aging actor was so *humbled* by the young child's brilliant performance that he gave his award to her instead.

Humbled (hŭm′bəld) is an adjective that means   (paragraph 1)

a. feeling less proud and important in comparison with someone else.
b. feeling upset and angry in comparison with someone else.
c. feeling confident in comparison with someone else.
d. feeling better and superior in comparison with someone else.

_____ 2. Some are afraid that your success will take you away from them, so they subtly *sabotage* your journey.

The terrorists planned to *sabotage* the president's inauguration by setting off an explosion, but they were caught before they could do anything.

Sabotage (săb′ə-täzh′) is a verb that means   (paragraph 4)

a. to share; participate in.
b. to disrupt; to interfere with.
c. to try to change.
d. to support.

_____ 3. You search to find good child care and *wrestle* with the guilt of being away from your kids even though you're going to college to better their lives as well.

Sometimes we *wrestle* with our consciences: we know the right thing to do, but we don't always want to do it.

Wrestle (rĕs′əl) is a verb that means   (paragraph 4)

a. encourage.
b. laugh at.
c. enjoy thinking about.
d. struggle.

_____ 4. More than almost anywhere in higher education, the *diversity* that strengthens us and inspires you will be there.

The *diversity* at our college is reflected in the fact that our students range from 16 to 80 years of age, many have disabilities of some sort, and all of our students together speak more than 60 different languages.

Diversity (dĭ-vûr′sĭ-tē, dī-) is a noun that means   (paragraph 5)

a. a collection of people with similar backgrounds and interests.
b. a collection of people from different countries.
c. a collection of people of various types and backgrounds.
d. a collection of people who are rich and poor.

_____ 5. For many of you, beginning with us fresh out of high school makes perfect sense because of where we're located, our cost, our size, or a *host* of other reasons.

A *host* of representatives from the college conducted tours for visitors and told them about the college's new programs.

Host (hōst) is a noun that means   (paragraph 6)

a. someone who interviews guests on a television or radio program.

b. a very large number of things or people.

c. a place or organization that provides space and facilities for a special event.

d. someone who invites, welcomes, and entertains guests.

_____ 6. It's time for a *radical* shift.

Rather than dieting sensibly and exercising, many people try *radical* approaches to losing weight.

Radical (răd′ĭ-kəl) is an adjective that means   (paragraph 7)

a. intelligent.

b. expensive.

c. harsh.

d. extreme.

_____ 7. You're going from waiting tables to mastering computer networking, or from working in a factory to spending sleepless nights *pursuing* a nursing degree.

Pursuing your dreams gives life meaning and purpose.

Pursuing (pər-sōō′ĭng) is a noun that means   (paragraph 7)

a. seeking.

b. chasing.

c. worrying about.

d. avoiding.

_____ 8. Your *persistence* in getting better teaches us that the time it takes to complete a course or program isn't really the issue.

Thomas Edison is known for his remarkable *persistence*: It took him approximately 1,000 attempts before he found the right filament to make an electric lightbulb.

Persistence (pər-sĭs′təns) is a noun that means   (paragraph 9)

a. refusal to try.

b. reluctance; hesitation.

c. going on in spite of opposition; not giving up.

d. speed and efficiency.

_____ 9. With each passing day, you continue on, riding with the *ebbs and flows.*

Despite *ebbs and flows* in the real estate business, my boss never gets overly excited when sales are good or upset when they are slow.

Ebbs and flows (ĕbz ən flōz) is an idiom that means   (paragraph 9)

a. comings and goings.
b. failures and disappointments.
c. departures and returns.
d. successes and setbacks.

_____ 10. *Obstacles* of all sorts flood your way from semester to semester or quarter to quarter: births, deaths, marriages, divorces, getting jobs, losing jobs, and just about every other kind of life experience you can imagine.

No matter how many *obstacles* life puts in your path, you can find ways to overcome them and achieve your dreams.

Obstacles (ŏb'stə-kəlz) is a noun that means   (paragraph 9)

a. permanent barriers.
b. things that interfere with progress or achievement.
c. interesting challenges.
d. amusing situations.

✔ **Comprehension Check**

Read each of the following questions. Then write the correct answer choice in the blank. *Base your answers on information in the selection.* You may refer to the selection as you answer the questions.

_____ 1. New college students can feel overwhelmed because they must

a. fill out forms.
b. take placement tests.
c. piece together a schedule.
d. do all of the above.

_____ 2. Many college students feel happy to have the support of family and friends but feel pressured by their expectations.

a. true
b. false

_____ 3. One pressure some college students face is

a. lack of adequate preparation in high school.
b. uncooperative supervisors and job schedules.
c. legal problems.
d. high interest rates on student loans.

_____ 4. More than almost anywhere in higher education, community colleges and technical colleges have

    a. greater diversity in their student populations.
    b. less diversity in their student populations.
    c. similar student populations.
    d. small student populations.

_____ 5. Many students choose a two-year college because of the college's

    a. cost.
    b. location.
    c. size.
    d. all of the above

_____ 6. Getting "better" means you

    a. complete a certification or two-year degree.
    b. move on to a university.
    c. get a job.
    d. do better than you did yesterday.

_____ 7. The time it takes to complete a course or program isn't really an issue since

    a. time will pass either way.
    b. you will remain at a dead end.
    c. obstacles of all sorts will flood your way semester to semester.
    d. fears and insecurities will discourage you at every turn.

_____ 8. People who make the decision to start college are

    a. confident.
    b. angry.
    c. courageous.
    d. mentally and physically tired.

_____ 9. Two-year college students who complete their program or degree

    a. typically do not pursue any further education.
    b. move on to work or other education.
    c. encourage their friends to start college.
    d. often have difficulty obtaining a job.

_____ 10. Once people decide to begin college and they make the first choice to try, they

    a. do not have to make any other choices.
    b. have the support of family, friends, and faculty.
    c. are assured of being successful.
    d. must continue to make this choice again and again as they take each step along their journey.

Writing to Make Connections

Respond to the following items, based on information in the reading selection and on your own experience. You may refer to the selection as you answer the questions.

If the item has this symbol, your instructor may assign you to work collaboratively on it with classmates:

In that case, you should form groups of three or four students as directed by your instructor and work together to complete the exercises. After your group discusses each item and agrees on the answer, have a group member record it. Every member of your group should be able to explain all of your group's answers.

1. The author, David Milliron, says that it takes "an incredibly courageous choice" to begin college. What led to your decision to start college? What is your reason for attending college, the goal you want to achieve? Did it (or does it still) seem a bit frightening or overwhelming to be attending college? If so, what in particular, makes you feel that way?

_____

_____

_____

_____

2. What has been your biggest surprise since you started college? In what ways has your experience been different from what you expected?

_____

_____

_____

_____

3. What obstacles, if any, did you face in starting college? What obstacles or challenges do you think you may face as you progress through college?

_____

_____

_____

_____

_____

_____

_____

4. What effect do you think your attending college will have on your family and friends? What effect do you think it will have on you a few years from now?

_____

_____

_____

_____

_____

_____

5. What advice would you give a friend or family member who is considering going to college?

_____

_____

_____

_____

_____

6. List at least five things colleges could do to make new students feel more welcome and confident.

_____

_____

_____

_____

_____

Web Resources

A search engine is a website that uses powerful data-searching techniques to help users locate websites that contain the types of information they are seeking. As of mid-2005, Google indexed more than 8 billion Web pages, so you can see the usefulness of having programs that let you focus your search!

Google is probably the most popular search engine. If you are not familiar with it or have used it to only a limited extent, take advantage of the tutorial at the Google website, www.google.com. Click on About Google. Then click on Help and How to Search. At the Google Help Center, click on Basic Search. You'll see clear explanations, along with examples. You may also want to check out the section on Search Features, as well as Services and Tips. Many users are unaware of Google's definition feature, maps and directions, weather, spell-check for words used in queries, translations of Web pages, calculator, phone book, websites for universities, movie reviews and show times near you, Q & A (to get answers to fact-based questions), travel information, and many other handy services. Need images for a class presentation? Google has those, too!

Whenever you go to *any* website, it is a good idea to evaluate it critically. Are you getting good information—information that is accurate, complete, and up-to-date? Who sponsors the website? How easy is it to use the features of the website?

For additional information related to the selection topic, see the following websites:

www.uu.edu/centers/faculty/resources/article.cfm?ArticleID=119

The College Board's nationwide study includes this profile of adult learners in America, half of whom are 25 years of age or older.

www.ecampustours.com

This website presents practical advice about college and college life. Click on the tabs for college planning, campus life, career exploration, and paying for college.

www.mhhe.com/entryways

For more complete descriptions of these websites, as well as additional web resources related to this selection, see the ORL Student Center.

(For more complete descriptions, as well as additional websites, consult the Online Reading Lab.)

Although the addresses (URLs) listed above were active at the time *Entryways* was published, URLs can change or go out of existence. To locate other websites related to the selection topic, use these descriptors with Google or another search engine of your choice: **first year college** or **successful transition to college**.

READING SELECTION 2

SUPERMAN AND ME

By Sherman Alexie

Connecting with What You Already Know

Do these exercises *before* you read the selection.

First, think about the title. Then preview this selection by reading the

- title
- introduction (in *italics*)
- the first sentence of each paragraph

1. Based on your preview, what do expect this selection to be about?

   _____

   _____

   _____

2. What was your first experience with learning to read? Do you remember when you first realized you could read? Describe your experiences.

   _____

   _____

   _____

3. In the selection, you'll encounter the following words. Mark any words you already know or think you know. Most words have more than one meaning. After you have read the selection, you will have an opportunity to deduce (reason out) their meanings according to how they are used in the selection. At that point, you will discover whether you were correct, and if not, you'll have a new word to add to your vocabulary.

villain	prodigy
avid	subverted
random	monosyllabic
clarity	submissively
narrative	pediatrician

SUPERMAN AND ME

By Sherman Alexie

Sherman Alexie is an award-winning Native American author, poet, and screenwriter. As of February 2006, he had written 17 books and three movies, including Smoke Signals *(1998). In the wonderful selection below, he reveals the surprising way he learned to read, how reading affected his childhood and, ultimately, his life.*

1 I learned to read with a *Superman* comic book. Simple enough, I suppose. I cannot recall which particular *Superman* comic book I read, nor can I remember which villain he fought in that issue. I cannot remember the plot, nor the means by which I obtained the comic book. What I can remember is this: I was three years old, a Spokane Indian boy living with his family on the Spokane Indian Reservation in eastern Washington state. We were poor by most standards, but one of my parents usually managed to find some minimum-wage job or another, which made us middle class by reservation standards. I had a brother and three sisters. We lived on a combination of irregular

paychecks, hope, fear, and government-surplus food.

2   My father, who is one of the few Indians who went to Catholic school on purpose, was an avid reader of westerns, spy thrillers, murder mysteries, gangster epics, basketball player biographies, and anything else he could find. He bought his books by the pound at Dutch's Pawn Shop, Goodwill, Salvation Army, and Value Village. When he had extra money, he bought new novels at supermarkets, convenience stores, and hospital gift shops. Our house was filled with books. They were stacked in crazy piles in the bathroom, bedrooms, and living room. In a fit of unemployment inspired creative energy, my father built a set of bookshelves and soon filled them with a random assortment of books about the Kennedy assassination, Watergate, the Vietnam War, and the entire twenty-three-book series of the Apache westerns. My father loved books, and since I loved my father with an aching devotion, I decided to love books as well.

3   I can remember picking up my father's books before I could read. The words themselves were mostly foreign, but I still remember the exact moment when I first understood, with a sudden clarity, the purpose of a paragraph. I didn't have the vocabulary to say "paragraph" but I realized that a paragraph was a fence that held words. The words inside a paragraph worked together for a common purpose. They had some specific reason for being inside the same fence. This knowledge delighted me. I began to think of everything in terms of paragraphs. Our reservation was a small paragraph within the United States. My family's house was a

paragraph, distinct from the other paragraphs of the LeBrets to the north, the Fords to our south, and the Tribal School to the west. Inside our house, each family member existed as a separate paragraph, but still had genetics and common experiences to link us. Now, using this logic, I can see my changed family as an essay of seven paragraphs: mother, father, older brother, the deceased sister, my younger twin sisters, and our adopted little brother.

4   At the same time I was seeing the world in paragraphs, I also picked up that *Superman* comic book. Each panel, complete with picture, dialogue, and narrative, was a three-dimensional paragraph. In one panel, Superman breaks through a door. His suit is red, blue, and yellow. The brown door shatters into many pieces. I look at the narrative above the picture. I cannot read the words, but I assume it tells me that Superman is breaking down the door. Aloud, I pretend to read the words and say, "Superman is breaking down the door." Words, dialogue, also float out of Superman's mouth. Because he is breaking down the door, I assume he says, "I am breaking down the door." Once again, I pretend to read the words and say aloud, "I am breaking down the door." In this way, I learned to read. This might be an interesting story all by itself. A little Indian boy teaches himself to read at an early age and advances quickly. He reads *Grapes of Wrath* in kindergarten when other children are struggling through *Dick and Jane*. If he'd been anything but an Indian boy living on the reservation, he might have been called a prodigy. But he is an Indian boy living on the reservation, and is simply an

oddity. He grows into a man who often speaks of his childhood in the third-person, as if it will somehow dull the pain and make him sound more modest about his talents.

5   A smart Indian is a dangerous person, widely feared and ridiculed by Indians and non-Indians alike. I fought with my classmates on a daily basis. They wanted me to stay quiet when the non-Indian teacher asked for answers, for volunteers, for help. We were Indian children who were expected to be stupid. Most lived up to those expectations inside the classroom, but subverted them on the outside. They struggled with basic reading in school, but could remember how to sing a few dozen powwow songs. They were monosyllabic in front of their non-Indian teachers, but could tell complicated stories and jokes at the dinner table. They submissively ducked their heads when confronted by a non-Indian adult, but would slug it out with the Indian bully who was ten years older. As Indian children, we were expected to fail in the non-Indian world. Those who failed were ceremonially accepted by other Indians and appropriately pitied by non-Indians.

6   I refused to fail. I was smart. I was arrogant. I was lucky. I read books late into the night, until I could barely keep my eyes open. I read books at recess, then during lunch, and in the few minutes left after I had finished my classroom assignments. I read books in the car when my family traveled to powwows or basketball games. In shopping malls, I ran to the bookstores and read bits and pieces of as many books as I could. I read the books my father brought home from the pawnshops and

secondhand stores. I read the books I borrowed from the library. I read the backs of cereal boxes. I read the newspaper. I read the bulletins posted on the walls of the school, the clinic, the tribal offices, the post office. I read junk mail. I read auto-repair manuals. I read magazines. I read anything that had words and paragraphs. I read with equal parts joy and desperation. I loved those books, but I also knew that love had only one purpose. I was trying to save my life.

7   Despite all the books I read, I am still surprised I became a writer. I was going to be a pediatrician. These days, I write novels, short stories, and poems. I visit schools and teach creative writing to Indian kids. In all my years in the reservation school system, I was never taught how to write poetry, short stories, or novels. I was certainly never taught that Indians wrote poetry, short stories, and novels. Writing was something beyond Indians. I cannot recall a single time that a guest teacher visited the reservation. There must have been visiting teachers. Who were they? Where are they now? Do they exist? I visit the schools as often as possible. The Indian kids crowd the classroom. Many are writing their own poems, short stories, and novels. They have read my books. They have read many other books. They look at me with bright eyes and arrogant wonder. They are trying to save their lives. Then there are the sullen and already defeated Indian kids who sit in the back rows and ignore me with theatrical precision. The pages of their notebooks are empty. They carry neither pencil nor pen. They stare out the window. They refuse and resist. "Books," I say to them.

"Books," I say. I throw my weight against their locked doors. The door holds. I am smart. I am arrogant. I am lucky. I am trying to save our lives.

✔ **Vocabulary Check**

Use the context clues from *both* sentences to reason out the meaning of the italicized words. *The answer you choose should make sense in both sentences.* You may use a dictionary to confirm your answer choice, but be sure the meaning you select fits the context of both sentences. Write your answer in the space provided.

Refer to page 402 for the pronunciation key.

_____ 1. I cannot recall which particular *Superman* comic book I read, nor can I remember which *villain* he fought in that issue.

In the *Batman* movies, Batman always defeats the Joker, the Penguin, and any other *villain* he encounters.

Villain (vĭl'ən) is a noun that means   (paragraph 1)
a. actor in a movie.
b. make-believe hero in a fairy tale.
c. real person who has magical powers.
d. fictional character who is at odds with the hero.

_____ 2. My father, who is one of the few Indians who went to Catholic school on purpose, was an *avid* reader of westerns, spy thrillers, murder mysteries, gangster epics, basketball player biographies, and anything else he could find.

My brothers are *avid* baseball fans who never miss a White Sox game.

Avid (ăv'ĭd) is an adjective that means   (paragraph 2)
a. rude and impatient.
b. easily upset.
c. having keen interest and enthusiasm.
d. professional.

_____ 3. In a fit of unemployment inspired creative energy, my father built a set of bookshelves and soon filled them with a *random* assortment of books about the Kennedy assassination, Watergate, the Vietnam War, and the entire twenty-three-book series of the Apache westerns.

The lottery winner is determined by drawing a *random* set of numbers.

Random (răn'dəm) is an adjective that means   (paragraph 2)

a. expensive; costly.
b. having no specific pattern or purpose.
c. having little value.
d. precise; exact.

_____ 4. The words themselves were mostly foreign, but I still remember the exact moment when I first understood, with a sudden *clarity*, the purpose of a paragraph.

I understand the concepts in my economics class because the instructor explains them with great *clarity*.

Clarity (klăr'ĭ-tē) is a noun that means   (paragraph 3)

a. enthusiasm.
b. interest.
c. energy.
d. clearness.

_____ 5. Each panel, complete with picture, dialogue, and *narrative*, was a three-dimensional paragraph.

The *narrative* of a person's life is called a biography.

Narrative (năr'ə-tĭv) is a noun that means   (paragraph 4)

a. story.
b. purpose.
c. length.
d. lesson.

_____ 6. If he'd been anything but an Indian boy living on the reservation, he might have been called a *prodigy*.

Mozart was a *prodigy* who began playing the piano and composing music as a young child.

Prodigy (prŏd'ə-jē) is a noun that means   (paragraph 4)

a. person with exceptional talents.
b. person with musical ability.
c. person with athletic ability.
d. person with artistic talent.

_____ 7. Most lived up to those expectations inside the classroom, but *subverted* them on the outside.

The employees appeared to go along with their boss's plan, but then *subverted* it by ignoring his instructions.

Subverted (seb-vûrt'əd) is a verb that means   (paragraph 5)
   a. ruined.
   b. copied.
   c. began.
   d. repeated.

_____ 8. They were *monosyllabic* in front of their non-Indian teachers, but could tell complicated stories and jokes at the dinner table.

Parents complain that teenagers answer questions with only "yes," "no," and other *monosyllabic* responses.

Monosyllabic (mŏn'ə-sĭ-lăb'ĭk) is an adjective that means
   a. spoken slowly.   (paragraph 5)
   b. difficult to pronounce.
   c. hard to understand.
   d. having only a single syllable.

_____ 9. They *submissively* ducked their heads when confronted by a non-Indian adult, but would slug it out with the Indian bully who was ten years older.

The frightened dog *submissively* obeyed its owner.

Submissively (səb-mĭs'ĭv lē) is an adverb that means   (paragraph 5)
   a. proudly.
   b. slowly.
   c. giving in to the will or authority of another.
   d. done in a brave manner.

_____ 10. I was going to be a *pediatrician*.

Because my sister has always loved children, she decided to go to medical school to become a *pediatrician*.

Pediatrician (pē'dē-ə-trĭsh'ən) is a noun that means   (paragraph 7)
   a. therapist who works with children.
   b. physician who specializes in the care of infants and children.
   c. day care provider.
   d. teacher who specializes in early childhood education.

✔ Comprehension Check

Read each of the following questions. Then write the correct answer choice in the blank. *Base your answers on information in the selection.* You may refer to the selection as you answer the questions.

True or False

_____ 1. Sherman Alexie grew up in eastern Washington, D.C.

_____ 2. Alexie knew his classmates were smarter than they let on in school.

_____ 3. Today Alexie visits schools to teach creative writing to Indian children.

_____ 4. As a child, Alexie was inspired by guest teachers who visited the reservation school.

_____ 5. Alexie's father read books of all kinds.

Multiple-Choice

_____ 6. Alexie decided to love books as a child because
   a. he wanted to read about Superman.
   b. his father owned a bookstore.
   c. he loved his father, and his father loved books.
   d. he had a teacher who encouraged him to read.

_____ 7. As a boy, Alexie realized that paragraphs were like
   a. common experiences that link us.
   b. a Native American reservation.
   c. a Catholic school.
   d. fences that held words.

_____ 8. Because Alexie was a "smart Indian," he was
   a. feared and ridiculed, and he fought daily with his classmates.
   b. admired by both Indians and non-Indians alike.
   c. allowed to skip a grade.
   d. reluctant to show how much he knew.

_____ 9. Besides books, Alexie read
   a. the backs of cereal boxes.
   b. bulletin boards in various offices.
   c. junk mail.
   d. all of the above.

_____ 10. When Alexie said he read to save his life, he meant he
   a. understood being educated was the key to succeeding in the non-Indian world.
   b. was trying to find out about a life-threatening illness he had.
   c. wanted to become a writer as an adult.
   d. knew his father would be very angry if he did not read as much as his father did.

Writing to Make Connections

Respond to the following items, based on information in the reading selection and on your own experience. You may refer to the selection as you answer the questions.

If the item has this symbol, your instructor may assign you to work collaboratively on it with classmates:

In that case, you should form groups of three or four students as directed by your instructor and work together to complete the exercises. After your group discusses each item and agrees on the answer, have a group member record it. Every member of your group should be able to explain all of your group's answers.

1. Describe some of the ways you think Sherman Alexie's life might have been different if he had not learned to love to read as a child.

   _____

   _____

   _____

2. Describe your earliest experiences and memories that concern reading. Was there someone who read to you when you were young? What do you remember about how you learned to read?

   _____

   _____

   _____

 ## Web Resources

A search engine is a website that uses powerful data-searching techniques to help users locate websites that contain the types of information they are seeking. As of mid-2005, Google indexed more than 8 billion Web pages, so you can see the usefulness of having programs that let you focus your search!

Google is probably the most popular search engine. If you are not familiar with it or have used it to only a limited extent, take advantage of the tutorial at the Google website, www.google.com. Click on About Google. Then click on Help and How to Search. At the Google Help Center, click on Basic Search. You'll see clear explanations, along with examples. You may also want to check out the section on Search Features, as well as Services and Tips. Many users are unaware of Google's definition feature, maps and directions, weather, spell-check for words used in queries, translations of Web pages, calculator, phone book, websites for universities, movie reviews and show times near you, Q & A (to get answers to fact-based questions), travel information, and many other handy services. Need images for a class presentation? Google has those, too!

For additional information related to the selection topic, see the following website:

www.mhhe.com/
entryways

For a more complete description of this website, as well as an additional web resource related to this selection, see the ORL Student Center.

http://www.fallsapart.com

The official Sherman Alexie website.

Although the address (URL) listed above was active at the time *Entryways* was published, URLs can change or go out of existence. To locate other websites related to the selection topic, use this descriptor with Google or another search engine: **Sherman Alexie**.

READING SELECTION 3

DO YOU HAVE WHAT IT TAKES TO SURVIVE ARMY BOOT CAMP?

Connecting with What You Already Know

Do these exercises *before* you read the selection.

Preview this selection by reading the

- title
- introduction (in *italics)*
- headings
- first paragraph
- first sentences of the other paragraphs
- last two paragraphs
- source

1. Based on your preview, what do you expect this selection to be about?

   _____

   _____

   _____

   _____

2. Have you or anyone you know been through military boot camp? If so, what was the experience like? If not, what have you heard about boot camp?

_____

_____

_____

_____

3. In the selection, you'll encounter the following words. Mark any words you already know or think you know. Most words have more than one meaning. After you have read the selection, you will have an opportunity to deduce (reason out) their meanings according to how they are used in the selection. At that point, you will discover whether you were correct, and if not, you'll have a new word to add to your vocabulary.

inundated	obstacle course
ramrod	rations
barracks	edible
chow	culmination
ingest	tactical

DO YOU HAVE WHAT IT TAKES TO SURVIVE ARMY BOOT CAMP?

Adapted from "Surviving Military Boot Camp, Part III, Army Basic Training" and "How to Survive Boot Camp," by Rod Powers

This selection is drawn from soldiers' accounts of their Basic Combat Training (BCT), more commonly known as "Boot Camp." The soldiers include advice to new enlistees for surviving the experience and getting the most out of it. Enlistees can take comfort in knowing that about 90 percent of recruits successfully complete Basic Training.

A more intense basic training program is currently being tested at Fort Benning, GA. Training is still nine weeks long, but there are significant changes in the way the time is spent. Field Exercises are expanded from the current 3 days to 10 days for one test group, and from 3 days to 23 days in the other test program. Recruits who are sent to Fort Benning will not know until they arrive which test group they've been assigned to.

1 They may be the hardest nine weeks of a person's life. You drill and march endlessly. For what seems like hours, you stand ramrod straight in formation, even if a fly annoys you, your nose itches, or sweat rolls into your eyes. You're inundated with information you must quickly memorize: information in the Soldier's Handbook, the names of officer and enlisted ranks, Army General Orders, and the seven Army Core Values (loyalty, duty, respect, selfless-service, honor, integrity, and personal courage—memory peg: the letters spell "LDRSHIP"). You will be yelled at constantly. Your muscles will ache. You will be dog-tired. You're a new Army recruit.

2   You'll be given a list of what you can and can't bring. If something isn't on the list, don't bring it. It will be taken away from you. Bring all the necessary papers. If you smoke or chew tobacco, quit ahead of time. All tobacco products are forbidden in boot camp.

3   Experienced soldiers advise recruits to bring foot powder and foot cream to boot camp. Also, bring a truckload of cough drops: your throat will be sore from yelling your responses; you and everyone else will be sick at some point. Moreover, cough drops are about the only "sweet" you'll taste for several weeks. Bring stamps. They can be more valuable than money during boot camp. Bring phone cards. Bring toothpaste that tastes good. Leave your iPod, radio, magazines, jewelry, and alcohol and food products at home. The Army doesn't take kindly to recruits who show up with forbidden items, or worse, try to hide them.

Reception

4   The enlistment period begins with Reception. It consists of 8–10 hours of processing spread over one to three weeks, a little each day, prior to the official start of basic training. You'll spend a lot of time waiting around. You'll go through physical fitness screening. You'll undergo dental and eye examinations. If you need glasses in order to have 20/20 vision, you'll be given ones with thick plastic lenses set in thick, hard-plastic frames to wear during basic training. No contact lenses are allowed. If you already wear glasses, they'll be taken away and you'll receive a government-issued pair. Other processing includes getting immunizations, completing paperwork, getting your hair cut off, and being issued uniforms. You learn barracks upkeep, including how to make your bunk with "hospital corners" so that the bed is smooth and tight. You'll also take classes in "drill"—marching.

5   Don't plan on sneaking around at night. There may be cameras in the halls. If you're spotted, the entire bay will be waked up by an officer yelling at you over the loudspeaker.

6   At this point, you're loaded onto a bus. You're on your way to boot camp, where your actual training will begin. You're about to meet someone who will have the greatest impact on your life for the next nine weeks: a drill sergeant who will watch your every move and control your every waking moment.

Boot Camp

Phase I

7 Phase I, also called the "Red Phase" and the "Patriot Phase," consists of the first three weeks. Your day starts at 4:30 a.m., with lights out at 9:00 p.m. Every minute of the day you will be told exactly what to do and when to do it, and you will do nothing that you are not told to do. You will be yelled at day-in and day-out. You will be "dropped" repeatedly— ordered to do push-ups. In the Army, you address the drill sergeant as "Drill Sergeant," not "Sir" or "Ma'am": "Yes, Drill Sergeant" and "No, Drill Sergeant." If you forget and use sir or ma'am, you'll find yourself doing push-ups while being screamed at by a loud, angry drill sergeant. If you look him or her directly in the eye, you'll find yourself in the same unfortunate situation.

8   You discover that you cannot do anything right. Leave your locker unlocked and your drill sergeant will ream you out, not to

mention dumping out the contents of your locker and continuing to scream at you while you do push-ups. Do anything wrong and you'll get "smoked," ordered to do extra exercise, usually push-ups.

9   In fact, no matter how well you perform, your drill sergeant will constantly tell you how much better his grandmother could do it. Everyone will take turns at Fire Guard duty, two-hour shifts of walking around the barracks. If you're not in shape physically when you report for boot camp, you'll wish you'd spent the previous couple of months running, doing push-ups, and sit-ups. Your physical fitness is assessed when you begin and finish basic training (push-ups, sit-ups, and a two-mile run). Physical training starts as soon as you arrive in boot camp.

10   You eat your meals in the chow hall. You'll have 20 minutes to eat each meal. Forget soft drinks and Gatorade during this phase. You'll be drinking water. Forget desserts. If you ingest any extra calories, your drill sergeant will notice and see to it that you burn them off.

11   The entire time, you're cramming information into your head on all kinds of military-related subjects that range from map reading and weapons to first aid. You'll memorize rules and regulations. You'll be introduced to your M16A2 rifle. (Never call it a "gun"! If you do, you'll be doing push-ups.) You'll learn how to hold your rifle, aim it, dismantle it, clean it, and reassemble it. You'll do these things over and over again. Learning to fire it comes later.

12   During the second week, you'll experience the gas chamber, a nasty experience that's guaranteed to make your eyes burn and sting, make you gag and cough, and cause you to wish you'd eaten a light lunch. For at least a minute or two, you'll be forced to lift your gas mask, open your eyes, and inhale a small amount of the tear gas. It's rough, but you learn to trust your equipment.

13   Toward the end of Phase 1, your drill sergeant will gradually begin to shift the emphasis from individuals to the "team." He will assign each person a "Battle Buddy," and throughout the rest of basic training, whenever one "buddy" does something wrong, both get blamed.

Phase II

14 Phase II, the second three weeks of Basic Training is called the "White Phase" or "Gunfighter Phase." The first week you learn marksmanship (how to shoot a rifle). You move from range to range, shooting at various types of targets (including ones that pop up) at various distances.

15   During the following week, you're introduced to the obstacle course. You'll run the course with your rifle, and you'll work as a team with your Battle Buddy. You'll also learn about anti-tank weapons and other heavy weapons. You spend time practicing how to use—stab with—your bayonet. In week 7, you learn how to launch and lob grenades. You go through live-fire exercises.

16   Physical training continues throughout this phase, as do the practice of basic drills and ceremonies. You notice, though, that your drill sergeant isn't yelling at everyone quite as much.

Phase III

17 The end is in sight! Phase III, known as the "Blue Phase" or "Warrior Phase," comprises the final three weeks of Basic. During

the first week, your physical fitness is reassessed. Anyone who doesn't pass the test (which is rare) is not allowed to go to the "Field" with the rest of the platoon.

18 In the Field, you learn to pitch tents, patrol at night, and carry out night operations. All of your meals are MREs, "meals ready to eat." The name says it all: they are rations that require no preparation other than opening or removing the packaging. Edible, to be sure, but definitely not culinary delights. And pay attention to your drill sergeant if he says not to chew the gum enclosed in the MREs. He will probably count them at the end, and if there are any pieces missing, the entire platoon will suffer the consequences. Listen to your drill sergeant whenever he tells you he'll be counting something or searching for something! He's looking for recruits who ignore orders or try to get around the rules, and he's sure to make examples of them.

19 The second week is the culmination: a tactical field exercise that requires you and your platoon to draw upon everything you've learned up to this point. Your platoon and squad leaders must make the tactical decisions, although the drill sergeants are there to keep anyone from being injured. The goal is to work 20 together as a skilled unit.

The Field experience ends with an informal celebratory ceremony. The final week of Phase III leads to the graduation ceremony. You and your platoon members have earned the right to feel confident and proud. Your family and friends are invited to this important life event. You have made the transition from civilian to a disciplined soldier 21 who is ready for basic combat.

As good as it feels to have completed Basic Training, know that your real training still lies ahead, when you move to AIT, Advanced Individual Training. This provides hands-on training in specific Army jobs and careers. There is an impressive number of choices. Among others, the choices include engineer school, signal corps (communications technology), air defense artillery school (high-tech missile systems), electronics, and military police.

Source: Rod Powers, "Surviving Military Boot Camp, and "How to Survive Boot Camp," *About, Inc.,* May 17, 2005. Reprinted with permission of *The New York Times.*

✔ **Vocabulary Check**

Use the context clues from both sentences to reason out the meaning of the italicized words. *The answer you choose should make sense in both sentences.* You may use a dictionary to confirm your answer choice, but be sure the meaning you select fits the context of both sentences. Write your answer in the space provided.

Refer to page 404 for the pronunciation key.

_____ 1. You're *inundated* with information you must quickly memorize: information in the Soldier's Handbook, the names of officer and enlisted ranks, Army General Orders, and the seven Army Core Values.

As soon as the company announced the new job openings, it was *inundated* with applications.

Inundated (ĭn'ŭn-dāt'əd) is a verb that means   (paragraph 1)

a. trusted with.
b. flooded; overwhelmed.
c. limited; restricted.
d. held responsible for.

_____ 2. You learn *barracks* upkeep, including how to make your bunk with "hospital corners" so that the bed is smooth and tight.

To prepare for the daily inspection of the *barracks*, the cadets scoured the floors, scrubbed the showers, and polished the windows.

Barracks (băr'əks) is a noun that means   (paragraph 4)

a. buildings used to house military personnel.
b. bathing facilities on military bases.
c. military weapons.
d. buildings used for meals on military bases.

_____ 3. If you *ingest* any extra calories, your drill sergeant will notice and see to it that you burn them off.

All parents should know what to do if their children accidentally *ingest* poison.

Ingest (ĭn-jĕst') is a verb that means   (paragraph 10)

a. to find or locate.
b. to seek out.
c. to take into the body by the mouth.
d. to hide or prevent the discovery of.

_____ 4. You'll learn how to hold your rifle, aim it, *dismantle* it, clean it, and reassemble it.

The workers will carefully *dismantle* and pack up the exhibit so that it can be shipped to the next museum.

Dismantle (dĭs-măn'tl) is a verb that means   (paragraph 11)

a. to label.
b. to take apart.
c. to polish.
d. to remove.

_____ 5. During the following week, you're introduced to the *obstacle course*.

To train for the *obstacle course*, the recruits practiced scaling barriers and climbing rope walls.

Obstacle course (ŏb′stə-kəl kôrs) is a noun that means   (paragraph 15)

a. a path soldiers cut through the woods or jungle.
b. a road soldiers construct through hostile or enemy territory, using the materials at hand.
c. a training course filled with impediments, such as ditches and walls, that troops must move through as quickly as possible.
d. a secret route troops use in order to avoid detection by the enemy.

_____ 6. Anyone who doesn't pass the test (which is rare) is not allowed to go to the "Field" with the rest of the *platoon*.

The lieutenant ordered the squads into position and then marched the entire *platoon* to the head of the president's inaugural parade.

Platoon (plə-toon′) is a noun that means   (paragraph 17)

a. a subdivision of a company of troops consisting of two or more squads and usually commanded by a lieutenant.
b. a group of military personnel who travel together.
c. a company of soldiers that is sent into combat as a single unit.
d. a specialized military team that functions together to carry out complex missions.

_____ 7. The name says it all: they are *rations* that require no preparation other than opening or removing the packaging.

The *rations* were not very tasty, but the famine victims were grateful to receive food of any sort.

Rations (răsh′ənz, rā′shənz) is a noun that means   (paragraph 18)

a. building supplies issued to members of a group.
b. medicine issued to members of a group.
c. food issued to members of a group.
d. equipment issued to members of a group.

_____ 8. *Edible*, to be sure, but definitely not culinary delights.

Some wild mushrooms are *edible*, but others are poisonous; be sure you know the difference before you prepare a meal with them.

Edible (ĕd′ə-bəl) is an adjective that means   (paragraph 18)

a. fit to be eaten.
b. fit to be cooked.
c. fit to be picked in the wild.
d. fit to be packaged.

_____ 9. The second week is the *culmination*: a tactical field exercise that requires you and your platoon to draw upon everything you've learned up to this point.

For students, graduation is the *culmination* of years of hard work.

Culmination (kŭl'mə-nā'shən) is a noun that means   (paragraph 19)

a. turning point.
b. highest point; climax.
c. test.
d. the reverse; opposite.

_____ 10. Your platoon and squad leaders must make the *tactical* decisions, although the drill sergeants are there to keep anyone from being injured.

The artillery soldiers used special signals to share *tactical* information with each other.

Tactical (tăk'tĭ-kəl) is an adjective that means   (paragraph 19)

a. clever; skillful.
b. related to smaller, closer to base, and less significant military operations.
c. pertaining to unfair strategies or tricks.
d. involving danger.

✔ **Comprehension Check**

Read each of the following questions. Then write the correct answer choice in the blank. *Base your answers on information in the selection.* You may refer to the selection as you answer the questions.

True or False

_____ 1. The people who are likely to have the greatest effect on recruits during basic training are the drill sergeants.

_____ 2. Recruits who try to get around the rules or who disobey are punished by being restricted to their barracks and not permitted to train with other recruits.

_____ 3. At the end of Phase I, each recruit is assigned two "Battle Buddies" that he will work with throughout the rest of basic training.

_____ 4. The gas chamber is part of the experience in Phase III.

_____ 5. Recruits can refer to their M16A2 weapon as either their rifle or their gun.

Multiple-Choice

_____ 5. It seems likely that the three phases of boot camp are called the red, white, and blue phases because these colors are

   a. associated with Independence Day (July 4).
   b. bright and cheerful.
   c. the three most popular colors.
   d. patriotic ones since they appear in the U.S. flag.

_____ 6. The time when recruits get physical assessments, immunizations, haircuts, and uniforms is

   a. Reception.
   b. Phase I.
   c. Phase II.
   d. Phase III.

_____ 7. The Field experience takes place

   a. on an athletic field at the military base.
   b. in the barracks.
   c. on the obstacle course.
   d. out in the open.

_____ 8. Recruits are part of

   a. a squad only.
   b. a platoon only.
   c. a squad and a platoon.
   d. none of the above.

_____ 9. During basic training, the emphasis gradually shifts from

   a. the individual to the group.
   b. the group to the individual.
   c. the individual to his or her buddy.
   d. the platoon to the squad.

_____ 10. Both buddies are punished whenever one of them does something wrong. The likely reason for this is that

   a. it causes recruits to begin to think of themselves as team members who are responsible for each other.
   b. drill sergeants like to punish as many recruits as possible.
   c. it causes recruits to turn on each other, and the drill sergeants can determine which recruits are not "team players."
   d. it helps drill sergeants determine which recruits have natural leadership ability.

Writing to Make Connections

Respond to the following items, based on information in the reading selection and on your own experience. You may refer to the selection as you answer the questions.

If the item has this symbol, your instructor may assign you to work collaboratively on it with classmates:

In that case, you should form groups of three or four students as directed by your instructor and work together to complete the exercises. After your group discusses each item and agrees on the answer, have a group member record it. Every member of your group should be able to explain all of your group's answers.

1. What did you learn about Army boot camp that was new information to you or that surprised you most?

   _____

   _____

   _____

   _____

2. Based on what you read about boot camp, how do you think you would respond to basic training? Do you think you would make it through the experience? Why or why not?

   _____

   _____

   _____

   _____

 3. In what ways do you think successfully completing boot camp and serving in the military could help a person later in life?

   _____

   _____

   _____

   _____

Web Resources

For additional information related to the selection topic, see the following websites:

www.goarmy.com
   Click on What's it like being a soldier?

www.baseops.net/basictraining/army.html

www.mhhe.com/ entryways

For more complete descriptions of these websites, as well as additional web resources related to this selection, see the ORL Student Center.

Information from 3D Basic Combat Training and U.S. Army websites.

Although the addresses (URLs) listed here were active at the time *Entryways* was published, URLs can change or go out of existence. To locate other websites related to the selection topic, use this descriptor with Google or another search engine: **surviving military boot camp.**

READING SELECTION 4

ROLLER-COASTER ATTENTION CYCLES

Connecting with What You Already Know

1. What do you think is being described by the title, "Roller-Coaster Attention Cycles"?

   _____

   _____

Do these exercises *before* you read the selection.

Preview the selection by reading the

- introduction (in *italics*)
- headings
- first paragraph (paragraph 1)
- first sentence of paragraphs 2–11
- last paragraph (paragraph 12)

2. Now that you have previewed the selection, what are "roller-coaster attention cycles"?

   _____

3. In the selection, you'll encounter the following words. Mark any words you already know or think you know. Most words have more than one meaning. After you have read the selection, you will have an opportunity to deduce (reason out) their meanings according to how they are used in the selection. At that point, you will discover whether you were correct, and if not, you'll have a new word to add to your vocabulary.

consistently	transports
drowsy	assess
cycles	productivity
practical	periodic
lethargy	dehydrating

ROLLER-COASTER ATTENTION CYCLES

Based on *Teaching with the Brain in Mind,* by Eric Jensen

Many students believe that there is something wrong with them because they cannot focus their attention for long periods of time. This selection is from a book on the brain and learning. It will help you understand more about how the brain pays attention and what is "normal." It also explains how you can take advantage of your brain's natural attention shifts. This selection will help you understand why the directions for chapter exercises encourage you to stand, stretch, and use certain other strategies to help you refocus your attention before starting the activities.

1   Are you consistently drowsy in a certain class? Do you wonder why? It may be as simple as the fact that the class meets at a time when you are in a low attention cycle. Although your attention will go back up, being at the bottom of your attention cycle is like being at the bottom of a roller-coaster ride: it's a real letdown.

2   Just as you experience light sleep and deep sleep, you experience cycles of high and low attention when you are awake. Everyone has natural high points and low points of attention throughout the day. The brain's attention cycles last about 90–110 minutes. That means that you have about 16 of these cycles in every 24-hour period.

3   If you are aware of times when you are usually at a low point, you can avoid taking classes at those times. That's not always practical, of course. A more practical solution is movement. A brisk walk—outside, if possible—can help. If you start to feel drowsy in class, stretching will make you feel more alert.

4   Simply drinking water is another way to boost your attention and alertness. Most students do not drink enough water, and to be at their best, learners need water. The brain is made up of a higher percentage of water than any other organ. Water helps supply the brain with the oxygen it must have in order to function efficiently and effectively. Without enough water, you lose attentiveness, and lethargy sets in. Water also helps keep your stress level in check.

5   There are differences in the blood flow and in breathing during high and low attention cycles. Blood transports oxygen to the brain, so these changes influence the amount of oxygen your brain receives. These changes in your oxygen level, in turn, affect learning.

6   Your attention cycles affect your performance on mental tasks. To assess your learning accurately, look at the work you have done over a period of time. In other words, instead of looking at how you did on one particular test to evaluate how well you are doing, look at your day-to-day performance. Look at how you do in class and on homework assignments. What if you studied appropriately for a test and felt you understood the material, but did not do as well as you had expected? One explanation: you may have been at a low point in your attention cycle when you took the test.

7   When your brain is at the bottom of a low attention cycle, its message is, "Take it easy." That's not always possible, but when it is, you should give yourself a mental break. Resting your mind will actually *increase* your overall productivity.

8   In general, the brain does a poor job of continuous, high-level attention. It can only pay constant attention at a high level for a short time, usually ten minutes or less! And, after a new learning experience, you need time for the learning to "imprint." This means that in class, you need time to process what you are learning. For this reason, your teacher may have you stop and discuss new material in small groups, ask questions about it, or do some other change-of-pace activity. When you are doing homework, take periodic breaks. Stop and reflect on what you have been reading or studying. Stand up, stretch, eat a high-protein snack (such as a low-fat dairy product), or get a drink of water.

9   You may be tempted to deal with your brain's low attention cycle by drinking coffee and soft drinks to stay alert. Bad solution! Both coffee and soft drinks contain caffeine. Both are dehydrating: they rob your body of water. As noted earlier, dehydration is a common problem that's linked to poor learning.

10   Rather than drink coffee or a soft drink, try to find a few moments for quiet time. If you are on campus, go to the library. If the weather is nice, find a pleasant place to sit outside. Other possibilities are moving around and doing a little deep breathing.

11   If you are at home, take a 20-minute "power nap." Cornell University sleep researcher James Maas says that power nappers think more clearly and perform much better than their overtired colleagues. Thomas Edison, one of this country's most creative inventors, was famous for taking quick naps during the day. Be sure not to sleep for more than 20 minutes or so, or you will not feel alert when you wake up.

12   It's normal to go through periods of high and low attention throughout the day. You can't get off the "attention roller coaster," but you can learn how to "ride" it.

Source: Eric H. Jensen, *Teaching with the Brain in Mind,* American Association for Supervision and Curriculum Development, 1998, pp. 26, 44–48. Copyright © 1998 ASCD. Reprinted by permission. The Association for Supervision and Curriculum Development is a worldwide community of educators advocating sound policies and sharing best practices to achieve the success of each learner. To learn more, visit ASCD at www.ascd.org.

✔ **Vocabulary Check**

Use the context clues from both sentences to reason out the meaning of the italicized words. *The answer you choose should make sense in both sentences.* You may use a dictionary to confirm your answer choice, but be sure the meaning you select fits the context of both sentences. Write your answer in the space provided.

Refer to page 402 for the pronunciation key.

_____ 1. Are you *consistently* drowsy in a certain class?

In contrast to the other employees who only exceed their sales goals occasionally, Marcella *consistently* exceeds hers.

Consistently (kən-sĭs′ tənt lē) is an adverb that means   (paragraph 1)

a. regularly.
b. partially.
c. rarely.
d. never.

_____ 2. Are you consistently *drowsy* in a certain class?

After the large Thanksgiving dinner, we felt so *drowsy* that we could barely keep our eyes open.

Drowsy (drou′zē) is an adjective that means   (paragraph 1)

a. full of energy.
b. upset.
c. sick; ill.
d. ready to fall asleep.

_____ 3. It may be as simple as the fact that the class meets at a time when you are in a low attention *cycle*.

The moon's *cycle* consists of several phases that move from a new moon to a full moon and then back again.

Cycle (sī′kəl) is a noun that means   (paragraph 3)

a. changing from a partially round shape to a round shape.
b. a device used for transportation.
c. a course of events that recur regularly and usually lead back to the starting point.
d. alertness.

_____ 4. That's not always *practical*, of course.

The first electric cars were a good idea, but because of their expense and other problems, they were not *practical*.

Practical (prăk′tĭ-kəl) is an adjective that means   (paragraph 3)

a. successful.
b. capable of being put into use.
c. attractive in appearance.
d. advertised for sale.

_____ 5. Without enough water you lose attentiveness, and *lethargy* sets in.

Lethargy was one side effect of Marco's allergy medication; he seemed to have no energy at all.

Lethargy (lĕth′ər-jē) is a noun that means   (paragraph 4)

a. nervousness; anxiety.
b. physical or mental sluggishness.

c. nausea.

d. a high level of interest.

_____ 6. Blood *transports* oxygen to the brain, so these differences affect the amount of oxygen your brain receives.

My uncle's trucking company *transports* vegetables from the farms where they are grown to the market where they will be sold.

Transports (trăns-pôrts′) is a verb that means   (paragraph 5)

a. transfers or conveys from one place to another.

b. changes or transforms.

c. prevents or blocks.

d. moves in an unpredictable manner.

_____ 7. To *assess* your learning accurately, look at the work you have done over a period of time.

An ophthalmologist is a doctor who is specially trained to *assess* patients' vision and to diagnose eye problems.

Assess (ə-sĕs′) is a verb that means   (paragraph 6)

a. to prevent.

b. to confuse.

c. to evaluate.

d. to minimize.

_____ 8. Resting your mind will actually increase your overall *productivity*.

When the factory installed new, efficient, high-tech equipment, *productivity* increased by 30 percent.

Productivity (prō′dŭk-tĭv′ĭ-tē) is a noun that means   (paragraph 7)

a. alertness; mental sharpness.

b. fatigue resulting from overwork.

c. complaints; dissatisfaction.

d. effectiveness in bringing about results.

_____ 9. When you are doing homework, take *periodic* breaks.

To be sure that drivers are qualified, states require *periodic* driver's license renewals.

Periodic (pîr′ē-ŏd′ĭk) is an adjective that means   (paragraph 8)

a. occurring at regular intervals.

b. occurring at uneven intervals.

c. lasting for a long time.

d. permanent; unchanging.

_____ 10. Both are *dehydrating*: they rob your body of water.

Exercising outdoors in hot weather can be extremely *dehydrating*, so be sure to drink enough water to replenish the water you lose through perspiration.

Dehydrating (dē-hī′drāt′ĭng) is an adjective that means   (paragraph 9)

a. causing loss of energy from the body.

b. causing loss of water from the body.

c. causing loss of muscle tissue from the body.

d. causing loss of fat from the body.

✔ Comprehension Check

Read each of the following questions. Then write the correct answer choice in the blank. *Base your answers on information in the selection.* You may refer to the selection as you answer the questions.

_____ 1. High and low attention cycles

a. are the same as light and deep sleep cycles.

b. are not normal.

c. are not understood by scientists.

d. are normal and occur in everyone.

_____ 2. The length of the brain's attention cycles is

a. 16 minutes.

b. 24 hours.

c. 90–110 minutes

d. 16–20 minutes.

_____ 3. Drinking water

a. helps you feel more alert if you get drowsy.

b. hydrates your brain.

c. provides the brain with oxygen.

d. all of the above.

_____ 4. Blood flow and breathing

a. are different during high and low attention cycles.

b. are not affected by high and low attention cycles.

c. cause high and low attention cycles.

d. are caused by attention cycles.

_____ 5. The brain is able to

a. maintain a high level of constant attention for 90–110 minutes.

    b. remain at a constant high attention level for only ten minutes or less.

    c. process new material very quickly when attention is high.

    d. "imprint" new material quickly.

_____ 6. A test grade may not be an accurate assessment of your learning because

    a. most tests are not fair.

    b. you may have studied for it when you were in low attention cycles.

    c. you may have been in a low attention cycle when you took the test.

    d. light and deep sleep cycles could have affected your performance on the test.

_____ 7. When you are in a low attention cycle, you should

    a. give yourself a mental break.

    b. keep going anyway.

    c. take a long nap.

    d. drink a cup of coffee.

_____ 8. Drinking coffee and soft drinks

    a. will switch you from a low attention cycle to a high attention cycle.

    b. has the same beneficial effect as relaxing for a few minutes.

    c. helps hydrate the brain.

    d. has several negative effects on the brain.

_____ 9. Twenty-minute "power naps"

    a. disrupt your attention cycles.

    b. are a bad idea for students.

    c. can help you think more clearly and perform better.

    d. should be at least an hour long.

_____ 10. Knowing about high and low attention cycles can

    a. help you avoid them altogether.

    b. enable you to work with them rather than against them.

    c. help you sleep better.

    d. put you on a roller coaster.

Writing to Make Connections

Respond to the following items, based on information in the reading selection and on your own experience. You may refer to the selection as you answer the questions.

    If the item has this symbol, your instructor may assign you to work collaboratively on it with classmates:

In that case, you should form groups of three or four students as directed by your instructor and work together to complete the exercises. After your group discusses each item and agrees on the answer, have a group member record it. Every member of your group should be able to explain all of your group's answers.

1. When are the typical downtimes (periods of low attention) during your day? Describe any regularly scheduled things you do at those times, such as attending class, working at your job, riding home, or studying. How do you feel during those times? How do they affect what you are doing at the time?

_____

_____

_____

_____

_____

_____

_____

2. Describe at least three things mentioned in the selection that people could do to help themselves when they are in a low attention cycle.

_____

_____

_____

_____

3. Explain why looking at your performance in a class over time gives you more accurate feedback than basing your assessment on a single test score.

_____

_____

_____

_____

_____

_____

_____

_____

_____

_____

_____

 4. In class, what do you think teachers could do to take into account the fact that students have alternating cycles of high and low attention? Try to think of at least three things that teachers could do to adjust the instruction to help students who might be in low attention cycles.

_____

_____

_____

_____

_____

_____

_____

_____

_____

_____

 Web Resources

For additional information related to the selection topic, see the following websites:

www.mhhe.com/
entryways

For more complete descriptions of these websites, as well as additional web resources related to this selection, see the ORL Student Center.

http://cms.psychologytoday.com/articles/index.php?term =pto-20040428-000001

This *Psychology Today* article explains the 90-minute brain cycles, what triggers them, and how to synchronize our internal cycles with day and night.

www.sciencemaster.com/wesson/pdfs/attention.pdf

This short selection about "Attention and the Brain" contains a wealth of useful information.

Although the addresses (URLs) listed above were active at the time *Entryways* was published, URLs can change or go out of existence. To locate other websites related to the selection topic, use this descriptor with Google or another search engine: **brain attention.**

READING SELECTION 5

THE LIKEABILITY FACTOR
By Tim Sanders

Connecting with What You Already Know

Do these exercises *before* you read the selection.

First, think about the title. Then preview this selection by reading the

- introduction (in *italics*)
- first three paragraphs
- words in special print
- last paragraph

1. Based on your preview, what do you expect this selection to be about?

   _____

   _____

2. What, if anything, have you read, heard, or experienced about "likeability"?

   _____

   _____

3. In the selection, you'll encounter the following words. Mark any words you already know or think you know. Most words have more than one meaning. After you have read the selection, you will have an opportunity to deduce (reason out) their meanings according to how they are used in the selection. At that point, you will discover whether you were correct, and if not, you'll have a new word to add to your vocabulary.

rejuvenation	exponentially
generating	irascible
spouse	sustainable
boosting	engrossed
authenticity	deliberate (verb)

THE LIKEABILITY FACTOR

By Tim Sanders

How likeable are you? How do you think your "likeability" affects your life? The following excerpt is from The Likeability Factor: How to Boost Your L-Factor and Achieve Your Life's Dreams. *In it, the author, explores the power of likeability and suggests ways a person can increase it. According to his research, likeable people bring out the best in others. In bringing out the best in others, they themselves receive recognition. Moreover, they outperform in their daily lives, they overcome life's challenges, and they even enjoy better health! What are the elements of likeability? This selection tells more about likeability and the four elements it consists of.*

1   Life is a series of popularity contests. The choices other people make about you determine your health, wealth, and happiness. And decades of research prove that people choose who they like. They vote for them, they buy from them, they marry them, and they spend precious time with them.

2   The good news is that you can arm yourself for the contest and win life's battles for preference. How? By being likeable.

3   The more you are liked—or the higher your likeability factor—the happier your life will be.

4   But exactly what is likeability? *Likeability* is a difficult term to define. Dictionary definitions can be as vague as "easy to like," "attractive," or "appealing." But after researching the worlds of psychology, physiology, and personality, I define it thus: Likeability is an ability to create positive attitudes in other people through the delivery of emotional and physical benefits.

5   Someone who is likeable can give you a sense of joy, happiness, relaxation, or rejuvenation. He or she can bring you relief from depression, anxiety, or boredom.

6   By being likeable, by generating positive feelings in others, you gain as well. The quality of your life and the strength of your relationships are the product of a choice—but not necessarily *your* choice. After all, if everything were a matter of choice, you'd select the best job, the best mate, and the best life in the world.

7   Your life is really determined by *other people's* choices. Do you want the job? It's up to the woman doing the hiring. Do you want to watch football all day on Sunday *and* stay happily married? It's up to your spouse or partner. Do you want the jury to find you guilty or innocent? It's their choice. The more likeable you are, the more likely you are to be on the receiving end of a positive choice from which you can profit.

8   You can raise your likeability factor by boosting four critical elements of your personality:

- *Friendliness*: your ability to communicate liking and openness to others
- *Relevance*: your capacity to connect with others' interests, wants, and needs
- *Empathy*: your ability to recognize, acknowledge, and experience other people's feelings
- *Realness*: the integrity that stands behind your likeability and guarantees its authenticity

9   How do these factors fit together? Let's say you're driving along an isolated road and you hit a stoplight. The first light represents *friendliness.* If you are not friendly, the light remains red and you can't go any farther. If you are friendly, the light turns green and you drive on.

10   Friendliness is the most fundamental element of likeability. If you are not friendly, you will have to work exponentially harder to be more likeable. Some people are able to do this—we all have had at least one irascible friend whom we nevertheless love. But we don't have many; there isn't enough time.

11   Back inside the car, imagine that you're driving along the highway again and arrive at a second stoplight. This one stands for *relevance*.

12   If you can find a way to be relevant to someone else, you get a green light and can drive on. Otherwise, the light stays red. That smiling, sweet doorman may be the friendliest man you've ever met, but if you have no contact with him, you really don't care whether he's friendly.

13   Now, in the car again, you hit a third light; this one represents *empathy*. If you are able to prove that you are an empathetic person who understands, and in a way actually senses, another person's feelings, you get a green light and can keep on driving. Empathy is possibly the least understood of the four factors, yet without it your friendliness and relevance will have a hard time finding a sustainable place in another person's heart.

14   There's one more stoplight, and this one stands for *realness*. Some people, trying to boost their L-factor, seem genuinely friendly, relevant, and empathetic. But eventually you discover that there's no one there; it's all an act. Over time you wonder, "Is this person for real?" If he or she isn't, then you have reached the end of the line.

15   Of course, most of us aren't conscious of these four lights. When we meet someone new, we seldom actually ask ourselves, "Is this person relevant, and if so, is he or she empathetic?"

16   We're all engrossed in the middle of life, and we're not thinking about every little detail we've learned. We simply combine all our information and talents and act, as when we drive a car or perform other skills we've mastered.

17   Similarly, when we meet a new person, we don't pause to deliberate about each element of his or her likeability factor. Yet for the most part, we won't become likeable to someone else, nor will that person be likeable to us, unless all four criteria are met.

Source: Tim Sanders, *The Likeability Factor*. New York: Crown Publishers, 2005, jacket, pp. 33, 98–100. Copyright © 2005 by Tim Sanders. Reprinted by permission of Crown Publishers, an imprint of the Crown Publishing Group, a division of Random House, Inc.

 Vocabulary Check

Use the context clues from both sentences to reason out the meaning of the italicized words. *The answer you choose should make sense in both sentences.* You may use a dictionary to confirm your answer choice, but be sure the meaning you select fits the context of both sentences. Write your answer in the space provided.

Refer to page 402 for the pronunciation key.

_____ 1. Someone who is likeable can give you a sense of joy, happiness, relaxation, or *rejuvenation*.

The *rejuvenation* I felt after a month-long vacation left me ready to tackle my work again.

Rejuvenation (rĭ-jōō′və-nā′shən) is a noun that means (paragraph 5)

a. taking revenge; getting even with someone.
b. feeling renewed energy or enthusiasm.
c. exhaustion; fatigue.
d. disappointment.

_____ 2. By being likeable, by *generating* positive feelings in others, you gain as well.

Generating attention for celebrities in magazines, newspapers, and on TV is the job of publicists.

Generating (jĕn′ə-rāt′ĭng) is a verbal noun that means (paragraph 6)

a. celebrating.
b. producing; creating.
c. blocking; limiting.
d. removing.

_____ 3. It's up to your *spouse* or partner.

Even after a divorce, a former *spouse* sometimes keeps in touch with former in-laws.

Spouse (spous) is a noun that means (paragraph 7)

a. best friend.
b. business partner
c. neighbor.
d. husband or wife.

_____ 4. You can raise your likeability factor by *boosting* four critical elements of your personality.

Boosting calcium intake can increase bone strength.

Boosting (bōōst′ĭng) is a verbal noun that means (paragraph 8)

a. maintaining.
b. limiting.
c. increasing.
d. ignoring.

_____ 5. Realness: the integrity that stands behind your likeability and guarantees its *authenticity*.

Once the art expert confirmed the *authenticity* of the painting, its value doubled.

Authenticity (ô′thĕn-tĭs′ĭ-tē) is a noun that means (paragraph 8)

a. insincerity.
b. ability to last.

c. falseness.
d. genuineness.

_____ 6. If you are not friendly, you will have to work *exponentially* harder to be more likeable.

People who frequently drink and drive increase *exponentially* their likelihood of being in an accident.

Exponentially (ĕk′spə-nĕn′shəl lē) is an adverb that means

a. only slightly.   (paragraph 10)
b. to a significantly greater degree.
c. not at all.
d. somewhat.

_____ 7. Some people are able to do this—we all have had at least one *irascible* friend whom we nevertheless love.

People who are under stress tend to be *irascible* and difficult to deal with.

Irascible (ĭ-răs′ə-bel) is an adjective that means   (paragraph 10)
a. easily embarrassed.
b. charming.
c. extremely lazy.
d. easily angered.

_____ 8. Empathy is possibly the least understood of the four factors, yet without it your friendliness and relevance will have a hard time finding a *sustainable* place in another person's heart.

Many people make New Year's resolutions that are not realistic or *sustainable*, and after only a few days, they give up.

Sustainable (sə-stā′nə-bəl) is an adjective that means

a. capable of being continued.   (paragraph 13)
b. annoying.
c. reasonable.
d. entertaining.

_____ 9. We're all *engrossed* in the middle of life, and we're not thinking about every little detail we've learned.

When my brother is *engrossed* in a video game, he doesn't seem to see or hear anything that is going on around him.

Engrossed (ĕn-grōs'd) is an adjective that means   (paragraph 16)

a. caught; trapped.
b. experimenting with.
c. learning from.
d. completely involved with.

_____ 10. Similarly, when we meet a new person, we don't pause to *deliberate* about each element of his or her likeability factor.

Rather than make snap judgments about major purchases, my father prefers to *deliberate*.

Deliberate (dĭ-lĭb'-ə-rāt') is a verb that means   (paragraph 17)

a. to guess.
b. to think carefully about a decision to be made.
c. to consult with other people.
d. to leave things to chance.

✔ **Comprehension Check**

Read each of the following questions. Then write the correct answer choice in the blank. *Base your answers on information in the selection*. You may refer to the selection as you answer the questions.

True or False

_____ 1. According to the author, how happy a person's life will be depends on how well he or she is liked.

_____ 2. The author believes people can increase their likeability factor.

_____ 3. To have a high likeability factor, a person needs to have any two of the four likeability elements.

_____ 4. Most people are consciously aware of the four elements of likeability.

_____ 5. Empathy is possibly the least understood of the four elements of likeability.

Multiple-Choice

_____ 6. The most fundamental aspect of likeability is

a. friendliness.
b. relevance.
c. empathy.
d. realness.

_____ 7. According to the author, a person's life is really determined by
      a. the person's choices.
      b. other people's choices.
      c. who hires the person.
      d. how accurately the person evaluates other people's likeability.

_____ 8. Likeability involves the ability to
      a. drive well.
      b. be irascible.
      c. be engrossed in life.
      d. create positive attitudes and feelings in others.

_____ 9. The capacity to connect with others' interests, wants, and needs is called
      a. friendliness.
      b. relevance.
      c. empathy.
      d. realness.

_____ 10. The rest of the elements will not make a person truly likeable if others sense the person lacks
      a. friendliness.
      b. relevance.
      c. empathy.
      d. realness.

Writing to Make Connections

Respond to the following items, based on information in the reading selection and on your own experience. You may refer to the selection as you answer the questions.

If the item has this symbol, your instructor may assign you to work collaboratively on it with classmates:

In that case, you should form groups of three or four students as directed by your instructor and work together to complete the exercises. After your group discusses each item and agrees on the answer, have a group member record it. Every member of your group should be able to explain all of your group's answers.

1. In your opinion, which element of likeability (friendliness, relevance, empathy, realness) is the most important? Explain why you think that.

_____

_____

_____

2. Think of someone you really like. You don't have to give a name, but tell who they are (your aunt, a former coach, your employer, etc.). What positive effects do you think that person's likeability has had on his or her life?

_____

_____

_____

3. Which likeability element—friendliness, relevance, empathy, and realness—do you think you need to increase in yourself? Why? How might it change your life if you significantly increased that element?

_____

_____

_____

_____

4. Why do you think likeable people tend to be healthier than people who are not very likeable?

_____

_____

_____

_____

 Web Resources

For additional information related to the selection topic, see the following website:

www.westaff.com/yourworkplace/yw47_story.html

This article, from the Westaff monthly e-newsletter about workplace trends, explains how likeability can help people get ahead in the corporate world.

Although the address (URL) listed here was active at the time *Entryways* was published, URLs can change or go out of existence. To locate other websites related to the selection topic, use these descriptors with Google or another search engine: **likeability** or **Tim Sanders.**

THE WALKING WEARY: WHAT TEENS AND YOUNG ADULTS NEED TO KNOW ABOUT SLEEP

Connecting with What You Already Know

Do these exercises *before* you read the selection.

Preview the selection by reading the

- title
- introduction (in *italics*)
- headings
- the first paragraph
- first sentence of the remaining paragraphs (2–16)

1. Think about the title. Why do you expect to learn about sleep as it pertains to teens and young adults?

    _____

    _____

2. Now that you have previewed the selection, tell why the article might be helpful to college students.

    _____

    _____

    _____

3. In the selection, you'll encounter the following words. Mark any words you already know or think you know. Most words have more than one meaning. After you have read the selection, you will have an opportunity to deduce (reason out) their meanings according to how they are used in the selection. At that point, you will discover whether you were correct, and if not, you'll have a new word to add to your vocabulary.

vital	prone
well-being	drawn
promotes	lapses
poll	chronic
deprived	zombies

THE WALKING WEARY: WHAT TEENS AND YOUNG ADULTS NEED TO KNOW ABOUT SLEEP

Based on "Sleep and Teens"; "'Generation Y' Is Significantly Sleepy, National Sleep Foundation Finds"; and "Tips for Teens"

Research suggests that adolescents need approximately 9 hours of sleep each night, and healthy adults need 7 to 9 hours. Are you among the millions of teens and young adults who do not get enough sleep? A 2000 poll by the National Sleep Foundation found that one-third of young adults (18- 29-year-olds) have difficulty getting up for work. One-fourth are occasionally or frequently late to work because of it. Moreover, one-third suffer significant daytime sleepiness. These numbers are higher than in any other age group.

How can you tell if you are getting the sleep you need? These are some clues: You have trouble staying alert in school, when you are reading, or when making a long drive. You have trouble concentrating or remembering things. You tend to be irritable or overly aggressive. (Because of these effects, sleep deprivation is often misdiagnosed as ADHD, attention deficit hyperactivity disorder.) If some or all of these describe you, you may need to increase your sleep!

Why Sleep Matters

1   Sleep is "food" for the brain, yet many brains are sleep starved. During sleep, important body functions and brain activity occur. Skipping sleep can be harmful— even deadly, particularly if you are behind the wheel. Inadequate sleep can make you look bad, feel moody, and perform poorly. Too little sleep can make it hard for you to get along with your family and friends. It can affect your grades and how well you play a sport. When you do not get enough sleep, you are more likely to have an accident, injury, and/or illness.

2   Sleep is vital to your well-being, as important as the air you breathe, the water you drink, and the food you eat. It can even help you make better food choices and handle the stress that comes with being a teen or a college student.

The Problems

3 During adolescence, biological sleep patterns shift toward later times. It is natural for teens and young adults not to be able to fall asleep before 11:00 p.m. Not surprisingly, their pattern is also to sleep later in the morning.

4   Teens need about 9 hours of sleep each night to function at their best, but most teens do not get enough sleep. One-third of them report that they sleep less than 7 hours a night. In fact, one study found that only 15% slept 8½ hours on school nights. Like high school students, many college students force themselves to get by on too little sleep.

5   Teens and college students are biologically "wired" to stay up late at night and wake up later in the morning, but this doesn't always work well with public school schedules. Most teens still have to get up early to go to school. The predictable result is sleep deprivation.

6   Having a consistent bedtime and wake-up time promotes good sleep. Teens and young adults,

however, tend to keep irregular hours. They stay up late and then try to make up for it by "sleeping in" (sleeping later) on the weekends. The bad news is that sleep doesn't average out. Sleeping 4 hours one night and 12 hours the next doesn't give the body the same benefits as sleeping 8 hours each night. The reason? Keeping an irregular schedule affects your biological clock and hurts the quality of your sleep.

7   Many teens suffer from undiagnosed, but treatable sleep disorders. These include narcolepsy, insomnia, restless legs syndrome, and sleep apnea. Unfortunately, doctors often fail to ask patients, especially younger patients, about sleep problems. Nor does it occur to most young adults to discuss sleep problems with their doctor. A 2000 poll by the National Sleep Foundation revealed that only 12% of 18- to 29-year-olds have raised the issue with their doctor.

Consequences of Sleep Deprivation

8   Not getting enough sleep can limit your ability to learn, listen, concentrate, and solve problems. You may even forget important information like names, phone numbers, your homework, or a date with a special person in your life. It may take you longer to complete assignments, and even though you work and study hard, your grades may suffer.

9   Sleep difficulties or inadequate sleep affects your health and your appearance. It can cause you to eat too much. When you feel tired and need quick energy, it's tempting to choose fattening, unhealthy food, such as sweets and fried foods. Lack of sleep may increase your use of stimulants such as nicotine and caffeine (especially caffeine in coffee, sodas, and chocolate). Being sleep deprived makes you more prone to acne and other skin problems. It causes you to look drawn and tired. It contributes to illness because it lowers your resistance to infection and disease. There are no vitamins, pills, or drinks that can make up for inadequate sleep.

10   A brain that is hungry for sleep will get it, even if you fight it. You can become drowsy and drift off to sleep without realizing it. Drowsiness creates lapses in attention and impairs your ability to react quickly. This can lead to accidents at home and on the job. It's even worse if the drowsiness hits while you are driving. According to the National Traffic Safety Administration, drowsiness and fatigue cause more than 100,000 police-reported accidents each year. These accidents kill more than 1,500 Americans and injure another 71,000. Drowsy young drivers (age 25 and under) cause more than half of all fall-asleep crashes. Driving drowsy is every bit as dangerous as driving drunk.

11   Chronic lack of sleep can also trigger aggressive or inappropriate behavior. For example, you might find yourself yelling at your friends or being impatient with family members. You might be more prone to road rage. In addition, being short of sleep heightens the effects of alcohol.

Sleep and School Schedules

12 Is your brain still on the pillow when school starts? As noted earlier, teens need about 9 hours of sleep to do their best. Most high school students need an alarm clock or a parent to wake them on school days. They are like zombies getting ready for school, and they

find it hard to be alert and pay attention in class. Because they are sleep deprived, they are sleepy all day and cannot do their best.

13   Since teens' normal sleep cycle causes them not to get sleepy until around 11:00 p.m., one way for them to get more sleep is to start school an hour or so later. In fact, some schools, such as those in Edina, Minnesota, have adopted later start times. This allows students to get one hour more of sleep per school night, which means five hours more per week. Students, teachers, administrators, and parents are enthusiastic about the results.

14   Schools that have adopted a later start time report that enrollment and attendance have improved, and students are more likely to be on time. Parents and teachers report that teens are more alert in the morning and in better moods. They are less likely to feel depressed or need to visit the nurse or school counselor.

15   As a college student, you are likely to have the same delayed sleep cycle as high school students. However, you have an advantage: You have more control over the time you start class each day. When you plan your schedule, choose realistic times. If you stay up late or work long hours, don't sign up for 8:00 a.m. classes.

Sleep Tips

16 Getting adequate, restful sleep affects every area of your life, so make it a priority. When you feel extremely sleepy, take a 15–20 minute nap. At night your bedroom should be quiet, cool, and dark. Try to go to bed and awaken at the same time each day. Avoid eating, drinking, exercising, watching TV, and using the computer in the hours before you go to bed. Avoid driving drowsy. If you follow these guidelines, you'll feel better, look better, and function better—great rewards for something as simple as giving your body the sleep it needs.

Sources: Based primarily on "Sleep and Teens," www.sleepfoundation.org/hottopics/ index.php?secid=18&id=264, with additional information from "'Generation Y' is Significantly Sleepy, National Sleep Foundation Finds," www.sleepfoundation. org/hottopics/index.php?secid=18&id=204, and "Tips for Teens," www.sleepfoundation. org/hottopics/index.php?secid=18&id=276. Accessed 1/20/06.

✔ **Vocabulary Check**

Use the context clues from both sentences to reason out the meaning of the italicized words. *The answer you choose should make sense in both sentences.* You may use a dictionary to confirm your answer choice, but be sure the meaning you select fits the context of both sentences. Write your answer in the space provided.

Refer to page 402 for the pronunciation key.

_____ 1. Sleep is *vital* to your well-being, as important as the air you breathe, the water you drink, and the food you eat.

It is *vital* that stroke victims receive immediate medical treatment.

Vital (vīt'l) is an adjective that means   (paragraph 2)

a. helpful, useful.
b. receptive to.
c. similar to, like.
d. necessary, essential.

_____ 2. Sleep is vital to your *well-being*, as important as the air you breathe, the water you drink, and the food you eat.

In general, living in a two-parent home contributes greatly to children's *well-being.*

Well-being (wĕl'bē'ĭng) is a noun that means   (paragraph 2)

a. the state of being healthy and happy.
b. the state of being mature and responsible.
c. the state of being awake and alert.
d. the state of being irritable and unpleasant.

_____ 3. Having a consistent bedtime and wake-up time *promotes* good sleep.

The Sierra Club is an environmental organization that *promotes* the protection of our communities and the planet.

Promotes (prə-mōts') is a verb that means   (paragraph 6)

a. ignores.
b. avoids
c. contributes to.
d. restricts or limits.

_____ 4. A 2000 *poll* by the National Sleep Foundation revealed that only 12% of 18- to 29-year-olds have raised the issue with their doctor.

CNN reported the results of a *poll* on the popularity of the presidential candidates.

Poll (pōl) is a noun that means   (paragraph 7)

a. a survey of the public.
b. a vote on an issue.
c. a campaign.
d. an argument.

_____ 5. Being sleep *deprived* makes you more prone to acne and other skin problems.

The school district announced a new program to help preschoolers from educationally *deprived* households get off to a good start.

Deprived (dǐ-prīvd′) is an adjective that means   (paragraph 9)

a. filled with.
b. kept from having.
c. supplied with.
d. enriched.

_____ 6. Being sleep deprived makes you more *prone* to acne and other skin problems.

People who exercise their bodies and minds are *prone* to live longer, healthier lives.

Prone (prōn) is an adjective that means   (paragraph 9)

a. resistant.
b. unconcerned about.
c. unwilling.
d. likely, inclined.

_____ 7. It causes you to look *drawn* and tired.

It was three days before the mountain climbers could be rescued; they were uninjured, but looked extremely pale and *drawn*.

Drawn (drôn) is an adjective that means   (paragraph 9)

a. appearing exhausted, as from fatigue or ill health.
b. very happy, ecstatic.
c. relaxed and calm.
d. appearing as if in a picture.

_____ 8. Drowsiness creates *lapses* in attention and impairs your ability to react quickly.

Test anxiety, which is caused by stress, can cause memory *lapses* during the test.

Lapses (lăp′səs) is a noun that means   (paragraph 10)

a. periods of time.
b. slips, temporary failures.
c. bursts of energy.
d. slow, gradual declines.

_____ 9. *Chronic* lack of sleep can also trigger aggressive or inappropriate behavior.

Sickle cell anemia is a *chronic* illness that must be treated throughout life.

Chronic (krŏn'ĭk) is an adjective that means   (paragraph 11)
a. continuing for a long time.
b. annoying.
c. preventable.
d. lasting briefly.

_____ 10. They are like *zombies* getting ready for school, and they find it hard to be alert and pay attention in class.

Because of the drugs they were given, the patients in the mental institution sat in chairs all day long and looked like *zombies*.

Zombies (zŏm'bēz) is a noun that means   (paragraph 12)
a. people who are always cheerful and optimistic.
b. people who behave like robots or as if under a spell.
c. people who are always busy.
d. people who move quickly and efficiently.

✔ Comprehension Check

Read each of the following questions. Then write the correct answer choice in the blank. *Base your answers on information in the selection.* You may refer to the selection as you answer the questions.

True or False

_____ 1. Sleep patterns are the same regardless of people's ages.

_____ 2. Good sleep is promoted by having a consistent bedtime and wake-up time.

_____ 3. It is possible to make up for nights of too little sleep because sleep averages out.

_____ 4. Body functions and brain activity continue during sleep.

_____ 5. Most teens sleep at least 9 hours per night.

Multiple-Choice

_____ 6. Approximately how many hours of sleep do teens need each night?
a. 7 hours
b. 8½ hours
c. 9 hours
d. 15 hours

_____ 7. Narcolepsy and insomnia are examples of
  a. sleep apnea.
  b. restless leg syndrome.
  c. sleep disorders.
  d. all of the above.

_____ 8. College students have an advantage over high school students because they
  a. do not have the same sleep cycle as older adults.
  b. can nap during the day.
  c. rarely have sleep problems.
  d. have more control over the time they start class each day.

_____ 9. For a few hours before going to sleep, it is wise to avoid
  a. eating and drinking.
  b. exercising.
  c. watching TV and using the computer.
  d. all of the above.

_____ 10. According to the National Traffic Safety Association, each year drowsiness and fatigue cause how many reported accidents?
  a. 1,500
  b. 71,000
  c. more than 10,000
  d. more than 100,000

Writing to Make Connections

Respond to the following items, based on information in the reading selection and on your own experience. You may refer to the selection as you answer the questions.

If the item has this symbol, your instructor may assign you to work collaboratively on it with classmates:

In that case, you should form groups of three or four students as directed by your instructor and work together to complete the exercises. After your group discusses each item and agrees on the answer, have a group member record it. Every member of your group should be able to explain all of your group's answers.

1. List at least three new things that you learned in this selection.

_____

_____

_____

_____

2. How many hours do you usually sleep each night? Is it enough? How well do you sleep? If you do not get at least 8½ to 9 hours sleep per night, what changes could you make to get more sleep? If you do not sleep well, what changes could you make to get better sleep?

_____

_____

_____

_____

_____

_____

3. Should all public high schools move to a later start time, perhaps closer to 9:00 a.m.? Why or why not? The benefits are obvious, but what problems could a later start time create?

_____

_____

_____

_____

_____

 ## Web Resources

For additional information related to the selection topic, see the following websites:

www.parent-teen.com/yourbody/sleep.html

This article, "Wake Up, Sleepy Teens," appears at this online magazine for families with teens.

http://health.discovery.com/centers/sleepdreams/basics/teens.html

"Helping Sleep-Deprived Teens" appears on the Discovery Health Channel website.

Although the addresses (URLs) listed above were active at the time *Entryways* was published, URLs can change or go out of existence. To locate other websites related to the selection topic, use these descriptors with Google or another search engine: **sleep** or **sleep and teens.**

www.mhhe.com/ entryways

For more complete descriptions of these websites, as well as additional web resources related to this selection, see the ORL Student Center.

READING SELECTION 7

LANDING THAT FIRST JOB
By Joyce Lain Kennedy

Connecting with What You Already Know

Do these exercises *before* you read the selection.

Preview by reading the

- title
- introduction (in *italics*)
- first two paragraphs
- sentences in bold

1. Based on your preview, what do you anticipate the article will be about?

   _____

   _____

2. How is the information in the article organized?

   _____

   _____

3. What do you know about strategies for finding an appropriate job?

   _____

   _____

   _____

   _____

4. In the selection, you'll encounter the following words. Mark any words you already know or think you know. Most words have more than one meaning. After you have read the selection, you will have an opportunity to deduce (reason out) their meanings according to how they are used in the selection. At that point, you will discover whether you were correct, and if not, you'll have a new word to add to your vocabulary.

annuity	prospects
smashing	trump
surplus	robust
digitized	jaded
abroad	mock (adjective)

LANDING THAT FIRST JOB

By Joyce Lain Kennedy

In this syndicated newspaper column, Joyce Lain Kennedy, a careers expert, responds to a question from a recent college graduate.

1   *Question:* I am slightly older, 25, and a new college graduate. I haven't been offered the right job yet. Suggestions? K.B.

2   *Answer:* Your first job doesn't define your career, but starting off on the right foot is an employment annuity. Here is my view of the 10 most important factors in pulling off a smashing job hunt for your first job.

1. Become a gold medal competitor.

3   Think about the big economic picture: A worldwide oversupply of workers meets technological change in a world interconnected as never before.

4   The labor surplus is primarily the result of the end of the Cold War, the breakdown of the socialist economic system and the merging, with the capitalist economic system, of separate labor forces. Even with strong world growth, the absorption of the surplus will take a decade, maybe 25 years. Where does that leave you as an American worker? Fighting off the whole world that wants a piece of your—until now—exclusive job pie.

5   You are the first generation in American history to face global competition. Any job that can be digitized can be given to workers who will do the work for less money, both abroad and at home. As you compete, remember that in your first job, great training

prospects trump salary. But on your second job, be sure you know the market rate of pay and get it.

2. Do a 360-degree search.

6   Today's job market is not your parents' job market. Many companies are doing more with less. The buzzword is "higher productivity" gained from trimmed-down workforces, technology, and automation. A wide search includes school career centers and teachers, as well as job ads and business news in newspapers and on the Internet and television.

3. Target your direction.

7   In fields where hiring is robust, focus on one to three choices of where you'd like to land in terms of occupation, industry, possible job titles, and locale. At the same time, be prepared to change directions if opportunity strikes.

4. Make a master list of job leads.

8   Identify potential employers that might be a good fit and the names of individuals at each company who hire people for the job you want. Keep good records, either on an Excel spreadsheet or on cards.

5. Research like an ace.

9   Use every investigative source, including business news, Internet, library databases and personal interviewing. No one should know more than you about choices on your master list of job leads. You will find out who is hiring and how your skills make you a competitor.

6. Practice nonstop networking.

10   As a new graduate, this is the best time in your life to benefit from informational interviews and referrals. Reach out and contact people who can make them happen. Even jaded executives are responsive to beginners who need a hand to get started. At the end of each meeting, ask, "Who else should I be talking to?"

7. Prepare targeted self-marketing materials.

11   Use self-assessment to know what you have to sell. Then create a core résumé and cover letter and, most important, tailor them for each prospective employer.

8. Polish online strategy.

12   Don't post your résumé online and passively wait for calls. Save days for interviews, but at night, work your computer. Job boards will bring your résumé up as "new" if you update it daily with a one-word change. Job boards will e-mail you openings that meet your criteria if you sign up for the alerts. And, when possible, apply for employment directly to company Web sites.

9. Rehearse closing the sale.

13   You won't be hired until you get before the person who has a job to offer and convince that person that you're the best fit. Prepare yourself to explain why you should be hired instead of the next person. Work out the bugs with a video camera or mock interview sessions.

10. Know when to say yes.

14   Before accepting a job offer, follow the Taxi Principle: Know what it will cost your career before you get into a job. Can it lead where you want to go? Many of today's jobs are temporary, which is acceptable if there's a realistic prospect for full-time employment or if you will learn a marketable skill in the temporary job.

Source: Joyce Lain Kennedy, "Weigh 10 Factors Before Job Hunt," *Dallas Morning News,* June 6, 2004, p. 1J. Copyright © Tribune Media Services. Reprinted by permission of the author.

✔ **Vocabulary Check**

Use the context clues from both sentences to reason out the meaning of the italicized words. *The answer you choose should make sense in both sentences.* You may use a dictionary to confirm your answer choice, but be sure the meaning you select fits the context of both sentences. Write your answer in the space provided.

Refer to page 404 for the pronunciation key.

_____ 1. Your first job doesn't define your career, but starting off on the right foot is an employment *annuity.*

My parents' financial advisor recommended they invest in an *annuity* that would help them throughout their retirement.

Annuity (ə-nōō'ĭ-tē) is a noun that means   (paragraph 2)

a. an event that happens once a year.

b. an offer that is made annually.

c. a risky investment.

d. an investment that returns a benefit for a number of years or throughout a lifetime.

_____ 2. Here is my view of the 10 most important factors in pulling off a *smashing* job hunt for your first job.

The press described the actor's Academy Award-winning performance as *smashing*.

Smashing (smăsh'-ĭng) is an adjective that means   (paragraph 2)

a. extremely destructive.

b. fabulously successful.

c. careful and thorough.

d. ineffective.

_____ 3. Even with strong world growth, the absorption of the *surplus* will take a decade, maybe 25 years.

The city food bank distributed food to the hungry and stored the *surplus*.

Surplus (sûr'pləs) is a noun that means   (paragraph 4)

a. a quantity or amount in excess of what is needed.

b. part that is unidentified.

c. part that is unrecognizable.

d. a shortage.

_____ 4. Any job that can be *digitized* can be given to workers who will do the work for less money, both abroad and at home.

Using computer technology, music can be *digitized* and stored on iPods and other MP3 players.

Digitized (dĭj'ĭ-tīz'd) is a verb that means   (paragraph 5)

a. divided into extremely small pieces.

b. put (something) into digital form so that a computer can make use of it.

c. done with the fingers or hands.

d. created.

_____ 5. Any job that can be digitized can be given to workers who will do the work for less money, both *abroad* and at home.

Before you travel *abroad*, it is a good idea to learn something about the countries you will be visiting.

Abroad (ə-brôd′) is an adverb that means   (paragraph 5)

a. in one's own country.
b. in a vast area.
c. in foreign countries.
d. in an unknown territory.

_____ 6. As you compete, remember that in your first job, great training *prospects* trump salary.

The treasure hunters hoped to find the ancient sunken ship, but the *prospects* don't look good.

Prospects (prŏs′pĕkts) is a noun that means   (paragraph 5)

a. ideas.
b. discoveries.
c. ocean currents.
d. possibilities; chances.

_____ 7. As you compete, remember that in your first job, great training prospects *trump* salary.

We were able to *trump* the competition because they didn't know we'd been secretly practicing for weeks.

Trump (trŭmp) is a verb that means   (paragraph 5)

a. to ignore; to pay no attention to.
b. to fade in importance.
c. to win over something or someone else.
d. to reduce.

_____ 8. In fields where hiring is *robust*, focus on one to three choices of where you'd like to land in terms of occupation, industry, possible job titles and locale.

Home sales were so *robust* last summer that most realtors in our firm set new sales records.

Robust (rō-bŭst′, rō′bŭst) is an adjective that means   (paragraph 7)

a. limited in scope.
b. unsuccessful.
c. vigorous; active.
d. slow or inactive.

_____ 9. Even *jaded* executives are responsive to beginners who need a hand to get started.

Some children are so indulged that they become bored and *jaded* by the time they are teenagers.

Jaded (jā'dĭd) is an adjective that means (paragraph 10)

   a. shy; reserved.
   b. outgoing; friendly.
   c. wealthy.
   d. emotionally hardened.

_____ 10. Work out the bugs with a video camera or *mock* interview sessions.

To understand what trial lawyers experience in the courtroom, the law students participated in a series of *mock* trials.

Mock (mŏk) is an adjective that means (paragraph 13)
   a. simulated; pretend.
   b. silly; childish.
   c. videotaped.
   d. inexpensive.

✔ Comprehension Check

Read each of the following questions. Then write the correct answer choice in the blank. *Base your answers on information in the selection.* You may refer to the selection as you answer the questions.

True or False

_____ 1. The author believes that a college grad's career will be determined by a person's first job.

_____ 2. It's important to keep accurate and complete records about potential employers and the individuals responsible for hiring people.

_____ 3. American workers today have a better chance of competing for jobs than Americans did in past decades.

_____ 4. The author advises choosing a job that offers great training opportunities over one that pays more, but doesn't provide any training.

_____ 5. Unlike job seekers of the past, job seekers today face global competition.

_____ 6. You should prepare a core résumé and cover letter that you can use for all prospective employers.

Multiple-Choice

_____ 7. A wide search includes
   a. school career centers and teachers.
   b. job ads and business news in newspapers.

c. the Internet and television.

d. all of the above.

_____ 8. The Taxi Principle refers to

     a. finding out ahead of time the effect a job might have on your career.

     b. learning to navigate the Internet efficiently.

     c. saying yes to any job offer, even if it is a temporary job.

     d. explaining why you should be hired instead of someone else.

_____ 9. The best time in life to network for a job is when you

     a. finish high school.

     b. finish college.

     c. are ready to change from your first job.

     d. have had several jobs.

_____ 10. With regard to the Internet, job seekers should

     a. post their résumé and wait to be contacted.

     b. e-mail any companies they are interested in.

     c. apply for jobs directly at company Web sites.

     d. sponsor a job board.

Writing to Make Connections

Respond to the following items, based on information in the reading selection and on your own experience. You may refer to the selection as you answer the questions.

If the item has this symbol, your instructor may assign you to work collaboratively on it with classmates:

In that case, you should form groups of three or four students as directed by your instructor and work together to complete the exercises. After your group discusses each item and agrees on the answer, have a group member record it. Every member of your group should be able to explain all of your group's answers.

1. List at least two new things that you learned in this selection.

    _____

    _____

    _____

    _____

2. Which two suggestions do you think are the most important ones for locating a good job at the beginning of your career?

    _____

_____

_____

_____

3. Which suggestions did you think were least helpful, and why?

_____

_____

_____

_____

 4. In addition to the author's suggestions, what ideas do you have for successfully landing a first job after you finish college?

_____

_____

_____

_____

Web Resources

For additional information related to the selection topic, see the following websites:

www.acinet.org/acinet/library.asp?category=2.1

A clearinghouse with links for all aspects of job searches.

www.collegecentral.com

"The nation's largest network of small, midsize, and community college job seekers." Résumé and interview pointers as well as other information of interest to college students.

Although the addresses (URLs) listed above were active at the time *Entryways* was published, URLs can change or go out of existence. To locate other websites related to the selection topic, use these descriptors with Google or another search engine: **job search, career guide,** or **getting your first job.**

www.mhhe.com/
entryways
For more complete descriptions of these websites, as well as additional web resources related to this selection, see the ORL Student Center.

READING SELECTION 8

WHAT YOUR CAR SAYS ABOUT YOU

By Dianne Hales

Connecting with What You Already Know

Do these exercises *before* you read the selection.

Preview the selection by reading the

- title
- headings
- first paragraph
- first sentence in paragraphs 2–10
- paragraph 11
- source

1. Based on your preview, what do you anticipate the selection will be about?

   _____

   _____

   _____

   _____

2. Based on your preview, what do you think is the overall message of the selection, the one point the author wants readers to come away knowing?

   _____

   _____

   _____

3. In the selection, you'll encounter the following words. Mark any words you already know or think you know. Most words have more than one meaning. After you have read the selection, you will have an opportunity to deduce (reason out) their meanings according to how they are used in the selection. At that point, you will discover whether you were correct, and if not, you'll have a new word to add to your vocabulary.

vehicular	telegraph (verb)
irrational	fiscal
epitomize	subtle
formidable	retro-styled
in the eye of the beholder	exuberance

WHAT YOUR CAR SAYS ABOUT YOU

By Dianne Hales

This selection appeared in a popular Sunday newspaper supplement. It is interesting and straightforward. The first paragraph serves as an introduction.

1   Stud or dud? Sassy or shy? Trendy or traditional? Soccer mom or sexy mama? Before you say a word, your car broadcasts the answer.

2   "Your car is the best way of advertising who you are and how well you're doing," says psychologist Carleton Kendrick of Mills, Mass. An analyst of auto trends, he notes that cars "are an extension of what we want to be" whether that's successful, cool or just different.

3   According to a national survey by Roper, almost half of Americans believe their cars match their personalities. And with more makes, models, sizes, styles, colors, and accessories available in every price range to buy or lease, any driver can make a vehicular statement. "If cars were just about transportation, we would all drive the same thing," says Stephen Roulac, a business strategist in San Rafael, Calif. "Everybody expresses something through their cars—even if they try not to."

Inkblots on Wheels

4   Most people think they choose a car rationally. Not so, says consumer psychology expert Charles Kenny of Memphis. "Car choice comes from the right side of the brain—the emotional, irrational side. It's driven by psychological needs that most of us don't recognize. That's why you go to the dealer to buy a subcompact but end up driving home in a racier model with four on the floor. The bottom line is, 'How does a car make you feel?'"

5   SUVs deliver the heady feeling of being independent and above it all. Convertibles epitomize wind-in-the-hair freedom. Rugged off-roaders convey outdoor adventure—even if most rarely take on anything more formidable than a speed bump.

6   "About 25% of people choose cars that make them feel powerful," says James Hazen, a psychologist in Wexford, Pennsylvania, who works in the auto industry. "They go for the big engines, the big tires. Some people want cars that look good and stand out. Others find comfort in blending in with all the other white Camrys on the road."

7   Colors, accessories and origins also send signals. "People with red Corvettes are different than those who opt for a power color like black," says Hazen. White minivan owners who buy a GPS (global positioning system) because they worry about getting lost are different from those who get roof racks because they ski. Import-car buyers are more likely to live in blue states; those who buy American autos tend to come from union families and red states.

Read My Ride

8   Our cars reflect not just who we are but also how we want others to see us. "Cars are the ultimate status symbol," says BJ Gallagher of Los Angeles, a consultant to automotive businesses. "But status lies in the eye of the beholder and varies with your peer group."

9   In high finance, cars so rare and pricey that they're made of what one expert calls

"unobtainium"—such as a Bentley or Maserati—telegraph fiscal triumph. Among political activists, an environmentally correct Toyota Prius hybrid commands respect. For the young and well-wheeled, individuality rules. "You don't want to look like you're driving anybody else's car, especially your parents'," says Bobby Jones, a hip-hop lifestyle expert for a marketing company. "You want a car they'd never drive—like a Scion xB or Dodge Magnum—tricked out to make a statement about you."

10   Car talk can be more subtle. A sports car hints of an inner James Bond. A woman in a pickup asserts anything-he-can-do competence.

Midlife men—and increasingly women—in convertibles tell the world they still have a lot of life left in them. Drivers of retro-styled cars like the Mini Cooper or Chrysler PT Cruiser "are trying to recapture the exuberance that comes so easily when you're young and carefree," says Charles Kenny.

11   At any age or life stage, automotive messaging is "natural, normal and healthy," he adds. "Expressing a unique identity is what makes us human, and that's what our cars let us do."

Source: Dianne Hales, "What Your Car Says about You," *Parade*, May 15, 2005, p. 8. Copyright © 2005 Diane Hales. All rights reserved. Reprinted by permission of Parade Publications and the author.

✔ **Vocabulary Check**

Use the context clues from both sentences to reason out the meaning of the italicized words. *The answer you choose should make sense in both sentences.* You may use a dictionary to confirm your answer choice, but be sure the meaning you select fits the context of both sentences. Write your answer in the space provided.

Refer to page 402 for the pronunciation key.

_____ 1. And with more makes, models, sizes, styles, colors and accessories available in every price range to buy or lease, any driver can make a *vehicular* statement.

The drunk driver who killed the pedestrian was charged with *vehicular* homicide.

Vehicular (vē-hĭk'yə-lər) is an adjective that means
a. pertaining to drivers.   (paragraph 3)
b. pertaining to driving while intoxicated.
c. pertaining to motor vehicles, such as cars, trucks, etc.
d. pertaining to speed.

_____ 2. Car choice comes from the right side of the brain—the emotional, *irrational* side.

My common sense told me not to lend my coworker money, but I was *irrational* and did it anyway.

Irrational (ĭ-răsh′ə-nəl) is an adjective that means   (paragraph 4)

a. not based on reason and sound judgment.
b. friendly; kind.
c. unhappy.
d. tired; exhausted.

_____ 3. Convertibles *epitomize* wind-in-the-hair freedom.

To Americans, Abraham Lincoln will always *epitomize* honesty and humility.

Epitomize (ĭ-pĭt′ə-mĭz′) is a verb that means   (paragraph 5)

a. to be the opposite of.
b. to be confused with.
c. to be a typical example of.
d. to make a joke of.

_____ 4. Rugged off-roaders convey outdoor adventure—even if most rarely take on anything more *formidable* than a speed bump.

When my brother and I were children, we had the *formidable* task of telling our mother that we'd accidentally broken her treasured antique teapot.

Formidable (fôr′mĭ-də-bəl) is an adjective that means

a. causing fear or dread.   (paragraph 5)
b. causing admiration or wonder.
c. causing anger.
d. causing confusion.

_____ 5. But status lies *in the eye of the beholder* and varies with your peer group.

The saying, "Beauty is *in the eye of the beholder*" means that each person has his or her own idea of what is beautiful.

In the eye of the beholder (bĭ-hōld′ər) is a phrase that means

a. in sight; in the line of vision.   (paragraph 8)
b. depends on whether a person wears glasses.
c. varies according to how well a person sees.
d. varies according to each person's individual perception.

_____ 6. In high finance, cars so rare and pricey that they're made of what one expert calls "unobtainium"—such as a Bentley or Maserati—*telegraph* fiscal triumph.

The drill sergeant could *telegraph* his disapproval simply by raising his eyebrow.

Telegraph (tĕl′ĭ-grăf′) is a verb that means   (paragraph 9)

a. to announce in a loud voice.
b. to make known by nonverbal means.
c. to cover up or conceal.
d. to overcome.

_____ 7. In high finance, cars so rare and pricey that they're made of what one expert calls "unobtainium"—such as a Bentley or Maserati—telegraph *fiscal* triumph.

The treasurer and bookkeeper are responsible for collecting the club dues, as well as handling the organization's other *fiscal* affairs.

Fiscal (fĭs′kəl) is an adjective that means   (paragraph 9)

a. related to cars.
b. related to organizations.
c. related to finance or finances.
d. related to buying and selling.

_____ 8. Car talk can be more *subtle*.

The difference between the actual painting and the copy of it was so *subtle* that only an expert could tell which was the original.

Subtle (sŭt′l) is an adjective that means   (paragraph 10)

a. obvious.
b. extremely large.
c. difficult to detect or describe.
d. uncertain.

_____ 9. Drivers of *retro-styled* cars like the Mini Cooper or Chrysler PT Cruiser "are trying to recapture the exuberance that comes so easily when you're young and carefree," says Charles Kenny.

Those *retro-styled* dresses looked like the ones flappers wore in the 1920s!

Retro-styled (rĕt′rō stīld) is an adjective that means   (paragraph 10)

a. styled in a way that is reminiscent of the past.
b. highly decorated.
c. extremely modern or futuristic.
d. extremely fancy and expensive.

_____ 10. Drivers of retro-styled cars like the Mini Cooper or Chrysler PT Cruiser "are trying to recapture the *exuberance* that comes so easily when you're young and carefree," says Charles Kenny.

The puppy was full of *exuberance*: He jumped up and down and wagged his tail nonstop.

Exuberance (ĭg-zōō'bər-əns) is a noun that means (paragraph 10)
a. inappropriate behavior.
b. nervous energy.
c. desire to be outside.
d. unrestrained joy or enthusiasm.

✔ **Comprehension Check**

Read each of the following questions. Then write the correct answer choice in the blank. *Base your answers on information in the selection.* You may refer to the selection as you answer the questions.

True or False

_____ 1. According to a Roper survey, nearly half of Americans think their cars match their personalities.

_____ 2. Americans who tend to buy cars made in this country are likely to live in red states.

_____ 3. In cars, black is a power color.

_____ 4. We choose cars based partly on how we want others to see us.

_____ 5. Most people choose a car rationally.

Multiple-Choice

_____ 6. "Signals" about a driver can come from a car's
a. origin.
b. color.
c. accessories.
d. all of the above.

_____ 7. A Maserati is the type of car that might be purchased by a person who
a. is young and attractive.
b. is extremely wealthy.
c. is a political activist.
d. has a hip-hop lifestyle.

_____ 8. What "message" is conveyed about the lifestyle of someone who drives a convertible?
   a. They feel independent and above it all.
   b. They enjoy a sense of freedom and feel they have lots of life in them.
   c. They like outdoor adventure.
   d. They are assertive.

_____ 9. An example of a car that is styled like one from the past is the
   a. Prius.
   b. Camry.
   c. PT Cruiser.
   d. Corvette.

_____ 10. Automotive messaging is
   a. normal.
   b. healthy.
   c. natural.
   d. all of the above.

Writing to Make Connections

Respond to the following items, based on information in the reading selection and on your own experience. You may refer to the selection as you answer the questions.

   If the item has this symbol, your instructor may assign you to work collaboratively on it with classmates:

In that case, you should form groups of three or four students as directed by your instructor and work together to complete the exercises. After your group discusses each item and agrees on the answer, have a group member record it. Every member of your group should be able to explain all of your group's answers.

1. Which make and model of car or truck do you drive? (If you do not have one, think of a relative who does.) What "message" do you think that vehicle communicates about the driver?

   _____

   _____

   _____

   _____

2. If you could have any vehicle (cost does not matter), which one would you choose and why?

   _____

_____

_____

_____

3. Of the reasons you listed in item 2, which ones are actually reasons (based on reason or logic) and which ones are actually based on feelings or other nonlogical "reasons" (such as image).

_____

_____

_____

_____

4. The Hummer ("Hum V") was originally designed for military use, but now tens of thousands of American citizens are driving around in them—despite the fact that these vehicles are quite expensive and get relatively poor gas mileage. Describe the kind of person you think would drive a Hummer. Why would it appeal to them?

_____

_____

_____

_____

 ## Web Resources

For additional information related to the selection topic, see the following websites:

www.hybridcars.com/hybrid-buyer-profile.html
   Mentions celebrities who drive hybrids and profiles the "typical" hybrid car buyer.

social.chass.ncsu.edu/~wiley/courses/com110/VanSUV.html
   This _New York Times_ article focuses on differences between minivan buyers and SUV buyers.

   Although the addresses (URLs) listed above were active at the time _Entryways_ was published, URLs can change or go out of existence. To locate other websites related to the selection topic, use these descriptors with Google or another search engine: **consumer research car buying psychology, car buyer profile marketing,** or **car buyer profiles.**

READING SELECTION 9

CREDIT CARDS: CONVENIENCE OR CALAMITY?

By William Nickels, James McHugh, and Susan McHugh

Connecting with What You Already Know

Do these exercises *before* you read the selection.

First, think about the title. Then preview this selection by reading the

- introduction (in *italics*)
- first three paragraphs
- words in special print
- last paragraph

1. Based on your preview, what do you expect this selection to be about?

   _____

   _____

   _____

   _____

   _____

2. What, if anything, have you read, heard, or experienced about credit card abuse?

   _____

   _____

   _____

   _____

3. In the selection, you'll encounter the following words. Mark any words you already know or think you know. Most words have more than one meaning. After you have read the selection, you will have an opportunity to deduce (reason out) their meanings according to how they are used in the selection. At that point, you will discover whether you were correct, and if not, you'll have a new word to add to your vocabulary.

traumatic	bail
substantial	over-the-top
initial	capital
delinquent	tap
issuers	debit

CREDIT CARDS: CONVENIENCE OR CALAMITY?

By William Nickels, James McHugh, and Susan McHugh

Visa, MasterCard, gasoline cards, store cards . . . credit cards have become part of everyday American life. If you're like most college students, you have at least one credit card, and perhaps several. And if you're like many students, you don't pay off your credit card bill at the end of each month. In other words, you're in debt.

When you make a purchase with a credit card, you're actually making a short-term, high-interest loan from the credit card company. A college student who would never consider going to a bank and taking out a high-interest $5,000 loan to spend on clothes and entertainment may very well owe that much credit card debt on the very same type of purchases.

This selection focuses on college students and credit cards. It sheds light on both the pitfalls and benefits of credit cards.

Give Me Credit or Give Me Death

1   College students today use cash for 42 percent of purchases. The rest are bought with credit, debit, or ATM cards or even their college IDs. Over 35 percent of freshmen and 60 percent of seniors have their own credit cards. The change from paying cash to buying things on credit is often a traumatic one for students. Often, they simply don't have the experience, or sometimes the self-control, to manage such freedom to buy what they want. Some students are taking on "substantial debt loads that will clearly affect them for the rest of their lives," says a law professor at the University of Houston. A student with a balance of $3,000 on a credit card with an annual percentage rate of 18–20 percent, who pays the minimum 3 percent monthly payment, would take about 15 years to pay off the debt (and that's without using the card again to purchase so much as a candy bar). In addition, the student would end up paying double the initial amount of the purchases.

2   Students are nearly three times as likely to be at least 90 days delinquent on their credit card payments as older adults. Yet credit card issuers don't experience large losses because parents often bail students out.

3   Nonetheless, the need for students to manage cards better is clear. One college junior was forced to drop out of school when her credit card charges got out of hand. She still has $10,000 in credit card debt and $23,000 in student loans taken out to pay down debt. Some students are better off with a debit card or stored-value card that sets limits on the amount that can be spent. In fact, debit cards and ATM cards are more popular on campus than credit cards.

4   Many adults experience similar problems handling the freedom of having credit cards available. Often that results in debt from buying expensive new cars and other over-the-top items. Changing from a lifestyle of free spending to one of carefully watching every dime is a major undertaking. Do you know people who suffer from credit card debt? How hard does it seem for them to get rid of that debt? Wouldn't it be a lot easier not to

get into such debt in the first place?

Learning to Manage Credit

5   Known as *plastic* to young buyers, credit cards are no doubt familiar to you. Names like Visa, MasterCard, American Express, Discover, and Diners Club are well known to most people. In a credit card purchase, finance charges usually amount to anywhere from 12 to 20 percent annually. This means that if you finance a TV, home appliances, and other purchases with a credit card, you may end up spending much more than if you pay with cash. A good manager of personal finances, like a good businessperson, pays on time and takes advantage of savings made possible by paying early. People who've established a capital fund can tap that fund to make large purchases and pay the fund back (with interest if so desired) rather than pay bank finance charges.

6   Credit cards are an important element in a personal financial system, even if they're rarely used. First, some merchants request credit cards as a form of identification. It may be difficult to buy certain goods or even rent a car without owning a credit card because businesses use them for identification and assured payment. Second, credit cards can be used to keep track of purchases. A gasoline credit card, for example, gives you records of purchases over time for income tax and financial planning purposes. Third, it's sometimes easier to write one check at the end of the month for several purchases than to carry cash when you shop. Besides, when cash is stolen or lost, it is simply gone; a stolen credit

card can be canceled to protect your account.

7   Finally, a credit card is more convenient than cash or checks. If you come upon a special sale and need more money than you usually carry, paying by credit is quick and easy. You can carry less cash and don't have to worry about keeping your checkbook balanced as often.

8   If you do use a credit card, you should pay the balance in full during the period when no interest is charged. Not having to pay 14 percent interest is as good as earning 14 percent tax free. Also, you may want to choose a card that pays you back in cash, like the Discover card, or others that offer paybacks like credits toward the purchase of a car, free long-distance minutes, or frequent-flier miles. The value of these givebacks can be from 1 to 5 percent. Rather than pay 14 percent, you earn a certain percentage—quite a difference. Some cards have no annual fees; others have lower interest rates. To compare credit cards, check out www.cardratings.com or www.angelfire.com/ ny/erte200l/cardinfo.html.

9   The danger of a credit card is the flipside of its convenience. Too often, consumers buy goods and services that they wouldn't normally buy if they had to pay cash or write a check on funds in the bank. Using credit cards, consumers often pile up debts to the point where they're unable to pay. If you aren't the type who can stick to a financial plan or household budget, it may be better not to have a credit card at all. There are alternatives to credit cards, such as debit cards. Debit

cards are like credit cards, but they won't let you spend more than a predetermined amount, a great benefit for those who are not as careful with their spending as they should be.

10   Credit cards are a helpful tool to the financially careful buyer. They're a financial disaster to people with little financial restraint and tastes beyond their income.

College students take note: Of the debtors seeking help at the National Consumer Counseling Service, more than half were between 18 and 32.

Source: From William Nickels, James McHugh, and Susan McHugh, *Understanding Business,* 7th ed., p. 679. Copyright © 2005 The McGraw-Hill Companies. Reprinted by permission of The McGraw-Hill Companies, Inc.

✔ Vocabulary Check

Use the context clues from both sentences to reason out the meaning of the italicized words. *The answer you choose should make sense in both sentences.* You may use a dictionary to confirm your answer choice, but be sure the meaning you select fits the context of both sentences. Write your answer in the space provided.

Refer to page 402 for the pronunciation key.

_____ 1. The change from paying cash to buying things on credit is often a *traumatic* one for students.

When parents divorce, it is usually a *traumatic* experience for children.

Traumatic (trô'-măt'ĭk) is an adjective that means   (paragraph 1)
a. causing distress and disruption.
b. pertaining to the family.
c. lengthy, occurring over a long period of time.
d. pleasant, enjoyable.

_____ 2. Some students are taking on "*substantial* debt loads that will clearly affect them for the rest of their lives," says a law professor at the University of Houston.

Authorities are alarmed at the *substantial* increase in methamphetamine use in the United States during the last few years.

Substantial (səb-stăn'shəl) is an adjective that means (paragraph 1)
a. small, unimportant.
b. occurring in a short period of time.
c. barely noticeable.
d. large in amount.

_____ 3. In addition, the student would end up paying double the *initial* amount of the purchases.

Filling out an application is the *initial* step for those who want to attend college.

Initial (ĭ-nĭsh′əl) is an adjective that means   (paragraph 1)

a. important, large.
b. first, occurring at the beginning.
c. pertaining to the first letter in a word.
d. difficult, challenging.

_____ 4. Students are nearly three times as likely to be at least 90 days *delinquent* on their credit card payments as older adults.

Because the man was two months *delinquent* on his apartment rent, he was evicted.

Delinquent (dĭ-lĭng′kwənt) is an adjective that means   (paragraph 2)

a. pertaining to bad behavior.
b. overdue in payment.
c. early.
d. in advance.

_____ 5. Yet credit card *issuers* don't experience large losses because parents often bail students out.

Various state and local agencies are the official *issuers* of drivers' licenses, hunting licenses, and building permits.

Issuers (ĭsh′o͞o ərz) is a noun that means   (paragraph 2)

a. those who become involved in conflicts.
b. those who hold a great deal of power.
c. those who offer or give something out.
d. those who manufacture products.

_____ 6. Yet credit card issuers don't experience large losses because parents often *bail* students out.

If parents *bail* their children out of every problem, the children grow up unable to cope effectively with the demands of adult life.

Bail (bāl) is a verb that means   (paragraph 2)

a. to get someone out of a difficult situation.
b. to put someone into a difficult situation.
c. to talk someone out of something.
d. to refuse to believe someone.

_____ 7. Often that results in debt from buying expensive new cars and other *over-the-top* items.

Many movie stars have *over-the-top* lifestyles: luxury cars, private jets, lavish homes, designer clothes, and fabulous jewelry.

Over-the-top is an adjective that means   (paragraph 4)
a. producing envy in others.
b. earned as the result of hard work.
c. excessively expensive or extravagant.
d. made in another country and imported.

_____ 8. People who've established a *capital* fund can tap that fund to make large purchases and pay the fund back (with interest if so desired) rather than pay bank finance charges.

The new company established a *capital* account from which to pay its bills.

Capital (kăp′ĭ-tl) is an adjective that means   (paragraph 5)
a. pertaining to money borrowed from others.
b. pertaining to money accumulated by a person or a business.
c. pertaining to money invested in the stock market.
d. pertaining to money gained illegally.

_____ 9. People who've established a capital fund can *tap* that fund to make large purchases and pay the fund back (with interest if so desired) rather than pay a bank finance charges.

Because I overspent on my spring break trip, I had to *tap* my savings account.

Tap (tăp) is a verb that means   (paragraph 5)
a. to hit or strike lightly.
b. to brag about.
c. to check.
d. to make use of.

_____ 10. *Debit* cards are like credit cards, but they won't let you spend more than a predetermined amount, a great benefit for those who are not as careful with their spending as they should be.

Accountants record unpaid expenses in the *debit* column of their accounting ledgers.

Debit (dĕb′ĭt) is an adjective that means   (paragraph 9)
a. pertaining to a column.
b. pertaining to a debt.

c. pertaining to something made of plastic.
d. pertaining to credit cards.

✔ Comprehension Check

Read each of the following questions. Then write the correct answer choice in the blank. *Base your answers on information in the selection.* You may refer to the selection as you answer the questions.

True or False

_____ 1. More college seniors than freshmen have their own credit cards.

_____ 2. Even though many college students get behind on their credit card payments, their parents often pay off the debt.

_____ 3. College students prefer credit cards over ATM cards and debit cards.

_____ 4. According to the selection, it would be better not to have or use credit cards.

_____ 5. Money you do not have to pay in credit card interest is like earning the same amount of money tax free.

Multiple-Choice

_____ 6. In credit card purchases, the annual finance charges are usually
a. 1 to 5 percent.
b. 12 to 20 percent.
c. 18 to 20 percent.
d. 35 to 60 percent.

_____ 7. A benefit of owning a credit card is
a. some merchants require one for identification and/or assured payment.
b. it can help you keep track of purchases.
c. it can be canceled if it is lost or stolen.
d. all of the above.

_____ 8. People who are not good at sticking to a financial plan or household budget should
a. talk with a financial counselor.
b. consider using a debit card instead of a credit card.
c. choose a credit card that charges no more than 20 percent interest.
d. take out a loan from a bank instead.

_____ 9. An example of a credit card that pays you back in cash for a percentage of your purchases is

a. American Express.

b. Diners Club.

c. Discover.

d. none of the above.

_____ 10. More than half of the debtors who seek help at the National Consumer Counseling Center are between the ages of

a. 16 and 20.

b. 18 and 32.

c. 28 and 40.

d. 42 and 56.

Writing to Make Connections

Respond to the following items, based on information in the reading selection and on your own experience. You may refer to the selection as you answer the questions.

If the item has this symbol, your instructor may assign you to work collaboratively on it with classmates:

In that case, you should form groups of three or four students as directed by your instructor and work together to complete the exercises. After your group discusses each item and agrees on the answer, have a group member record it. Every member of your group should be able to explain all of your group's answers.

1. In your opinion, should college students own a credit card? More than one credit card? Explain your position.

_____

_____

_____

2. List at least two characteristics a person should look for when selecting a credit card.

_____

_____

_____

_____

3. There is a downside to credit cards, but what are some advantages? List at least three.

_____

_____

_____

_____

_____

_____

_____

_____

4. What are some steps college students can take to learn to use credit cards wisely?

_____

_____

_____

_____

_____

_____

_____

_____

 ## Web Resources

For additional information related to the selection topic, see the following websites:

www.bankrate.com/brm/news/cc/19980803.asp

This page contains the first of a helpful, readable five-part series about college life and money.

http://beginnersinvest.about.com/od/studentcredit/

Articles on pitfalls of student credit cards, avoiding credit card debt, financial management for beginners, and many more.

Although the addresses (URLs) listed above were active at the time _Entryways_ was published, URLs can change or go out of existence. To locate other websites related to the selection topic, use these descriptors with Google or another search engine: **college students credit cards, credit card debt,** or **debt management.**

READING SELECTION 10

PULLING THE PLUG ON TV

Connecting with What You Already Know

Do these exercises *before* you read the selection.

Preview this selection by reading the

- title
- introduction (in *italics*)
- first sentence of paragraphs 1–8
- last paragraph

1. Based on your preview, what do you think the selection is going to be about?

_____

_____

_____

2. What do you think is the author's purpose in writing the selection?

_____

_____

_____

3. What, if anything, have you heard or read about the effects that excessive TV watching has on children and adults?

_____

_____

_____

4. In the selection, you'll encounter the following words. Mark any words you already know or think you know. Most words have more than one meaning. After you have read the selection, you will have an opportunity to deduce (reason out) their meanings according to how they are used in the selection. At that point, you will discover whether you were correct, and if not, you'll have a new word to add to your vocabulary.

quipped	undermines
mind-numbing	empathy
blaring	pledge
epidemic	forgoing
engaging	recreationally

PULLING THE PLUG ON TV

Based on TV Turnoff Network

Television is bubblegum for the eyes.
—Frank Lloyd Wright, American architect

How much television do you watch every day? Every week? How much time do you spend watching DVDs and playing video games? Have you ever considered going without TV or even giving it up altogether? What might happen if you did? The following selection focuses on these issues.

1   Someone once quipped that the United States is a "nation of vidiots," referring to the astonishing number of mind-numbing hours that the typical American spends watching TV. The average American has the TV blaring nearly 8 hours a day and watches it more than 4 hours. Although the American Pediatric Association recommends children two and under watch no TV or other screen media, American one-year-olds average 6 hours per week. It quickly gets worse: children under age two tend to sit in front of TVs 2 hours a day. For ages 2–17, it mushrooms to approximately 20 hours a week, with the vast majority of 2- to 7-year-olds watching alone or unsupervised. According to www.tvturnoff.org, U.S. children spend an average of 900 hours per year in school, but spend a whopping 1,023 hours glued to the TV. Think about what that adds up to over a lifetime.

2   Barbara Brock, recreation management professor at Eastern Washington University, reports that 98 percent of Americans spend 40 percent of their time sitting and watching TV. It's no wonder that obesity has reached epidemic proportions: one-third of adults are obese, and U.S. children today are the most overweight in history. Nearly half of all American families report that they frequently or always watch TV while eating dinner, time that could be spent engaging in conversation with each other.

3   Besides slicing into family time, TV has a negative effect on the development of children's academic skills, including lower reading levels. It also has a negative effect on the development of social skills. The time wasted in front of the TV could be spent reading, pursuing creative outlets, playing, dreaming, enjoying the outdoors, and interacting with others. At the end of your life, what would you give to have back the *years* you spent watching TV? Years you could have spent with friends and people you love? Doing activities that you truly enjoy? Using your talents to make the world a better place?

4   Excessive TV watching is associated with bullying. Is it any wonder? Kids tend to imitate the behaviors of TV and video game characters. By age 18, the average American child has seen 200,000 violent acts on TV. They've witnessed 16,000 murders on TV. The TV-Turnoff Network puts it bluntly:

> When it comes to children's behavior, it is abundantly clear that excessive screen time is just what the doctor *didn't* order. It provides numerous models of violent and aggressive behavior, and at the same time reduces children's interaction with real people—caring adults and peers. As a result, it undermines children's empathy and suggests that acting out in anger is acceptable and even desirable.

5   What would happen to people if they voluntarily gave up TV for a week? Might they discover that their lives could be much better? Questions like that led to TV-Turnoff Week. It is sponsored once a year in the spring by a Washington, D.C. headquartered nonprofit organization, TV-Turnoff Network. Their slogan is "Turn off TV. Turn on life." They encourage children and adults to cut back on TV so their lives will be healthier and more fulfilling. More than 70 national organizations sponsor TV-Turnoff Week. Among these respected organizations are the National Education Association, American Academy of Pediatrics, American Medical Association, and President's Council on Physical Fitness and Sports.

6   The organization's website, www.tvturnoff.org, provides suggestions for month-by-month activities to replace watching television. There are also tips on TV-proofing your home, as well as tips for turning off TV and suggestions for coping with "withdrawal."

7   Since TV-Turnoff Week was launched in 1995, more than 24 million people have answered those questions for themselves. They come from every background, occupation, and socioeconomic level. Millions of students have participated through their schools. Millions of children and adults became involved through churches and community organizations. Still others undertook the project as families or individuals. More than 19,000 organizers planned events in 2004, with approximately seven-and-a-half million participants. In some communities, local newspapers publish the names of the proud preschool and elementary school students who lived up to their pledge to watch no TV, video or DVD, or video games during TV-Turnoff Week. The success rate is encouraging: in follow-up surveys, 90 percent of the respondents said as a result of their participation, they reduced their TV viewing.

8   Does forgoing TV mean becoming glued to the computer instead? Professor Brock, whose research on 385 TV-free families is included at the TV-Turnoff Network website, found that non-TV watchers do not substitute the computer for the TV. Adults, in fact, said that they used the computer recreationally only 1–3 hours a week. Nearly half of their children use the computer less than TV-watching kids. Parents in the study also reported that they spend about an hour a day in meaningful conversation with their children. That's approximately 11 times the national average of 38 *minutes a week!* Moreover, Brock found that both parents and children in the study tended to be readers. (TV-Turnoff Network also sponsors "More Reading, Less TV," a four-week elementary school program that fosters enthusiasm for and a deep enjoyment of reading.) Brock made several other important discoveries about these TV-free children: More than half of them make straight As. They have fewer fights with their siblings. They can play for hours by themselves or with others. They don't feel deprived or that they're missing out on anything because they don't watch TV.

9   The TV-Turnoff Network states that the research is clear, and sums up the problem this way: "Excessive screen time is simply unhealthy for growing minds, growing bodies, and for our families." Is it time for you to rise

to the challenge and pull the plug for a week? If you feel you can't do it by yourself, enlist friends or family members to join you. There's no time like the present to "Turn off TV and turn on life."

✔ **Vocabulary Check**

Use the context clues from both sentences to reason out the meaning of the italicized words. *The answer you choose should make sense in both sentences.* You may use a dictionary to confirm your answer choice, but be sure the meaning you select fits the context of both sentences. Write your answer in the space provided.

Refer to page 402 for the pronunciation key.

_____ 1. Someone once *quipped* that the United States is a "nation of vidiots," referring to the astonishing number of mind-numbing hours that the typical American spends watching TV.

When the author asked, "Did you read my last book?" the reviewer *quipped*, "I hope so."

Quipped (kwĭpt) is a verb that means   (paragraph 1)
a. lied.
b. reported.
c. made a kind, gracious remark.
d. made a clever, sarcastic remark.

_____ 2. Someone once quipped that the United States is a "nation of vidiots," referring to the astonishing number of *mind-numbing* hours that the typical American spends watching TV.

The topic was boring, and the long lecture was filled with statistics; it was *mind-numbing*.

Mind-numbing (mīnd nŭm-ĭng) is an adjective that means
a. energizing; renewing.   (paragraph 1)
b. producing the inability to respond mentally or emotionally.
c. adding to one's knowledge or understanding.
d. fresh; innovative.

_____ 3. The average American has the TV *blaring* nearly 8 hours a day and watches it more than 4 hours.

Every night we hear the stereo *blaring* in the next apartment, and it makes it impossible to sleep.

Blaring (blâr'-ĭng) is an adjective that means   (paragraph 1)

  a. making loud, annoying sound.
  b. making a low, steady sound.
  c. silent; muted.
  d. shining or flashing brightly.

_____ 4. It's no wonder that obesity has reached *epidemic* proportions: one-third of adults are obese, and U.S. children today are the most overweight in history.

In 1918 influenza reached *epidemic* levels worldwide, killing between 20 and 40 million people.

Epidemic (ĕp'ĭ-dĕm'ĭk) is an adjective that means   (paragraph 2)

  a. reduced or decreased.
  b. unknown because it cannot be measured.
  c. stable or unchanging.
  d. spreading quickly and affecting many people at the same time.

_____ 5. Nearly half of all American families report that they frequently or always watch TV while eating dinner, time that could be spent *engaging* in conversation with each other.

In the research study, a shockingly high number of people admitted to *engaging* in shoplifting.

Engaging (ĕn-gāj'ĭng) is a verbal noun that means   (paragraph 2)

  a. learning about; taking instruction in.
  b. refusing to be part of.
  c. participating in; being involved in.
  d. making promises about.

_____ 6. As a result, it *undermines* children's empathy and suggests that acting out in anger is acceptable and even desirable.

Not getting enough sleep *undermines* the health of many college students.

Undermines (ŭn'dər-mīnz') is a verb that means   (paragraph 4)

  a. goes deeper into.
  b. gradually weakens or diminishes.
  c. has no noticeable effect upon.
  d. improves or enhances.

_____ 7. As a result, it undermines children's *empathy* and suggests that acting out in anger is acceptable and even desirable.

My mother has so much *empathy:* she cries at sad movies and joyful weddings, and when she reads novels, she feels whatever the main character is feeling.

Empathy (ĕm'pə-thē) is a noun that means   (paragraph 4)

   a. rejection of another's feelings.
   b. understanding and identification with another's feelings.
   c. feeling sorry for someone.
   d. misinterpretation of another's feelings.

_____ 8. In some communities, local newspapers publish the names of the proud preschool and elementary school students who lived up to their *pledge* to watch no TV, video or DVD, or video games during TV-Turnoff Week.

At many schools, teens and young adults sign a *pledge* not to drink and drive.

Pledge (plĕj) is a noun that means   (paragraph 7)

   a. wish or desire.
   b. solemn promise.
   c. something written on paper.
   d. an article appearing in print.

_____ 9. Does *forgoing* TV mean becoming glued to the computer instead?

By *forgoing* dessert and saving the money instead, the fourth-graders raised $150 for the World Hunger Fund last year.

Forgoing (fôr-gō'ĭng) is a verbal noun that means   (paragraph 8)

   a. keeping oneself from doing something.
   b. preventing.
   c. choosing with care.
   d. enjoying; taking pleasure in.

_____ 10. Adults, in fact, said that they used the computer *recreationally* only 1–3 hours a week.

I swim *recreationally,* but my brother swims competitively.

Recreationally (rĕk'rē-ā'shə-nəl lē) is an adverb that means

   a. in a formal way.   (paragraph 8)
   b. in a way that is time consuming.
   c. in a way that amuses or refreshes; for play.
   d. in a cheerful, positive manner.

✔ **Comprehension Check**

Read each of the following questions. Then write the correct answer choice in the blank. *Base your answers on information in the selection.* You may refer to the selection as you answer the questions.

True or False

_____ 1. U.S. children spend approximately 100 hours more per year in school than they do watching TV.

_____ 2. As children get older, the amount of TV they watch tends to increase.

_____ 3. Bullying is associated with excessive TV watching in children.

_____ 4. TV-Turnoff Week is sponsored by a government agency.

_____ 5. Family members would probably have more communication and better communication if they turned off the TV during dinner.

Multiple-Choice

_____ 6. Excessive TV has a negative effect on children's
    a. academic skills.
    b. social skills.
    c. empathy.
    d. all of the above

_____ 7. The annual TV-Turnoff Week is held every
    a. winter.
    b. spring.
    c. summer.
    d. fall.

_____ 8. By the age of 18, the average American child has seen how many violent acts on TV?
    a. 16,000
    b. 19,000
    c. 200,000
    d. 7,500,000

_____ 9. One researcher found that adults in TV-free homes use the computer
    a. very few hours per week.
    b. the same number of hours per week as TV watchers.
    c. more hours per week than TV watchers.
    d. more than twice as many hours per week as TV watchers.

_____ 10. Parents in TV- free homes report that they spend approximately how much time per week talking with their children?

    a. 11 minutes

    b. 38 minutes

    c. 1 hour

    d. 7 hours

Writing to Make Connections

Respond to the following items, based on information in the reading selection and on your own experience. You may refer to the selection as you answer the questions.

If the item has this symbol, your instructor may assign you to work collaboratively on it with classmates:

In that case, you should form groups of three or four students as directed by your instructor and work together to complete the exercises. After your group discusses each item and agrees on the answer, have a group member record it. Every member of your group should be able to explain all of your group's answers.

1. On average, how much TV do you currently watch each day? What time of day or evening do you watch the most? Do you watch more TV on weekdays or on weekends?

_____

_____

_____

_____

2. If you stopped watching TV, how might your life change for the better? How would you use that time instead?

_____

_____

_____

_____

3. Do you think it would be hard to go without TV for a week? What would help you get through the week successfully?

_____

_____

_____

4. Should colleges encourage students to watch less TV? Should they sponsor a TV Turnoff week? Why or why not?

_____

_____

_____

_____

Web Resources

For additional information related to the selection topic, see the following websites:

www.tvturnoff.org

> Website for the national nonprofit organization that sponsors the annual TV-Turnoff Week.

www.usatoday.com/news/health/2003-11-10-tv-study_x.htm

> This _USA Today_ article focuses on TV's effect on very young children.

Although the addresses (URLs) listed above were active at the time _Entryways_ was published, URLs can change or go out of existence. To locate other websites related to the selection topic, use this descriptor with Google or another search engine: **turning off TV.**

www.mhhe.com/
entryways

For more complete descriptions of these websites, as well as an additional web resource related to this selection, see the ORL Student Center.

Master Vocabulary List for Reading Selections

The selection number is given after each word.

abroad, 7
annuity, 7
assess, 4
authenticity, 5
avid, 2

bail, 9
barracks, 3
blaring, 10
boosting, 5

capital, 9
chow, 3
chronic, 6
clarity, 2
consistently, 4
culmination, 3
cycles, 4

debit, 9
dehydrating, 4
deliberate (verb), 5
delinquent, 9
deprived, 6
digitized, 7
diversity, 1
drawn, 6
drowsy, 4

ebbs and flows, 1
edible, 3
empathy, 10
engaging, 10
engrossed, 5
epidemic, 10
epitomize, 8
exponentially, 5
exuberance, 8

fiscal, 8
forgoing, 10
formidable, 8

generating, 5

host (noun), 1
humbled, 1

in the eye of the beholder, 8
ingest, 3
initial, 9
inundated, 3
irascible, 5
irrational, 8
issuers, 9

jaded, 7

lapses, 6
lethargy, 4

mind-numbing, 10
mock (adj.), 7
monosyllabic, 2

narrative, 2

obstacle course, 3
obstacles, 1
over-the-top, 9

pediatrician, 2
periodic, 4
persistence, 1
pledge, 10
poll, 6
practical, 4
prodigy, 2
productivity, 4
promotes, 6
prone, 6
prospects, 7
pursuing, 1

quipped, 10

radical, 1
ramrod, 3
random, 2
rations, 3
recreationally, 10
rejuvenation, 5
retro-styled, 8
robust, 7

sabotage, 1
smashing, 7
spouse, 5
submissively, 2
substantial, 9
subtle, 8
subverted, 2
surplus, 7
sustainable, 5

tactical, 3
tap, 9
telegraph (verb), 8
transports, 4
traumatic, 9
trump, 7

undermines, 10

vehicular, 8
villain, 2
vital, 6

well-being, 6
wrestle, 1

zombies, 6

Glossary of Key Terms

abridged dictionary a shortened dictionary that focuses on useful words and contains fewer definitions per word (*Chapter 4*)

adjective a word that describes a noun or pronoun; tells what kind, how many, or which one (*Chapters 4 and 6*)

adverb a word that describes or limits a verb, adjective, or another adverb; tells how, where, or when (*Chapters 4 and 6*)

after-reading strategies strategies for reviewing and rehearsing material that has been read in order to remember the material (*Chapter 12*)

annotating writing explanatory notes in the margin of your textbook to organize and remember information (*Chapter 12*)

article the words *a, an,* and *the* (*Chapters 4 and 6*)

auditory learner person who prefers to learn by hearing information (*Identifying Your Learning Style*)

auditory-sequential learner person who learns well by hearing and from step-by-step learning (*Identifying Your Learning Style*)

authors' writing patterns (*See* writing patterns)

cause-effect pattern writing pattern in which the author presents reasons (causes), results (effects), or both (*Chapter 11*)

chapter introduction textbook feature at the beginning of a chapter that describes the overall purpose and major topics (*Chapter 12*)

chapter objectives textbook feature at the beginning of a chapter that tells what you should know or be able to do after studying the chapter (*Chapter 12*)

chapter summary textbook feature in which the author consolidates most of the main ideas; may also be called "Chapter Highlights," "Key Points," "Chapter Recap," or other such names (*Chapter 12*)

collegiate dictionary medium-sized, desktop hardcover dictionary that focuses on words useful to the typical college student and adult (*Chapter 4*)

comparison-contrast pattern writing pattern in which the author presents similarities (comparisons), differences (contrasts), or both (*Chapter 11*)

complex sentence sentence that consists of an independent clause and one or more dependent clauses (*Chapter 6*)

compound sentence sentence made of two or more independent clauses (equal sentences) joined by a coordinating conjunction (*Chapter 6*)

comprehension understanding what you read (*Introduction to Part Three*)

comprehension monitoring evaluating your understanding as you read and correcting the problem whenever you realize that you are not comprehending (*Chapter 12*)

conjunction word used to join other words or groups of words (*Chapters 4 and 6*)

connotations implied meanings or emotions associated with a word (*Chapter 4*)

consonant any alphabet letters other than *a, e, i, o, u* (*Chapter 4*)

context clues words in a sentence or paragraph that help the reader reason out the meaning of an unfamiliar word (*Chapter 3*)

contrast clue type of context clue in which a word or phrase in a sentence has a meaning that is the opposite of an unfamiliar word (*Chapter 3*)

coordinating conjunction a word that connects two equal grammatical elements (*for, and, nor, but, or, yet, so*) (*Chapter 6*)

definition clue type of context clue in which a definition or synonym provides a clue to the meaning of an unfamiliar word (*Chapter 3*)

definition pattern writing pattern in which the author presents the meaning of an important term and then discusses it throughout the paragraph (*Chapter 11*)

denotation dictionary definition of a word (*Chapter 4*)

dependent clause a clause that depends on the rest of the sentence in order to make sense (*Chapter 6*)

details (*See* supporting details)

direct object the object that receives the action of the verb; the word or phrase in a sentence that refers to the person or thing receiving the action of a transitive verb (*Chapter 6*)

during-reading strategies asking and answering questions as you read in order to increase and monitor comprehension *(Chapter 12)*

entry an item in the dictionary that appears in bold print and is defined *(Chapter 4)*

etymology part of a dictionary entry that appears at the end in brackets and explains the origin and history of a word *(Chapter 4)*

example clue type of context clue in which one or more examples in the sentence illustrate the meaning of an unfamiliar word *(Chapter 3)*

FAN BOYS memory peg for recalling the seven coordinating conjunctions (*for, and, nor, but, or, yet,* and *so*) *(Chapter 6)*

feedback information that comes back in response to something you have done *(Chapter 2)*

formulated main idea (*See* implied main idea)

general characteristic of a larger category; broad in nature *(Chapter 7)*

general sense clue type of context clue in which the overall meaning of the sentence, along with the reader's knowledge and experience, provides a clue to the meaning of an unfamiliar word *(Chapter 3)*

glossary a minidictionary of the important terms in a textbook that is usually located near the end of the textbook *(Chapter 4)*

goals (*See* intermediate goals, long-term goals, short-term goals)

guidewords words at the top of a dictionary page that tell the first word and last word on the page, between which all words on the page come alphabetically *(Chapter 4)*

homonyms words that sound the same but have different spellings and meanings (*our* and *hour*), or words that have the same spelling but different meanings (tree *bark* and dog's *bark*) *(Chapter 5)*

idiom expression whose meaning cannot be deduced by "adding up" the meaning of the parts *(Chapter 4)*

implied main idea sentence formulated by the reader that expresses the author's most important point about the topic; also called a *formulated main idea, unstated main idea,* or *indirectly stated main idea* *(Chapter 10)*

independent clause clause that has a subject and a verb and can stand alone (makes sense by itself) *(Chapter 6)*

index a listing at the back of a book that tells the specific page on which information appears *(Chapter 12)*

inductive reasoning a way of reasoning that moves from specific examples to a general rule or principle *(Special Features of This Book)*

information from another sentence type of context clue provided by information in a different sentence from the one that contains the unfamiliar word *(Chapter 3)*

interjection a word used by itself to express strong feeling or emotion *(Chapters 4 and 6)*

intermediate goals goals to be accomplished during the next two to five years *(Chapter 2)*

intransitive verb verb that does not take an object *(Chapter 6)*

introduction a feature at the beginning of a textbook in which the author describes the book, how it is organized, its special features, what certain symbols mean, and so forth *(Chapter 12)*

learning style the modality through which an individual learns best *(Identifying Your Learning Style)*

list pattern writing pattern in which the author presents a group of items in no particular order because the order is unimportant *(Chapter 11)*

long-term goals goals to be accomplished during a person's lifetime *(Chapter 2)*

main idea (*See* implied main idea and stated main idea sentence)

major detail detail that is essential for understanding the main idea completely; also called a *primary detail* *(Chapter 9)*

marking textbooks underlining or highlighting topics, main ideas, and important terms and definitions in textbooks *(Chapter 12)*

minor detail less important detail that explains another detail; also called a *secondary detail* *(Chapter 9)*

noun word that names a person, place, thing, or idea *(Chapters 4 and 6)*

overall main idea a very general sentence that sums up the main ideas of a selection; the general point of an entire selection (such as a section of a textbook chapter); also called a *thesis sentence* *(Chapters 8 and 10)*

paragraph a group of sentences that all pertain to the same topic; a division of written or printed matter that begins on a new, usually indented line, consists of one or more sentences, and typically develops a single thought *(Chapter 7)*

part of speech any of the eight categories (noun, pronoun, verb, adjective, adverb, preposition, conjunction, and interjection) used to describe the function of words in context *(Chapters 4 and 6)*

phrasal verb verb followed by an adverb, a preposition, or both, such as *turn down* and *turn away,* forming a term with an idiomatic meaning that is often quite different from the meaning of the individual words *(Chapter 4)*

phrase group of words that is shorter than a sentence but functions together as a meaningful unit *(Chapter 4)*

pocket dictionary a small, less complete dictionary with fewer and shorter definitions than a standard dictionary *(Chapter 4)*

predicate the part of a sentence that tells what the subject is doing or what is being said about the subject; also called the *verb (Chapter 6)*

predictions educated guesses about what a textbook assignment will be about and how the material will be organized *(Chapter 12)*

prefix word part attached to the beginning of a word that adds its meaning to that base word *(Chapter 4)*

preposition a word used to show the relationship between a noun or pronoun and another word *(Chapters 4 and 6)*

prereading strategies previewing an assignment, planning your reading session, and assessing your prior knowledge before actually reading a textbook assignment in order to increase comprehension *(Chapter 12)*

previewing looking through an assignment before reading it to see what it is about, how the information is organized, and what is important *(Chapter 12)*

prior knowledge the information a person already knows about the topic; also called *background knowledge (Chapter 12)*

pronoun a word used in place of a noun *(Chapters 4 and 6)*

pronunciation key dictionary feature that explains the phonetic symbols and diacritical marks that indicate the way a word is spoken *(Chapter 4)*

rehearsing information to remember it saying or writing information to transfer it into long-term memory *(Chapter 12)*

sentence a group of words that expresses a complete thought; a basic sentence consisting of a subject and a predicate *(Chapter 6)*

sequence pattern writing pattern in which a group of items are presented in a specific order because the order is important; also known as *time order, chronological order, a process,* or a *series (Chapter 11)*

sequential learner person who prefers to learn information step-by-step *(Identifying Your Learning Style)*

setting priorities making decisions about what is most important *(Chapter 2)*

short-term goals goals to be accomplished during the next six months to a year *(Chapter 2)*

signal words words that indicate the author's writing pattern or organization *(Chapter 11)*

spatial learner person who can visualize how things fit together or can imagine what an object looks like from another perspective *(Identifying Your Learning Style)*

specific used to describe distinctive, individual things that are part of a larger category *(Chapter 7)*

stated main idea sentence a sentence in a paragraph that tells the author's most important point about the topic *(Chapter 8)*

subject the part of a sentence that tells who or what the sentence is about or is talking about *(Chapter 6)*; the topic of a paragraph or longer selection *(Chapter 7)*

supporting details additional information the author provides so the reader can understand the main idea completely *(Chapter 9)*

syllabication dividing words into syllables *(Chapter 4)*

syllable a word or word part that consists of one vowel sound, along with any consonant sounds, that is pronounced as a single unit *(Chapter 4)*

syllabus an instructor-prepared document that describes a course, its requirements, and other important information about a course; also called a *course description (Chapter 1)*

synonym a word that has the same meaning as another word (*little* is a synonym for *small*) *(Chapters 3 and 4)*

tactile-kinesthetic learner person who learns by touching or manipulating objects, as well as through movement *(Identifying Your Learning Style)*

textbook features devices authors use to emphasize important material or to show how it is organized *(Chapter 12)*

thesaurus a book or software program that gives synonyms *(Chapter 4)*

thesis sentence   overall main idea of a selection that summarizes the individual main ideas of the selection *(Chapters 6 and 10)*

topic   word, name, or phrase that tells who or what is discussed throughout a paragraph; also known as the *subject* or *subject matter* *(Chapter 7)*

transition words   words and phrases that show relationships among ideas in sentences, paragraphs, and longer selections *(Chapter 11)*

transitive verb   verb that expresses an action carried from the subject to the object; verb that requires a direct object to complete the meaning *(Chapter 6)*

unabridged dictionary   large, complete, full-length dictionary *(Chapter 4)*

verb   word that shows physical action, mental action, or a state of being *(Chapters 4 and 6)*

visual learner   person who learns well by seeing things *(Identifying Your Learning Style)*

visual-spatial learner   person who thinks in pictures rather than words *(Identifying Your Learning Style)*

vowels   the letters *a, e, i, o, u,* and sometimes *y* *(Chapter 4)*

writing patterns   ways authors organize material they present; also called *organizational patterns* *(Chapter 11)*

Index

*Note: Page numbers in **bold** indicate pages on which definitions appear; page numbers followed by f indicate figures, and page numbers followed by t indicate tables.*

auditory learners and, 387, Visual Summary 2
highlighting/underlining, 378, 389
reading and marking, 377–398
visual-spatial learners and, 387, Visual Summary 2
textbook features, **381**
thesauruses, **135**
on computers, 113, 129, 135
dictionaries and, 113, 129, 134–135
etymology of, 135
synonyms and, 129, 134–135
thesis sentence, 261
thumb index tabs, 112f, 116, 117f
time management, 42–47, 53
time order pattern, 350
titles
of chapters, 385
of textbooks, 381–382
as topic clue, 213–218, 226, 230, 231, 248
To Do lists, 44–45, 46
topic sentence, 248, 253
topics, 207–240, **213**
clues to, 211–212, 213–232, 234, 248, 259, Visual
Summary 1
general *vs.* specific, 212, 226–231, 227f
identifying, 177
overall, 230, 261
of paragraphs, 207–240, 281
rap about, 231
repeated phrases/words as clue to, 220–222,
231, 259
titles as, 213–218, 226, 230, 231, 248
transition words, 194
transitive verbs, 126, **185**, 187
tutoring, 13, 37, 53, 55, 388

U

unabridged dictionaries, 111
underlining textbook assignments, 378, 389
usage labels in dictionary definitions, 129–130

V

verbs
as confused/misused words, 164–167
intransitive, **185**
as part of speech, 125–127, 185–186
phrasal, **131**, 132
in sentences, 185, 190–191
transitive, **185**
video games, 75–76
Vision of Success form, 39, 41
visual learners, **11**, Visual Summary 2

assignment management strategies for,
49–50
learning new words and, 110
visualization
of context clues, 95
for deep processing of words, 137–139
of goals, 38–41, 40t
learning new words and, 110
of studying, 45
visual-spatial learners, **11**
learning new words and, 110
textbook assignments and, 387
vocabulary building and, 67
vocabulary. *See also* dictionaries.
background knowledge and, 88, 102
building, 22, 65–174
cards, 66, 67f
games, 167
learning styles and, 66, 67, 106, 110
vowels, **119,** 125

W

"The Walking Weary: What Teens and Young Adults
Need to Know About Sleep," 445–453
"What Your Car Says About You" (Hales), 462–469
word(s). *See also* confused/misused words; signal
words; terms; vocabulary.
academic, 74
alphabetizing, 107, 114–118
in bold/italics/color, 79–80, 93, 219, 361, 385
coding, into memory, 136–138, 139t
confused/misused, 149–174
context of, 65–67, 69–103
core vocabulary, 136–138
deep processing of, understanding and, 136–138,
139t
formal/informal, 129–131, 155
history/origin of, 132–134
insulting/vulgar, 129–130
irregular forms of, 118, 127
misused, 129–130, 149–174
nonstandard, 130
related forms of, 118, 119f, 132
special labels for, 118, 129–131
transition, 194
wall, 93, 113, 138
word meanings
confused/misused, 65–66, 74, 109, 149–174, Visual
Summary 1
definitions and, 65–67, 69–102
multiple, 110, 127–129
Wright, Frank Lloyd, 480
writing

Notes

Notes

Notes

Notes

Notes

Notes

Notes

Notes